Proceedings
1992 Symposium on Interactive 3D Graphics
Cambridge, Massachusetts
29 March - 1 April 1992

Program Co-Chairs

Marc Levoy   Edwin E. Catmull
Stanford University   Pixar

Symposium Chair

David Zeltzer
MIT Media Laboratory

Sponsored by the following organizations:

Office of Naval Research
National Science Foundation
USA Ballistic Research Laboratory
Hewlett-Packard
Silicon Graphics
Sun Microsystems
MIT Media Laboratory

In Cooperation with ACM SIGGRAPH

ndiana Univers
Library
Northwe

T
385

D1445388

mc

The Association for Computing Machinery
1515 Broadway
New York, New York 10036 USA

Soft Cover   ISBN: 0-89791-467-8
Series Hard Cover   ISBN: 0-89791-471-6
Additional copies may be ordered prepaid from:

ACM Order Department
P.O. Box 64145   1-800-342-6626
Baltimore, MD 21264, USA   1-410-528-4261 (Outside U.S.,
+1 301-528-4261   MD and AK)

ACM Order Number: 429920

Image Credits

Proceedings Front Cover

Title: *Umbilic Torus NIST*
Design & Sculpture: *Helaman Ferguson*
Dimensions: *Ht. 24", W. 24", D. 9"*
Material: *Carrera Marble*
Photography: *Noelle Ferguson*
Engineering Support: *Jim Albus, Roger Bostleman, NIST*
Software Support: *Sam Ferguson, BYU*
Produced at the Studio of Helaman Ferfuson, Laurel, MD
© Copyright 1990 by Helaman Ferguson

Proceedings Rear Cover Top

Title: *Constrained Gestural Translation Using 3D Handles*
Design: *Frank Graf, Kenneth P. Herndon, Daniel C. Robbins, Scott S. Snibbe*
Rendering: *Real time on a Hewlett Packard 835 Turbo SRX workstation*
Photography: *Scott S. Snibbe*
Support: *Robert C. Zeleznik, Nate Huang*
Produced at the Brown University Computer Graphics Group
© Copyright 1991 Brown University Computer Graphics Group

Proceedings Rear Cover Bottom

Title: *Interactive Drumming*
Design: *Martin Friedmann*
Produced at the MIT Media Laboratory
© Copyright 1991 by Martin Friedmann–MIT Media Laboratory, Cambridge, MA

Contents and Symposium Program

Wednesday, 1 April 1992

1:30pm - 3:00pm   **Closing Session**

Closing Remarks
David Zeltzer, Ed Catmull, Marc Levoy

Preface

These proceedings contain the papers presented at the 1992 Symposium on Interactive 3D Graphics held at the Royal Sonesta Hotel in Cambridge, Massachusetts on March 29 - April 1, 1992.

The symposium focuses on innovative 3D graphics architectures and hardware, algorithms for generating visual, haptic and auditory output, perceptual and psychological issues of viewing and operating in complex virtual spaces, interactive simulations distributed over local and long-haul networks, real-time dynamics, and innovative human-machine interface technologies and paradigms.

The call for participation was written in April, 1991, distributed at Siggraph '91, and disseminated throughout the graphics community. The deadline for submission of extended abstracts was September 18, 1991 at 5:00pm. In keeping with the rule applied for Siggraph conferences, this deadline was strictly enforced. On September 19, the 69 submitted abstracts were scanned by program co-chairs Ed Catmull and Marc Levoy and distributed to a committee consisting of 24 prominent researchers from the graphics, human-computer interaction, and psychology research communities. Each abstract received at least four reviews, and many received five. On October 28, the program committee met at Stanford University and selected 30 papers to be published in the proceedings and presented at the symposium. Submissions were accepted either as short or long papers (4 pages or 12 pages respectively) and were designated as short or long symposium presentations (15 minutes or 25 minutes respectively).

To insure a lively symposium and close interaction among the participants, attendance was limited to under 200 participants, and the program was spiced with frequent panels, live demonstrations, and social events. We were also privileged to have as our keynote speaker Andries van Dam, 1991 recipient of the Steven A. Coons Award for Outstanding Creative Contributions to Computer Graphics, and as our capstone speaker Stuart Card of Xerox PARC.

There are many people without whose volunteer efforts this symposium could not have succeeded. The chairs would first of all like to thank the members of the program committee for their reviews, their hard day's work at Stanford, and their numerous suggestions on the format of this and future symposia:

Kurt Akeley, Silicon Graphics
Norm Badler, U. of Pennsylvania
Eric Bier, Xerox PARC
Elain Cohen, U. of Utah
Tom DeFanti, U. of Illinois - Chicago
Tony DeRose, U. of Washington

Tom Ferrin, U. of California at San Francisco
Alain Fournier, U. of British Columbia
Henry Fuchs, U. of N. Carolina at Chapel Hill
Paul Haeberli, Silicon Graphics
Pat Hanrahan, Princeton University
Paul Heckbert, U. of California at Berkeley
Leo Hourvitz, NeXT Computer
S. Kicha Ganapathy, AT&T Bell Labs
Margaret Minsky, MIT
Eben Ostby, Pixar
Alex Pentland, MIT
Rich Reisenfeld, U. of Utah
Carlo Sequin, U. of California at Berkeley
Spencer Thomas, University of Michigan
Brian Wandell, Stanford University
Lance Williams, Apple Computer
Andrew Witkin, Carnegie Mellon University
Mike Zyda, Naval Postgraduate School

Special thanks are due to Dee Bell of Pixar, whose organizational skills kept the work flowing smoothly throughout her advancing pregnancy, Kay Seirup of Pixar, who picked up the torch and formatted these proceedings when Dee's pregnancy became maternity, and Rhea Zdimal of Stanford, who organized the program committee meeting with skill and style. In Boston, Janette Noss of the MIT Media Lab provided administrative and organizational support, and handled an infinity of details for the symposium itself. Greg Tucker, also of the Media Lab, valiantly provided support for the audio/visual and demonstration equipment.

We thank Judy Brown and Steve Cunningham for their help in obtaining ACM SIGGRAPH "in cooperation" status and publication of these proceedings. Thanks to Nicholas Negroponte and the MIT Media Lab for providing generous support for color reproduction in the proceedings. In addition, we also wish to acknowledge the generous contributions of the following organizations:

Office of Naval Research
National Science Foundation
USA Ballistic Research Laboratory
Hewlett-Packard
Silicon Graphics
Sun Microsystems

It has been a privilege to work with such an enthusiastic and dedicated crowd of people. Although it is only December as these proceedings go to press, inquiries concerning registration have been running at fever pitch. As with the previous two symposia, the strict attendance limit has generated controversy and occasionally disappointment, but the program committee feels that the small size and narrow focus of the symposium are keys to its continuing success. We anticipate a provocative and inspiring symposium in March, and we look forward to many repetitions in the coming years.

David Zeltzer, Symposium Chair
Ed Catmull and Marc Levoy, Program Co-Chairs
December 1991

Escaping Flatland in User Interface Design

Andries van Dam, Brown University

Fast and inexpensive computers and many productivity-enhancing applications have made computer users of a significant percentage of our population, professional and casual users alike. And the advances in ease of learning and ease of use made possible by modern user interfaces have helped immeasurably in this process. These superior interfaces, made possible by hardware such as bitmap graphics and the mouse, depend on the contributions of user interface designers who have created a new design discipline with its own tools and methodologies.

Hardware advances continue unabated, and decreases by a factor of two in price/performance occur almost yearly. Multimedia is today's buzzword and the hardware support for it, as usual, outpaces the software to exploit it. Low-level hardware support for 3D realtime shaded graphics is already built into a commodity CPU chip (the Intel i860) and will soon not just be part of workstations specialized for the nascent 3D market but be integrated into entry-level workstations and, shortly thereafter, personal computers. Indeed, distinctions between workstations and personal computers will all but disappear as they share more and more hardware and software features. As forecast by Raj Reddy and others, affordable 3G machines (gigaIPS/FLOPS, gigabyte of main memory, gigabaud communication) will appear on our desks before the end of the decade. They will also smooth-shade the equivalent of 1 megapolygon/sec. Thus multimedia support and 3D graphics will finally become mainstream, integrated into every desktop computer.

What new opportunities do these exciting technology developments make possible?

Can we expect paradigm shifts in computing akin to those arising from Xerox PARC's pioneering work on bitmap workstations in the early seventies?

Those attending this symposium understand the importance and potential of 3D. They will therefore not be surprised by my claim that one of the next major frontiers in computing is the introduction of realtime 3D graphics into existing everyday applications and the creation of new 3D applications. The eighties were the decade in which computers and 2D graphics finally became fast enough to run a host of 2D interactive applications. These include drawing/painting programs, WYSIWYG word processors and desktop publishing programs. The nineties will see a rapidly growing set of interactive 3D applications, both the traditional applications for specialists (e.g., 3D CAD/CAM, scientific visualization) and those for both professional and casual users (e.g., 3D illustration and animation programs, interior design and walkthrough programs). There need not even be a 'killer application' for 3D, akin to 2D's spreadsheets or wordprocessing, to justify its importance as a new dimension in computer applications: I believe 3D will be found useful in many applications today considered 2D.

Spreadsheets are 2-1/2D already, and Xerox PARC has used 3D widgets that exploit real-time animation to visualize data that is not intrinsically spatial, let alone 3D. CASE tools that provide program and algorithm visualization will reap the same benefits from realtime 3D graphics that science and engineering obtain from scientific visualization technology today. Electronic books, to be used, for example, for technical documentation, education and entertainment, will contain 'interactive illustrations', i.e., user-controlled, model-driven, real-time animation, in addition to video. Many of these models will be 3D virtual worlds; 2D illustrations can then become an important special case of the more general 3D illustrations.

While 3D has been prevalent for many years in such fields as mechanical CAD/CAM and scientific visualization, even in such applications the user interface has been largely 2D: menus, dialogue boxes, sliders, etc. There are surprisingly few 3D widgets beyond 3D cursors, virtual sphere simulations of 3D joysticks, and gestural selection, translation and rotation. Why this paucity? Among the reasons are that until very recently 3D has been unavailable to interface and application designers except on specialized, expensive platforms. Another reason is that 3D (and realtime animation) introduce not only new modalities of use but also new complexities. Furthermore, user interface designers have not had 3D toolkits for constructing 3D widgets. Finally, little research has been done thus far on creating new 3D metaphors and interaction paradigms. Even virtual reality research has had to focus on using and improving the still primitive hardware technology. Yet it is necessary not just for input and output hardware to continue to evolve dramatically; it is equally important that we stretch our imagination to think of new ways of interacting with our objects and data items and their interrelationships.

Among the issues that arise in designing 3D interfaces are the tradeoffs between direct manipulation and indirect manipulation through a widget. Direct manipulation involves widgets that have behavior but little or no geometry, such as gestural control for selection, translation and rotation. Indirect manipulation is done using 2D and 3D widgets that have both geometry and behavior such as object handles in a drawing program. Such widgets abstract out the salient parameters of the objects to be manipulated and/or of the operations themselves. Another issue is the separation between interface and application objects. Current user interface design favors separating widgets from the objects they control. Such widgets are constructed with their own design tools. In our paper in these proceedings we advocate making widgets first-class objects in the same environment that contains the application objects, and constructed with the same tools. Examples of our 3D widgets will be shown, which we hope will stimulate the 3D research community to consider realtime 3D not only as a technology or application domain but also as a means for creating engaging, productive user interfaces.

Management of Large Amounts of Data in Interactive Building Walkthroughs

Thomas A. Funkhouser, Carlo H. Séquin and Seth J. Teller
University of California at Berkeley[‡]

Abstract

We describe techniques for managing large amounts of data during an interactive walkthrough of an architectural model. These techniques are based on a spatial subdivision, visibility analysis, and a display database containing objects described at multiple levels of detail. In each frame of the walkthrough, we compute a set of objects to render, i.e. those potentially visible from the observer's viewpoint, and a set of objects to swap into memory, i.e. those that might become visible in the near future. We choose an appropriate level of detail at which to store and to render each object, possibly using very simple representations for objects that appear small to the observer, thereby saving space and time. Using these techniques, we cull away large portions of the model that are irrelevant from the observer's viewpoint, and thereby achieve interactive frame rates.

CR Categories and Subject Descriptors:
[Information Systems]: H.2.8 Database Applications.
[Computer Graphics]: I.3.5 Computational Geometry and Object Modeling – *geometric algorithms, languages, and systems*; I.3.7 Three-Dimensional Graphics and Realism – *visible line/surface algorithms*.

Additional Key Words and Phrases: architectural simulation, virtual reality.

[‡]Computer Science Department, Berkeley, CA 94720

1 Introduction

Interactive computer programs that simulate the experience of "walking" through a building interior are useful for visualization and evaluation of building models before they are constructed. However, realistic-looking building models with furniture may consist of tens of millions of polygons and require gigabytes of data - far more than today's workstations can render at interactive frame rates or fit into memory simultaneously. In order to achieve interactive walkthroughs of such large building models, a system must store in memory and render only a small portion of the model in each frame; that is, the portion seen by the observer. As the observer "walks" through the model, some parts of the model become visible and others become invisible; some objects appear larger and others appear smaller. The challenge is to identify the relevant portions of the model, swap them into memory and render them at interactive frame rates (at least ten frames per second) as the observer's viewpoint is moved under user control.

Using the design of Soda Hall, a planned computer science building at UC Berkeley, as a test object, we have completed the first version of a system that supports interactive walkthroughs of large, fully furnished building models. Our system builds upon pioneering work by Airey and Brooks [1,2,5] and uses conceptual ideas going back to Jones [8] and Clark [6]. The special features of our system are 1) a hierarchical display database that describes the building model as a set of objects represented at multiple levels of detail; 2) a spatial subdivision and visibility analysis in which the building model is divided into cells, and cell-to-cell and cell-to-object visibility information is computed; 3) a real-time memory management algorithm for swapping objects in and out of memory as the observer moves through the model; and 4) a real-time refresh algorithm for choosing which objects to render at which levels of detail in each frame.

1.1 System Overview

Our system is divided into three distinct phases as shown in Figure 1. First, during the *modeling phase*, we construct the building model from AutoCAD floor plans and elevations, and populate the model with furniture. Next, during the *precomputation phase*, we perform a spatial subdivision and observer-independent lighting and visibility calculations. Finally, during the *walkthrough phase*, we simulate an observer moving through the building model under user control with the mouse, rendering the model as seen from the observer's viewpoint in each frame. The *display database* is the link between these three phases. It stores the complete building model, along with the results of the precomputation phase, for use during the walkthrough phase.

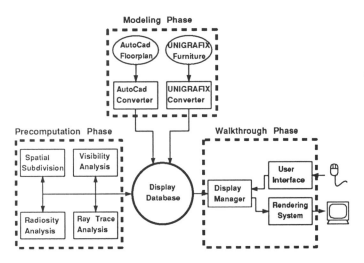

Figure 1: System overview.

2   Modeling Phase

Our walkthrough system requires a detailed 3D model of a building, complete with furniture and realistic material and lighting information.

We first convert the raw $2\frac{1}{2}$D model received from the architects in AutoCAD DXF format [3] into a consistent 3D representation in Berkeley UNIGRAFIX format [10]. Unfortunately, the raw architectural models that we received were not true three-dimensional models and contained non-planar faces, coincident coplanar faces, improper face intersections, and inconsistent face orientations. During conversion, our programs [9] detect and automatically correct many of these anomalies. Any remaining modeling errors are corrected manually using interactive tools.

We then populate the architectural model with stairs, furniture and other objects that a user would expect to find in a typical building. We have generated highly detailed descriptions for several pieces of furniture using interactive modeling programs, and received others from Greg Ward of Lawrence Berkeley Laboratories. We place instances of these objects into the building model using both automatic and interactive placement programs. We have written several programs that automatically place objects into specific types of rooms

based on sets of parameters. For instance, the "conference room generator" places a rectangular or elliptical table in the middle of a room, chairs all around it, a blackboard on one wall, a transparency projector on the table, and so on. The "office generator" places a desk against one wall, a chair in front of the desk, some bookshelves against the walls, and so on. Numerous parameters are available for the user to control the size, number and placement of objects with each of these programs. We have also written a program for interactively placing objects into a three-dimensional model. It allows a user to add, delete, or move object instances with real-time visual feedback.

Gradually, we load the walls and furniture of the building model into the walkthrough display database. The display database represents the building model as a set of *objects* (e.g. walls, desks, chairs, telephones, pencils, etc.), each of which can be described at multiple levels of detail [6]. We construct less detailed representations of objects from the highly detailed originals using an interactive design tool that allows a user to simplify 3D objects by deleting and merging vertices and faces. For instance, we construct five representations of a desk: 1) a highly detailed desk with faces subdivided along gradients of radiosity, 2) a slightly less-detailed desk with simple handles and larger faces, 3) an even less-detailed desk without any handles at all, 4) a coarsely detailed desk with only legs and drawers, and 5) a simple box. These object abstraction hierarchies are adjusted interactively so that transitions between levels are barely noticeable as one zooms closer to an object and detail is refined. Levels of detail are chosen dynamically during the interactive walkthrough phase to improve refresh rates and memory utilization.

So far, we have built a completely furnished model of the sixth floor of Soda Hall, the planned computer science building at U.C. Berkeley. This floor model has a total of 2,320 objects, represented at up to five levels of detail, and contains over 400,000 faces, requiring 68MB of storage. Color Plate I shows a top-view of the model.

3   The Precomputation Phase

After the complete building model has been loaded into the display database, we distribute the model into a *spatial subdivision* and perform a *visibility analysis* of the model cells and objects. The resulting information is stored in the display database for use by the display and memory management algorithms during the walkthrough phase.

3.1   Spatial Subdivision

We subdivide the model using a variant of the k-D tree data structure [4]. Splitting planes are introduced along the major opaque elements in the model, namely the walls, door frames, floors, and ceilings (details are given in [11]).

The subdivision terminates when all sufficiently large, axial opaque elements in the model are coplanar with an axial boundary plane of at least one subdivision leaf cell.

After subdivision, cell *portals* (i.e., the transparent portions of shared boundaries) are identified and stored with each leaf cell, along with an identifier for the neighboring cell to which the portal leads (Figure 2). Enumerating the portals in this way amounts to constructing an *adjacency graph* over the leaf cells of the subdivision; two leaves (nodes) are adjacent (share an edge) if and only if there is a portal connecting them. All the visibility computations to be described exploit the adjacency graph data structure.

This procedure can be applied quickly. At the cost of performing an initial $O(n \lg n)$ sort, the split dimension and abscissa can be determined in time $O(f)$ at each split, where f is the number of faces stored with the node. We have found that these subdivision criteria yield a tree whose cell structure reflects the "rooms" of our architectural model. For our floor model with 1920 split faces, the subdivision created 1280 cells and 3600 portals in 23 seconds.

3.2 Cell-to-Cell Visibility

Once the spatial subdivision has been constructed, we compute and store *cell-to-cell visibility* for each leaf cell, i.e. the set of cells visible to an observer able to look in all directions from any position within the cell. The cell-to-cell visibility for a cell C contains exactly those cells to which an unobstructed *sightline* leads from C. Such a sightline must be disjoint from any opaque elements and must intersect, or *stab*, a portal in order to pass from one cell to the next (Figure 2). Sightlines connecting cells that are not immediate neighbors must traverse a *portal sequence*, each member of which lies on the boundary of an intervening cell. We have implemented a procedure that finds sightlines through axial portal sequences, or determines that no such sightline exists, in $O(n \lg n)$ time, where n is the number of portals in the sequence [7].

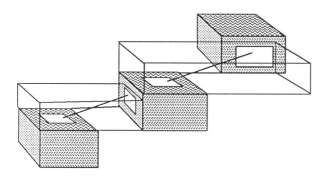

Figure 2: Stabbing an axial portal sequence in three dimensions.

We compute the cell-to-cell visibility by constructing a *stab tree* for each leaf cell C of the subdivision [11] as shown in Figure 3. Each node of the stab tree corresponds to a cell

visible from C; each edge of the stab tree corresponds to a portal stabbed as part of a portal sequence originating on a boundary of C. The stab tree is constructed incrementally using a constrained depth-first search on the adjacency graph. As each cell is encountered by the depth first search, it is effectively marked "visible" by its inclusion into the source cell's stab tree. For any source cell C, we say that a cell R is *reached* if R is in C's cell-to-cell visibility set.

3.3 Cell-to-Object Visibility

Cells that are immediate neighbors of the source cell are entirely visible to it, since the eyepoint can be placed on the shared portal. Cells farther away from the source, however, are in general only partially visible to an observer in the source cell. This is due to the fact that, as the length of a portal sequence increases, the collection of lines stabbing the entire sequence typically narrows.

Casting the sightline search as a graph traversal yields a simple method for computing the partially visible portion of each reached cell. First, the traversal *orients* each portal encountered, since the portal is traversed in a known direction. Thus each portal contributes a "lefthand" and a "righthand" constraint to the set of sightlines stabbing the sequence. The result, after stepping through n portals in the plane, is a bowtie-shaped bundle of lines that stabs every portal of the sequence, and which "fans out" beyond the final portal into an infinite wedge. This wedge can then be clipped to the boundary of the reached cell. In our three dimensional models, all portals are axial rectangles, so any portal sequence can generate at most three pairs of bowtie constraints (one from each collection of portal edges parallel to the x, y, and z axes). Color Plate II depicts the clipped polyhedral wedges for a source cell in three dimensions.

We define *cell-to-object* visibility as the set of *objects* that can be seen by an observer constrained to a given source cell C (but, again, free to move anywhere in C and look in any direction). For each reached cell R, we compute a *superset* of C's cell-to-object visibility in R by assembling a set of *halfspaces* bounding the portion of R visible from C. We then store with C those objects in R that are completely or partially inside the assembled halfspaces. One special case exists: all objects in C's neighbor cells are tagged as visible from C without any bowtie computations.

Figure 5 depicts this process in two dimensions, using a simplified floorplan of our three-dimensional test model. The objects found potentially visible from the source (the filled squares in Figure 5) are associated with the source cell and reached cell in a compacted representation of the stab tree. Later, in the interactive walkthrough phase, this object list will be retrieved and culled dynamically based on the observer's position and view direction.

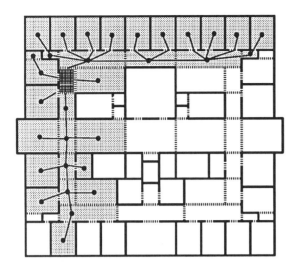

Figure 3: Cell-to-cell visibility and stab tree.

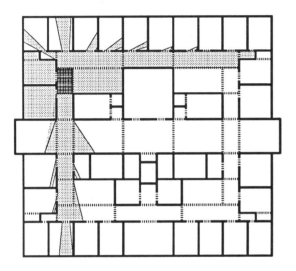

Figure 4: In general, only a fraction of the reached cell is visible to the source.

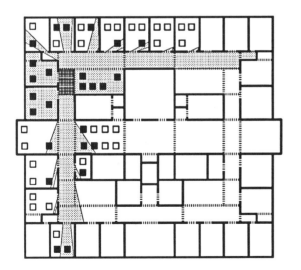

Figure 5: Computing cell-to-object visibility; the filled squares are marked visible.

4 The Display Database

The results of the modeling and precomputation phases are stored in a display database designed specifically to identify and swap relevant objects into memory quickly as the observer moves through the model during the interactive walk-through phase. The structure of the display database is shown in Figure 6.

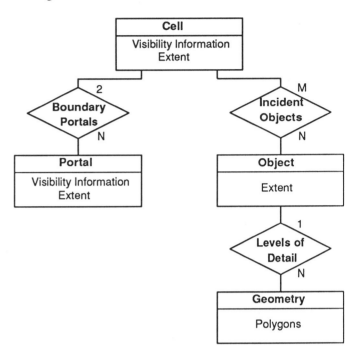

Figure 6: A structural diagram of the display database showing entities (boxes) and relationships (diamonds).

4.1 Segments

All entities (e.g. cells, portals, objects, etc.) are stored in *segments* in the display database. A segment is simply an abstraction for a variable-sized contiguous group of bytes in a display database file that can be read and released as a unit. Each segment is represented by its size, a byte offset into a file, and a pointer into memory, as shown in Figure 7. The arrangement of bytes in a segment is identical in memory and on disk so that only pointers within a segment must be updated when a segment is read (requiring one addition per pointer); there is no need to allocate extra memory or to move or copy bytes. With these properties, segments can be swapped quickly in and out of memory.

All relationships (e.g. adjacent, incident, visible, etc.) are stored in *segment references* in the display database. A segment reference can be represented by either an integer segment ID (if it has not yet been read into memory) or a pointer to a segment's data in memory. At any time, a segment reference may be read (converted from an ID to a pointer) or released (converted from a pointer to an ID). A reference count is stored with each segment so that segments can be read and released through multiple segment references quickly and transparently.

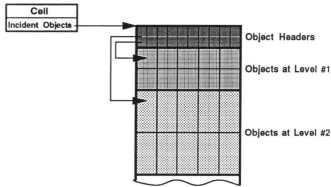

Figure 8: The layout of objects incident upon the same cell in the display database.

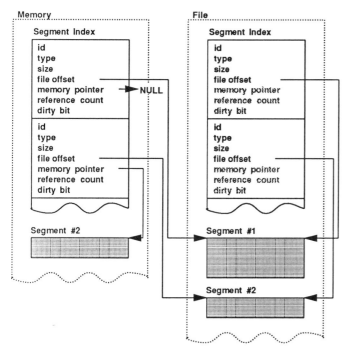

Figure 7: The implementation of display database segments.

4.2 Layout

Since the latency overhead of each read operation is relatively large, we group the segments for all objects incident upon the same cell contiguously in the display database file. This layout allows us to utilize the cell-to-cell visibility information from the precomputation phase to load groups of objects (those likely to become visible at the same time) into memory in a single IO operation. If an object is incident upon more than one cell (i.e. straddles a cell boundary), then we store it redundantly, once for each cell.

Furthermore, we store descriptions of all objects incident upon the same cell at the same level of detail contiguously in the display database, as shown in Figure 8. Within a single cell, the object headers appear first, followed by descriptions of the objects at increasing levels of detail. As a result, all objects incident upon a cell at or up to any level of detail may be read at once in a single read operation during the interactive walkthrough phase.

5 The Walkthrough Phase

During the walkthrough phase, we simulate an observer moving through the architectural model under user control. The goal is to render the model as seen from the observer's

viewpoint in a window on the workstation display at interactive frame rates as the user moves the observer's viewpoint through the model.

The primary problem is that building models are very large and so 1) do not fit into memory, and 2) cannot be rendered completely in an interactive frame time. Thus we must identify a small, but relevant, portion of the model to store in memory and to render in each frame. We use the results of the visibility precomputation along with the object hierarchy of the display database and dynamic culling algorithms to identify which objects are visible to the observer, and choose an appropriate level of detail for each one. We load into memory and render only relevant levels of detail for potentially visible objects.

5.1 Display Management

We use two techniques to reduce the amount of data rendered in each frame: 1) we compute the subset of objects visible to the observer using a real-time visibility analysis based on the results of the precomputation phase, and 2) we choose an appropriate level of detail at which to render each visible object from the object hierarchy constructed during the modeling phase. Using these techniques, we are able to cull away large portions of the model that are irrelevant from the observer's viewpoint, and therefore achieve much shorter refresh times. Moreover, computations are done in parallel with the display of the previous frame and do not increase the effective frame time.

Visibility Analysis

To compute the set of objects to render for a given observer viewpoint, we first identify the cell containing the observer's position and fetch its cell-to-object visibility from the display database. Since the cell-to-object visibility contains all objects visible from any viewpoint in a given cell, it is always a superset of the objects actually visible to a particular observer in that cell. It is typically a small subset of the entire model.

Since the observer is at a known point and has vision limited to a *view cone* emanating from this point, we can cull the set of visible objects even further. We define the *eye-to-cell* visibility as the set of all objects incident upon any cell partially or completely visible to the observer (the light stippled regions in Figure 9). Clearly, the eye-to-cell visibility is also a superset of the objects actually visible to the observer. The visible area in any cell is always the intersection of that (convex) cell with one or more (convex) wedges emanating through portals from the eyepoint. To compute the eye-to-cell visibility, we initialize the visible area wedge to the interior of the view cone, and the eye-to-cell visibility to the source cell. Next, we perform a constrained depth-first-search (DFS) of the stab tree, starting at the source cell, and propagating outward. Upon encountering a portal, the wedge is suitably narrowed, and the newly reached cell is added to the eye-to-cell visibility set. If the wedge is disjoint from the portal, the active branch of the DFS is terminated.

Finally, we estimate the *eye-to-object* visibility, a narrower superset of the objects actually visible to the observer, by generating the intersection of the cell-to-object and eye-to-cell sets. For example, consider the observer viewpoint shown in Figure 9. The eye-to-object visibility set (filled squares) contains all objects in the intersection between the cell-to-object (all squares) and eye-to-cell (gray regions) sets. It is a small subset of all objects in the model, but still an over-estimate of the actual visibility of the observer. In Figure 9, only one square lies in a cell visible to the observer and can be seen from some point inside the cell containing the observer, but is not visible from the observer's current viewpoint. Color Plate III depicts the eye-to-object visibility set for this observer viewpoint in three dimensions.

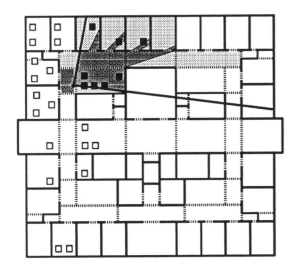

Figure 9: Eye-to-object visibility. Shown are only the potentially visible objects, i.e. the black objects from Figure 5.

Object Hierarchy

After we have culled away portions of the model that are invisible from the observer's viewpoint, we can further reduce the number of faces rendered in each frame by choosing an appropriate level of detail at which to render each visible object. Since the image must ultimately be displayed in pixels, it is useless to render very detailed descriptions of objects that are very small or far away from the observer and which map to just a few pixels on the display (Figure 10). Likewise, it is wasteful to render details in objects that are moving quickly across the screen and which appear blurred or can be seen for only a short amount of time (Figure 11). Instead, we can achieve the same visual effect by rendering simpler representations of these objects, consisting of just a few faces with appropriate colors. This is a technique used by commercial flight simulators, however little has been published on these systems [12].

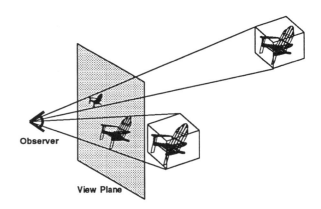

Figure 10: Perceptible detail is related to apparent size.

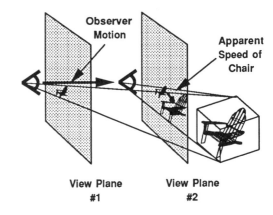

Figure 11: Perceptible detail is related to apparent speed.

Rather than rendering all objects at the highest level of detail in every frame, we choose a level of detail at which to render each object based on its apparent size and speed from the point of view of the observer. For each level of detail, we estimate the size of an average face in pixels, and the speed of an average face in pixels per frame. We render an object at the lowest level of detail for which the average size of a face is greater than some threshold, and the size of an average face divided by its speed is greater than another threshold. If either of these values is less than the corresponding threshold for all available levels of detail of an object, we render the object at its lowest level of detail.

As the observer moves through the model, an object may be rendered at different levels of detail in successive frames. Rather than abruptly snapping from one level of detail to the next, we blend successive levels of detail using partial transparency. Since the complexity of any level is typically small compared to the one of the next higher higher level (by more than a factor of two), the extra time spent blending the two levels during transition does not constitute an undue overhead, considering the small fraction of objects making a transition at the same time.

5.2 Memory Management

Since the entire model cannot be stored in memory at once, we must choose a subset of objects to store in memory for each frame, and swap objects in and out of memory in real-time as the observer moves through the model. As a minimum, we must store in memory all objects to be rendered in the next frame. However, since it takes a relatively large amount of time to swap data from disk into memory, we must also predict which objects might be rendered in future frames and begin swapping them into memory in advance. Otherwise, frame updates might be delayed, waiting for objects to be read from disk before they can be rendered.

As described in Section 4.2, we group each level of detail for all objects incident upon the same cell contiguously in the display database. To take advantage of the relative efficiency of large IO operations, we always load all objects incident upon the same cell into memory together at the same level of detail. Thus, our memory management algorithm must compute for each frame which cell contents to store in memory at which levels of detail.

In general, we store in memory the contents of the cells containing the objects most likely to be rendered in upcoming frames. Specifically, we determine which cells are most likely to contain the observer in upcoming frames, and store in memory all objects incident upon cells visible from any of these cells. Each time the observer steps across a cell boundary, we traverse the cell adjacency graph, considering cells in order of the minimum amount of time before the cell can possibly contain the observer using a shortest path algorithm. The user interface also enforces some limits on the size of a step or turn that the observer may take in a single frame. For each cell C, visited in the search, we mark and claim memory for the contents of all cells visible from C in the direction of the observer's frustum up to the precomputed maximum level of detail at which any object incident upon the cell might be rendered for an observer in C. Our search terminates when all available memory has been claimed or when we have considered all possible observer viewpoints

more than some maximum amount of time in the future. We then read the contents of all newly marked cells into memory, possibly replacing the contents of unmarked cells.

For instance, consider the observer viewpoint shown in Figure 12. Cells are labeled by the minimum amount of time (in seconds) before they can possibly become visible to the observer; and shaded by the level at which their contents are stored in memory – darker shades represent higher levels. The cells surrounded by the thick-dashed line represent the cells visited during the search, i.e. the range of observer positions for which we store visible objects in memory.

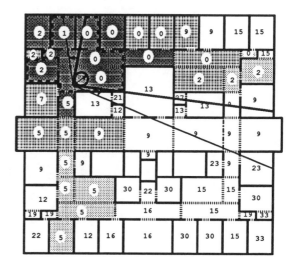

Figure 12: Cells labeled by the number of seconds before they can possibly become visible to the observer, and shaded by level of detail stored in memory (a darker shade represents a higher level of detail). White cells are not loaded into memory.

6 Results and Discussion

In this section we present and analyze test results collected during real interactive walkthroughs performed with our system. During these tests, we logged statistics regarding the performance of our display and memory management algorithms in real time as a user walked through the building model.

We present results for one observer viewpoint used as an example in the previous discussion (marked by an 'A' in Figure 13), as well as for a full sequence of observer viewpoints generated during an actual walkthrough along the path shown in Figure 13). The path is about 300 feet long, and a realistic physical walk along it should take approximately one minute. All tests were performed on a VGX 320 Silicon Graphics workstation with two 33 MHz processors and 64 MB of memory.

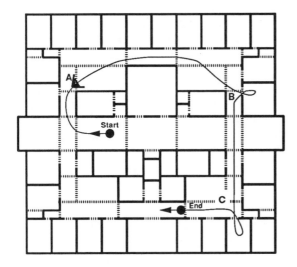

Figure 13: Test path through the building model.

Display Management

As discussed in Section 5.1, we compute the set of potentially visible objects by generating successively smaller supersets, culling away objects invisible to the observer. The sizes of these sets, and the times (in seconds) required to render them are shown for viewpoint 'A' in Table 1 and averaged over the test walkthrough path in Table 2. On average, we are able to cull away 94% of the model and reduce rendering time by a factor of 17 by rendering only objects in the eye-to-object visibility set rather than the entire building model.

Culling Method	# Objs.	# Faces	Draw Time	% of Model
Entire model	2,320	242,668	3.77	100%
Cell-to-cell	1,065	109,227	1.77	45%
Cell-to-object	558	40,475	0.65	17%
Eye-to-cell	241	30,265	0.52	12%
Eye-to-object	165	18,927	0.33	7.8%

Table 1: Visibility cull results for viewpoint 'A'.

Culling Method	# Objs.	# Faces	Draw Time	% of Model
Entire model	2,320	242,668	3.66	100%
Cell-to-cell	778	78,475	1.22	32%
Cell-to-object	440	36,921	0.59	15%
Eye-to-cell	207	20,657	0.34	8.5%
Eye-to-object	141	13,701	0.23	5.6%

Table 2: Average visibility cull results for test walkthrough.

We further reduce the number of faces rendered at each frame by choosing an appropriate level of detail at which to render each potentially visible object based on its apparent size and speed to the observer. Statistics regarding the number of faces and the time required to render each frame using different pixels-per-face thresholds for viewpoint 'A' and averaged over the test path are shown in Tables 3 and 4, respectively. Usable rendering modes for which little or no degradation in image quality is perceptible ($\geq$ 256 pixels per face), are shown in bold typeface.

Color Plates IV, V and VI show the difference between a static image produced using the highest level of detail for all objects (Plate IV) and one generated with reduced levels of detail for objects with fewer than 256 pixels per face (Plate V). Plate IV has 23,468 faces and took 0.34 seconds to render, whereas Plate V has 7,555 faces and took 0.17 seconds. These images were rendered without interpolated shading or antialiasing in order to accentuate differences – notice the reduced tessellation of the chairs further from the observer. Plate VI shows which level of detail was used for each object in Plate V (a darker shade represents a higher level of detail).

Overall, after computing the set of potentially visible objects and choosing an appropriate level of detail for each object, we are able to cull away an average of 97% of the building model and reduce rendering time by an average factor of 39 in each frame.

Min. Pixels Per Face	# Objs.	# Faces	Draw Time	% of Model
0	**165**	**18,927**	**0.33**	**7.8%**
64	**165**	**11,763**	**0.26**	**4.8%**
128	**165**	**8,861**	**0.22**	**3.6%**
256	**165**	**6,204**	**0.17**	**2.6%**
512	165	3,889	0.13	1.6%
1024	165	2,871	0.12	1.2%

Table 3: Average detail cull results for viewpoint 'A'.

Min. Pixels Per Face	# Objs.	# Faces	Draw Time	% of Model
0	**141**	**13,701**	**0.23**	**5.6%**
64	**141**	**9,700**	**0.18**	**4.0%**
128	**141**	**7,979**	**0.16**	**3.3%**
256	**141**	**6,176**	**0.14**	**2.5%**
512	141	4,745	0.12	2.0%
1024	141	3,427	0.10	1.4%

Table 4: Average detail cull results for test walkthrough.

Memory Management

As described in Section 5.2, the memory manager tries to store in memory the objects incident upon the cells that are

18

most likely to be visible to the observer in upcoming frames in order of decreasing urgency. One of the two processors of the VGX is used for pre-fetching data concurrently with the rendering of the current frame. The results presented here were gathered from a walk along the test path shown in Figure 13. Since the current floor model is not very large compared to the memory capacity of our machine, we impose an artificial 8MB limit on the amount of object data that can be stored in memory at any one time. As the observer, "walks" along the path, we swap data in and out of memory, never exceeding the 8MB limit. We are still experimenting with techniques to control the interaction between our memory management algorithm and the paging of the operating system. Thus the data below must be regarded as tentative and rather preliminary. More reliable data will be gathered once the fully furnished model of the whole building becomes available.

Figure 14 shows a plot of the number of bytes that must be in memory in order to render the visible parts of the scene (lower curve); superimposed is a plot of the number of bytes our algorithm loads into memory in preparation for possible near-term observer moves. As expected, these amounts of data fluctuate strongly depending on whether the observer is in a relatively simple part of the model with rather confined views, or whether the visible cells stretch out to great depth along several directions. In all, we read 52MB during the 261 frames.

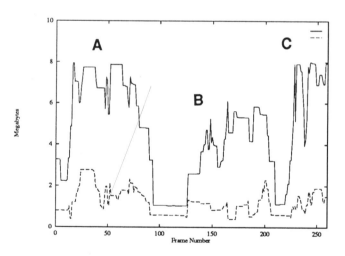

Figure 14: Comparison of the amounts of data fetched from disk (top curve) and actually needed for rendering (bottom curve) while following the walkthrough test path; marked spots correspond to the labels shown in Figure 13.

In general, we are able to pre-fetch objects before they are rendered, and so the observer can move smoothly through the model. However, there are a few cases in which the memory manager is not able to predict which objects are going to become visible to the observer far enough in advance to pre-fetch them, and so the user may have to wait while they are read into memory. As the observer turns a corner in a corridor, the visible set of objects can change dramatically This prompts a request for a large amount of new data to be loaded into memory. For the worst-case corners (labels 'B' and 'C'), the coprocessor is busy for about 8 seconds to prefetch on the order of 2 MB of data that might be used in the near future. However, the amount of data needed immediately for the rendering of the next frame is much smaller; because of parallel processing, resulting observable delays are on the order of a couple of seconds for a worst-case situation in our model. We are developing more sophisticated pre-fetching techniques that use a better prediction of the observer's motion.

7 Conclusion

Our paper describes a system for interactive walkthroughs of very large architectural models. It builds a hierarchical display database containing objects represented at multiple levels of detail during the modeling phase, performs a spatial subdivision and visibility analysis during a precomputation phase, and uses real-time display and memory management algorithms during a walkthrough phase to judiciously select a relevant subset of data for rendering. We have implemented a first version of this system, and tested it in real walkthroughs of a completely furnished model of the sixth floor of the planned Computer Science building at UC Berkeley. Our initial results show that these display and memory management techniques are effective at culling away substantial portions of the model, and make interactive frame rates possible even for very large models.

8 Acknowledgements

We are grateful to Delnaz Khorramabadi for her efforts constructing the building model, and to Paul Haeberli for his help in producing the color plates. Silicon Graphics, Inc., donated a 320 VGX workstation to this project as part of a grant from the Microelectronics Innovation and Computer Research Opportunities (MICRO) program of the State of California.

References

[1] Airey, John M. *Increasing Update Rates in the Building Walkthrough System with Automatic Model-Space Subdivision and Potentially Visible Set Calculations*. Ph.D. thesis, UNC Chapel Hill, 1990.

[2] Airey, John M., Rohlf, John H., and Brooks, Jr., Frederick P. Towards image realism with interactive update rates in complex virtual building environments. *ACM SIGGRAPH Special Issue on 1990 Symposium on Interactive 3D Graphics*, 24, 2 (1990), 41-50.

[3] *Autocad Reference Manual*, Release 10, Autodesk Inc., 1990.

[4] Bentley, J.L. Multidimensional Binary Search Trees Used for Associative Searching. *Communications of the ACM*, 18 (1975), 509-517.

[5] Brooks, Jr., Frederick P. Walkthrough - A Dynamic Graphics System for Simulating Virtual Buildings. *Proceedings of the 1986 Workshop on Interactive 3D Graphics.*

[6] Clark, James H. Hierarchical Geometric Models for Visible Surface Algorithms. *Communications of the ACM*, 19, 10 (October 1976), 547-554.

[7] Hohmeyer, Michael E., and Teller, Seth J. Stabbing Isothetic Rectangles and Boxes in $O(n \lg n)$ Time. Technical Report UCB/CSD 91/634, Computer Science Department, U.C. Berkeley, 1991. Also to appear in *Computational Geometry: Theory and Applications*, 1992.

[8] Jones, C.B. A New Approach to the 'Hidden Line' Problem. *The Computer Journal*, 14, 3 (August 1971), 232-237.

[9] Khorramabadi, Delnaz. A Walk through the Planned CS Building. Masters Thesis UCB/CSD 91/652, Computer Science Department, U.C. Berkeley, 1991.

[10] Séquin, Carlo H. Introduction to the Berkeley UNIGRAFIX Tools (Version 3.0). Technical Report UCB/CSD 91/606, Computer Science Department, U.C.Berkeley, 1991.

[11] Teller, Seth J., and Séquin, Carlo H. Visibility Preprocessing for Interactive Walkthroughs. *Computer Graphics (Proc. SIGGRAPH '91)*, 25, 4 (August 1991), 61-69.

[12] Zyda, Michael J. Course Notes, Book Number 10, Graphics Video Laboratory, Department of Computer Science, Naval Postgraduate School, Monterey, California, November 1991.

Fast Object-Precision Shadow Generation for Area Light Sources Using BSP Trees

Norman Chin
Steven Feiner

Department of Computer Science
Columbia University
New York, New York 10027

nc@cs.columbia.edu
feiner@cs.columbia.edu

Abstract

This paper introduces an efficient object-precision shadow generation algorithm for static polygonal environments directly illuminated by convex area light sources. Penumbra and umbra regions are calculated analytically and represented as a pair of BSP trees for each light source. As the trees are built, convex scene polygons are filtered down the trees, and split into fragments that are wholly lit, in penumbra, or in umbra. The illumination due to the light source is calculated at selected points within the wholly lit and penumbra regions by contour integration with the visible parts of the light source. We use a fast analytic algorithm to compute the fragments of the area light source visible from a point in penumbra. Rendering is done using hardware-supported linear interpolated shading on a 3D graphics workstation.

Because the scene itself is represented as a BSP tree, visible-surface determination may be performed by using either workstation-supported hardware (e.g., a z-buffer) or software BSP-tree traversal. We provide sample images created by our implementation, including timings and polygon counts.

CR Categories and Subject Descriptors: I.3.3 [**Computer Graphics**]: Picture/Image Generation—*Display algorithms*; I.3.5 [**Computer Graphics**]: Computational Geometry and Object Modeling—*Constructive solid geometry (CSG)*; I.3.7 [**Computer Graphics**]: Three-Dimensional Graphics and Realism—*Color, shading, shadowing, and texture*

General Terms: Algorithms

Additional Keywords and Phrases: shadow volume, area light source, BSP tree, penumbra, umbra

Introduction

Shadow generation is a classic problem in 3D computer graphics that has been addressed by a wide variety of algorithms [13, 22]. Point light-source shadow algorithms essentially compute the visibility of parts of the environment from a point at the light source; therefore any point in the environment is either fully in or out of shadow. In contrast, in an environment lit by area light sources, a point in the environment may be either visible to the entirety of the light source, visible to no part of the light source (i.e., in the light source's *umbra*), or visible to only a portion of the light source (i.e., in the light source's *penumbra*). In this latter case, to compute the point's illumination, it is also necessary to determine which portions of the area light source are visible from the point. Since real light sources are not points and therefore cast both umbrae and penumbrae, an area light-source shadow algorithm can be used to create pictures that are more photorealistic in appearance than those created with a point light-source shadow algorithm.

Shadows from area light sources have been computed using radiosity approaches [9, 6], by summing the contributions of an approximating set of point light sources [5], by ray tracing shadow cones from points in a scene to spherical light sources [1], by distributed ray-tracing [10], and by an object-precision algorithm developed by Nishita and Nakamae [17]. With the exception of this single object-precision algorithm, all the other algorithms approximate the shadow boundaries on the objects in the scene. For each pair of a light source and a polyhedral object, Nishita and Nakamae compute the volume that the object fully shadows from the light source (its *umbra volume*) and the volume that the object partially shadows from the light source (its *penumbra volume*). The intersections of these volumes with the other objects in the environment are computed and guide the calculation of the illumination at selected points on the objects. For example, a point is fully shadowed if it is included in at least one umbra volume.

The algorithm that we describe here is inspired in part by this work; unlike Nishita and Nakamae, however, we build a single merged umbra volume and penumbra volume for each light source. Furthermore, these volumes are represented as

BSP trees [14, 15, 21, 16] using an efficient extension of the earlier BSP-tree-based shadow algorithm for point light sources [7]. Although subdivision is always done along exact shadow boundaries, further subdivision may be necessary to compute illumination more accurately. We have used both regular gridding and adaptive subdivision of fragments in the penumbra and wholly lit regions to compute the illumination at additional points.

Background

The binary space-partitioning (BSP) tree visible-surface algorithm was developed by Fuchs, Kedem, and Naylor [14], based in part on the work of Schumacker [19, 20]. A BSP tree defines a recursive partitioning of space by planes that embed the polygons in the scene. The tree's root is a polygon chosen from those in the scene. This polygon's plane partitions space into two half-spaces: the "positive" half-space contains all other polygons in front of the root's plane (on the side into which its normal points); the "negative" half-space contains all polygons behind the root's plane. If a polygon straddles the root's plane, it is cut by it and each of its pieces is assigned to the appropriate half-space. One polygon each from the positive and negative half-spaces are then selected to become the root's children. Each child is then recursively used to divide the remaining children in its half-space in the same way. The tree is complete when each leaf node contains a single polygon whose half-spaces are both empty. The BSP tree visible-surface algorithm is a modified inorder traversal of the scene's BSP tree, guided by a simple comparison of the eyepoint with each polygon's plane; this determines in $O(n)$ time a back-to-front ordering of the polygons for any eyepoint.

Thibault and Naylor [21] showed that BSP trees can be used to represent polyhedral solids. Each of the empty regions at the leaves is associated with a value of either "in" or "out". Assuming that each polygon that bounds a polyhedron has a normal that points out of the polyhedron, then an "in" region is bounded in part by the polygon's negative (back) half-space and an "out" region is bounded in part by the polygon's positive (front) half-space. The BSP tree's leaf nodes tessellate space into a set of convex polyhedral regions, a subset of which (the "in" regions) represent the solid.

The point light-source shadow algorithm described in [7, 8] uses BSP trees to model the polyhedral shadow volumes [11] cast by convex polygons. We call the BSP tree representation of the shadow volume the SVBSP (Shadow Volume BSP) tree. A regular BSP tree is first constructed for all polygons in the scene. (Note that if the scene is modified, then the scene BSP tree must be recalculated.) The scene BSP tree allows the shadow algorithm to obtain all scene polygons efficiently in front-to-back order relative to an arbitrary point light source. Only scene polygons that face the light are selected. The point light source and the first scene polygon chosen define together a shadow volume that is a semi-infinite pyramid. Each of the pyramid's faces is embedded in a plane defined by the light source and an edge of the scene polygon. A point will be in shadow if it lies within the pyramid and in the scene polygon's negative half-space. The scene polygon is itself fully lit.

Because of the front-to-back order imposed by the BSP tree traversal, each new scene polygon processed is guaranteed not to block any of the previously selected scene polygons from the light. It may be wholly or partially in shadow itself, however. To determine which parts of the new polygon are visible from the light source, we must partition the polygon into parts that are inside and outside the current SVBSP-tree shadow volume. Note that there is no need to compare the new polygon with the planes that embed the previous scene polygons, since the BSP-tree traversal order ensures that the new polygon does not lie between the light source and the preceding scene polygons. Those parts of the new polygon that are inside the shadow volume are in shadow; those parts that are outside it are lit. Furthermore, any parts that are outside define additional shadow volumes that must be added to the SVBSP tree. The point light-source algorithm efficiently combines these two steps of classifying polygon fragments and enlarging the SVBSP tree by using a simplified version of the Boolean set union operation algorithm presented in [21]. Each remaining polygon is processed in this fashion to determine which of its parts are shadowed.

Like the BSP-tree point light-source shadow algorithm, our BSP-tree convex area light-source algorithm supports multiple light sources. The area light-source algorithm extends the point light-source algorithm by classifying polygons into fragments that are wholly lit, in penumbra (partially blocked from the light source), or in umbra (wholly blocked from the light source). To do this, we must first define the umbra and penumbra volumes of an area light source.

Constructing Penumbra and Umbra Volumes

In environments composed of convex polygons illuminated by convex light sources, the penumbra and umbra volumes associated with a single scene polygon can be constructed entirely from three kinds of planes:

- *scene polygon planes*, a single one of which is defined by the scene polygon itself.

- *light-source vertex planes*, defined by a vertex of the light source and an edge of a scene polygon, oriented so that the scene polygon is entirely in the plane's negative half-space or on the plane.

- *light-source edge planes*, defined by an edge of the light source and a vertex of a scene polygon, oriented so that the scene polygon is entirely in the plane's negative half-space or on the plane.

We use Nishita and Nakamae's criteria for determining those planes that define the penumbra and umbra volumes of a scene polygon. The penumbra volume is the intersection of the scene polygon's negative half-space with the negative half-spaces of certain light-source vertex planes and light-source edge planes. These light-source vertex planes and light-source edge planes are those for which the vertices of the light source are entirely in the plane's positive half-space or on the plane. (The penumbra volume actually encloses points in umbra, as well as those in penumbra.)

Figure 1 shows the penumbra cast on a large polygon by a triangle light source illuminating a quadrilateral scene polygon. Dashed lines passing from each light source vertex to

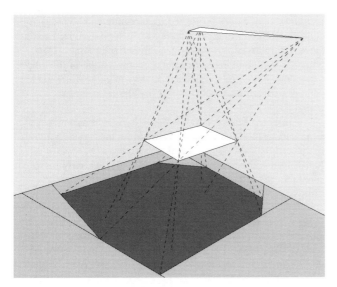

Figure 1: Penumbra of area light source, with light-source vertex planes and light-source edge planes.

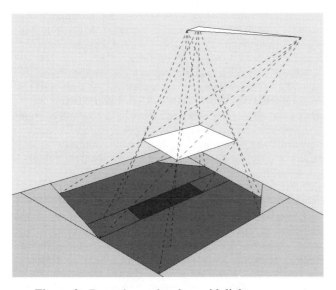

Figure 2: Penumbra and umbra, with light-source vertex planes and light-source edge planes.

all scene polygon vertices define the light-source vertex planes and light-source edge planes. (The additional fragmentation surrounding the penumbra outline is caused by the algorithm's classification process, which we describe later.) Note that the planes that bound the penumbra volume are those that have the light source in their positive half-space and the scene polygon in their negative half-space. Thus, any point in the positive half-space of such a plane cannot be blocked from any part of the light source by the scene polygon.

The umbra volume, which is contained entirely within the penumbra volume, is the intersection of the scene polygon's negative half-space with the negative half-spaces of certain light-source vertex planes. These light-source vertex planes are those for which the vertices of the light source are entirely in the plane's negative half-space or on the plane. No light-source edge planes contribute to the umbra volume.

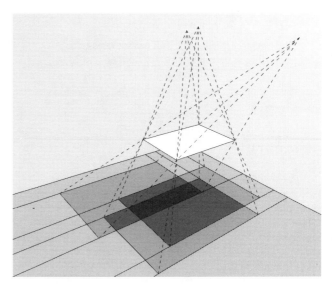

Figure 3: Shadows cast by 3 point light sources at the vertices of an area light source.

Figure 2 shows the same scene as Figure 1 with the umbra included. Note that the dashed lines that lie in the planes that define the umbra outline do not always pass through the umbra outline's vertices.

Figure 3 shows an alternative, but exactly equivalent, way to define the umbra and penumbra volumes. They can be derived from the shadow volumes generated when the convex scene polygon is illuminated by point light sources at the convex area light source's vertices. (The additional fragmentation of the ground plane is caused by the BSP-tree point light-source shadow algorithm used to create this figure.) The area light source's umbra volume contains those points that are blocked from all of the area light source's vertices. This corresponds to the intersection of the point light-source shadow volumes, which is defined by the set of light-source vertex planes specified previously.

The union of the point light-source shadow volumes encloses all points that are blocked from one or more vertices of the area light source. This is only a subset of the light source's penumbra volume, however, since it does not include those points that are visible from all the area light source's vertices, but are blocked from part of the area light source's interior. It can be shown that to enclose these points the penumbra volume must be the convex hull of the point light-source shadow volumes. The convex hull is defined by the set of light-source vertex planes and light-source edge planes specified previously.

Overview

Instead of the single SVBSP tree required by the point light-source shadow algorithm, we use two BSP trees: a *penumbra tree* and an *umbra tree* [8]. Each BSP-tree internal node is defined by a light-source vertex plane or light-source edge plane.

Much like the point light-source shadow algorithm, two steps must be performed for each scene polygon:

- Classifying the polygon into wholly lit, penumbra, and umbra fragments.

- Enlarging the penumbra and umbra trees with light-source vertex planes and light-source edge planes defined by the polygon.

The classified fragments must then be illuminated and scan-converted.

Algorithm

Preprocess. An obvious approach to classification would be to compare each scene polygon with the shadow volume of every other scene polygon. However, polygons that are not in the same half-space of a polygon as the light source cannot cast shadows on that polygon or any other polygon in the light source's half-space. Therefore, as in the point light-source shadow algorithm, we first compute a BSP tree for the entire scene. This allows us to perform a modified inorder traversal of the tree to process scene polygons in front-to-back order relative to the light source.

Unlike a point light source, an area light source may not lie entirely in a single half-space of a scene polygon. If this occurs, choosing different points on the area light source will generate different BSP-tree traversal orders. To obtain a unique order, we first split each area light source by those scene polygons that intersect it and that are in the lit half-space of the light source's plane. Since each of the resulting light sources is wholly on one side of each scene polygon, any point within the light source will generate the same front-to-back ordering of the scene polygons. For convenience, we pick the centroid of each resulting area light source as the point from which to compute the ordering. We must also ensure that each scene polygon that straddles a light source plane is split by the plane.

Classification. Classification and tree enlargement are interleaved as they are performed incrementally for each scene polygon in front-to-back order. Therefore, the two shadow trees represent the merged penumbra and umbra volumes of all the scene polygons processed thus far. Classification occurs by filtering each polygon down one or both shadow trees. This process is applied recursively until all of a polygon's fragments reach the "in" and "out" leaves.

A polygon is first filtered down the penumbra tree. Any fragment that reaches an "out" cell is marked as wholly lit and will not be compared with the umbra tree. (Recall that the umbra volume is wholly contained within the penumbra volume, so any fragment outside the penumbra volume cannot be in umbra.) Any fragment that reaches an "in" cell is at least in penumbra and may be in umbra. Each such fragment must then be filtered down the umbra tree. Any fragment that reaches an umbra tree "out" cell is in penumbra, whereas any fragment that reaches an umbra tree "in" cell is in umbra. The penumbra and umbra BSP trees are enlarged by unioning them with the penumbra volume and umbra volume, respectively, defined by the full scene polygon. We trivially classify as in umbra any polygon that is in the back half-space of a light source, without any need for filtering. In addition, if we assume that polygons are "one-sided" and that they bound closed polyhedra, we can also trivially classify as in umbra all polygons that are back-facing relative to the light source.

As in the earlier point light-source algorithm, multiple area light sources are supported by pipelining. The fragments classified relative to one light source must be used as input to the algorithm when processing the next light source. Thus, when all light sources have been processed, each of the output fragments is uniquely classified relative to each of the light sources. (See the pseudocode for the algorithm in the appendix.)

Example. Figure 4 shows how the algorithm handles a simple example. For ease of explanation, the figure is drawn in 2D and thus shows umbra and penumbra areas cast by a linear light source on lines in the plane. (In 2D, only light-source vertex edges are needed, but the definitions are the same otherwise.)

Initially, both shadow trees are null ("out"), as shown in Figure 4(a). Polygon 1 is first filtered down the penumbra tree and is trivially classified as fully lit. Because no part of the polygon was classified as in penumbra, no classification is done using the umbra tree. Next, as shown in Figure 4(b), polygon 1's penumbra is used to enlarge the penumbra tree. Rather than using the many lit fragments that may have been identified, the original polygon is used instead. In 2D, this results in a union with polygon 1 and light-source vertex planes a and b, which define polygon 1's penumbra volume. Although polygon 1 was not classified using the umbra tree, it must be used to enlarge the umbra tree and results in a union with volume defined by polygon 1 and the light-source planes u and v.

Next, polygon 2 is classified, as shown in Figure 4(c). Much like polygon 1, polygon 2 is classified as wholly lit relative to the penumbra tree and is not classified using the umbra tree. The penumbra tree is then enlarged with polygon 2 and planes c and d, and the umbra tree is enlarged using polygon 2 and planes w and x. (Figure 4d). Unlike polygon 1, however, polygon 2's addition to the merged umbra volume is not semi-infinite.

Polygon 3 is more interesting. When it is classified against the penumbra tree, as shown in Figure 4(e), it is split by face a into fragments 3.1 and 3.2. Fragment 3.1 is classified as "out" (i.e., wholly lit), while fragment 3.2 is classified as "in" (i.e., in some combination of penumbra and umbra). Therefore, only fragment 3.2 must be filtered down the umbra tree. When this is accomplished, the umbra tree's v plane further subdivides fragment 3.2 into fragments 3.2.1 (in penumbra) and 3.2.2 (in umbra). At this point, both shadow trees are enlarged using the original polygon 3, as shown in Figure 4(f). This results (in 2D) in the polygon fragment 3.1 and plane e being added to the penumbra BSP tree and a volume defined by planes y and z and 3*, the fraction of polygon 3 not in umbra, being added to the umbra BSP tree.

Illumination

After classifying all fragments by all light sources, we need to illuminate them. We use an analytic direct diffuse illumination model [17] based on contour integration, which is evaluated at polygon vertices within the penumbra and wholly lit regions. Unlike full global illumination algorithms, interreflections are not computed. Points in umbra are lit by an ambient light component alone. In our implementation, interpolated shading is performed using 3D graphics hardware.

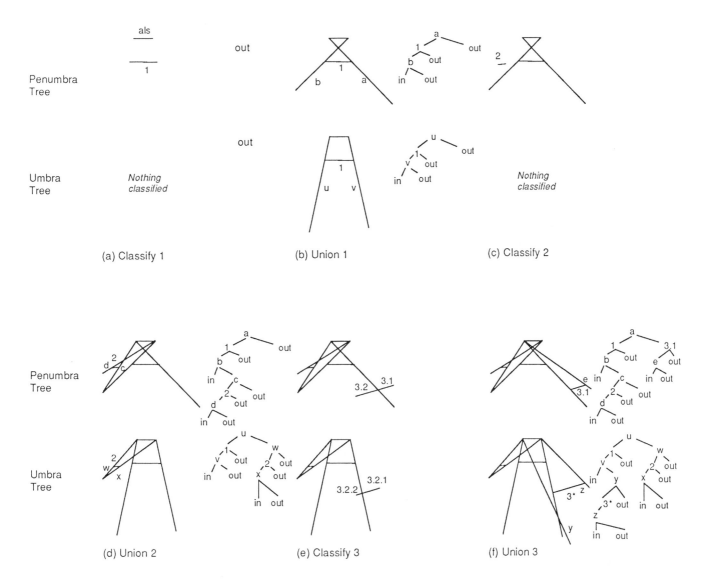

Figure 4: Classifying polygons and enlarging the penumbra and umbra BSP trees. Parts (a–f) show penumbra and umbra volumes (areas) and their trees during the classification of three polygons (lines).

Although the classification process divides polygons along precise shadow boundaries, large polygons may remain that are homogeneously lit or in penumbra. While direct illumination should vary continuously across these surfaces, linear interpolation does not adequately represent these changes and does not allow any polygon interior pixel to be brighter than the polygon's vertices. Therefore, illumination must be computed at additional points within the scene. In the pictures included here, we subdivide wholly lit and penumbra regions using regular grids of user-specified granularity. We generally use a finer grid in the penumbra region, since the intensity typically changes more quickly than in an equivalent wholly lit region. The umbra region is not subdivided because it receives only constant ambient illumination. Subdivision is performed after classification, since it has no effect on the precision at which classification occurs and would increase the classification overhead if performed first. BSP-tree subdivision can often generate thin sliver polygons that can cause shading anomalies. Better results would be obtained with an adaptive subdivision algorithm that attempted to generate well-shaped fragments from these potentially problematic fragments [3].

Diffuse illumination equation. To determine the illumination at a point that is wholly lit, we perform contour integration with the light source from the point being lit, as described in [17]. The diffuse illumination at point p due to the light-source is computed as

$$I_p = \frac{I_l}{2} \sum_{v=1}^{n} \alpha_v \cos(\beta_v),$$

where I_l is the light source intensity, n is the number of vertices of the light source, α_v is the angle between the vector from p to light-source vertex v and the vector from p to light-source vertex $v+1$, and β_v is the angle between the plane defined by the two vectors used to compute α and the plane on which p lies. (The cosine of β_v may be computed as the dot product of the normalized surface normal at p with the cross product of the normalized vectors used to define α_v.)

25

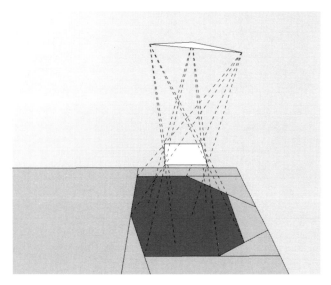

Figure 5: Penumbra volume of a single polygon.

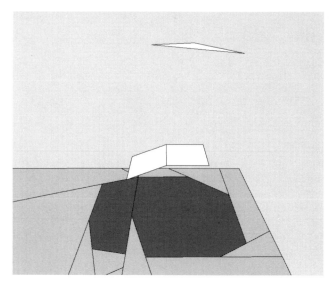

Figure 6: Incorrect merged penumbra volume of two polygons.

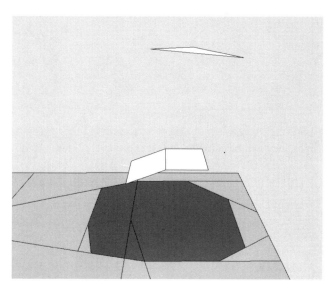

Figure 7: Correct merged penumbra volume of two polygons.

Analytic visibility for penumbra vertices. For points in penumbra, we must determine the fragments of the light source that are visible from the point. We accomplish this with a simplified version of the earlier point light-source shadow algorithm. By traversing the scene BSP tree, we can obtain all polygons between the point whose illumination is being computed and the plane of the light source. (Whether the traversal order is back-to-front or front-to-back is unimportant.) As before, we consider only those scene polygons that are front-facing relative to the light source (i.e., back-facing relative to the point being illuminated).

For each scene polygon, we clip the light-source polygon by the point light-source shadow volume defined by the point in penumbra and the edges of the scene polygon. The portion of the light source that is inside this volume is discarded and the portions that are outside are retained for comparison with the next scene polygon's volume. (Since the original light-source polygon bounds any light-source fragments produced, it can be used to do an extent check if desired.) The fragments remaining when the BSP-tree traversal encounters the light-source polygon are those that are visible from the point in penumbra and we sum the illumination contributed by each light-source fragment.

Discussion and Implementation

In the BSP-tree point light-source algorithm, the SVBSP tree was enlarged to reflect a polygon's contribution to the shadow volume by using a simplified version of the set union algorithm described in [21]. This simplification ignored any part of a polygon that fell within the existing volume. It used only planes determined by those fragments of the polygon that were wholly lit. For a point light source, the volume determined by these planes is guaranteed not to intersect the existing shadow volume. (In other words, no fragment lit by a point light source casts a shadow that falls within the shadow cast by any other lit fragment.) This is not the case for penumbra volumes, however. The penumbra volume cast by one polygon may intersect the volume cast by another. Therefore, a regular BSP-tree set union operation [21] must be performed.

Figure 5 shows the penumbra volume defined by a single scene polygon. Figure 6 shows the incorrect results that occur if a second scene polygon is added and the planes defining its penumbra volume are not continued into the penumbra volume of the original polygon. In this case, the penumbra volume of the second polygon considered by itself is similar to that of the first polygon and overlaps the first polygon's penumbra volume. This new penumbra volume crosses over the leftmost light-source vertex plane bounding the first polygon's penumbra volume. Part of the second polygon's contribution to the merged penumbra volume is ignored, resulting in the penumbra gap shown at the bottom of the figure. Figure 7 shows the correct merged penumbra volume that results when the original volume is enlarged properly by unioning the second polygon's penumbra volume with the current penumbra BSP tree, taking into account the possibility of

Plate	# lights	input polygons	shadow time (sec)	grid time (sec)	illum time (sec)	total time (sec)	output polygons	actual vertices	illuminated vertices
1,2	1	14	0.3	0.6	2.2	3.1	747	1341, 1668, 231	494, 437, 61
3,4	1	149	13.4	5.3	105.4	124.1	3348	3125, 8556, 3043	1576, 2512, 839
5	2	70	8.6	10.2	30.8, 37.9	87.5	4085	6768, 4627, 5791	2211, 1140, 1823
								7969, 5847, 3370	2608, 1429, 1132
6	2	151	35.8	23.2	178.1, 247.2	484.3	9344	10821, 14938, 13458	3904, 3839, 4008
								12599, 16594, 10024	4352, 4424, 2944

Figure 8: Statistics for color plates. All timings are given in elapsed wall-clock seconds for an HP 9000 380 (22 MIPS, 2.6 MFLOPS). Input polygon count takes into account splits caused by building the scene BSP tree. Shadow time is the time to classify the input polygons. Grid time is the time to subdivide the wholly lit and penumbra regions to produce the output polygons. Illumination time is the time to determine illumination values for the output vertices. Actual vertices lists the numbers of wholly lit, penumbra, and umbra vertices. Illuminated vertices lists the numbers of wholly lit, penumbra, and umbra calculations performed, which is lower than the actual vertex count because of vertex sharing. (Figures 5 and 6 have one illumination time for each light source, and one set of vertex statistics for each light source. Note that the sum of the actual wholly lit, penumbra, and umbra vertices is the same for each light source in these figures.)

overlapping volumes.

If the penumbra volume were incomplete, fragments that were contained in the volume's missing parts would be marked as wholly lit and would be incorrectly illuminated. Therefore, it is essential that the entirety of the actual penumbra volume be represented. In contrast, since the umbra volume is contained within the penumbra volume, if the umbra volume were incomplete, fragments that were contained in the umbra volume's missing parts would be marked as being in penumbra. Since the illumination algorithm correctly determines that these fragments are wholly blocked from the light, they will be correctly (albeit expensively) illuminated.

It is interesting to note that unioning each polygon's umbra volume with the existing umbra volume does *not* create the complete set of all points that are fully blocked from the light source. Instead, it creates the set of all points p such that there is at least one polygon that fully blocks p from the light source. That is, the union of the individual polygon umbra volumes does not contain those points that are fully blocked from the light source only because of the contributions of multiple blocking polygons. An example of this occurs in Figure 4(f). Points in the gap between planes v and y at the bottom of the volume are fully blocked from the light source because of the combined effect of polygons 1 and 3, yet do not lie in the merged umbra volume.

As with most analytic algorithms, care must be taken to contend with finite floating-point precision. To avoid problems, as polygons are split, the plane equations are copied, not recomputed. A similar method can be used to guarantee that split edges remain truly collinear. When a polygon edge is split, we also insert the new vertex in any other polygon that shares the edge. This prevents the shading discontinuities that would be caused by a "T" vertex. The vertex at which a split occurs is also shared among the polygon's fragments. This allows each vertex's illumination computation to be performed only once. It also makes it easy to determine the kinds of fragments that share a given vertex. If a vertex is shared by a wholly lit fragment and a penumbra fragment, we treat the vertex as wholly lit for both, eliminating the need for the light-source visibility test. If a vertex is shared by a wholly lit fragment and an umbra fragment, it is treated differently in each to preserve the boundary. We

currently do not promote vertices shared by both penumbra and umbra fragments to umbra vertices. This avoids the possibility of smearing a full umbra shadow into a penumbra fragment when the umbra fragment is blocked by an object that does not block the penumbra fragment. This is similar to the problem of "light leaks" [6], in which a polygon is straddled by a partition that blocks light from some of its vertices, even though illumination leaks under the partition through interpolated shading.

Another possible optimization that would reduce fragmentation is to merge fragments together when both subtrees were classified as "in" or as "out" [8]. Since a penumbra volume extends infinitely far past the object that casts it, we have also considered some approaches to restricting its extent, similar to Bergeron's use of end caps on shadow volumes to eliminate the need to perform shadow computations outside of a light's "sphere of influence." [4].

The area light-source algorithm has been implemented in C on an HP 9000 380 TurboSRX workstation, and the results are displayed interactively using hardware interpolated shading. Because the scene polygons are represented as a BSP tree, either the hardware z-buffer or a software BSP-tree visible-surface algorithm can be used to render the scene.

Pictures. Color Plate 1 shows two objects floating in air and one triangle light source with their penumbra and umbra regions. The light grey and dark grey fragments are in penumbra and umbra respectively, while the colored fragments are wholly lit. The wholly lit and penumbra fragments have been gridded after classification. Note the band of penumbra separating the umbra regions of both objects. As described above, this strip should be in umbra, but will be properly illuminated because the illumination computation determines that its vertices are unlit. The same scene after illumination and interpolated shading is shown in Color Plate 2.

Color Plate 3 shows a room with one quadrilateral area light source and gray fragments to represent the regions identified as being in penumbra and umbra. Color Plate 4 shows the room as it appears after illumination and shading. Color Plate 5 shows a different view of a simpler version of the room without the playpen, illuminated by two quadrilateral light sources. Color Plate 6 shows the same scene as Color

Figure 9: Room scene classified, 2 lights.

Plate 4, illuminated by both light sources. Figure 8 provides statistics for the color plates. Figure 9 shows the room depicted in Color Plate 6, prior to illumination, with the fragments produced by classification with both light sources and gridding.

Note that the most expensive part of the algorithm is the illumination phase, which need not be accomplished if the user is interested only in classifying objects according to their visibility, which is necessary in a number of applications in areas such as computer vision and graphics [12].

Conclusions and Future Work

The algorithm described here analytically generates penumbra and a subset of the umbra for static convex polygonal environments illuminated by convex area light sources. It is relatively simple to implement, places no restrictions on the location of objects and light sources, and runs efficiently for small scenes on modern workstations with hardware 3D graphics support. To generate further points at which illumination is sampled, we have implemented both regular gridding and simple adaptive subdivision of those fragments that are wholly lit or in penumbra.

We believe that an efficient analytic shadow algorithm would be useful in multiple passes of a radiosity approach (not just for the initial light-source calculations, as implemented in [18]). If selected radiators were treated as area light sources, object-precision shadow boundaries could be determined, instead of the relatively coarse boundaries obtained with current adaptive meshing techniques. This may make it possible to create more accurate images, with the illumination contour integral used to calculate analytic form factors [2] that properly take into account obstructions, guided by the shadow (i.e., visibility) classification phase.

Acknowledgments

This work was supported in part by the Office of Naval Research under Contract N00014-91-J-1872, the Defense Advanced Research Projects Agency under Contract N00039-84-C-0165, and an equipment grant from the Hewlett-Packard Company. Thanks to Clark Still and Tim Lee of the Columbia University Department of Chemistry, and Marilyn Noz of the NYU School of Medicine for generously allowing us to use their workstations.

References

1. Amanatides, J. Ray Tracing with Cones. *Proc. SIGGRAPH '84* (Minneapolis, MN, July 23–27, 1984). In *Computer Graphics*, 18(3), July 1984, 129–135.

2. Baum, D., Rushmeier, H., and Winget, J. Improving Radiosity Solutions Through the Use of Analytically Determined Form-Factors. *Proc. SIGGRAPH '89* (Boston, MA, July 31–August 4, 1989). In *Computer Graphics*, 23(3), July 1989, 325–334.

3. Baum, D., Mann, S., Smith, K., and Winget, J. Making Radiosity Usable: Automatic Preprocessing and Meshing Techniques for the Generation of Accurate Radiosity Solutions. *Proc. SIGGRAPH '91* (Las Vegas, NV, July 28–August 2, 1991). In *Computer Graphics*, 25(4), July 1991, 51–60.

4. Bergeron, P. A General Version of Crow's Shadow Volumes. *IEEE CG&A*, 6(9), September 1986, 17–28.

5. Brotman, L. and Badler, N. Generating Soft Shadows with a Depth Buffer Algorithm. *IEEE CG&A*, 4(10), October 1984, 5–12.

6. Campbell, A.T., III, and Fussell, D.S. Adaptive Mesh Generation for Global Diffuse Illumination. *Proc. SIGGRAPH '90* (Dallas, TX, August 6–10, 1991). In *Computer Graphics*, 24(4), August 1990, 155–164.

7. Chin, N. and Feiner, S. Near Real-Time Shadow Generation Using BSP Trees. *Proc. SIGGRAPH '89* (Boston, MA, July 31–August 4, 1989). In *Computer Graphics*, 23(3), July 1989, 99–106.

8. Chin, N. *Near Real-Time Object-Precision Shadow Generation Using BSP Trees.* MS Thesis, Dept. of Computer Science, Columbia University, New York, NY, 1990.

9. Cohen, M.F. and Greenberg, D.P. The Hemi-Cube: A Radiosity Solution for Complex Environments. *Proc. SIGGRAPH '85* (San Francisco, CA, July 22–26, 1985). In *Computer Graphics*, 19(3), July 1985, 31–40.

10. Cook, R.L., Porter, T., and Carpenter, L. Distributed Ray Tracing. *Proc. SIGGRAPH '84* (Minneapolis, MN, July 23–27, 1984). In *Computer Graphics*,

18(3), July 1984, 137–145.

11. Crow, F. Shadow Algorithms for Computer Graphics. *Proc. SIGGRAPH '77* (San Jose, CA, July 20–22, 1977). In *Computer Graphics*, 11(2), Summer 1977, 242–248.

12. Feiner, S. and Seligmann, D. Dynamic 3D illustrations with visibility constraints. In Patrikalakis, N. (ed.), *Scientific Visualization of Physical Phenomena* (*Proc. Computer Graphics International '91*, Cambridge, MA, June 26–28, 1991), Springer-Verlag, Tokyo, 1991, 525–543.

13. Foley J., van Dam, A., Feiner, S., and Hughes, J. *Computer Graphics: Principles and Practice, Second Edition*, Addison-Wesley, Reading MA, 1990.

14. Fuchs, H., Kedem, A., and Naylor, B. On Visible Surface Generation by A Priori Tree Structures. *Proc. SIGGRAPH '80* (Seattle, WA, July 14–18, 1980). In *Computer Graphics*, 14(3), July 1980, 124–133.

15. Fuchs, H., Abram, G., and Grant, E. Near Real-Time Shaded Display of Rigid Objects. *Proc. SIGGRAPH '83* (Detroit, MI, July 25–29, 1983). In *Computer Graphics*, 17(3), July 1983, 65–72.

16. Naylor, B., Amanatides, J., and Thibault, W. Merging BSP Trees Yields Polyhedral Set Operations. *Proc. SIGGRAPH '90* (Dallas, TX, August 6–10, 1991). In *Computer Graphics*, 24(4), August 1990, 115–124.

17. Nishita, T. and Nakamae, E. Half-Tone Representation of 3-D Objects Illuminated by Area Sources or Polyhedron Sources. *Proc IEEE COMPSAC*, November 1983, 237–241.

18. Nishita, T. and Nakamae, E. Continuous Tone Representation of Three-Dimensional Objects Taking Account of Shadows and Interreflection. *Proc. SIGGRAPH '85* (San Francisco, CA, July 22–26, 1985). In *Computer Graphics*, 19(3), July 1985, 23–30.

19. Schumacker, R., Brand, B., Gilliland, M., and Sharp, W. Study for Applying Computer-Generated Images to Visual Simulation. Technical Report AFHRL-TR-69-14, NTIS AD700375, US Air Force Human Resources Lab, Air Force Systems Command, Brooks AFB, TX, September 1969.

20. Sutherland, I., Sproull, R., and Schumacker, R. A Characterization of Ten Hidden-Surface Algorithms. ACM Computing Surveys, 6(1), March 1974, 1–55.

21. Thibault, W. and Naylor, B. Set Operations on Polyhedra Using Binary Space Partitioning Trees. *Proc. SIGGRAPH '87* (Anaheim, CA, July 27–31, 1987). In *Computer Graphics*, 21(4), July 1987, 153–162.

22. Woo, A., Poulin, P. and Fournier, A. A Survey of Shadow Algorithms. *IEEE CG&A*, 10(6), November 1990, 13–32.

Appendix: Pseudocode

```
procedure generateShadows (ALSlist, BSPtree)

    for each node n in BSPtree ; scene BSP tree
        copy n.scenePolygon into n.fragmentList
    endfor

    for each als in ALSlist
        centroid := centroid of als

        pBSP := OUT_CELL ; penumbra BSP tree
        uBSP := OUT_CELL ; umbra BSP tree

        for each node n in BSPtree in front-to-back order
            relative to centroid

            ; move n.fragmentList to fragmentList
            ; so that n.fragmentList can be recreated
            ; with fully classified and subdivided fragments
            fragmentList := n.fragmentList
            n.fragmentList := NULL

            for each fragment f in fragmentList
                if f not facing centroid OR als not facing f
                    mark f in umbra
                    n.fragmentList := append(n.fragmentList,f)
                else
                    ; split f into wholly lit & shadowed fragments
                    ; by filtering down pBSP

                    tempFragmentList := NULL
                    classifyWhollyLitOrShadowed
                        (als,pBSP,f,&tempFragmentList)

                    ; partition shadowed fragments into penumbra
                    ; and umbra

                    for each fragment t in tempFragmentList
                        if t is shadowed
                            classifyPenumbraOrUmbra
                                (als,uBSP,t,&n.fragmentList)
                        else
                            n.fragmentList :=
                                append(n.fragmentList,t)
                        endif
                    endfor

                    ; enlarge pBSP and uBSP trees

                    pv :=
                        constructPolygonPenumbra(als,n.scenePolygon)
                    pBSP := union(pBSP,pv) ; see [21]
                    uv :=
                        constructPolygonUmbra(als,n.scenePolygon)
                    uBSP := union(uBSP,uv)
                endif
            endfor ; fragment
        endfor ; node

        discard pBSP and uBSP

    endfor ; als
endproc
```

```
procedure classifyWhollyLitOrShadowed          procedure classifyPenumbraOrUmbra
    (als,pBSP,f,fragmentList)                      (als,uBSP,f,fragmentList)

  if (pBSP is a leaf)                             if (uBSP is a leaf)
    if (pBSP == OUT_CELL)                           if (uBSP == OUT_CELL)
      mark f as wholly lit                            mark f as penumbra
    else                                            else
      mark f as shadowed                              mark f as umbra
    endif                                           endif
    fragmentList := append(fragmentList,f)          fragmentList := append(fragmentList,f)
  else                                            else
    splitPolygon(pBSP.plane,f,&negPart,&posPart)    splitPolygon(uBSP.plane,f,&negPart,&posPart)
    if (negPart != NULL)                            if (negPart != NULL)
      classifyWhollyLitOrShadowed(als,pBSP.negChild,   classifyPenumbraOrUmbra(als,uBSP.negChild,
        negPart,&fragmentList)                           negPart,&fragmentList)
    endif                                           endif
    if (posPart != NULL)                            if (posPart != NULL)
      classifyWhollyLitOrShadowed(als,pBSP.posChild,   classifyPenumbraOrUmbra(als,uBSP.posChild,
        posPart,&fragmentList)                           posPart,&fragmentList)
    endif                                           endif
  endif                                           endif

endproc                                         endproc
```

Lights from Highlights and Shadows

Pierre Poulin
Alain Fournier

Department of Computer Science
University of British Columbia
{poulin | fournier} @cs.ubc.ca

Abstract

Designing the illumination of a scene is a difficult task because one needs to render the whole scene in order to look at the result. Obtaining the correct lighting effects may require a long sequence of modeling/rendering steps. We propose to use directly the highlights and shadows in the modeling process. By creating and altering these lighting effects, the lights themselves are indirectly modified. We believe this new technique to design lighting is more intuitive and can lead to a reduction of the number of modeling/rendering steps required to obtain the desired image.

CR Categories and Subject Descriptors: I.3.7 [Computer Graphics]: Three-Dimensional Graphics and Realism. Interaction techniques.
General Terms: Algorithms.
Additional Key Words and Phrases: extended light source, shadow volume, soft shadows, hard shadows, interactive light modeling.

1 Introduction

An important research area of computer graphics consists in simulating realistic pictures. Reality is modeled by observing and measuring its attributes. In a next step, the models are rendered onto an image. In that sense, computer graphics models the causes and renders the effects onto an image. On the other hand, computer vision is interested in analyzing an image. It tries to isolate certain effects in an image in order to identify the causes. While the two processes might seem to go on totally opposite directions, it is interesting to consider how advances in one direction might actually help the reverse process.

In computer vision, highlight information has been used to determine light direction or local shape orientation. Babu et al. [babu85] study contours of constant intensity in an image to determine the orientation of planar surfaces under the illumination of a directional light source. Buchanan [buch87] fits ellipses to the highlights to obtain the same information

for planar surfaces illuminated by point light sources.

One important aspect of most of these algorithms consists in identifying the highlight area. This is not an easy task as many of the algorithms for shape from shading [horn88] require almost entirely diffuse surfaces.

When techniques are not restricted to diffuse surfaces, they often rely on some kind of thresholding. The unfortunate reality with thresholding is that different values of threshold can lead to relatively different shape of the highlight and therefore, to different shape/light recovery. Other techniques like Wolff's use of polarization [wolf91] are promising although require the presence of polarizing lenses on the cameras capturing the scene.

Much useful information can also be extracted from the shadow areas in an image [walt75] [shaf85]. These areas provide additional information on the shape of the object casting a shadow and even on the shape of the object on which the shadow is cast. Moreover, they provide information on the direction and the shape of the light sources. Unfortunately, very little work has been involved in recovering the shape of an extended light source, as recovering shape from shading under a directional or a point light source is already a difficult task.

Shadows are not easy to extract from an image. Detecting shadows can be done in a similar way than edge detection by applying various edge enhancing filters. For extended lights, the shadow edges are soft and the shadow must be detected based on changes in the gradients of the shading. Gershon [gers87] use gradients in color space to determine if the region corresponds to a shadow region or simply to a change of material. Textures can also defeat most of the techniques and must be carefully handled.

While modeling a scene, a user has access to important information unavailable to computer vision, i.e. the geometry of the scene and the viewing projection parameters. To better understand a 3D scene, the user can therefore move the camera around, use at the same time several views of the same scene, move objects, remove hidden surfaces, and all of this in real time; however, so far, few applications use information about highlights and shadows in order to improve on the modeling step in computer graphics.

This paper proposes to investigate how we can use highlight and shadow information in order to help a user to define the shape and position of a light source. It does not preclude the previous ways of defining and positioning the light sources, but enhances the whole process.

2 Defining and Manipulating Light Sources

With the advent of high performance graphics hardware, it becomes possible to interactively create and manipulate more and more complex models with a higher degree of realism. Yesterday's simple wireframe models can now be replaced by flat shaded polygons, Gouraud shaded and even Phong shaded polygons, allowing for real time interaction with the models. Hanrahan and Haeberli [hanr90] demonstrate with their system how today's graphics hardware could be used to "paint" textures and various other surface parameters (transparency, perturbation of surface normals, etc.) in a fully interactive system. This increase in rendering power provides us with the possibility to investigate light definition and manipulation from the highlights and shadows it produces.

2.1 Lights from Highlights

In this section, the process of defining a light from its highlights is described. Its advantages are demonstrated and its restrictions explained so one could better understand the implications of using such a process.

Highlights are usually defined in the reflection models by the specular term. Consider the specular term of Phong's shading [phon75] as expressed by Blinn [blin77]:

$$\left(\vec{N} \cdot \vec{H}\right)^n \tag{1}$$

where $\vec{N}$ is the surface normal at a given point[1]

$\vec{H}$ is the bisector vector of the eye direction and the light direction

n is the surface roughness coefficient.

This formulation tells us that for a given point on the surface specified as the *maximum intensity* of the highlight, a unique directional light source can be determined as

$$\vec{L} = 2\left(\vec{N} \cdot \vec{E}\right)\vec{N} - \vec{E} \tag{2}$$

where $\vec{E}$ is the eye direction.

The term *maximum intensity* is not properly correct if we think of it in the context of a complete shading model. However we will use it here meaning maximizing equation (1). It is interesting to note that other points on the surface might reach this maximum but will never surpass it.

This simple relationship between the maximum intensity of the highlight and light direction has been used in the past. Hanrahan and Haeberli [hanr90] mention how they can specify a light direction by dragging a highlight on a sphere. This technique has also been previously implemented in some modelers like a light modeler developed in 1983 at NYIT by Paul Heckbert (manipulating highlights on a sphere) and a light editor written by Richard Chuang around 1985 at PDI, which was used among others, to get highlights to appear at the right time on flying logos. It also came to the attention of the authors that a similar approach to Chuang's was used at LucasFilm to get the glare to appear at the crucial moment on a sword in the movie *Young Sherlock Holmes*.

Our technique extends the basic approach in the above systems by indirectly and interactively determining the surface roughness coefficient n in relation with the size of the highlight. Here is how it works.

---

[1] All vectors in this paper are assumed normalized

Once the maximum intensity point of the highlight has been chosen, the user drags the cursor away from this point. At a new position on the surface, the surface normal is computed. This new point is used to determine the boundary of the highlight, i.e. where the specular term of (1) reaches a fixed threshold t. To satisfy this threshold, n, the only unknown, is easily computed as

$$n = \frac{\log t}{\log(\vec{N} \cdot \vec{H})}. \tag{3}$$

While only these two points on a surface are necessary to orient a directional light source and establish the surface roughness coefficient, they give almost no information on the shape of the highlight. To approximate the contour of the highlight, the pixel with the maximum intensity is used as a seed point and the neighboring pixels covered by this surface are visited in a *boundary fill* fashion until pixels on both sides of the threshold are identified or until the boundary of the surface is found. With this technique, the second point might not appear within the contour of the highlight determined from the seed point. If this happens, the second point is also used as a seed. Unfortunately, unless each pixel covered by this surface is visited, some of the other highlights produced by this light on this surface might be missed. If the position of every highlight is necessary, the whole surface is visited by the filling algorithm only on request from the user because such a request can lead to considerable increase in computation time.

When n has already been determined for a given surface, care must be taken in order to keep a unique value for n. If another highlight is created on this surface, as soon as the point with the maximum intensity is selected, the contour of this new highlight is computed with the previous value for n. However this value for n and the position of the highlights are not fixed and can be interactively changed because some information is kept in a temporary frame buffer. In this frame buffer, each previously visited pixel contains information about its surface normal. The contour can therefore be scaled down (i.e. a smaller highlight but a larger value for n) very efficiently. If the contour is increased, only the unvisited pixels need to have their surface normal determined. Moving the contour on the surface is also possible although more expensive if the highlight is moved to a completely different location on the surface as many surface normals might have to be computed. On some graphics hardware like the VGX from SGI, information on the surface normals can be obtained directly from the hardware and therefore allows for even faster highlight manipulation. Figure 1 shows the highlight produced by a directional light source over a patch of the teapot. The white segment within the highlight region represents the point of maximum intensity and points towards the light direction.

Unfortunately, highlight information is dependent on the eye position. Therefore, if the camera is moved, every highlight in the scene must be recomputed. Also, the points of maximum intensity are not valid any more and consequently every surface has to be scanned to recover every highlight, an expensive process that one should try to avoid as much as possible. This means also that a highlight computed in one window would have a different definition in another window with a different projection. To avoid confusion and increasing too much the computing time, we decided to remove every highlight information when the viewing parameters are changed although we keep the light definitions. These highlights are recomputed on request from the user.

Figure 1: Creating a light by its highlight

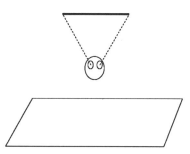

Figure 2: Incomplete highlight information

Another limitation of using highlight information to describe a light source resides in the fact that a highlight specifies only a direction. We therefore need more constraints to use it to determine other types of light source. Such constraints exist for instance for polygonal light sources. Assume a plane on which a polygonal light resides. By adding a highlight, a direction is established. The intersection between this direction and such a plane[2] defines a point light source, a vertex of a linear or polygonal light source.

To represent highlights created by extended light sources, the contribution of each vertex of the light is not sufficient to determine the shape of the complete highlight. To display this information, the boundary fill algorithm would have to compute the specular integral for a linear light [poul91] or a polygonal light [tana91] for each pixel to visit. Such integrals are rather expensive to compute and in order to achieve real time, cheaper approximations based on precomputed tables could be of some use here. We did not investigate this approach in the context of this paper, relying solely on the partial information provided by the light vertices as shown in figure 2.

As it can be observed, highlight information can be very useful to specify directional light sources and surface roughness coefficients. With extra constraints, they can even be

used to define point, linear and polygonal light sources although creating an arbitrary plane in 3D is not necessarily an easy task. Another technique, more flexible for extended light sources, consists in using the shadow information to define the light sources.

2.2 Lights from Shadows

Shadows are very important clues to help understanding the geometry of the scene and the interrelationship between objects; in the context of this paper, shadows can reveal important information about the nature of the light sources. We will define light sources by manipulating their *shadow volumes*.[3] These shadow volumes have the advantage to depend only on the lights and objects positions. Therefore, as opposed to the case of the highlights, the camera position can be changed without altering their description. Moreover, their definition is consistent for every projection, allowing for multiple windows open with different orthographic and perspective projections as used in most of the modeling systems.

The shadow volume created by an object illuminated by a directional light source consists of a sweep of the object silhouette in the direction the light source shines. This silhouette can be analytically determined for simple primitives, computed for moderately complicated objects with algorithms like in [bonf86], sampled by studying the variation of surface normals at the vertices of a tessellated object or sampled using the information in a z-buffer projection of this object. Specifying the direction of a directional light is simply a question of choosing two arbitrary, although different, points in the scene. The second point will be along the shadow cast by the first one. To move this shadow volume once defined, one needs to select a point on the shadow

---

[2]Note that there might not be any intersection

[3]A shadow volume formed by a single object and a directional or a point light is the 3D volume within which every point is in shadow of this object [crow77] [berg86]. For extended light sources (linear, polygonal), the shadow volume is the 3D volume within which every point is at least partly in shadow of this object.

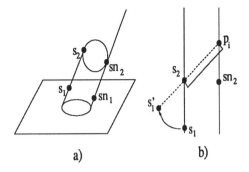

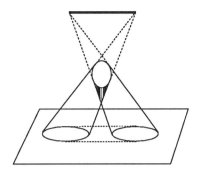

Figure 4: Going from a directional light source to a point light source

Figure 5: Umbra region in hatched undetected in the projection domain

volume. The point on the object casting this shadow is then identified. By dragging the cursor to a new location, a new direction is computed, the direction of a directional light source. Figure 3 shows a cylinder illuminated by a directional light source. For some primitives, computing the exact silhouette can be expensive and not carry much more information. In the case of this cylinder, each polygon vertex forming the cylinder is simply projected in the direction the light shines.

A directional light source can be viewed as a point light source at infinity. If the point light source is not at infinity, the silhouette defining the shadow volume can be different than the silhouette defined by a directional light source. Figure 4 illustrates the process of going from a directional light source (figure 4a) to a point light source (figure 4b) by modifying its shadow volume.

A point sn_1 on the shadow volume is chosen. The point sn_2 on the silhouette casting shadow on the point sn_1 is identified. This *shadow segment* $sn_1 - sn_2$ will now be considered as nailed and the point light source will reside on the line extending this segment. By selecting another point s_1 on the shadow volume, the point s_2 casting this shadow on this point is identified. The nailed segment $sn_1 - sn_2$ and the point s_2 define a plane $(sn_1 - sn_2 - s_2)$. By moving the cursor, a point s'_1 on this plane is located. s'_1 now is on the shadow cast by s_2. The point light source is therefore moved to p_i as shown in figure 4b.

Once a point light source is created, it can be manipulated in the scene by manipulating its volume shadow. This can be done by fixing any shadow segment as previously explained, or, if no shadow segment is nailed, by adding a new constraint to the system by assuming for instance the distance d from the light p_i to the point s_2 casting a shadow is constant. Combinations of these two actions are sufficient to position almost any point light source in a scene.

In some rare configurations of a scene, some positions might not be accessible. For instance, assume a scene is made of a single flat polygon and of a directional light parallel to the plane of the polygon. In such a situation, the light will never be able to escape the plane of the polygon. Fortunately, this situation does not occur often in general 3D scenes, and so far combinations of moving the shadow volumes with and without nailed segments proved to be sufficient to position our lights.

It is important to note that the point s_2 might not lie on the boundary of the shadow volume while the point light source is moved around. However the real shadow volume is always displayed so the user has a direct view of the altered shadow.

To create extended light sources like linear or polygonal, new point light sources are needed, defining the vertices of the light source. The shadow volumes of each light vertex are handled as normal point light sources although for polygonal light sources with more than three vertices, care must be taken so each light vertex will reside on the light plane.

Shadows of extended light sources are formed by the umbra and penumbra regions. The whole shadow region is defined by the convolution of the object and the light source in the projection domain [guib83]. The umbra is defined by the intersection of each shadow volume (one shadow volume per light vertex); the penumbra is the difference between the whole shadow and the umbra. Nishita et al. [nish83] studied the various parts of these shadow regions in 2D, once projected onto polygonal surfaces for shadow culling purposes. Some problems occur when neither the object casting the shadow or the light are limited to being convex. It can be shown however that if both the light and the object are divided into convex elements, the whole shadow is the *union* in 3D of all the shadow convex hulls as:

```
For each convex light element
    For each convex object element
        Compute the convex hull of the shadow
        volumes created by these two elements
    Compute the 3D union of all these convex hulls
```

For now on, assume a polygonal convex light and a convex object.

Assume an object does not intersect the light plane. All the shadows lie on a plane parallel to the light plane but located at infinity. As such, 2D convex hull algorithms can be used to determine which part of the shadow volumes form the 3D convex hull of the shadow volumes.

However computing the umbra region, i.e. the intersection of the convex hulls for each light vertex cannot be done in 2D. Figure 5 shows an example where using only the information in the 2D projection plane would fail to identify the umbra region showed in hatched.

To recover the umbra region, one could intersect each shadow polygon[4] of a light vertex shadow volume with each other shadow volume of the other vertices of a single light. This process can be very expensive as it is $O((ps)^2)$ where p is the number of vertices of the light and s is the number

---

[4]The silhouette of the object can be discretized. Each point cast its shadow in one direction. Two consecutive points on this silhouette and their shadow direction define a quadrilateral with two of its vertices at infinity.

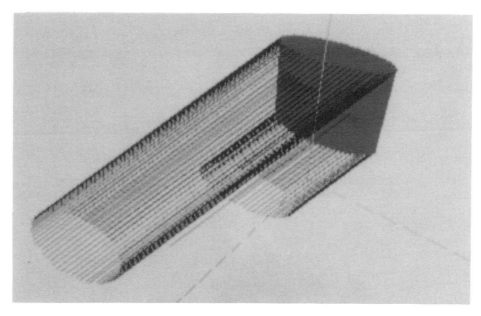

Figure 3: Creating a directional light by its shadow

of shadow polygons forming the shadow volume. However some improvements can be obtained by first projecting the shadow quadrilateral onto the plane containing the convex hull on the 2D projection plane.

Since we use Graham's 2D convex hull algorithm [sedg90], the points of the shadow quadrilateral, once projected in 2D, are converted in pseudo angles and an efficient combination of angle comparisons and boxing allows for faster intersection culling.

This process could also be improved by using a different data structure that might be more suitable for faster intersections of half planes defined by the shadow quadrilaterals. In object space, the binary space subdivision algorithm handling shadow volumes as presented by Chin and Feiner [chin89] would be a good candidate to investigate, while in screen space the algorithm described by Fournier and Fussell [four88] could be of use.

3   Results

A very simple modeler has been implemented in order to test the techniques presented in this paper. The modeler includes primitives like conics (sphere, disk, cone, cylinder), squares, cubes, triangular meshes and Bézier patches. Figure 6 shows a global view of the modeler itself.

The code, far from being optimized, is written under GL and was developed and tested on an Iris 4D/20 with z-buffer. This machine handles well a few primitives (≈ 10) but as the scene complexity increases, a 4D/240 VGX becomes very handy. The VGX also allows for real time Phong shading which is very useful to model a scene and when creating/manipulating shadows, but it can lead to some minor difficulties when creating highlights, because the threshold t must be adjusted to the SGI's Phong's shading implementation.

Figures 7 to 9 show a cone under a triangular light source. At first, no convex hull is applied. In this image (figure 7), it is easier to associate each shadow with a light vertex. Once the convex hull is applied (figure 8), the silhouette

of the penumbra is easier to detect. Notice the umbra region just under the cone, within the penumbra region. In figure 9, the umbra and penumbra volumes are filled with a semi-transparent mask. This representation gives a more complete impression of the shadows that can not really be shown here with a single image.

4   Conclusion

In this paper, we investigated using lighting effects, i.e. highlights and shadows, to define the lights themselves and specify their location. We showed some inherent limitations with these approaches but also demonstrated a powerful new technique. This technique allows a user to interactively manipulates highlights and shadows, which can be very important when designing a scene. In previous modeling systems, these effects were too often neglected. Therefore a user needed to iterate between rendering the whole scene and modifying the lights. It is a process that can be expensive depending of the quality of the rendering required. Incorporating highlights and shadows in the modeling process adds more information on the geometry of the scene and its illumination which should help the user to understand better the scene before even rendering it.

Our system, although simple, gives during the modeling process direct information to the user on the lighting effects since these effects are the objects being manipulated. This direct manipulation is crucial as getting the right effect by manipulating the causes is generally more difficult than manipulating the effects themselves.

We foresee that, as the graphics hardware improves and as the CPU becomes faster, more and more effects available once only at the rendering stage will become an inherent part of the modeling stage itself. Real time Phong shading is now becoming common with high-end modelers. These improvements will lead us to investigate more intuitive ways of defining and controlling these special effects. Although the separation between computer graphics and computer vision is still strong, we believe this will lead us to more and more

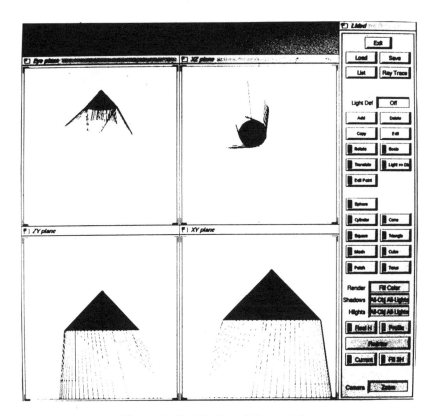

Figure 6: Global view of the modeler

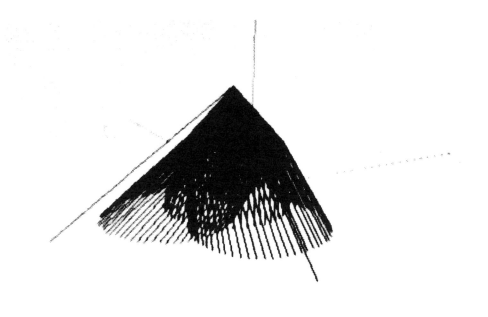

Figure 7: Cone under a triangular light: No convex hull

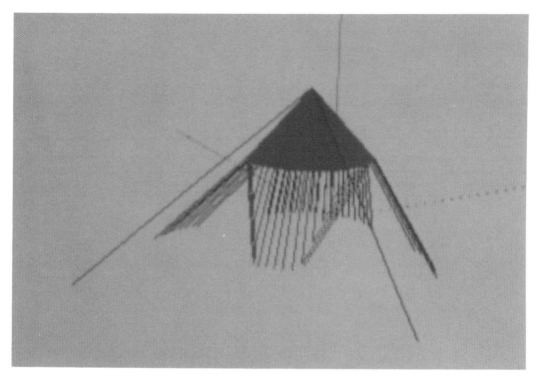

Figure 8: Cone under a triangular light: Convex hull applied

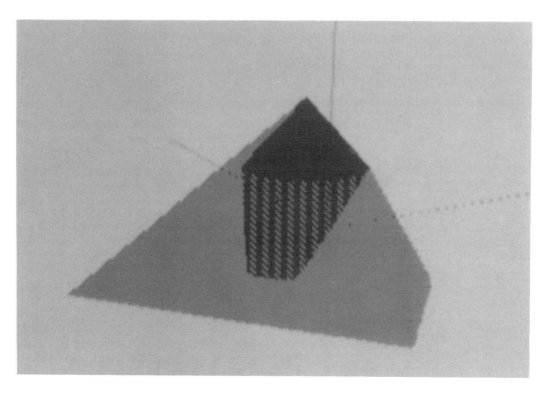

Figure 9: Cone under a triangular light: Convex hull with filled shadows

graphics in vision and more and more vision in graphics for greater benefits to realism in graphics and scene analysis of natural phenomena in vision.

Acknowledgements

Thanks to Mikio Shinya for interesting "brainstorming" sessions while the first author spent a summer at NTT Japan. Thanks also go to Paul Heckbert for informing us on related but unpublished work and for commenting on previous drafts of this paper. We acknowledge financial support from NSERC, UGF and the University of British Columbia.

References

[babu85] Mohan D.R. Babu, Chia-Hoang Lee, and Azriel Rosenfeld. "Determining Plane Orientation from Specular Reflectance". *Pattern Recognition*, Vol. 18, No. 1, pp. 53–62, January 1985.

[berg86] P. Bergeron. "A General Version of Crow's Shadow Volumes". *IEEE Computer Graphics and Applications*, Vol. 6, No. 9, pp. 17–28, September 1986.

[blin77] James F. Blinn. "Models of Light Reflection For Computer Synthesized Pictures". *Computer Graphics (SIGGRAPH '77 Proceedings)*, Vol. 11, No. 2, pp. 192–198, July 1977.

[bonf86] L. Bonfigliolo. "An Algorithm for Silhouette of Curved Surfaces based on Graphical Relations". *Computer-Aided Design*, Vol. 18, No. 2, pp. 95–101, March 1986.

[buch87] Craig Stuart Buchanan. "Determining Surface Orientation from Specular Highlights". M.Sc. Thesis, Department of Computer Science, University of Toronto, August 1987.

[chin89] Norman Chin and Steven Feiner. "Near Real-Time Shadow Generation Using BSP Trees". *Computer Graphics (SIGGRAPH '89 Proceedings)*, Vol. 23, No. 3, pp. 99–106, July 1989.

[crow77] Franklin C. Crow. "Shadow Algorithms for Computer Graphics". *Computer Graphics (SIGGRAPH '77 Proceedings)*, Vol. 11, No. 2, pp. 242–248, July 1977.

[four88] Alain Fournier and Donald Fussell. "On the power of the frame buffer". *ACM Transactions on Graphics*, Vol. 7, No. 2, pp. 103–128, April 1988.

[gers87] Ron Gershon. *The use of color in computational vision*. Ph.D. thesis, Dept. of Computer Science, University of Toronto, 1987.

[guib83] Leo Guibas, Lyle Ramshaw, and Jorge Stolfi. "A kinetic framework for computational geometry". *Proceedings of the 24th Annual IEEE Symposium on the Foundations of Computer Science*, pp. 100–111, 1983.

[hanr90] Pat Hanrahan and Paul Haeberli. "Direct WYSIWYG Painting and Texturing on 3D Shapes". *Computer Graphics (SIGGRAPH '90 Proceedings)*, Vol. 24, No. 4, pp. 215–223, August 1990.

[horn88] Berthold K. P. Horn and M.J. Brooks, editors. *Shape from Shading*. MIT Press, 1988.

[nish83] Tomoyuki Nishita and Eihachiro Nakamae. "Half-Tone Representation of 3-D Objects Illuminated by Area or Polyhedron Sources". *Proc. of IEEE Computer Society's Seventh International Computer Software and Applications Conference (COMPSAC83)*, pp. 237–242, November 1983.

[phon75] Bui-T. Phong. "Illumination for Computer Generated Pictures". *Communications of the ACM*, Vol. 18, No. 6, pp. 311–317, June 1975.

[poul91] Pierre Poulin and John Amanatides. "Shading and shadowing with linear light sources". *Computers and Graphics*, Vol. 15, No. 2, pp. 259–265, 1991.

[sedg90] Robert Sedgewick. *Algorithms in C*. Addison-Wesley, 1990.

[shaf85] Steven A. Shafer. *Shadows and Silhouettes in Computer Vision*. Kluwer Academic Publishers, 1985.

[tana91] Toshimitsu Tanaka and Tokiichiro Takahashi. "Shading with Area Light Sources". *Eurographics '91*, pp. 235–246, September 1991.

[walt75] David Waltz. "Understanding Line Drawings of Scenes with Shadows". *The Psychology of Computer Vision*, pp. 19–91. Mc-Graw Hill, New York, 1975.

[wolf91] Lawrence B. Wolff. *Polarization Methods in Computer Vision*. Ph.D. thesis, Columbia University, 1991.

The Effect of Shadow Quality on the Perception of Spatial Relationships in Computer Generated Imagery.

Leonard Wanger

SimGraphics Engineering
South Pasadena, California 91030

ABSTRACT

The effect of shadow sharpness and shadow shape on the perception of spatial relationships was studied in three psychophysical experiments. In each experiment, the accuracy with which subjects were able to perform spatial estimation tasks was measured while either the sharpness or shape of the shadow was varied.

The effects of shadow sharpness and shadow shape on the accuracy of size and position estimations were tested in the first and second experiments respectively using fixed scaling tasks. Neither variations in shadow sharpness or shadow shape had a significant effect on the accuracy of performance in the experiments.

The third experiment tested the effect shadow sharpness on the accuracy of performance in a shape matching task. In this experiment, shadow sharpness had a significant effect on the accuracy of performance with soft edged shadows significantly reducing the number of correct shape matches.

These results indicate that less physically accurate hard edged shadow rendering techniques may be preferable in tasks requiring accurate perception of an object's shape.

CR categories and Subject Descriptors:
D.2.2 [Software Engineering]: Tools and Techniques - User interfaces;
H.1.2 [Models and Principals]: User/Machine Systems - Human information processing;
I.3.6 [Computer Graphics]: Methodology - interaction techniques;
I.3.7 [Computer Graphics]: Three-dimensional graphics and realism - color, shading, shadowing, and texture.

General Terms: Interactive 3-D Graphics, Visual Perception, Psychophysics, Human Factors.

Additional Key Words and Phrases: Interactive tasks, Spatial relations, Cue theory.

1. INTRODUCTION

One of the difficult decisions facing the designers of applications for the interactive viewing and manipulation of virtual spaces is determining the combination of rendering techniques to use for the generation of displays. Each rendering technique provides a subset of the perceptual cues used in determining spatial relations. The job of the designer is to maximize the spatial information perceived by the user, without exceeding the computational limitations of real-time image generation in the target computing environment.

Wanger, Ferwerda, and Greenberg [6],[7] ran several formal psychophysical experiments to measure the relative effects of a number of spatial cues on the performance of several spatial manipulation tasks in a virtual space. One result of their experiments was that shadows had a significant positive effect on the performance of tasks requiring the determination of an object's position and size.

Although these results indicate that shadows are a powerful cue for determining spatial relationships in many tasks, they do not address the effect of the quality of the shadow on the perception of the space. Since accurate shadow generation is computationally expensive, it would be useful to understand the repercussions of various shadow approximations on the perception of spatial relationships. This paper describes three psychophysical experiments conducted to measure the effect of shadow sharpness and shadow shape on the perception of spatial relationships in static computer generated images.

2. THE EXPERIMENTS

This section describes the experiments performed. Specific details on the methods used for each of the experiments can be found in Appendix A.

2.1 EXPERIMENT 1: EFFECT OF SHADOW SHARPNESS ON THE PERCEPTION OF OBJECT SIZE AND POSITION

The first experiment tested the effect of shadow sharpness on the perception of object size and position estimations in a fixed scaling task. In each trial subjects were presented with a display of a virtual room on a monitor (Figure 1). Four blue lines were displayed on the floor of the room to provide a scale for object depth (two at the front and two at the rear of the room), and four yellow lines were displayed on the back wall to provide a unitless scale for object height. Five balls, increasing linearly in radial size from left to right, were displayed on the floor near the front of the room to provide a scale for object size. Additionally a sixth ball, the test ball, was suspended in the room. In each trial subjects were asked to type the answers to the following three questions on a keyboard:

1. Using the blue lines at the front and back of the floor of the room as depths of 0.0 and 10.0 respectively, what is the depth of the test object?

2. Using the yellow lines at the bottom and top of the back wall of the room as heights of 0.0 and 10.0 respectively, what is the height of the test object?

3. Using the right-most object in the line of objects at the front of the room as a size of 1 and the left-most as a size of 5, what is the size of the test object?

In addition to varying the size, height, and depth of the test ball, one of the following three shadow sharpness levels was used for the test ball in each trial (Figure 2):

1. No shadows - The test object did not cast a shadow.

2. Hard shadows - The test object cast a shadow with a sharp boundary (i.e. no penumbral region).

3. Soft shadows - The test object cast a complete shadow with both umbral and penumbral regions accurately rendered.

Twelve subjects were each run through 56 trials representing one trial for each of the combinations of shadow level, test ball size, test ball depth, and test ball height.

2.2 EXPERIMENT 2: EFFECT OF SHADOW SHAPE ON THE PERCEPTION OF OBJECT SIZE AND POSITION

The second experiment tested the effect of shadow shape on the perception of object size and position in a fixed scaling task. The displays for Experiment two utilized the same virtual room as Experiment 1. However, barbells were used instead of balls for both the size scale objects and the test object (Figure 3). For each trial subjects were asked the same three questions as those asked in Experiment 1.

In addition to varying the size, height, and depth of the test object, one of the following three shadow shape levels was used for the test object in each trial (Figure 4):

1. No shadows - The test object did not cast a shadow.

2. Bounding volume shadows - The test object cast a shadow based on the its rectangular bounding volume. This produced normal looking objects with "boxy" shadows.

3. "True" shadows - The test object cast a shadow based on its actual geometry to produce properly shaped shadows.

Twelve subjects were each run through 56 trials representing one trial for each of the combinations of shadow shape level, test ball size, test ball depth, and test ball height.

2.3 EXPERIMENT 3: EFFECT OF SHADOW SHARPNESS ON THE PERCEPTION OF OBJECT SHAPE

Experiment three tested the effect of shadow sharpness on the perception of object shape in a shape matching task. The displays used in Experiment 3 consisted of two windows (Figure 5). In the lower window five objects of revolution, numbered from 1 to 5 from left to right respectively, were represented. Each of these shapes were unique in both their shape and height, but were identical as viewed from the base along their major axis. The top window displayed a plane with the test object suspended above it. The test object in the upper window was one of the shapes from the lower window rotated such that only its base could be seen. In each trial subjects were asked to type the identifying number of the shape from the lower window which corresponded to the test object in the upper window. In addition to changing the light position, the shape of the test object, and the elevation of the test object above the plane, either the hard or soft shadow sharpness levels described in Experiment 1 was used in each trial.

Twelve subjects were each run through 90 trials representing one trial for each of the combinations of shadow sharpness level, test object elevation, test object shape, and light position. In addition, 5 trials without shadows were added as a control condition to verify that the test object's shadow was the only cue provided regarding the test objects shape. This brought the total to 95 trials per subject.

3. EXPERIMENTAL RESULTS

This section describes the results of the experiments performed. Details on the methods used to analyze the experiments can be found in Appendix B. A detailed listing of the quantitative results of the analysis can be found in [6].

3.1 EXPERIMENT 1

Statistical analysis of the results of Experiment 1 indicated that the size, depth, and height of the test ball were all significant factors in size, depth, and height estimation, but that shadow sharpness was not a significant factor in any of the three estimation tasks. Although the existence of shadows greatly increased the accuracy of size and position (height and depth) estimations, the sharpness of the shadow did not have a statistically significant effect on the accuracy of the estimations.

A small, but statistically, significant interaction $(F(2,10)=4.296, p=0.0353)$[1] between shadow sharpness and test object elevation was seen in the position estimation task. When the test object was at the middle elevation (one inch above the ground plane) hard shadows significantly increased the accuracy of positional estimations. The reason for this anomaly is unknown.

---

[1]The F statistic is a measure of the variation in a set of observations due to a particular experimental factor. The p-value is the probablity that the amount of variation seen for by a factor in the data could have arisen merely by random variation.

3.2 EXPERIMENT 2

Similar to the results of Experiment 1, the size, depth, and height of the test object were all significant factors in the size and position estimations in Experiment 2, but shadow shape did not have a significant effect on the accuracy of either size or position estimations. Although shadow shape by itself was not a significant factor, higher order interactions between shadow shape and other factors (such as shadow shape by light position and shadow shape by test object elevation) indicate that shadow shape may have some subtle effect on the perception of size and position. It is unclear what these effects may be as post hoc analysis showed no clear directional trends for these interactions.

3.3 EXPERIMENT 3

All of the factors tested in Experiment 3 had a significant effect on the determination of object shape (object shape, light position, object elevation, and shadow sharpness: $F_{(4,8)}=4.829$ $p=0.028$, $F_{(2,10)}=10.603$ $p=0.003$, $F_{(2,10)}=32.440$ $p<0.001$, and $F_{(1,11)}=16.234$ $p=0.002$ respectively).

The shape matching task appears to be dependent on identifying features in the shape. Since each of the factors tested had some effect on the prominence of the features, it is logical that all of the factors were significant.

The position of the light affected the shape of the resulting shadow. The percentage of correct responses were 47.9%, 78.4%, and 73.6% as the light moved from the front, middle, and back light positions respectively. The increase in accuracy when the light was in the middle and back positions is explained by the fact that the light's normal came close to being perpendicular to the test object's major axis in these positions. This increased shape matching accuracy as the differences in the shape of shadow contours for the various shapes became more pronounced as the light's normal moved towards being perpendicular to the test object's major axis.

The elevation of the object above the ground plane also affected the prominence of object features when soft shadows were present. As the test object moved higher above the plane, the object's shadow became more diffuse - blurring identifying features. This explains why the percentage of correct shape matches decreased from 74.2%, to 70.1%, to 55.7% as the object moved from the lowest, to the highest position respectively. The percentage of correct matches stayed well above chance (20%) for all three elevations as some identifying features, such as the aspect ratio of the shadow, were visible in even the most diffuse shadows..

Support for the use of identifying features is seen in the fact that incorrect responses were not distributed uniformly among different shape pairs, but instead were concentrated between specific pairs of shapes. Confusion between shapes 1 and 2 (the ball and pear - figure 6) accounted for 18.6% of all incorrect responses, while confusion between shapes 3 and 5 (the cup and capsule) accounted for 65.9% of all of the incorrect responses. In both of these cases incorrect matches occurred when the identifying feature of one object was mimicked by the other object. For example, some projections of the flat top of the cup shape produced a shadow with two curved end - much like the shadow of capsule shape. The lack of identifying features was compunded even further by perspective foreshortening causing the cup to often be mistaken for the capsule and vice versa.

Perhaps the most dramatic result is the fact that 82.6% of all incorrect matches took place in trials where soft shadows were present. It is clear from this result that soft shadows can be detrimental to determining an object's shape in the absence of other cues.

4. CONCLUSION

Although it is likely that the patterns seen in these experiments would be present in many other situations, one must be careful in extrapolating the results of perceptual experiments such as those represented here. In order to allow these experiments to be accurately controlled and measured they were necessarily contrived. Assuming that these results are applicable to other situations the following conclusions can be reached:

1. These experiments support the earlier result that shadows are indeed a useful cue for indicating the size and position of objects. In addition, shadows can be a powerful cue for indicating an object's three dimensional shape.

2. It appears that the sharpness of a shadow does not have any appreciable effect in tasks based on the perception of the size and position of an object, however, soft shadows can have a strong negative effect in tasks requiring accurate perception of object shape.

3. Although the shape of a shadow has no appreciable effect on the perception of object size and position, higher order interactions indicate that it cannot be completely ignored.

These results indicate that in many cases, computationally cheaper hard shadow generation techniques are adequate and in fact may actually be more beneficial than more expensive soft shadow techniques.

ACKNOWLEDGMENTS

This work was performed while I was at the Cornell University Program of Computer Graphics. My appreciation goes out to Kathy Dorries and Dick Darlington who were invaluable for help with the statistical analysis, and to the subjects who participated in the experiments. I would particularly like to acknowledge Jim Ferwerda and Don Greenberg. Without Jim and Don this work could never have happened. This work was performed on equipment generously donated by Hewlett Packard and Digital Equipment, and was partially funded by the National Science Foundation under grant No. DCR8203979 -"Interactive Input and Display Techniques".

REFERENCES

[1] Blinn, James F. "Me and My (Fake) Shadow," IEEE Computer Graphics and Applications, January 1988, pg 82-86.

[2] Crow, Franklin C. "Shadow Algorithms For Computer Graphics,"Computer Graphics, 18(2), Summer 1977.

[3] Darlington, Richard B. Regression and Linear Models, McGraw Hill Series in Psychology, McGraw Hill, New York, 1990.

[4] Gibson, James J. The Perception of the Visual World, Houghton Mifflin Company, Boston, 1950.

[5] Luis. The Psychophysical Response of Human Beings When Subjected to Imploring Visual Stimuli, Master's thesis, Cornell University, Ithaca, New York, 1982.

[6] Wanger, Leonard R. Perceiving Spatial Relationships in Computer Generated Images, Master's thesis, Cornell University, Ithaca, New York, 1991.

[7] Wanger, Leonard R., James A. Ferwerda, and Donald P. Greenberg, "Perceiving Spatial Relationships in Computer Generated Images," in press.

[8] Woo, Andrew, Pierre Poulin, and Alain Fournier. "A Survey of Shadow Algorithms," IEEE Computer Graphics and Applications, November 1990, pg 13-31.

APPENDIX A: EXPERIMENTAL SETUP

The same twelve subjects, six men and six women, participated in each of the three experiments. Six of the subjects were experienced in using three dimensional computer graphics and six were not. The order of presentation of the three experiments was varied among the subjects to eliminate ordering bias. All subjects were either graduate students or faculty members at Cornell University and had normal or corrected to normal vision.

Displays were pre-computed using stochastic ray tracing, and were displayed on a HP 98752A 19 inch color monitor under controlled lighting conditions. Color and brightness were set by the experimenter and held constant for all trials.

Displays were rendered to correspond to the physical area of a 6 inch by 6 inch window located in the center of the monitor. The window subtended 9.5 degrees of visual angle both horizontally and vertically. The camera was set to be coincident with the eye point of the subjects looking towards the center of the virtual room, with the frustum of view corresponding to the physical space of the monitor, and proper perspective projection for a viewing distance of 18 inches. The scene was illuminated by a white ,ambient light source and a 2.5 inch by 2.5 inch, uniformly distributed, white, area light source with its normal parallel to the view vector.

In Experiments 1 and 3, shadow sharpness levels were created by varying the number of sample points used for the light source for shadow ray light intersection testing. Hard edged shadows were rendered using a single sample point located at the center of the area light. Soft edged shadows were rendered using a jittered 3x3 grid of sample points. Each grid was then sampled for light visibility testing. Images without shadows were produced by ignoring shadow rays which only intersected the test object.

In Experiment 2 shadow shape levels were created by varying the geometry of the object used to test object shadow ray intersections. Shadow rays were intersected with the test object to render properly shaped shadows, and were intersected with the test object's bounding box to create bounding volume shadows. Images without shadows were produced by ignoring shadow rays which only intersected the test object.

A more rigorous description of the experimental setup can be found in [6].

APPENDIX B: STATISTICAL METHODS

Results were analyzed using a multivariate analysis of variance (MANOVA), with a significance level cut-off of $p<0.05$. Post hoc tests for the direction of effects were performed with two tailed matched pairs T-tests.

In all three experiments trials without shadows were treated as control conditions and were left out of the final analysis. Subjects performed at chance on non-shadow trials in all three experiments verifying that subjects were making their spatial estimations solely on the basis of the shadow information.

Detailed descriptions of the methods used can be found in [6].

A Demonstrated Optical Tracker With Scalable Work Area for Head-Mounted Display Systems

Mark Ward[†], Ronald Azuma, Robert Bennett, Stefan Gottschalk, Henry Fuchs

Department of Computer Science
Sitterson Hall
University of North Carolina
Chapel Hill, NC 27599-3175

Abstract

An optoelectronic head-tracking system for head-mounted displays is described. The system features a scalable work area that currently measures 10' x 12', a measurement update rate of 20-100 Hz with 20-60 ms of delay, and a resolution specification of 2 mm and 0.2 degrees. The sensors consist of four head-mounted imaging devices that view infrared light-emitting diodes (LEDs) mounted in a 10' x 12' grid of modular 2' x 2' suspended ceiling panels. Photogrammetric techniques allow the head's location to be expressed as a function of the known LED positions and their projected images on the sensors. The work area is scaled by simply adding panels to the ceiling's grid. Discontinuities that occurred when changing working sets of LEDs were reduced by carefully managing all error sources, including LED placement tolerances, and by adopting an overdetermined mathematical model for the computation of head position: space resection by collinearity. The working system was demonstrated in the Tomorrow's Realities gallery at the ACM SIGGRAPH '91 conference.

CR categories and subject descriptors: I.3.1 [Computer Graphics]: Hardware Architecture - *three-dimensional displays*; I.3.7 [Computer Graphics]: Three-Dimensional Graphics and Realism - *Virtual Reality*

Additional Key Words and Phrases: Head-mounted displays, head tracking

1   Introduction

It is generally accepted that deficiencies in accuracy, resolution, update rate, and lag in the measurement of head position can adversely affect the overall performance of a HMD [17][24][25]. Our experience suggests that an additional specification requires more emphasis: range.

† Present address: Structural Acoustics, 5801 Lease Lane, Raleigh, NC, 27613.   (919) 787-0887

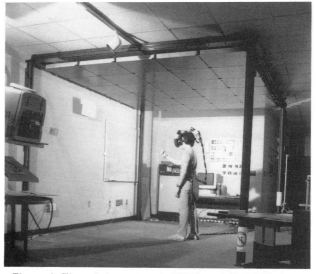

Figure 1: The existing system in UNC's graphics laboratory

Most existing HMD trackers were built to support situations that do not require long-range tracking, such as cockpit-like environments where the user is confined to a seat and the range of head motion is limited. But many virtual worlds applications, such as architectural walkthroughs, would benefit from more freedom of movement (Figure 2). Long-range trackers would allow greater areas to be explored naturally, on foot, reducing the need to resort to techniques such as flying or walking on treadmills.

Such techniques of extending range work adequately with closed-view HMDs that completely obscure reality. With see-through HMDs [9][11], however, the user's visual connection with reality is intact and hybrid applications are possible where physical objects and computer-generated images coexist. In this situation, flying though the model is meaningless. The model is registered to the physical world and one's relationship to both must change simultaneously.

This paper describes the second generation of an optoelectronic head-tracking concept developed at the University of North Carolina at Chapel Hill. In the concept's first generation, the fundamental design parameters were explored and a bench-top prototype was constructed [28]. Building on this success, the second-generation tracker is a fully functional prototype that significantly extends the workspace of an HMD wearer.

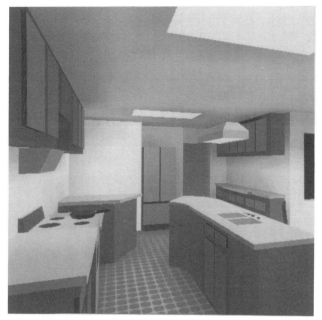

Figure 2: Walkthrough of Brooks' kitchen design that runs with the tracker. Actual resolution of images seen in the HMD is much lower than this picture's resolution.

The current system (Figure 1) places four outward-looking image sensors on the wearer's head and locates LEDs in a 10' x 12' suspended ceiling structure of modular 2' x 2' ceiling panels. Each panel houses 32 LEDs, for a total of 960 LEDs in the ceiling. Images of LEDs are formed by lateral-effect photodiode detectors within each head-mounted sensor. The location of each LED's image on a detector, or *photocoordinate*, is used along with the known LED locations in the ceiling to compute the head's position and orientation. To enhance resolution, the field of view of each sensor is narrow. Thus, as shown in Figures 3 and 7, each sensor sees only a small number of LEDs at any instant. As the user moves about, the working set of visible LEDs changes, making this a *cellular* head-tracking system.

Measurements of head position and orientation are produced at a rate of 20-100 Hz with 20-60 ms of delay. The system's accuracy has not been measured precisely, but the resolution is 2 mm and 0.2 degrees. It was demonstrated in the Tomorrow's Realities gallery at the ACM SIGGRAPH '91 conference, and is, to our knowledge, the first demonstrated scalable head-tracking system for HMDs.

The system is novel for two reasons. First, the sensor configuration is unique. Other optical tracking systems fix the sensors in the environment and mount the LEDs on the moving body [30]. The outward-looking configuration is superior for it improves the system's ability to detect head rotation. The scalable work space is the system's second contribution. If a larger work space is desired, more panels can be easily added to the overhead grid.

2   Previous work

Many tracking systems precede this effort, and we will briefly survey representative examples. The essence of the problem is the realtime measurement of the position and orientation of a rigid moving body with respect to an absolute reference frame, a six-degree-of-freedom (6DOF) measurement problem. Solutions are relevant to many other fields.

To our knowledge, four fundamentally different technologies have been used to track HMDs: mechanical, magnetic, ultrasonic, and optical.

The first HMD, built by Ivan Sutherland [27], used a mechanical linkage to measure head position. A commercial product, The Boom [12], uses a mechanical linkage to measure the gaze direction of a hand-held binocular display. The Air Force Human Resources Laboratory (AFHRL) uses a mechanical linkage to measure the position and orientation of a HMD used for simulation [24]. Mechanical systems have sufficient accuracy, resolution, and frequency response, yet their range is severely limited, and a mechanical tether is undesirable for many applications.

Magnetic-based systems [3][21] are the most widely used hand and head trackers today. They are small, relatively inexpensive, and do not have line-of-sight restrictions. Their primary limitations are distortions caused by metal or electromagnetic fields, and limited range [13].

Ultrasonic approaches have also been successful, such as the commercially-available Logitech tracker [20]. Time-of-flight measurements are used to triangulate the positions of sensors mounted on the HMD. The strength of this technology is minimum helmet weight [13]. Physical obscuration as well as reflections and variations of the speed of sound due to changes in the ambient air density make it difficult to maintain accuracy [5].

Because of the potential for operation over greater distances, optical approaches are plentiful, and it is helpful to categorize them on the basis of the light source used. Visible, infrared, and laser light sources have each been exploited.

Ferrin [13] reports the existence of a prototype helmet tracking system using visible light. Although it only tracks orientation, it is worth mentioning here because of its unique approach. A patterned target is placed on the helmet and a cockpit-mounted video camera acquires images in real time. The pattern is designed to produce a unique image for any possible head orientation. The strength of this approach is the use of passive targets which minimize helmet weight. Reflections and other light sources are potential sources of error.

Bishop's Self-Tracker [7] is a research effort involving visible light. A Self-Tracker chip senses incremental displacements and rotations by imaging an unstructured scene. A head-mounted cluster of these chips provide sufficient information for the computation of head position and orientation. Although still under development, the concept is mentioned here because it would allow an optical tracking system to operate outdoors, where a structured environment, such as our ceiling of LEDs, would be impossible to realize.

Because of the difficulties associated with processing information in an unstructured scene, most high-speed optical measurement systems use highly-structured infrared or laser light sources in conjunction with solid-state sensors. The sensor is a often a lateral-effect photodiode as opposed to a true imaging device, because the photodiode produces currents that are directly related to the location of a light spot's centroid on its sensitive surface [32]. The resultant sensor is relatively insensitive to focus, and the light spot's location, or photocoordinate, is immediately available without the need for image processing.

During the 1970's, Selspot [23] popularized the use of infrared LEDs as targets and lateral-effect photodiodes as sensors in a commercially-available system. Their primary emphasis was, and still is, on the three-dimensional locations of individual targets. That is, the Selspot system does not automate the computation of a rigid body's orientation. In a response to this shortcoming, Antonsson [2] refined the Selspot system for use in dynamic measurements of mechanical systems. The resultant system uses two Selspot cameras to view a moving body instrumented with LEDs. Similar approaches have been applied to HMD systems in cockpits [13] and in simulators [11].

The use of an LED light source limits the range of these systems. Typically, the distance between source and detector can be no greater than several feet. Longer distances can be spanned with laser light sources.

The only known example of a 6DOF tracker using laser sources is the Minnesota Scanner [26]. With this sytem, scanning mirrors are used to sweep orthogonal stripes of light across the working volume. Photodiodes are both fixed in space and placed on the moving body. By measuring the time between a light stripe's contact with a fixed and moving photodiode, the diode's three-dimensional location can be computed. Given the location of three or more moving diodes, the moving body's orientation can be computed. Similar technology has been applied to the cockpit, although orientation was the only concern [13].

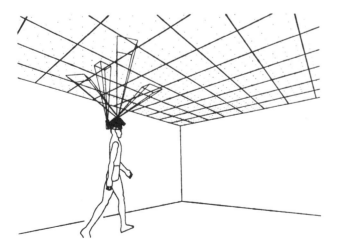

Figure 3: Conceptual drawing of outward-looking system and the sensors' fields of view

3   System overview

Wang demonstrated the viability of head-mounted lateral-effect photodiodes and overhead LEDs. This system extends his work in several ways. First, an overhead grid of 960 LEDs was produced with well-controlled LED location tolerances, and more attention was paid to controlling other error sources as well. Second, mathematical techniques were developed that allow an arbitrary number of sensors and an arbitrary number of LEDs in the field of view of each sensor to be used in the computation of head location. This resulted in an overdetermined system of equations which, when solved, was less susceptible to system error sources than the previous mathematical approach [10]. Third, the analog signals emerging from the sensors were digitally processed to reject ambient light. Finally, techniques for quickly determining the working sets of LEDs were developed.

3.1   Sensor   configuration

Typically, optical trackers are *inward-looking*; sensors are fixed in the environment within which the HMD wearer moves. With Self-Tracker, Bishop and Fuchs introduced the concept of *outward-looking* trackers that mount the image sensors on the head, looking out at the environment (Figure 3).

If a large work area is required, outward-looking configurations have an advantage over inward-looking techniques when recovering orientation. The two are equivalent for measuring translation: moving the sensor causes the same image shift as moving the scene. Rotations are significantly different. Unless targets are mounted on antlers, an inward-looking sensor perceives a small image shift when the user performs a small head rotation. The same head rotation creates a much larger image shift with a head-mounted sensor. For a given sensor resolution, an outward-looking system is more sensitive to orientation changes.

Figure 4: Remote Processor and head unit with four sensors

To improve resolution in general, long focal lengths must be used with an optical sensor regardless of whether the configuration is inward or outward-looking. Thus, a wide-angle lens cannot significantly extend the work area of an inward-looking system without sacrificing resolution and accuracy.

Narrow fields of view are a consequence of long focal lengths. Therefore, the HMD wearer cannot move very far before an LED leaves a given sensor's field of view. One solution is a cellular array of either LEDs or detectors. For an infrared system using LEDs and lateral-effect photodiodes, system cost is minimized by replicating LEDs as opposed to sensors. This is a result of both the device cost as well as the required support circuitry.

In the current system, four Hamamatsu (model S1880) sensors are mounted atop the head, as shown in Figure 4. Each sensor consists of a camera body to which a Fujinon lens (model CF 50B) is attached. The focal length of each lens is 50mm. Their principal points were determined experimentally by an optical laboratory. An infrared filter (Tiffen 87) is used to reject ambient light.

3.2 Beacon configuration

Experience with simulations and an early 48-LED prototype revealed the problem of *beacon switching error*: as the user moved around and the working set of beacons changed, discontinuous jumps in position and orientation occurred. These are caused by errors in the sensor locations, distortions caused by the lens and photodiode detector, and errors in the positions of the beacons in the ceiling.

To control beacon locations, we housed the LEDs in carefully constructed ceiling panels. Each 2' x 2' panel is an anodized aluminum enclosure that encases a 20" x 20" two-sided printed circuit board. On this board are electronics to drive 32 LEDs. The LEDs are mounted in the front surface with standard plastic insets. Using standard electronic enclosure manufacturing techniques, it was relatively easy to realize an LED-to-LED centerline spacing tolerance of .005" on a given panel.

The panels are hung from a Unistrut superstructure (Figure 1). At each interior vertex of a 2' x 2' grid, a vertically adjustable hanger mates with four panels. Four holes in the face of a panel slide onto one of four dowels on each hanger. The entire array of panels is levelled with a Spectra Physics Laser-Level, which establishes a plane of visible red light several inches below the panels' faces. Each hanger is designed to accept a sensor (Industra-Eye) that measures the vertical position of the laser relative to its own case. By moving the hangers up or down, they can be aligned to within .006" of the light beam.

The panels are electrically connected by a data and power daisy chain. The data daisy chain allows an individual LED to be selected. Once selected, the LED (Siemens SFH 487P) can be driven with a programmable current that ranges from 0-2 amperes. The programmable current allows an electronic iris feature to be implemented. Typically, an LED will be on for no more than 200 μsec. During this time period, the current is adjusted to achieve a desired signal level at the sensor (see Section 4).

3.3 Data Flow

As shown in Figure 5, the signals emerging from the head-mounted sensors are connected to the Remote Processor. Worn as a belt pack, the Remote Processor functions as a remote analog-to-digital conversion module. It can accept the four analog voltages emerging from a lateral-effect photodiode, for up to eight sensors. On command, the Remote Processor will simultaneously sample the four voltages on a selected sensor and relay four, 12-bit results to the LED Manager. The Remote Processor was used to alleviate the need for long runs of analog signals emerging from multiple sensors.

The LED Manager is a 68030-based processing module that controls the Remote Processor as well as the ceiling. A TAXI-based serial datalink [1] provides access to the Remote Processor while the ceiling's data daisy chain terminates at the LED Manager. Software executing on this module is responsible for turning LEDs on and for extracting data from the sensors. The LED Manager resides in a remote VME chassis that must be located near the ceiling structure.

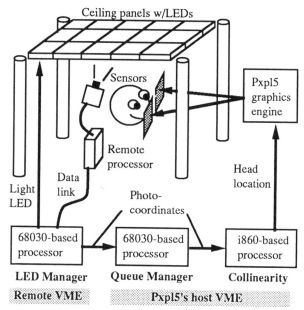

Figure 5: System Dataflow

For each measurement of head location, the LED Manager produces a list of visible LEDs and their associated photocoordinates. This list is transferred via shared memory to the Collinearity module, which resides in the graphics engine's VME chassis. The i860-based Collinearity module translates the list of photocoordinates into the current estimate of head location. For reasons explained in Section 6, an additional 68030-based processor is used to aid the transfer of data from the remote system to the host. In theory, this is not required. The VME systems are connected by a Bit-3 VME buslink.

The sampled head position is communicated to the Pixel-Planes 5 graphics engine [14], which in turn updates the images on the user's displays.

4   Low-level software

A library of low-level routines running on the LED Manager, called the Acquisition Manager, controls the beacons and detectors. Given an LED and a photodiode unit, these routines light an LED and determine if a photodiode's detector sees that LED. The detector returns four analog signals, which the Remote Processor board digitizes. A simple formula [16] converts these four numbers into the x,y photocoordinates of the LED's projection on the detector.

Hamamatsu datasheets specify 1 part in 40 accuracy and 1 part in 5000 resolution for the lateral-effect diode-based detectors used. As with Antonsson [2], we were able to achieve approximately 1 part in 1000 accuracy for the combined photodiode-lens assembly. Achieving this result required significant efforts to improve the signal-to-noise ratio and compensate for distortion, including:

Ambient light rejection: The voltage values with the LED off (called the "dark current") are subtracted from the voltage values with the LED on. Sampling with the LED off both before and after the samples with the LED on and averaging the two yields substantially improved ambient light rejection.

Random noise rejection: Averaging several measurements reduces random noise effects, but costs time. A good compromise between accuracy and sampling speed is to take 8 samples with the LED off, 16 samples with the LED on and 8 more samples with the LED off.

Current scaling: The distance between a photodiode and an LED depends on the user's location. To maximize the signal without saturating the photodiode detector, the Acquisition Manager dynamically adjusts the amount of current used to light an LED. Acquisition Manager routines estimate the threshold of current that will saturate the detector and use 90% of this value during sampling.

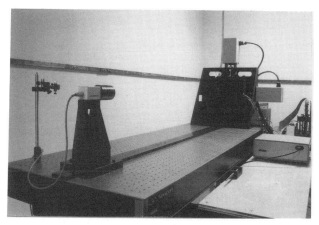

Figure 6: Optical bench for photodiode calibration

Calibration: Both the lens and the photodiode detector suffer from nonlinear distortions. By placing the photodiodes on an optical bench and carefully measuring the imaged points generated by beacons at known locations (Figure 6), we built a lookup table to compensate for these distortions. Bilinear interpolation provides complete coverage across the detector. More sophisticated calibration techniques should be investigated. Accurate calibration is required to reduce beacon switching error.

Programming techniques: Techniques such as list processing, cache management and efficient code sequencing result in a substantially improved sampling rate. In addition, expedited handling of special cases, such as when an LED is not within the field of view of a photodiode unit, further helps system performance.

Using 32 samples per LED, we compute a visible LED's photocoordinate in 660 μsec and reject a non-visible LED in

100 μsec. LEDs are tested in groups; each group carries an additional overhead of 60 μsec.

Figure 7: Sensors viewing LEDs in the ceiling. Each of the four groups is the set of LEDs that a sensor can see. Picture taken with a camera that is sensitive to infrared light.

5   LED Manager

The LED Manager uses the low-level Acquisition Manager routines to determine which LEDs each photodiode unit sees and where the associated imaged points are on the photodiode detectors. We usually want to collect data from all visible LEDs, since larger sample sets ultimately yield less noisy solutions from the Collinearity module (Section 7). Because the number of visible LEDs is small (see Figure 7) compared to the total number of LEDs in the ceiling, something faster than a brute-force scan of the entire ceiling array is called for. Two assumptions help us design a more efficient method:

1) Spatial coherence: The set of beacons visible to a photodiode unit in a given frame will be contiguous.

2) Temporal coherence: The user's movement rate will be slow compared to the frame rate. This implies that the field of view of a given photodiode unit does not travel very far across the ceiling between frames, so its set of visible beacons will not change much from one frame to the next.

5.1   The basic method

In each frame, the LED Manager goes through each photodiode unit in sequence, sampling beacons until it is satisfied that it has captured most of each photodiode unit's visible set. A basic difficulty is that we cannot be sure whether a beacon is visible or not until we attempt to sample it. The LED Manager remembers which beacons were in the camera's visible set from the previous frame. The set is called the *last visible set*. If the last visible set is nonempty, all beacons in that set are tested. The next action depends on how many of those beacons are actually visible:

1) All: We assume the field of view has not moved much and not many more beacons will be visible. We stop with this set and go on to the next photodiode unit.

2) Some: We assume that the field of view has shifted significantly, possibly enough to include previously unseen beacons. A *shell fill* (described later) is conducted, beginning with the set of beacons verified to be visible.

3) None: The field of view has moved dramatically, gone off the edge of the ceiling, or is obscured. We check the neighbors of the last visible set. If any of these beacons are visible, they are used to start a shell fill. If none are visible, we give up on this photodiode unit until the next frame.

What if the last visible set is empty? Our course of action depends on whether we were able to compute a valid position and orientation for the head in the last frame:

1) Valid previous location: We can predict which LEDs should be visible to our photodiode unit, if the user's head is actually at the computed location, because the geometry of the head unit is known. If no LEDs are predicted to be visible, we go on to the next photodiode unit, otherwise we sample those beacons and use them as the start of a shell fill, if any of them were actually visible.

2) No valid previous location: Now we have no way to guess which beacons are visible, so we resort to a simple *sweep search*, which lights the beacons in the ceiling row by row, until we have tried the entire ceiling or an LED is found to be visible. In the former case, we give up, and in the latter case, we use the visible beacon as the start of a shell fill.

5.2 Shell fill

A *shell fill* starts with a set of beacons known to be visible to a sensor and sweeps outward until it has found all the beacons in the field of view.

We do this by first sampling the neighbors of the initial set of beacons. If none are found visible, the shell fill terminates, concluding that the beacons in the initial set are the only visible ones. If any are found visible, we then compute the neighbors of the beacons we just sampled, excluding those which have already been tried, and sample those. We repeat this process of sampling beacons, computing the neighbors of those found visible, and using those neighbors as the next sample set, until an iteration yields no additional visible beacons.

Assumption 1, that visible sets are contiguous, suggests that this procedure should be thorough and reasonably efficient.

5.3 Startup

At startup, the head location is not known and all of the last visible sets are empty. We do a sweep search, as previously described, for each photodiode unit to locate the initial visible sets.

6 Communications

Communication between the various processors in our system is done using shared memory buffers, which offer low latency and high speed. The buffers are allocated and deallocated via a FIFO queue mechanism. Data is "transmitted" when it is written to the buffer: no copying is necessary. The only communication overhead is the execution of a simple semaphore acquisition and pointer management routine. Furthermore, all processors use the same byte ordering and data type size, so no data translation is needed.

The queuing mechanism lets all modules in the system run asynchronously. LED Manager, the Collinearity module, and Pixel-Planes 5 run as fast as they can, using the most recent data in the queue or the last known data if the queue is empty.

The various processors in our system are split between two separate VME buses, which are transparently linked together by Bit-3 bus link adapters (Figure 5). A subtle bus loading problem prevents the i860 board and the '030 board that runs LED Manager from operating in the same VME cage. This configuration increases latency because inter-bus access is significantly slower than intra-bus access, but increases throughput because the bus link allows simultaneous intra-bus activity to occur. Because the i860 processor cannot directly access the VME bus, a second '030 board, which runs the Queue Manager, moves data between the LED Manager and the Collinearity module.

A simpler and less expensive system could be built if we acquired an i860 board that can run on the same bus as the LED Manager '030 board. This configuration would not require the Queue Manager board or the Bit-3 links and would reduce both latency and throughput.

7 Space Resection by Collinearity

Given the observations of beacons, we compute the position and orientation of the user's head by using a photogrammetric technique called space resection by collinearity. The basic method for a single camera is in [31]; what we describe here is our extension for using it in a multi-sensor system. Because of space limitations, the description is necessarily brief. Full details are provided in [6].

7.1 Definitions

Three types of coordinate systems exist: one World space (tied to the ceiling structure), one Head space (tied to the HMD), and several Photodiode spaces (one for each photodiode unit).

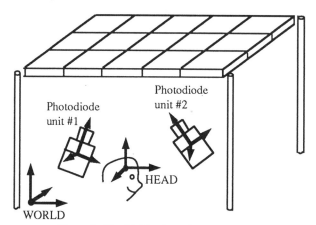

Figure 8: World, Head and Photodiode spaces

Changing representations from one space to another is done by a rotation followed by a translation. We use two types of 3x3 rotation matrices:

$\mathbf{M}$ = Head space to World space
$\mathbf{M}_i$ = Photodiode space i to Head space

48

with each matrix specified by Euler angles ω, α, and κ.

The optical model for each photodiode unit is simple: a light ray strikes the front principal point and leaves the rear principal point at the same angle (Figure 9).

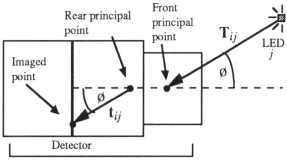

Figure 9: Optical model

Finally, we list the points and vectors we will need, segregated by the coordinate system in which they are represented. Given photodiode unit i sees LED number j,

Photodiode space:

$[x_{ij}, y_{ij}, 0]$ = imaged point on photodiode detector

Head space:

$\mathbf{t}_{ij}$ = vector from rear principal point to imaged point
$\mathbf{H}_0$ = origin of Head space
$\mathbf{d}_i$ = vector from $\mathbf{H}_0$ to center of photodiode detector
$\mathbf{e}_i$ = vector from $\mathbf{H}_0$ to rear principal point
$\mathbf{f}_i$ = vector from $\mathbf{H}_0$ to front principal point

World space:

$[X_0, Y_0, Z_0]$ = coordinates of the origin of Head space
$[X_j, Y_j, Z_j]$ = coordinates of LED j
$\mathbf{T}_{ij}$ = vector from LED j to front principal point

7.2 Geometric relationships

Figure 9 shows that $\mathbf{T}_{ij}$ and $\mathbf{t}_{ij}$ differ only by a scale factor; if they were placed at the same start point, they would be collinear. In equations:

$$\mathbf{T}_{ij} = \lambda \, \mathbf{M} \, \mathbf{t}_{ij} \qquad (1)$$

We now express $\mathbf{T}_{ij}$ and $\mathbf{t}_{ij}$ in terms of the other vectors in equations (2) and (3) and Figures 10 and 11:

$$\mathbf{T}_{ij} = \begin{bmatrix} X_0 - X_j \\ Y_0 - Y_j \\ Z_0 - Z_j \end{bmatrix} + \mathbf{M} \, \mathbf{f}_i \qquad (2)$$

$$\mathbf{t}_{ij} = \mathbf{d}_i - \mathbf{e}_i + \mathbf{M}_i \begin{bmatrix} x_{ij} \\ y_{ij} \\ 0 \end{bmatrix} \qquad (3)$$

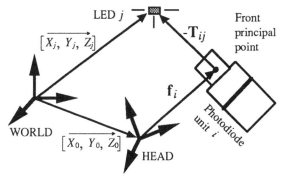

Figure 10: Expressing $\mathbf{T}_{ij}$ through other vectors

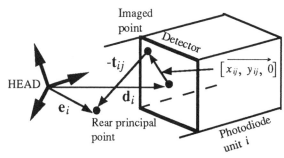

Figure 11: Expressing $\mathbf{t}_{ij}$ through other vectors

Substituting (2) and (3) into (1) yields the collinearity condition equation c_{ij} :

$$c_{ij}: \begin{bmatrix} X_0 - X_j \\ Y_0 - Y_j \\ Z_0 - Z_j \end{bmatrix} + \mathbf{M} \, \mathbf{f}_i = \lambda \, \mathbf{M} \left(\mathbf{d}_i - \mathbf{e}_i + \mathbf{M}_i \begin{bmatrix} x_{ij} \\ y_{ij} \\ 0 \end{bmatrix} \right)$$

7.3 System of equations

When a photodiode unit i sees an LED j, it generates a c_{ij}, which represents three independent equations. If we see N LEDs in all, the total number of unknowns in our system is $6+N$: 3 for position, 3 for orientation, and N scale factors. The first six are what we are trying to find, but we do not care about the scale factors. We eliminate these by rearranging the c_{ij} equations, then dividing the first and second equations by the third. This leaves two independent equations, of the form

$$G1_{ij}(\mathbf{L}) = 0, \quad G2_{ij}(\mathbf{L}) = 0$$

where $\mathbf{L}$ is a vector composed of the six unknowns: position (X_0, Y_0, Z_0) and orientation (ω, α, κ for matrix $\mathbf{M}$). We generate a linear approximation to these two equations by applying Taylor's theorem:

$$-G1_{ij}(\mathbf{L}) = \left(\frac{\partial G1_{ij}(\mathbf{L})}{\partial X_0} \right) dX_0 + \left(\frac{\partial G1_{ij}(\mathbf{L})}{\partial Y_0} \right) dY_0 + \left(\frac{\partial G1_{ij}(\mathbf{L})}{\partial Z_0} \right) dZ_0$$
$$+ \left(\frac{\partial G1_{ij}(\mathbf{L})}{\partial \omega} \right) d\omega + \left(\frac{\partial G1_{ij}(\mathbf{L})}{\partial \alpha} \right) d\alpha + \left(\frac{\partial G1_{ij}(\mathbf{L})}{\partial \kappa} \right) d\kappa$$

and a similar expansion for the linearized $G2$ equation.

Now we have six total unknowns, and every LED that we see generates two independent linear equations. Thus, we need to see at least three LEDs. If we see a total of N LEDs, we can write our system of N linearized $G1$ equations and N linearized $G2$ equations in matrix form:

$$-G_0 = \partial G * D \qquad (4)$$
$$2N\text{x}1 \quad 2N\text{x}6 \quad 6\text{x}1$$

where $D = [dX_0, dY_0, dZ_0, d\omega, d\alpha, d\kappa]^T$,
∂G is the matrix of partial derivatives of the $G1$ and $G2$,
and $-G_0$ contains the values of the $G1$ and $G2$ at a specific L.

7.4 Iteration and convergence

Collinearity takes an initial guess of L (the unknowns) and generates correction values (in D) to make a more accurate L, iterating until it converges to a solution. Thus, we need to extract D from equation (4). If $N = 3$, then we can solve for D directly. If $N > 3$, then the system is overdetermined and we approximate D through singular value decomposition [24]. Simulations show that using more than the minimum of 3 LEDs can reduce average error caused by non-systematic error sources. In pseudocode, our main loop is:

> Generate an initial guess for L
> repeat
> > Given L, compute G_0 and ∂G
> > Estimate D using singular value decomposition
> > $L = L + D$
>
> until magnitude of D is small
> return L

How do we generate the initial guess of L? Normally we use the last known position and orientation, which should be an excellent guess because we track at rates up to 100 Hz. Collinearity usually converges in 1 or 2 iterations when the guess is close. But in degenerate cases (at system startup, or when we lose tracking because the photodiode units are pointed away from the ceiling), we have no previous L. Collinearity will not converge if the guess is not close enough to the true value; we empirically found that being within 30° and several feet of the true L is a good rule of thumb. So in degenerate cases, we draw initial guesses for L from a precomputed lookup table with 120 entries, trying them sequentially until one converges. We can double-check a result that converges by comparing the set of LEDs used to generate that solution to the theoretical set of LEDs that the photodiode units should see, if the head actually was at the location just computed. When these two sets match, we have a valid solution.

8   Performance

A "typical situation" is defined as a user of average height standing erect underneath the ceiling, with at least three photodiode units aimed at the ceiling, moving his head at moderate speeds. All measurement bounds assume that the user remains in tracker range with at least two sensors aimed at the ceiling.

Update rate: The update rate ranges between 20–100 Hz. Under typical situations, 50-70 Hz is normal, depending on the height of the user. The wide variation in the number of LEDs seen by the sensors causes the variation in update rate. The more LEDs used, the slower the update rate, because LED Manager is the slowest step in the pipeline. If the head remains still and the sensors see a total of B beacons, LED Manager requires $3.33 + 0.782*B$ ms to run. Rapidly rotating the head increases this time by a factor of about 1.33, since additional time is required to handle the changing working sets of LEDs. Slower head movement rates have correspondingly smaller factors.

Lag: Lag varies between 20–60 ms, with 30 ms being normal under typical situations. Lag is measured from the time that LED Manager starts to the time when the Collinearity module provides a computed head location to the graphics engine. Therefore, tracker latency is a function of the number of LEDs seen and the quality of the initial guess provided to the Collinearity module. As B gets smaller, both the LED Manager and Collinearity modules become faster, reducing latency. This mutual dependence on B means that update rate and lag are closely tied: faster update rates correspond with lower latency values.

Resolution: When moving the head unit very slowly, we observed a resolution of 2 mm in position and 0.2 degrees in orientation. Measuring accuracy is much harder, and we do not have any firm numbers for that yet. At SIGGRAPH '91, users were able to touch a chair and the four ceiling support poles based solely on the images they saw of models of the chair and the poles in the virtual environment.

9   Evaluation

The system provides adequate performance but has several limitations and problems that must be addressed. The most noticeable is the combination of excessive head-born weight and limited head rotation range. Rotation range depends heavily on the user's height and position under the ceiling. A typical maximum pitch range near the center of the ceiling is 45 degrees forward and 45 degrees back. When the user walks near an edge of the ceiling, head rotation range becomes much more restricted. To accommodate the full range of head motion, multiple image sensors must be oriented such that wherever the head is pointed, two or more sensors are able to view LEDs on the ceiling. Given the current focal lengths, simulations show that as many as eight fields of view are required for a respectable rotation range [29]. The weight of each sensor must be significantly reduced to achieve this goal.

To reduce weight, we are trying to replace the current lenses (11 oz. each) with smaller, lighter lenses (2 oz. each). Other approaches are possible. Wang proposed optically multiplexing multiple fields of view onto a single lateral-effect photodiode [29]. Reduced signal strength, distortions, and view identification ambiguities make this a nontrivial task. It may be easier to design a helmet with integral photodiodes and lenses. Given that each photodiode is about the size of a quarter, the entire surface of a helmet could be studded with sensors.

Beacon switching error has been greatly reduced, but not eliminated. Small observable discontinuities occasionally occur, and while they are not a major disturbance, they are annoying. Calibration techniques are being explored to estimate error sources and compensate for their effects. Photogrammetric techniques like the bundle adjustment method [8] or an alternate scheme suggested by our colleagues [18] may provide the answer.

Infrared light sources in the environment surrounding the tracker, such as sunlight or incandescent light, must be controlled for the system to operate correctly. Specifically, any light source whose wavelengths include 880 nm will be detected by the photodiodes as if it were an LED. For this reason, fluorescent ambient lighting is preferred. Extreme caution is not required, however. Whereas a sensor pointed directly at an infrared light source other than the LEDs will confuse the system, a certain level of indirect infrared background light is tolerable due to the combination of optical filters and the ambient light rejection techniques described in Section 4.

Surprisingly, the bottleneck in the system is the time required to extract data from the photodiode detectors, not the time required to compute the head's location. The i860 processor performs the latter task adequately, and even faster and cheaper processors will be available in the future. But getting accurate photocoordinates from the detectors takes longer than expected, because of the time spent in current scaling and in sampling multiple times per LED. Further experimentation is required to see if we can safely reduce the number of samples. Optimizing the low-level software may improve sampling speed by 20-30%.

The use of Euler angles in the collinearity equations opens the possibility of gimbal lock. The current system avoids this because the head rotation range is too limited to reach gimbal lock positions, but a future version may. If we cannot place the gimbal lock positions out of reach, we can solve for the nine rotation matrix parameters individually, subject to six constraints that keep the matrix special orthogonal, or we may be able to recast the rotations as quaternions.

Since this tracker encourages the user to walk around large spaces, tripping over the supporting cables is a danger. We will investigate the feasibility of a wireless datalink to remove this problem.

Under certain circumstances, the sensors can see large numbers of beacons, such as a total of 30 or more. While using many LEDs usually improves the solution from the Collinearity module, it also slows down the update rate and increases the lag. Further experiments are needed to explore this tradeoff and determine rules of thumb that provide a reasonable balance between resolution and update rate.

Cellular systems using different technologies or configurations could be built to achieve similar scalable work areas. For example, Ascension has announced a cellular magnetic system [4]. Regardless of the technology, any cellular approach creates the problem of beacon switching error or its equivalent. Steps we took to control these errors would apply to other technologies as well: 1) precise positioning and measurement of system components, 2) averaging techniques to reduce random error sources, and 3) calibration routines to compensate for systematic error sources.

10   Future work

We intend to continue improving this system. In addition to the tasks listed in Section 9, we would eventually like to expand the ceiling size to around 20' x 20', to provide much greater range of movement, both quantitatively and psychologically. Also, ample room exists to improve the heuristics and optimize the code, increasing the update rate and reducing latency.

But beyond these incremental improvements, we do not expect to pursue this particular technology further. The system is a vehicle for further research and provides room-sized tracking capability today for HMD applications that require it. For example, the UNC Walkthrough team has begun interview-based user studies on what impact large-environment tracking has on the architectural design of a kitchen. In the future, emphasis will be placed on technologies that allow unlimited tracking volumes in unstructured environments. This potential exists in systems that measure only the relative differences in position and orientation as the user moves, integrating these differences over time to recover the user's location. Examples include inertial technologies and Self-Tracker. Since these technologies suffer from drift problems, initial versions may be hybrid systems reliant on the optical tracker for auxiliary information. Thus, the optical tracking system will serve as a testbed for its own successor.

Tracking HMDs will only get harder in the future. The higher resolution displays being developed demand higher resolution trackers. See-through HMDs add additional requirements. In the completely-enclosed HMDs commonly used today, the entire world is virtual, so resolution is much more important than accuracy. But for a see-through HMD, accurate registration of the HMD to the real world is vital. The effects of latency will also become more disturbing in see-through HMDs. Viewing computer-generated objects superimposed upon the real world, where those objects move with significant lag but the real world does not, will not provide a convincing illusion. People can perceive as little as 5 ms of lag [15], and it is unlikely that the combined tracker and graphics engine latency will be below that anytime soon. Therefore, compensation techniques need to be explored [19][24]. If HMDs are to achieve their potential of making a user truly feel immersed inside a virtual world, significant advances in tracking technologies must occur.

References

[1]   Advanced Micro Devices, Am7968/Am7969 TAXIchip Article Reprints, Sunnyvale, CA.

[2]   Antonsson, E. K., and R.W. Mann. Automatic 6-D.O.F. kinematic trajectory acquisition and analysis. *J. Dynamic Systems, Measurement, and Control*, 111, (March 1989) pp. 31–39.

[3]   Ascension Technology Corporation. The Bird 6D Input Device, Burlington, Vermont, 1989.

[4]   Ascension Technology Corporation. A Flock of Birds product description sheet, Burlington, Vermont, April 1991.

[5]   Axt, Walter E. Evaluation of a pilot's line-of-sight using ultrasonic measurements and a helmet mounted display. Proceedings IEEE National Aerospace and Electronics Conf. (Dayton, OH, May 18-22, 1987) pp. 921-927.

[6] Azuma, Ronald, and Mark Ward. Space-resection by collinearity: mathematics behind the optical ceiling head-tracker. UNC Chapel Hill Dept. of Computer Science technical report TR 91-048, Nov. 1991.

[7] Bishop, Gary and Henry Fuchs. The self-tracker: A smart optical sensor on silicon. *Proceedings of the 1984 MIT Conference on Advanced Research on VLSI* (Dedham, MA: Artech House, Jan 1984) pp. 65-73.

[8] Burnside, C. D. *Mapping from Aerial Photographs.* Granada Publishing Limited, G. Britain, 1979, pp. 248-258.

[9] Chung, Jim, Mark Harris, Fred Brooks, et al. Exploring Virtual Worlds with Head-Mounted Displays. SPIE Proceedings vol. 1083 Non-Holographic True 3-Dimensional Display Technologies (Los Angeles, CA, Jan 15-20, 1989).

[10] Church, Earl. Revised geometry of the aerial photograph. *Bulletins on Aerial Photogrammetry*, No. 15, Syracuse University, 1945.

[11] Cook, Anthony. The helmet-mounted visual system in flight simulation. Proceedings Flight simulation: Recent developments in technology and use. (Royal Aeronautical Society, London, England, Apr. 12-13, 1988) pp. 214-232.

[12] Fake Space Labs, Binocular Omni-Orientation Monitor (BOOM), Menlo Park, CA.

[13] Ferrin, Frank J. Survey of helmet tracking technologies. SPIE Vol. 1456 Large-Screen Projection, Avionic, and Helmet-Mounted Displays (1991) pp. 86-94.

[14] Fuchs, Henry, John Poulton, John Eyles, et. al. Pixel-Planes 5: A Heterogeneous Multiprocessor Graphics System Using Processor-Enhanced Memories. Proceedings of SIGGRAPH '89 (Boston, MA, July 31-Aug 4, 1989). In *Computer Graphics* 23, 3 (July 1989) pp. 79-88.

[15] Furness, Tom, and Gary Bishop. Personal communication.

[16] Hamamatsu. Hamamatsu Photonics, Hamamatsu City, Japan, 1985.

[17] Hardyman, G. M. and M. H. Smith. Helmet mounted display applications for enhanced pilot awareness. Proceedings of AIAA Flight Simulation Technologies Conference (Boston, MA, Aug. 14-16, 1989) pp. 221-225.

[18] Hughes, John F., and Al Barr. Personal communication.

[19] Liang, Jiandong, Chris Shaw, Mark Green. On Temporal-Spatial Realism in the Virtual Reality Environment. Proceedings of the 4th annual ACM Symposium on User Interface Software & Technology (Hilton Head, SC, Nov 11-13 1991) pp. 19-25.

[20] Logitech, Inc. Logitech 3-D Mouse news release. July 30, 1991.

[21] POLHEMUS 3SPACE User's Manual, OPM3016-004B, Colchester, Vermont, 1987.

[22] Press, William, Brian Flannery, Saul Teukolsky, William Vetterling. *Numerical Recipes in C*. Cambridge University Press, USA, 1988.

[23] SELCOM. SELSPOT II HARDWARE and MULTILab Software, Southfield, Michigan, 1988.

[24] Smith Jr., B. R. Digital head tracking and position prediction for helmet mounted visual display systems. Proceedings of AIAA 22nd Aerospace Sciences Meeting, (Reno, NV, Jan. 9-12, 1984).

[25] So, Richard H., and Michael J. Griffin. Effects of time delays on head tracking performance and the benefits of lag compensation by image deflection. Proceedings of AIAA Flight Simulation Technologies Conference (New Orleans, LA, Aug. 12-14, 1991) pp. 124-130.

[26] Sorensen, Brett, Max Donath, Guo-Ben Yang, and Roland Starr. The Minnesota scanner: a prototype sensor for three-dimensional tracking of moving body segments. *IEEE Transactions on Robotics and Automation,* 5, 4, (August 1989), pp. 499–509.

[27] Sutherland, Ivan. A head-mounted three dimensional display. Fall Joint Computer Conference, AFIPS Conference Proceedings, 33 (1968) pp. 757-764.

[28] Wang, Jih-Fang, Vernon Chi, and Henry Fuchs. A real-time 6D optical tracker for head-mounted display systems. Proceedings of 1990 Symposium on Interactive 3D Graphics (Snowbird, Utah, 1990). In *Computer Graphics* 24, 2 (March 1990) pp. 205-215.

[29] Wang, Jih-Fang, Ronald Azuma, Gary Bishop, Vernon Chi, John Eyles, Henry Fuchs. Tracking a head-mounted display in a room-sized environment with head-mounted cameras. SPIE Proceedings Vol. 1290 Helmet-Mounted Displays II (Orlando, FL, Apr 19-20 1990) pp. 47-57.

[30] Welch, Brian, Ron Kruk, Jean Baribeau, et al. Flight Simulator: Wide-Field-Of-View Helmet-Mounted Infinity Display System, Air Force Human Resources Laboratory technical report AFHRL-TR-85-59, May 1986, pp. 48-60.

[31] Wolf, Paul. *Elements of Photogrammetry, With Air Photo Interpretation and Remote Sensing*, 2nd ed., McGraw-Hill, New York, 1983.

[32] Woltring, Herman. Single- and Dual-Axis Lateral Photodetectors of Rectangular Shape. *IEEE Trans. on Electron Devices*, (August 1975) pp. 581–590.

Acknowledgements

This system would not exist today without the support of the Microelectronics System Laboratory, the Graphics Laboratory staff, and the other members of the Tracker group. The authors wish to thank Gary Bishop, Vern Chi, Carney Clegg, John Eyles, David Harrison, John Hughes, Jack Kite, Mark Mine, John Poulton, C. A. Stone, John Thomas, and Norm Vogel for all of their help. We also thank Fred Brooks and the UNC Walkthrough group for providing architectural applications to use with our tracker.

Accu-Tool Corporation of Cary, NC was responsible for the head frame's design and fabrication. Panel enclosures were fabricated by Southeastern Machine Tool of Raleigh, NC. All circuit boards were fabricated by Multilayer Technologies, Inc. of Irvine, CA. This work was partially supported by ONR contract N00014-86-K-0680, DARPA contract DAEA 18-90-C-0044, NSF contract ASC-8920219, and a Pogue Fellowship.

Interactive Viewpoint Control and Three-Dimensional Operations

Michael McKenna

Computer Graphics and Animation Group
The Media Laboratory
Massachusetts Institute of Technology
Cambridge, MA 02139

ABSTRACT

Techniques are discussed for creating a rendered view into a 3D scene, interactively based on the locations and orientations of the observer's head and the display surface. Stereoscopic head-mounted displays (HMDs) demonstrate a simplified, special case of these techniques, because the eyes and monitors move in unison. A largely overlooked class of interactive displays uses the relative positions between the eyes and monitor as input. These displays can be stereo or monoscopic, fixed or mobile, and the rendering process should incorporate the correct perspective distortion, which depends on the locations of the viewpoint(s) and the display monitor.

Three real-time graphics display systems were prototyped and examined: a high-resolution display which corrects the perspective projection based on the location of the observer's eye; the same display, extended to modify the view as the monitor is tilted and swiveled; and a handheld LCD display which can be freely moved and rotated as it displays a view based on the eye and monitor positions.

A simple experiment indicates that tracking the head and providing the appropriate view improves the ability to pick specific 3D locations in space using a 2D display, when compared to a fixed view and a mouse-controlled view.

1. INTRODUCTION

In the everyday world, we continually shift our visual attention from place to place. We rotate the eyes and head, scanning different regions of our field of view. In addition, we move our heads to different locations in space, changing our *viewpoints*. As an observer changes his or her viewpoint, objects at different relative depths appear to move with respect to each other. This effect is known as *motion parallax*, a powerful depth cue [5;7]. Changing one's viewpoint also allows an observer to "look around" objects, and to see the different sides of objects, obtaining multiple perspective views. Perspective and motion parallax are both *monocular* depth cues; the sensation of depth we derive from them requires only one eye, and thus, requires only a 2D display.

Motion parallax can be used to increase the visual correspondence between an operator and a remote or synthetic telerobotic manipulator. An important aspect in the design of displays and controls is creating *isomorphisms* between the local and remote operations [8]. (See Figure 1.) For example, the movement of a control should create a movement of the corresponding manipulator in the same direction, of the same apparent magnitude, on the display. An intelligent display should provide the operator with a view "corrected" for his or her relative position to the display, so that the displayed manipulator movements always appear isomorphic with her or his own movements. An uncorrected view requires

that the operator remain exactly centered in front of the display, in order to remain isomorphic. One way to provide the correct view is through the use of a "true" 3D display— i.e. an *autostereoscopic* display, which does not require viewing aids such as glasses [7]. Real-time autostereoscopic displays are problematic, especially concerning bandwidth and computational requirements. For tele-operations, a more difficult problem is the development of the camera required to record the spatial information for an autostereoscopic display. An alternate means of supplying the correct view is to track the locations of the eyes, and then provide the appropriate imagery. For a teleoperator, this requires that the remote camera be servoed to the operator's head movements. In addition, views in which the operator moves off-axis from the center of the monitor require that the displayed image be distorted, either by translating the receptors on the image-focus plane of the camera, providing a sub-image from a wide field-of-view, or by approximating the distortion in hardware/software. The use of head-mounted display systems bypasses the problem of distortion, since the eyes do not move relative to the displays.

The modification to the rendering process to generate off-axis perspective projections is straightforward, using parameters already built into most rendering systems. This can easily be implemented on today's real-time rendering workstations, through the addition of any number of tracking methods. Unfortunately, this technique has been largely overlooked, despite its ease of implementation and perceptual benefits. It is important that the

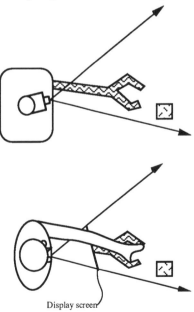

Figure 1: Isomorphisms between a remote robotic manipulator and human operator. Measures that appear equal between the two diagrams are, in fact, equal. The operator cannot put his or her hand through the display, obviously. However, the use of a head-mounted or a flat panel display allows the optical image of the display to share the same space as the operator's hand. Adapted from Sheridan [8].

correct perspective distortion be incorporated in the rendering process. This is not a type of "eye-in-hand" or "eye-on-head" camera control paradigm, in which only the eyepoint and viewing direction are modified [13]. Instead, it is an accurate way of modeling the visual characteristics of a 3D scene.

Prototype display systems were developed by the author to examine the use of tracking techniques to provide an accurate perspective projection, based on the relative positions of the viewer's eyes, the display surface, and the "real," inertial reference frame. Qualitatively, these displays add a great deal of depth perception via motion parallax. The ease of "look around" by moving the head is also a very attractive feature. Providing for a mobile display creates even greater flexibility for "look around" and the exploration of 3D scenes.

A simple experiment was conducted in order to explore the importance of isomorphic imaging on perceiving and interacting with three-dimensional information. Specifically, the experiment tested how many times a subject could move a three-dimensional cursor to a three-dimensional target within a given time period while viewing a 2D display. Different phases of the experiment tested the subject's responses when the view was fixed, when the view could be interactively changed using a mouse, and when the view could be interactively changed by moving the head.

By adding tracked objects in real space which have matching computer representations, important applications can be developed. For example, for medical examination and surgical planning and assist, computer models and scanned data of internal body features can be isomorphically displayed in the "patient space," along with tracked surgical instruments. Similarly, for training and repair, real world objects can be augmented with computer models to guide, instruct, and inform the user.

2. BACKGROUND

Head-mounted displays have been used to interactively view and explore 3D data and scenes for a number of years, recently gaining more popularity [3;11]. The head is tracked, and imagery is generated appropriate for the viewing location and direction. Boom-mounted displays provide similar functionality, allowing for more-massive, high-resolution displays and greater ease of use in certain situations [6].

A different approach was taken by Fisher, who used a monitor fixed in place, allowing the eyes to move relative to the display. Videodisc technology was used to store and playback multiple images of a scene, from different viewpoints. The observer's head was tracked and the appropriate image for that viewpoint location was displayed on a CRT display, creating what Fisher termed *viewpoint dependent imaging* [2].

About the same time, a similar system was demonstrated by Diamond, *et al.*, using real-time image generation. Wire-frame rendering was used to generate the perspective projection appropriate for the observer's eyepoint, tracked by a light bulb on the head using a video camera. The authors described the effect of their monoscopic system as "dynamic parallax" [1].

The above technique was extended by Suetens, *et al.*, to provide a stereoscopic image, using electro-optical shutter glasses. A Polhemus sensor was used to track the head, and a stereoscopic wire-frame rendering was generated in real-time [10].

Venolia and Williams created a similar system, which provided for real-time shaded stereoscopic imagery. In order to provide more complex imagery than could be generated in real-time, they employed a "viewpoint array" similar to Fisher's approach. The precomputed images were stored in memory and were displayed based on the observer's horizontal location [12].

This paper provides more details than the above references on the transformations used to generate viewpoint dependent images. It also extends this technique to allow for a mobile display surface. By tracking both the head and monitor, greater flexibility is

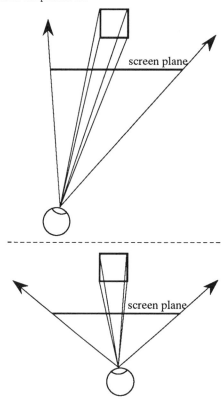

Figure 2: The perspectives and sizes of the 2D projections of 3D objects change as the viewpoint moves.

achieved in the exploration of 3D information, while retaining an isomorphic correspondence between the synthetic space and the real, laboratory space.

3. FIXED-DISPLAY MONOCULAR SYSTEM

Figure 2 shows an example of how the perspective projection of a 3D object is modified as the view changes. Points which lie at the same depth as the screen are the only ones which do not "move" relative to the screen as the viewpoint changes. Figure 3 depicts a stereoscopic, viewpoint dependent display. The display screen acts like a "window" into the three-dimensional space, cutting off the view of objects which lie outside the current viewing volume. Objects "behind" the screen are cut off just as we expect a real window to obscure objects. Objects in front of the screen and outside the viewing volume are also clipped. However, this is not a phenomenon we are familiar with from our everyday experiences. The "closer" objects are seemingly obscured by the screen, "further" back. This is often called a "window violation" and can significantly disrupt the depth perception of the scene, whether using a stereoscopic or monoscopic display.

To generate a viewpoint dependent image, a normal perspective rendering takes place, using a "window" onto the view-plane, which is off center from the vector which passes through the eye-point and is normal to the display surface. Figure 4 shows an example viewing setup. The *window center* rendering parameter is used to shift the area to be rendered away from the view normal [4;9].

The monitor's and the observer's locations and dimensions are tracked and located in the rendering "world-space" with the 3D objects. The eye location is established as a constant translational offset within the head tracking coordinate frame. A coordinate frame is established for the monitor, which has its origin at the center of the display surface. Matters are simplified if the coordinate axes are aligned with the display normal and the "vertical"

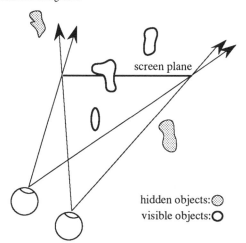

Figure 3: An off-axis view onto a stereoscopic, viewpoint dependent display. The screen acts as a "window" into the space— clipping objects both in the foreground and background.

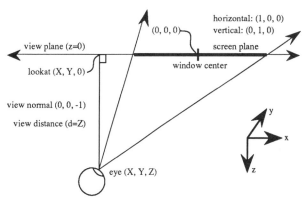

Figure 4: Shifting the "window center" based on the position of the eye generates the appropriate perspective for that viewpoint. The "window center" parameter is used in the rendering pipeline to control a shear transformation, which aligns the center-line of the viewing pyramid with the z-axis, in the coordinate system shown here.

and "horizontal" directions, such as the coordinate frame depicted in Figure 4.

The viewing parameters are set as follows: the *eyepoint* is set to the tracked location of the eye, in world space; the *view normal* is set to the "inwards" monitor normal, rotated (and not translated) into world space; the *view up* is set to the "vertical" monitor vector, rotated into world space; the *window half-size* is set to one half of the monitor's actual size; the *view distance* is set to the distance of the eye from the monitor plane, easily attainable by transforming the world-space location of the eye into the monitor's coordinate frame, and using the "height" of the eye, along the display normal ($-normal \bullet eye$); and the *window center* is set to offset the eye's position relative to the display surface's center: ($-horiz \bullet eye$, $-vertical \bullet eye$). These calculations assume that the display surface is planar.

This system was implemented using a Hewlett Packard Model 835 UNIX workstation, with a "Turbo-SRX" real-time polygonal rendering system (performance approximately 12 MIPS CPU, 38,000 shaded triangles per second). A Polhemus sensor was used to track the head. The display surface is fairly large (13" x 11"), with a resolution of 1280x1024.

This is the display system used in the experiment described in Section 6. The system has been used to view 3D objects and animations, qualitatively enhancing 3D perception significantly.

4. MOBILE DISPLAY MONOCULAR SYSTEM

By tracking the position and orientation of the display monitor, we can accommodate changes in its location in the rendering process, so that isomorphism is retained between the imagery and the real-world. The monitor can be moved to attain a better view of the data, or simply shifted to a more comfortable viewing position, without losing the correspondence to the real world coordinates.

The fixed-display method is extended simply by tracking the monitor, and adding the appropriate transformations. A monitor coordinate frame is established as above, only in this case, the monitor frame is a "child" of the display's tracking device coordinate frame, rotating to the normalized monitor space, and translating to the display center.

Two mobile display systems were implemented. The first used the high-resolution HP display, allowing it to tilt and swivel. The display could be translated as well, but it is quite bulky. The Polhemus sensor was mounted on a "boom," away from the EM field of the CRT. It is an important issue to mount the sensor as close as possible to the monitor's center, however, since error and noise in the orientation sensing will be amplified by distance. Movement of the monitor proved useful for adjusting the view, and for exploring

the data without losing the correspondence between object space and real space. The display was quite "jittery," unfortunately, due to tracking noise. However, a mode can be employed to deactivate monitor tracking when it is not being moved, to reduce the overall noise. Ideally, a low-noise tracking system would be employed, such as measuring the joint angles in the monitor base.

The second mobile display used a small (2.5"x1.8"), hand-held LCD screen, tracked by a Polhemus, which could be freely moved in space. This system was interesting due to its high mobility— the user could quickly explore 3D data, from many different positions and orientations. The small screen is certainly limiting, but the results indicate that larger screens are worth exploring in this context.

5. STEREOSCOPIC SYSTEM

The extension of the above systems to include stereo is very simple. The second eyepoint is located in world-space in the same manner as the first eye, with a different translational shift from the tracked point (e.g. the polhemus sensor). A second rendering is generated from the second viewpoint, and the left and right eye images are displayed in the appropriate manner for the type of stereoscopic display used.

A tracking device should be used which detects orientation, as well as position, so that the two eyes are accurately located in space. In addition, the "roll" of the head can be detected, as it tilts towards the sides, and the stereo imagery is automatically offset in the appropriate direction. This can be especially important when the display is mobile, since it may take on unusual viewing configurations. The stereoscopic display must be able to support these types of rotations— for example, some polarized systems use linear polarization, which will not allow "rolls."

Due to a lack of equipment, we have not, as yet, experimented with a non-HMD stereoscopic display.

6. EXPERIMENT

An informal experiment was conducted to test the effect of viewpoint dependent control on the speed required to manually locate a three dimensional target location. The fixed-monitor, moving viewpoint system was used, as described in Section 3. A second Polhemus sensor was used to track the hand location.

The experiment progresses as follows: A red cube, 2 cm per side (in modeling space and "real" space), appears on the display to act as the target. A blue cube, also 2 cm per side, is displayed, and acts as a cursor, tracking the motions of the hand. The cursor, in the depicted 3D space, moves with the same magnitude and directions as the tracked hand, simply offset by a translation. The task is to align the cursor cube to the target cube (translation only,

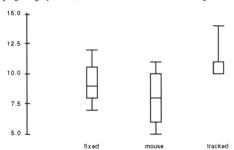

Figure 5: The experiment results from the "expert" subjects. The different phases of the experiments are shown across the plot on the x axis, and the number of successful target matches is shown on the y axis. The mean score is indicated by the central horizontal bar. The line boxes, partially overlapping the grey boxes, indicate the median 25%-75% range of the scores.

no orientation) within a given distance tolerance (1 cm). Once aligned, the target moves to a new random location within the workspace. The subject is instructed to reach the target as many times as he or she can, within the given, fixed time limit.

There are three phases of the experiment: one in which the view is fixed and unchanging, one in which the viewpoint can be moved using a mouse, and one in which the viewpoint is directly controlled by head movements.

Eleven subjects were run through the experiment, four novices and seven experts (subjects familiar with real-time rendering and tracking systems). Figure 5 shows the data from the expert subjects. The novice subjects had the lowest scores, and their results were more widely varying than the experts. In general, performance did increase under viewpoint dependent control, although not dramatically. Use of the mouse generally decreased the score.

Qualitatively, the subjects preferred the viewpoint dependent control, especially as compared to the mouse control, which most found confusing. Some subjects considered the "jitter" in the view, due to the noise from the polhemus tracker, to be distracting; others thought it helped give a better sense of the depth, due to the small amount of resulting motion parallax. This effect could be tested experimentally.

7. DISCUSSION

Providing renderings based on the true viewing parameters of the observer and display has proven to enhance the 3D perception of real-time graphics, in our applications and experiments. Qualitatively, these displays significantly enhanced depth perception via motion parallax, and the ability to "look around" objects and explore the 3D scene, using intuitive motions. These displays generated significant interest and excitement in the lab.

The mobile LCD prototype display is too small to be of use for many applications, but it demonstrates very intriguing viewing qualities. The objects displayed on it are convincingly 3D, not so much in that they "look" 3D, but rather, in that the 3D nature of the data is so easy to explore.

There are interesting differences between these displays and HMDs. These displays are particularly non-intrusive and non-disorienting, since most of the eyes' FOV remains within the real world, and visual jitter does not, therefore, strongly conflict with the vestibular system. Higher effective resolutions are achieved, since the pixels occupy smaller visual angles.

Tracking noise is currently a problem in these prototypes, especially in the mobile-monitor systems. Tracking systems are available which generate significantly lower noise than Polhemus trackers. In particular, articulated arms could be used to measure monitor positions with high accuracy and low noise.

The experiment helped confirm the utility of viewpoint dependent imaging in 3D picking operations. Further experiments should be designed in which a more complete understanding of the 3D scene is required, perhaps adding orientation criteria and more

complex environments. In this experiment, the task seemed too simple and quick to execute, in that the subjects would not take the extra time to obtain multiple views unless it was required. An experiment which "rewards" visual exploration would be more appropriate to investigate the perceptual benefits derived from interactive display techniques.

8. ACKNOWLEDGMENTS

This research was initiated through the class *Telerobotics and Human Supervisory Control*, taught by Thomas Sheridan at MIT. The rendering software was written by David Chen. The Polhemus interface code is by David Sturman. I also wish to thank my advisor, David Zeltzer. Thanks to everyone who took the experiment, and to everyone in the lab who helped out. This work was supported in part by grants from NHK (Japan Broadcasting, Co.), and equipment grants from Hewlett-Packard and Apple Computer.

9. BIBLIOGRAPHY

1. Diamond, R., A. Wynn, K. Thomsen and J. Turner. Three-Dimensional Perception for One-Eyed Guys. *Computational Crystallography*. Oxford, Clarendon Press (1982).

2. Fisher, S. S. *Viewpoint Dependent Imaging: An Interactive Stereoscopic Display*. Master's Thesis, Massachusetts Institute of Technology. (1981). Also see: *Proc. SPIE- Display of Three-Dimensional Data* (Bellingham, WA, 1982). Vol. 367.

3. Fisher, S. S., M. McGreevy, J. Humphries and W. Robinett. Virtual Environment Display System. *Proc. 1986 ACM Workshop on Interactive Graphics* (Chapel Hill, NC, October, 1986), 77-87.

4. Foley, J. D., A. van Dam, S. K. Feiner and J. F. Hughes. *Computer Graphics: Principles and Practice*. Reading, MA, Addison-Wesley (1990).

5. Goldstein, E. B. *Sensation and Perception* (3rd edition). Belmont, CA, Wadsworth Publishing (1989).

6. McDowall, I. E., M. Bolas, S. Pieper, S. S. Fisher and J. Humphries. Implementation and Integration of a Counterbalanced CRT-Based Stereoscopic Display for Interactive Viewpoint Control in Virtual Environment Applications. *Proc. SPIE Stereoscopic Displays and Applications* (San Jose, 1990) (1990).

7. Okoshi, T. *Three Dimensional Imaging Systems*. Academic Press (1976).

8. Sheridan, T.B. *Telerobotics and Human Supervisory Control: Cooperative Action by People and Computers*. MIT Press. (In press).

9. Smith, A. R. The Viewing Transformation. Technical Memo No. 84. Computer Division, Lucasfilm, Ltd. (May 4, 1984).

10. Suetens, P., D. Vandermeulen, A. Oosterlinck, J. Gybels and G. Marchal. A 3-D Display System with Stereoscopic, Movement Parallax and Real-time Rotation Capabilities. *Proc. SPIE-Medical Imaging II: Image Data Management and Display* (Part B) (Newport Beach, CA, January, 1988). Vol. 914, 855–861.

11. Sutherland, I. E. A Head-Mounted Three-Dimensional Display. *Proc. the Fall Joint Computer Conference* (1968), 765-776.

12. Venolia, D. and L. Williams. Virtual Integral Holography. *Proc. SPIE- Extracting Meaning from Complex Data: Processing, Display, Interaction* (Santa Clara, CA, February, 1990), 99–105.

13. Ware, C. and S. Osborne. Exploration and Virtual Camera Control in Virtual Three Dimensional Environments. *Proc. 1990 Symposium on Interactive Graphics* (Snowbird, Utah, 1990). In *Computer Graphics* 24, 2 (1990), 175-183.

Device Synchronization Using an Optimal Linear Filter

Martin Friedmann, Thad Starner and Alex Pentland [†]

Abstract

In order to be convincing and natural, interactive graphics applications must correctly synchronize user motion with rendered graphics and sound output. We present a solution to the synchronization problem that is based on optimal estimation methods and fixed-lag dataflow techniques. A method for discovering and correcting prediction errors using a generalized likelihood approach is also presented. And finally, MusicWorld, a simulated environment employing these ideas is described.

CR Categories and Subject Descriptors : I.3.6 [Computer Graphics]: Methodology and Techniques - *Interaction Techniques*; D.2.2 [Software Engineering]: Tools and Techniques - *User Interfaces*

Additional Keywords: Real-time graphics, artificial reality, interactive graphics, Kalman filtering, device synchronization.

1 Introduction

In order to be convincing and natural, interactive graphics applications must correctly synchronize user motion with rendered graphics and sound output. The exact synchronization of user motion and rendering is critical: lags greater than 100 msec in the rendering of hand motion can cause users to restrict themselves to slow, careful movements while discrepancies between head motion and rendering can cause motion sickness [3; 5]. In systems that generate sound, small delays in sound output can confuse even practiced users. This paper proposes a suite of methods for accurately predicting sensor position in order to more closely synchronize processes in distributed virtual environments.

Problems in synchronization of user motion, rendering, and sound arise from three basic causes. The first cause is noise in the sensor measurements. The second cause is the length of the processing pipeline, that is, the delay introduced by the sensing device, the CPU time required to calculate the proper response, and the time spent rendering output images or generating appropriate sounds. The third cause is unexpected interruptions such as network contention or operating system activity. Because of these factors, using the raw output of position sensors leads to noticeable lags and other discrepancies in output synchronization.

[†] Vision and Modeling Group, The Media Laboratory,
Massachusetts Institute of Technology, Cambridge, MA 02139.
{martin,testarne,sandy}@media-lab.media.mit.edu

Unfortunately, most interactive systems either use raw sensor positions, or they make an ad-hoc attempt to compensate for the fixed delays and noise. A typical method for compensation averages current sensor measurements with previous measurements to obtain a smoothed estimate of position. The smoothed measurements are then differenced for a crude estimate of the user's instantaneous velocity. Finally, the smoothed position and instantaneous velocity estimates are combined to extrapolate the user's position at some fixed interval in the future.

Problems with this approach arise when the user either moves quickly, so that averaging sensor measurements produces a poor estimate of position, or when the user changes velocity, so that the predicted position overshoots or undershoots the user's actual position. As a consequence, users are forced to make only slow, deliberate motions in order to maintain the illusion of reality.

We present a solution to these problems based on the ability to more accurately predict future user positions using an optimal linear estimator and on the use of fixed-lag dataflow techniques that are well-known in hardware and operating system design. The ability to accurately predict future positions eases the need to shorten the processing pipeline because a fixed amount of "lead time" can be allotted to each output process. For example, the positions fed to the rendering process can reflect sensor measurements one frame ahead of time so that when the image is rendered and displayed, the effect of synchrony is achieved. Consequently, unpredictable system and network interruptions are invisible to the user as long as they are shorter than the allotted lead time.

2 Optimal Estimation of Position and Velocity

At the core of our technique is the optimal linear estimation of future user position. To accomplish this it is necessary to consider the *dynamic* properties of the user's motion and of the data measurements. The Kalman filter [4] is the standard technique for obtaining optimal linear estimates of the state vectors of dynamic models and for predicting the state vectors at some later time. Outputs from the Kalman filter are the maximum likelihood estimates for Gaussian noises, and are the optimal (weighted) least-squares estimates for non-Gaussian noises [2].

In our particular application we have found that it is initially sufficient to treat only the translational components (the x, y, and z coordinates) output by the Polhemus sensor, and to assume independent observation and acceleration noise. In this section, therefore, we will develop a Kalman filter that estimates the position and velocity of a Polhemus sensor for this simple noise model. Rotations will be addressed in the following section.

2.1 The Kalman Filter

Let us define a dynamic process

$$\mathbf{X}_{k+1} = \mathbf{f}(\mathbf{X}_k, \Delta t) + \xi(t) \tag{1}$$

where the function $\mathbf{f}$ models the dynamic evolution of state vector $\mathbf{X}_k$ at time k, and let us define an observation process

$$\mathbf{Y}_k = \mathbf{h}(\mathbf{X}_k, \Delta t) + \eta(t) \tag{2}$$

where the sensor observations $\mathbf{Y}$ are a function $\mathbf{h}$ of the state vector and time. Both ξ and η are white noise processes having known spectral density matrices.

In our case the state vector $\mathbf{X}_k$ consists of the true position, velocity, and acceleration of the Polhemus sensor in each of the x, y, and z coordinates, and the observation vector $\mathbf{Y}_k$ consists of the Polhemus position readings for the x, y, and z coordinates. The function $\mathbf{f}$ will describe the dynamics of the user's movements in terms of the state vector, *i.e.* how the future position in x is related to current position, velocity, and acceleration in x, y, and z. The observation function $\mathbf{h}$ describes the Polhemus measurements in terms of the state vector, *i.e.*, how the next Polhemus measurement is related to current position, velocity, and acceleration in x, y, and z.

Using Kalman's result, we can then obtain the optimal linear estimate $\hat{\mathbf{X}}_k$ of the state vector $\mathbf{X}_k$ by use of the following *Kalman filter*:

$$\hat{\mathbf{X}}_k = \mathbf{X}_k^* + \mathbf{K}_k(\mathbf{Y}_k - \mathbf{h}(\mathbf{X}_k^*, t)) \tag{3}$$

provided that the Kalman gain matrix $\mathbf{K}_k$ is chosen correctly [4]. At each time step k, the filter algorithm uses a state prediction $\mathbf{X}_k^*$, an error covariance matrix prediction $\mathbf{P}_k^*$, and a sensor measurement $\mathbf{Y}_k$ to determine an optimal linear state estimate $\hat{\mathbf{X}}_k$, error covariance matrix estimate $\hat{\mathbf{P}}_k$, and predictions $\mathbf{X}_{k+1}^*$, $\mathbf{P}_{k+1}^*$ for the next time step.

The prediction of the state vector $\mathbf{X}_{k+1}^*$ at the next time step is obtained by combining the optimal state estimate $\hat{\mathbf{X}}_k$ and Equation 1:

$$\mathbf{X}_{k+1}^* = \hat{\mathbf{X}}_k + \mathbf{f}(\hat{\mathbf{X}}_k, \Delta t)\Delta t \tag{4}$$

In our graphics application this prediction equation is also used with larger times steps, to predict the user's future position. This prediction allows us to maintain synchrony with the user by giving us the lead time needed to complete rendering, sound generation, and so forth.

2.1.1 Calculating The Kalman Gain Factor

The Kalman gain matrix $\mathbf{K}_k$ minimizes the error covariance matrix $\mathbf{P}_k$ of the error $\mathbf{e}_k = \mathbf{X}_k - \hat{\mathbf{X}}_k$, and is given by

$$\mathbf{K}_k = \mathbf{P}_k^* \mathbf{H}_k^T (\mathbf{H}_k \mathbf{P}_k^* \mathbf{H}_k^T - \mathcal{R})^{-1} \tag{5}$$

where $\mathcal{R} = \mathbf{E}[\eta(t)\eta(t)^T]$ is the $n \times n$ observation noise spectral density matrix, and the matrix $\mathbf{H}_k$ is the local linear approximation to the observation function $\mathbf{h}$,

$$[\mathbf{H}_k]_{ij} = \partial \mathbf{h}_i / \partial x_j \tag{6}$$

evaluated at $\mathbf{X} = \mathbf{X}_k^*$.

Assuming that the noise characteristics are constant, then the optimizing error covariance matrix $\mathbf{P}_k$ is obtained by solving the *Riccati equation*

$$0 = \mathbf{P}_k^* + \mathbf{F}_k \mathbf{P}_k^* + \mathbf{P}_k^* \mathbf{F}_k^T - \mathbf{P}_k^* \mathbf{H}_k^T \mathcal{R}^{-1} \mathbf{H}_k \mathbf{P}_k^* + \mathcal{Q} \tag{7}$$

where $\mathcal{Q} = \mathbf{E}[\xi(t)\xi(t)^T]$ is the $n \times n$ spectral density matrix of the system excitation noise ξ, and $\mathbf{F}_k$ is the local linear approximation to the state evolution function $\mathbf{f}$,

$$[\mathbf{F}_k]_{ij} = \partial \mathbf{f}_i / \partial x_j \tag{8}$$

evaluated at $\mathbf{X} = \hat{\mathbf{X}}_k$.

More generally, the optimizing error covariance matrix will vary with time, and must also be estimated. The *estimate* covariance is given by

$$\hat{\mathbf{P}}_k = (\mathbf{I} - \mathbf{K}_k \mathbf{H}_k)\mathbf{P}_k^* \tag{9}$$

From this the predicted *error* covariance matrix can be obtained

$$\mathbf{P}_{k+1}^* = \mathbf{\Phi}_k \hat{\mathbf{P}}_k \mathbf{\Phi}_k^T + \mathcal{Q} \tag{10}$$

where $\mathbf{\Phi}_k$ is known as the state transition matrix

$$\mathbf{\Phi}_k = (\mathbf{I} + \mathbf{F}_k \Delta t) \tag{11}$$

2.2 Estimation of Displacement and Velocity

In our graphics application we use the Kalman filter described above for the estimation of the displacements P_x, P_y, and P_z, the velocities V_x, V_y, and V_z, and the accelerations A_x, A_y, and A_z of Polhemus sensors. The state vector $\mathbf{X}$ of our dynamic system is therefore $(P_x, V_x, A_x, P_y, V_y, A_y, P_z, V_z, A_z)^T$, and the state evolution function is

$$\mathbf{f}(\mathbf{X}, \Delta t) = \begin{bmatrix} V_x + A_x \frac{\Delta t}{2} \\ A_x \\ 0 \\ V_y + A_y \frac{\Delta t}{2} \\ A_y \\ 0 \\ V_z + A_z \frac{\Delta t}{2} \\ A_z \\ 0 \end{bmatrix} \tag{12}$$

The observation vector $\mathbf{Y}$ will be the positions $\mathbf{Y} = (P_x', P_y', P_z')^T$ that are the output of the Polhemus sensor. Given a state vector $\mathbf{X}$ we predict the measurement using simple second order equations of motion:

$$\mathbf{h}(\mathbf{X}, \Delta t) = \begin{bmatrix} P_x + V_x \Delta t + A_x \frac{\Delta t^2}{2} \\ P_y + V_y \Delta t + A_y \frac{\Delta t^2}{2} \\ P_z + V_z \Delta t + A_z \frac{\Delta t^2}{2} \end{bmatrix} \tag{13}$$

Calculating the partial derivatives of Equations 6 and 8 we obtain

$$\mathbf{F} = \begin{bmatrix} 0 & 1 & \frac{\Delta t}{2} & & & & & & \\ & 0 & 1 & & & & & & \\ & & 0 & & & & & & \\ & & & 0 & 1 & \frac{\Delta t}{2} & & & \\ & & & & 0 & 1 & & & \\ & & & & & 0 & & & \\ & & & & & & 0 & 1 & \frac{\Delta t}{2} \\ & & & & & & & 0 & 1 \\ & & & & & & & & 0 \end{bmatrix} \tag{14}$$

and

$$\mathbf{H} = \begin{bmatrix} 1 & \Delta t & \frac{\Delta t^2}{2} & & & & & & \\ & & & 1 & \Delta t & \frac{\Delta t^2}{2} & & & \\ & & & & & & 1 & \Delta t & \frac{\Delta t^2}{2} \end{bmatrix} \tag{15}$$

Finally, given the state vector $\mathbf{X}_k$ at time k we can predict the Polhemus measurements at time $k + \Delta t$ by

$$\mathbf{Y}_{k+\Delta t} = \mathbf{h}(\mathbf{X}_k, \Delta t) \tag{16}$$

and the predicted state vector at time $k + \Delta t$ is given by

$$\hat{\mathbf{X}}_{k+\Delta t} = \mathbf{X}_k^* + \mathbf{f}(\hat{\mathbf{X}}_k, \Delta t)\Delta t \tag{17}$$

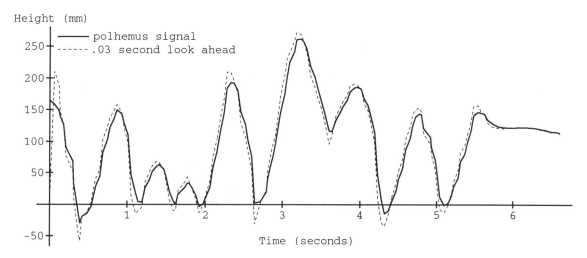

Figure 1: Output of a Polhemus sensor and the Kalman filter prediction of that output for a lead time of 1/30th of a second.

2.2.1 The Noise Model

We have experimentally developed a noise model for user motions. Although our noise model is not verifiably optimal, we find the results to be quite sufficient for a wide variety of head and hand tracking applications. The system excitation noise model ξ is designed to compensate for large velocity and acceleration changes; we have found

$$\xi(t)^T = \begin{bmatrix} 1 & 20 & 63 & 1 & 20 & 63 & 1 & 20 & 63 \end{bmatrix} \quad (18)$$

(where $\mathcal{Q} = \xi(t)\xi(t)^T$) provides a good model. In other words, we expect and allow for positions to have a standard deviation of $1mm$, velocities $20mm/sec$ and accelerations $63mm/sec^2$. The observation noise is expected to be much lower than the system excitation noise. The spectral density matrix for observation noise is $\mathcal{R} = \eta(t)\eta(t)^T$; we have found that

$$\eta(t)^T = \begin{bmatrix} .25 & .25 & .25 \end{bmatrix} \quad (19)$$

provides a good model for the Polhemus sensor.

2.3 Experimental Results and Comparison

Figure 1 shows the raw output of a Polhemus sensor attached to a drumstick playing a musical flourish, together with the output of our Kalman filter predicting the Polhemus's position $1/30th$ of a second in the future.

As can be seen, the prediction is generally quite accurate. At points of high acceleration a certain amount of overshoot occurs; such problems are intrinsic to any prediction method but can be minimized with more complex models of the sensor noise and the dynamics of the user's movements.

Figure 2 shows a higher-resolution version of the same Polhemus signal with the Kalman filter output overlayed. Predictions for 1/30, 1/15, and 1/10 of a second in the future are shown. For comparison, Figure 3 shows the performance of the prediction made from simple smoothed local position and velocity, as described in the introduction. Again, predictions for 1/30, 1/15, and 1/10 of a second in the future are shown. As can be seen, the Kalman filter provides a more reliable predictor of future user position than the commonly used method of simple smoothing plus velocity prediction.

3 Rotations

With the Polhemus sensor, the above scheme can be directly extended to filter and predict Euler angles as well as translations.

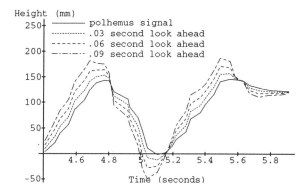

Figure 2: Output of Kalman filter for various lead times

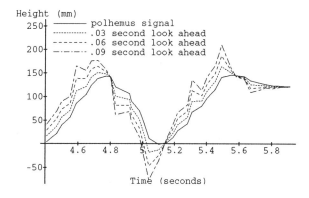

Figure 3: Output of commonly used velocity prediction method.

59

However with some sensors it is only possible to read out instant-by-instant *incremental rotations*. In this case the absolute rotational state must be calculated by integration of these incremental rotations, and the Kalman filter formulation must altered as follows [1]. See also [6].

Let ρ be the incremental rotation vector, and denote the rotational velocity and acceleration by ϑ and α. The rotational acceleration vector α is the derivative of ϑ which is, in turn, the derivative of ρ, but only when two of the components ρ are exactly zero (in some frame to which both ρ and ϑ are referenced). For sufficiently small rotations about at least two axes, ϑ is approximately the time derivative of ρ.

For 3D tracking one cannot generally assume small absolute rotations, so an additional representation of rotation, the unit quaternion $\overset{\circ}{\mathbf{q}}$ and its rotation submatrix $\mathbf{R}$, is employed. Let

$$\overset{\circ}{\mathbf{q}} = \begin{pmatrix} q_0 \\ q_1 \\ q_2 \\ q_3 \end{pmatrix}, \tag{20}$$

be the unit quaternion. Unit quaternions can be used to describe the rotation of a vector $\mathbf{v}$ through an angle ϕ about an axis $\hat{\mathbf{n}}$, where $\hat{\mathbf{n}}$ is a unit vector. The unit quaternion associated with such a rotation has *scalar part*

$$q_0 = \sin\left(\phi/2\right) \tag{21}$$

and vector part

$$\begin{pmatrix} q_1 \\ q_2 \\ q_3 \end{pmatrix} = \hat{\mathbf{n}} \cos\left(\phi/2\right). \tag{22}$$

Note that every quaternion defined this way is a unit quaternion.

By convention $\overset{\circ}{\mathbf{q}}$ is used to designate the rotation between the global and local coordinate frames. The definition is such that the orthonormal matrix

$$\mathbf{R} = \tag{23}$$
$$\begin{bmatrix} q_0^2 + q_1^2 - q_2^2 - q_3^2 & 2(q_1q_2 - q_0q_3) & 2(q_1q_3 + q_0q_2) \\ 2(q_1q_2 + q_0q_3) & q_0^2 - q_1^2 + q_2^2 - q_3^2 & 2(q_2q_3 - q_0q_1) \\ 2(q_1q_3 - q_0q_2) & 2(q_2q_3 + q_0q_1) & q_0^2 - q_1^2 - q_2^2 + q_3^2 \end{bmatrix}$$

transforms vectors expressed in the local coordinate frame to the corresponding vectors in the global coordinate frame according to

$$\mathbf{v}_{global} = \mathbf{R}\mathbf{v}_{local}. \tag{24}$$

In dealing with incremental rotations, the model typically assumes that accelerations are an unknown "noise" input to the system, and that the time intervals are small so that the accelerations at one time step are close to those at the previous time step. The remaining states result from integrating the accelerations, with corrupting noise in the integration process.

The assumption that accelerations and velocities can be integrated to obtain the global rotational state is valid only when ρ_k is close to zero and ρ_{k+1} remains small. The latter condition is guaranteed with a sufficiently small time step (or sufficiently small rotational velocities). The condition $\rho_k = 0$ is established at each time step by defining ρ to be a correction to a nominal (absolute) rotation, which is maintained externally using a unit quaternion $\overset{\circ}{\mathbf{q}}$ that is updated at each time step.

4 Unpredictable Events

We have tested our Kalman filter synchronization approach using a simulated musical environment (described below) in which we track a drumstick and simulate the sounds of virtual drums. For smooth motions, the drumstick position is accurately predicted, so that sound, sight, and motion are accurately synchronized, and the user experiences a strong sense of reality.

The main difficulties that arise with this approach derive from unexpected large accelerations, which produce overshoots and similar errors. It is important to note, however, that overshoots are *not* a problem as long the drumstick is far from the drum. In these cases the overshoots simply exaggerate the user's motion, and the perception of synchrony persists. In fact, such overshoots seem generally to enhance, not degrade, the user's impression of reality.

The problem occurs when the predicted motion overshoots the true motion when the drumstick is near the drumhead, thus causing a false collision. In this case the system generates a sound when in fact no sound should occur. Such errors detract noticeably from the illusion of reality.

4.1 Correcting Prediction Errors

How can we preserve the impression of reality in the case of an overshoot causing an incorrect response? In the case of simple responses like sound generation, the answer is easy. When we detect that the user has changed direction unexpectedly — that is, that an overshoot has occurred — then we simply send an emergency message aborting the sound generation process. As long as we can detect that an overshoot has occurred before the sound is "released," there will be no error.

This solution can be implemented quite generally, but it depends critically upon two things. The first is that we must be able to very quickly substitute the correct response for the incorrect response. The second is that we must be able to accurately detect that an overshoot has occurred.

In the case of sound generation due to an overshoot, it is easy to substitute the correct response for the incorrect, because the correct response is to do nothing. More generally, however, when we detect that our motion prediction was in error we may have to perform some quite complicated alternative response. To maintain synchronization, therefore, we must be able to detect possible trouble spots beforehand, and begin to compute all of the alternative responses sufficiently far ahead of time that they will be available at the critical instant.

The strategy, therefore, is to predict user motion just as before, but that at critical junctures to compute several alternative responses rather than a single response. When the instant arrives that a response is called for, we can then choose among the available responses.

4.2 Detecting Prediction Errors

Given that we have computed alternative responses ahead of time, and that we can detect that a prediction error has occurred, then we can make the correct response. But how are we to detect which of (possibly many) alternative responses are to be executed?

The key insight to solving this detection problem is that *if* we have the correct dynamic model then we will always have an optimal linear estimate of the drumstick position, and there should be nothing much better that we can to do. The problem, then, is that in some cases our model of the event's dynamics does not match the true dynamics. For instance, we normally expect accelerations to be small and uncorrelated with position. However in some cases (for instance, when sharply changing the pace of a piece of music) a drummer will apply large accelerations that are exactly correlated with position.

The solution is to have *several* models of the drummer's dynamics running in parallel, one for each alternative response. Then at each instant we can observe the drumstick position and velocity, decide which model applies, and then make our response based on that model. This is known as the *multiple model* or *generalized likelihood* approach, and produces a generalized maximum likelihood estimate of the current and future values of the state variables [10]. Moreover, the cost of the Kalman filter calculations is sufficiently small to make the approach quite practical.

Figure 4: MusicWorld's drum kit.

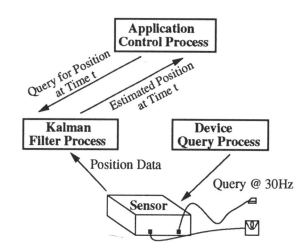

Figure 5: Communications used for control and filtering of Polhemus sensor.

Intuitively, this solution breaks the drummer's overall behavior down into several "prototypical" behaviors. For instance, we might have dynamic models corresponding to a relaxed drummer, a very "tight" drummer, and so forth. We then classify the drummer's behavior by determining which model best fits the drummer's observed behavior.

Mathematically, this is accomplished by setting up one Kalman filter for the dynamics of each model:

$$\hat{\mathbf{X}}_k^{(i)} = \mathbf{X}_k^{*(i)} + \mathbf{K}_k^{(i)}(\mathbf{Y}_k - \mathbf{h}^{(i)}(\mathbf{X}_k^{*(i)}, t)) \qquad (25)$$

where the superscript (i) denotes the ith Kalman filter. The *measurement innovations process* for the ith model (and associated Kalman filter) is then

$$\Gamma_k^{(i)} = \mathbf{Y}_k - \mathbf{h}^{(i)}(\mathbf{X}_k^{*(i)}, t) \qquad (26)$$

The measurement innovations process is zero-mean with covariance $\mathcal{R}$.

The ith measurement innovations process is, intuitively, the part of the observation data that is unexplained by the ith model. The model that explains the largest portion of the observations is, of course, the most model likely to be correct. Thus at each time step calculate the probability $P^{(i)}$ of the m-dimensional observations $\mathbf{Y}_k$ given the ith model's dynamics,

$$P^{(i)}(\mathbf{Y}_k) = \frac{1}{(2\pi)^{m/2}\mathrm{Det}(\mathcal{R})^{1/2}} \exp\left(-\frac{1}{2}\Gamma_k^{(i)T}\mathcal{R}^{-1}\Gamma_k^{(i)}\right) \quad (27)$$

and choose the model with the largest probability. This model is then used to estimate the current value of the state variables, to predict their future values, and to choose among alternative responses.

When optimizing predictions of measurements Δt in the future, equation 26 must be modified slightly to test the predictive accuracy of state estimates from Δt in the past.

$$\Gamma_k^{(i)} = \mathbf{Y}_k - \mathbf{h}^{(i)}(\mathbf{X}_{k-\Delta t}^{*(i)} + \mathbf{f}^{(i)}(\hat{\mathbf{X}}_{k-\Delta t}^{(i)}, \Delta t)\Delta t, t)) \qquad (28)$$

by substituting equation 17.

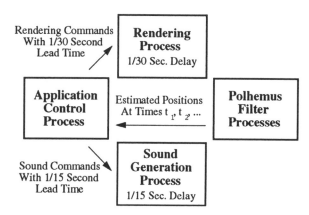

Figure 6: Communications and lead times for MusicWorld processes.

5 MusicWorld

Our solution is demonstrated in a musical virtual reality, an application requiring synchronization of user, physical simulation, rendering, and computer-generated sound. This system is called *MusicWorld*, and allows users to play a virtual set of drums, bells, or strings with two drumsticks controlled by Polhemus sensors. As the user moves a physical drumstick the corresponding rendered drumstick tracks accordingly. The instant the rendered drumstick strikes a drum surface a sound generator produces the appropriate sound for that drum. The visual appearance of MusicWorld is shown in Figure 4, and a higher quality rendition is included in the color section of these proceedings.

Figure 5 shows the processes and communication paths used to filter and query each Polhemus sensor. Since we cannot insure that the application control process will query the Polhemus devices on a regular basis, and since we do not want the above Kalman loop to enter into the processing pipeline, we spawn two small processes to constantly query and filter the actual device. The application control process then, at any time, has the opportunity to make a fast query to the filter process for the most up to date, filtered, polhemus position. Using shared-memory between these two processes makes the final queries fully optimal.

MusicWorld is built on top of the ThingWorld system [7; 8], which has one process to handle the problems of real-time physical simulation and contact detection and a second process to handle rendering. Sound generation is handled by a third process on a separate host, running CSound [9]. Figure 6 shows the communication network for MusicWorld, and the lead times employed.

The application control process queries the Kalman filter process for the predicted positions of each drumstick at 1/15 and 1/30 of a second. Two different predictions are used, one for each output device. The 1/15 of a second predictions are used for sound and are sent to ThingWorld to detect stick collisions with drums and other sound generating objects. When future collisions are detected, sound commands destined for 1/15 of a second in the future are sent to CSound. Regardless of collisions and sounds, the scene is always rendered using the positions predicted at 1/30 of a second in the future, corresponding to the fixed lag in our rendering pipeline. In general, it would be more optimal to constantly check and update the lead times actually needed for each output process, to insure that dynamic changes in network speeds, or in the complexity of the scene (rendering speeds) do not destroy the effects of synchrony.

6 Summary

The unavoidable processing delays in computer systems mean that synchronization of graphics and sound with user motion requires prediction of the user's future position. We have shown how to construct the optimal linear filter for estimating future user position, and demonstrated that it gives better performance than the commonly used technique of position smoothing plus velocity prediction. The ability to produce accurate predictions can be used to minimize unexpected delays by using them in a system of multiple asynchronous processes with known, fixed lead times. Finally, we have shown that the combination of optimal filtering and careful construction of system communications can result in a well-synchronized, multi-modal virtual environment.

7 Acknowledgements

This research was made possible by ARO Grant No. DAAL03-87-K-0005. First thanks go to the ACM for this publication. Thanks are due to Barry Vercoe and Mike Hawley for their help with CSOUND. Thanks! Special mention to Ali Azarbayejani, our newest member. And last but not least, shouts go out to the rest of the real-time programming posse: Irfan Essa, Bradley Horowitz and Stan Sclaroff.

References

[1] Azarbayejani, Ali. *Model-Based Vision Navigation for a Free-Flying Robot*. Masters Thesis, M.I.T. Dept. of Aero. and Astro. (1991).

[2] Friedland, Bernard. *Control System Design*. McGraw-Hill, (1986).

[3] Held, Richard. Correlation and decorrelation between visual displays and motor output. In *Motion sickness, visual displays, and armored vehicle design*, (pp. 64-75). Aberdeen Proving Ground, Maryland: Ballistic Research Laboratory. (1990).

[4] Kalman, R. E. & Bucy, R. S. New results in linear filtering and prediction theory. In *Transaction ASME (Journal of basic engineering)*, 83D, 95-108. (1961).

[5] Oman, Charles M. Motion sickness: a synthesis and evaluation of the sensory conflict theory. In *Canadian Journal of Physiology and Pharmacology*, 68, 264-303. (1990).

[6] Liang, Jiandong. Shaw, Chris & Green, Mark. On temporal-spatial realism in the virtual reality environment. In *Proceedings of the ACM Symposium on User Interface Software and Technology*, pp. 19-25, Hilton Head SC. (1991).

[7] Pentland, Alex & Williams, John. Good vibrations: Modal dynamics for graphics and animation. In *Computer Graphics* 23, 4, pp. 215-222. (1989).

[8] Pentland, A., Friedmann, M., Horowitz, B., Sclaroff, S. & Starner, T. The ThingWorld modeling system. In E.F. Deprettere, (Ed.). *Algorithms and parallel VLSI architectures*, Amsterdam : Elsevier. (1990).

[9] Vercoe, Barry & Ellis, Dan. Real-time CSOUND: Software synthesis with sensing and control. In *ICMC Glasgow 1990 Proceedings*, pp. 209-211. (1990).

[10] Willsky, Alan S.. Detection of Abrupt Changes in Dynamic Systems. In M. Basseville and A. Benveniste, (Ed.). *Detection of Abrupt Changes in Signals and Dynamical Systems*, Lecture Notes in Control and Information Sciences, No. 77, pp. 27-49, Springer-Verlag. (1986).

Manipulating the Future: Predictor Based Feedback for Velocity Control in Virtual Environment Navigation

Dale Chapman and Colin Ware

Faculty of Computer Science
P.O. Box 4400
University of New Brunswick
Fredericton, N.B.
CANADA E3B 5A3
Address correspondence to Ware
at above address or cware@UNB.ca

Abstract

This paper introduces a predictor based visual feedback aid for navigating through virtual environments using velocity control. The predictor indicates to the user where and how fast he or she is travelling and has a direct manipulation feel to it. Experiences using the predictor to navigate over digital terrain maps are discussed, which show it to be an aide in learning to use velocity control and in creating smooth flight paths over thinned wire frame representation of a scene for subsequent single frame animation. Measurements of performance in using the predictor to fly through a tube scene show a benefit for the less experienced users.

Introduction

For the past six years our work has focussed on methods for exploring "fishtank" virtual environments. These are not the full-blown environments with head mounted displays, coupled to head position (Sutherland, 1968; Blanchard, et al, 1990), but rather the (currently) far more useful environments where the virtual 3D world is perceived to be behind the monitor window. Given this common configuration, the user requires a means to move through the virtual environment and manipulate objects within it - both of these are 6 degree of freedom (6DF) tasks. Previous work on viewpoint manipulation in our laboratory using the Bat input device has established that control over viewpoint velocity to be a preferred exploration mode (Ware and Osborne, 1990). The Bat (like a mouse that flies or *fledermaus*) senses the user's hand position and orientation. We use the button as a kind of engagement device and while the button is held down relative position

and orientation is converted to viewpoint velocity; translational position is converted to translational velocity and orientation is converted to rotational velocity. We use a quadratic function to map hand displacement to both translational and rotational velocities and this gives control through changes of scale of up to four orders of magnitude.

The hand position is computed relative to the 6D coordinates of the initial change to the button down state. Using relative position in this way has advantages and disadvantages. It allows the user to work comfortably. If the user finds a position awkward, letting go of the Bat button instantly stops motion; the hand can be then moved to a more convenient position, usually fairly close to the body without undue arm extension, and motion can be resumed relative to this new position. The disadvantage of the relative mode is that the user is not likely to remember the starting position of the hand (button down transition). If you knew where your hand was your could infer your velocity. As it is there are only visual cues available from the virtual environment about the current viewpoint velocity and these are often not adequate, especially when the environment has little texture.

The present project was initiated to develop a viewpoint navigation aid by providing the user with feedback on his or her current velocity. The most important source of inspiration came from experimental heads-up cockpit displays designed to illustrate the aircraft attitude in the pilot's field of view. In some experimental studies it has been found useful to display the aircraft's predicted attitude in addition to the current aircraft attitude (Gallagher et al, 1977; Kelley, 1968). Taking this a step further is the "quickened" display which only shows the aircraft's future position (for a discussion see Wickens 1984).

The notion of quickening was especially attractive to us since we felt it might give a direct object manipulation feel to the interface. Even though the user is in fact directly manipulating the current velocities, he or she may feel that it is the predictor that is being manipulated and the predictor shows a future position and orientation based on extrapolation. Assuming success, the user will feel in control over the predictor and, in a sense, control over the future view point with a guaranteed

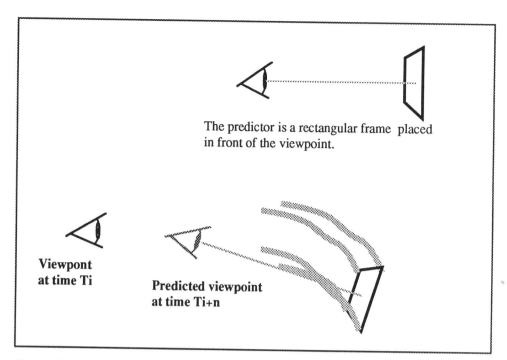

Figure 1. The predictor which is perceived at time Ti is based on the predicted position of the viewpoint at time Ti+n. The streamers from the corners of the predictor trace out the path of the predictor over the previous frames.

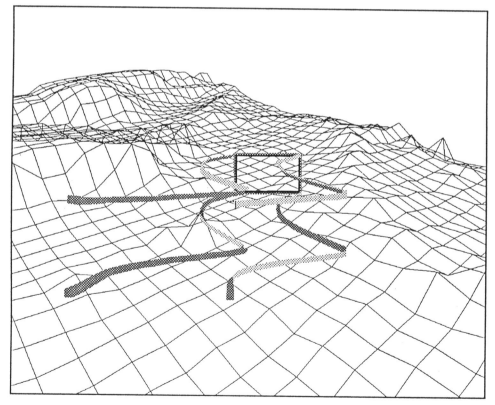

Figure 2. The predictor is seen in use over a digital terrain map representing the North Atlantic

smooth transition from the current viewpoint. To arrive at a particular location it will be only necessary to point the predictor at it, and changes of orientation may be achieved in a similar fashion. In this respect the display would be like Mackinlay et al's (1990) technique for viewpoint navigation relative to specified points on the surfaces of objects, only without the necessity of tieing navigation directly to objects.

Predictor design

The aircraft problem and the fishtank interaction problem are not exactly isomorphic. An aircraft has complex flight dynamics whereas our interface was designed for complete freedom of motion with ease of use being the only consideration. We are able to move up down forwards,backwards and sideways with equal facility. Because a conventional predictor will not be visible except in the case of forward motion we gave our predictor a neutral point in front of the viewpoint, as illustrated in Figure 1. To add velocity and trajectory feedback we added tails to the four corners of the predictor frame. Although these tails actually look like ribbons, they behave like smoke trails. That is, they mark the course of the predictor frame through space. Figure 2 illustrates the predictor being used to create a motion path over a digital terrain map.

Uses

Our first real application of the predictor is in virtual camera control. We are involved in a major Canadian ocean mapping project at UNB and we have created part of an animated videotape for the Canada pavilion in the upcoming World's Fair in Seville Spain. We used the predictor with the velocity control interface to create a motion path in real-time over a thinned wire frame representation of the topographic data. We can then reused the saved motion path with single frame animation and high quality rendering techniques to create the required movie.

We are also building the predictor into a data visualization and editing system for oceanographic research.

Evaluation

Our experience in using the predictor to explore various kinds of terrain data suggest that the predictor tails help in providing feedback about velocity, smoothness and direction of travel which is invaluable in the specification of a motion path for a flyby animation. In this kind of scene the terrain consists of a wire mesh which means that the tails were always visible to the user. In addition, the visual feedback from the predictor tails are especially useful in graphically impoverished scenes, they make up for the lack of visual motion parallax information (Gibson, et al, 1959)

The first stages of predictor design were an iterative process without formal evaluation. However, it is obvious to us already that it is a valuable navigation aid and as anticipated it has a direct manipulation feel to it. It has had additional benefits which were not anticipated. Because our system uses the standards Z buffering for hidden elimination. it gives a collision cue. The predictor can be seen to enter an object, leaving it's tail still visible allowing for avoidance action.

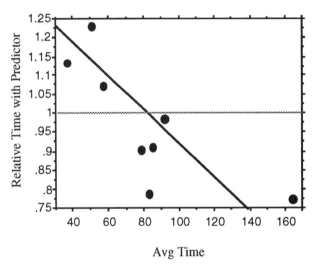

Figure 3. At a particular time setting, the presence of the predictor allows inexperineced subjects to perform better. Experienced subjects perform worse. See text for explanation

We are beginning a series of formal studies to evaluate various predictor parameters such as optimal extrapolation time and streamer length. The results we have thus far come from a task in which subjects navigate through a tunnel which is made up of a sequence of eight curves each having a diffferent radius. Each time the subject does the task a different randomly connected sequence of curves is used. The subject's task is to navigate the tunnel as fast as possible without flying through a wall. We measure both time to completion and errors under the three conditions:

No predictor
Predictor without tails
Predictor with tails.

The most interesting results obtained to date are plotted in Figure 3 which shows data from eight subjects. The relative time to completion for the predictor without tails condition is plotted agains average time to completion. The negative correlation shows that subjects who did the task slowly (on average) were did significantly better with the predictor - they are represented by the five points below the line, while subjects who did the task fast were actually hindered in their performance of the task. The subjects who did the task slowly were ones with no prior experience with our velocity navigation system and they clearly benefited from the presence of the predictor. The reason for the degradation of performance with the more experienced subjects became clear on detailed analysis. The speed with which they navigated through the tube was such that the predictor was projected right out of sight beyond the next bend, most of the time. Because of this the subject only occasionally obtained glimpses of the predictor which proved to be a distraction rather than a help. It appears likely that for experienced subjects the predictor should be projected a shorter time into the future.

The data obtained we have obtained thus far with the tails give a confusing picture which suggest that some subjects benefit while other subject find them to be a hindrance, irrespective of experience. We are continuing our investigation.

What has been achieved

We feel that the combination of Bat, fishtank environments and predictor has immediate utility for Scientific visualization and Cad systems. It lacks many of the motion constraints of full blown, head mounted virtual reality while it allows for almost as much functionality, although, of course the feeling of immersion in the graphical environment is absent - but this saves on Gravol. There are now three Bat devices in or close to production: the SimGraphics Flying Mouse™, the Ascension Technologies Bird™, the Logitech™ 3D mouse, and the Gyration GyroPoint™. In other studies we have found that Bats are good for object manipulation (Ware and Jessome, 1988, Ware, 1990) and superior to the SpaceBall™ for 3D navigation (Ware and Slipp, 1991)

Acknowledgements

Thanks are due to Pat Cavanaugh for part of the code used to display the digital terrain model and to Kevin Marinelli for software support.

References

1. Blanchard, C., Burgess, S., Harvill, Y., Lanier, J., Lasko, A., Oberman, M., Teitel, M., (1990) Reality Built for Two A Virtual Reality Tool. Computer Graphics 24(2), 35-36.

2. Brooks, F.P. (1986) Walkthrough - A Dynamic Graphics System for Simulating 3. Virtual Buildings, Proc 1986 Workshop on interactive 3D Graphics, F. Crow and S.M. Pizar, eds, 1986, ACM, New York, 77-88.

4. Gallagher, P.D., Hunt, R.A., and Williges, R.C. (1977) A regression approach to generate aircraft predictive information. Human Factors, 19, 549-566.

5. Kelley, C.R. (1968) Automatic and manual control. New York, Wiley.

6. Mackinlay, J.D., Card, S.K., and Robertson, GG. (1990) "Rapid Controlled Movement Through a Virtual 3D Workspace. Proceedings of SIGGRAPH'90 (Dallas, Texas, August 1990). In Computer Graphics, 24, 3, 171-176.

7. Sutherland, I.E. (1968) Head Mounted Three Dimensional Display. Proc of the Fall Joint Computer Conference, 33, 757-764.

8. Ware, C. (1990) Using hand position for virtual object placement. The Visual Computer, 6, 245-253.

9. Ware, C., and Osborne, S., Exploration and virtual camera control in virtual three dimensional environments. Proceedings of the 1990 Symposium on Interactive 3D Graphics (Snowbird, Utah, March 1990). In Computer Graphics 24, 2, 175-183.

10. Ware, C. and Slipp, L. (1991) Using Velocity Control to navigate 3D graphical environments: a comparison of three interfaces. Proceedings of Human Factors Society Meeting, San Francisco, Sept. 35, 300-304.

11. Ware, C., and Jessome, D.R. (1988)Using the Bat: A Six Dimensional Mouse for Object Placement. IEEE Computer Graphics and Applications, 8(6), 155-160.

12. Wickens, C.D.(1984) Engineering Psychology and Human Performance. Scott Foresman/Little Brown,

Videotape

The videotape that accompanied this paper showed sequences are shown:

1) The predictor is seen in use in the Duct Maze environment used to evaluate performance. The manouvers being carried out show how the predictor behaves when it is flown in and out of walls.

2) The predictor is used in an interface which allows the exploration of a digital terrain map of the North Atlantic and the west coast of North America. When motion stops the surface is rendered at successive levels of detail. The colour coding of the surface illustrates gravity anomalies.

In the version illustrated in the videotape, the predictor tails extend from 20 frames in the future to 10 frames into the past. At a frame rate of 20 frames/second this yields a one second predictor which seems about right

CINEMA: A System for Procedural Camera Movements

Steven M. Drucker, Tinsley A. Galyean, and David Zeltzer

Computer Graphics and Animation Group
MIT Media Lab
Cambridge, MA. 02139
(smd | tag | dz)@media-lab.media.mit.edu

Abstract

This paper presents a general system for camera movement upon which a wide variety of higher-level methods and applications can be built. In addition to the basic commands for camera placement, a key attribute of the CINEMA system is the ability to inquire information directly about the 3D world through which the camera is moving. With this information high-level procedures can be written that closely correspond to more natural camera specifications. Examples of some high-level procedures are presented. In addition, methods for overcoming deficiencies of this procedural approach are proposed.

1. Introduction

Camera control is an integral part of any 3D interface. In recent years a number of techniques for interactively specifying camera movement have been implemented or proposed. Each of these techniques has provided an interface for solving a problem for a particular domain, but all of them have remained independent making it impossible to use them across domains. These domains include keyframe based computer graphic animation techniques [8, 11], navigation of virtual environments [1, 2, 9, 12, 13], general 3D interaction [3, 12], automatic presentation [6] (in which computers generate a presentation), and synthetic visual narratives [4] (in which users author presentations). The CINEMA system described in this paper is a camera protocol that supports camera interface paradigms useful for all these domains, and provides a framework on which new interfaces can be developed.

The CINEMA system has a procedural interface for specifying camera movements relative to objects, events, and the general state of an environment. This task level approach enables the implementation of many common interactive metaphors and provides the ability to build higher level parameterized procedures that are reusable.

After a brief introduction to the problem, we will review related work in camera control, and then describe the CINEMA system, including the underlying support structure, the implemen-

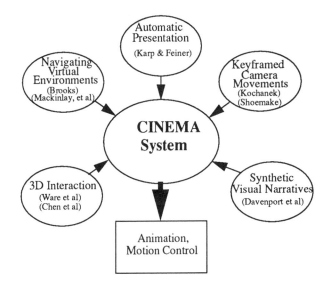

tation, and several examples that demonstrate the system. Finally, we will discuss problems with this approach and suggest alternatives based upon our findings. We will work under the assumption that the actions in the environment are occurring independently from the observer. By making this assumption, the specification of the camera is independent from the 3D world, or can be treated as a window into the world that does not impact on it. This simplification is made by many of the existing camera interfaces reviewed in this paper, and although limiting, it is appropriate for a variety of situations.

An effective camera protocol must support interfaces that investigate/explore and interfaces that present/illustrate the 3D world. Although we have only begun to explore the uses of this system, there are many applications in which it could be used. In both scientific and architectural visualization there is the need to explore the virtual environment interactively and then to later author a set of illustrative camera movements to be shown to clients or colleagues. In electronic books there will be the need for a designer or knowledge based system to generate an interface through which a reader can view the information. In the entertainment industry an animator could use it to direct or specify camera movements. Live action film makers may use it to create interactive story boards of their scenes, plan camera movements, or even to generate commands for motion controlled cameras. Telerobotic or virtual environment applications require a task level camera protocol in order to allow a human operator to efficiently and intuitively control the view while performing or directing some remote operation. All of these interfaces can be supported on top of the camera protocol described in this paper.

2. Previous Work

Early work in animation is devoted to making the movement of the camera continuous and to developing the proper representation for camera movements along a path [8, 11]. These works are devoted to giving the animator greater control in creating smooth movements and to finding ways to interpolate between user specified keyframes. Although generating spline curves for camera movement can produce smooth paths, it can be difficult to relate the movements of the camera to objects in the environment.

With the advent of virtual environments and related 3D interactive worlds, a great deal of effort has been spent on presenting convenient metaphors through which to change the user's view of an object or the world. A metaphor, as discussed in Ware et al [12] provides the user with a model that enables the prediction of system behavior given different kinds of input actions. A good metaphor is both appropriate and easy to learn. Some examples of metaphors are the 'eyeball in hand' metaphor, the 'scene in hand' or 'dollhouse' metaphor, and 'flying vehicle control.'

In the 'eyeball in hand' metaphor, a 6 degree of freedom device is used to position and orient a camera by directly translating and rotating the input device. Ware et al found this method somewhat awkward to use but easy to learn. The 'scene in hand' metaphor allows the user to rotate and translate the scene based on the position of the input device. This was found to be very convenient for hand sized objects, but nearly impossible to use for navigating inside closed spaces. Another scheme discussed by Ware et al was to control a simulated flying vehicle. The user's position and orientation respectively affected the linear and angular velocity of the camera viewpoint and direction of gaze. This metaphor makes it easy to navigate, but difficult to examine a particular object. Although 3D input devices such as a Polhemus Isotrack system or a Spatial Systems Spaceball enable the user to specify 6 degrees of freedom simultaneously, simulations of these devices can be done using only 2D devices [3].

Mackinlay et al [9] discuss the problem of scaling camera movements appropriately. They develop methods to select an object of interest and to move exponentially towards or away from the object. In this way, when the user is close to an object, the viewpoint changes only a little, while when they are far from an object, the viewpoint changes rapidly. By selecting 'point of interest,' the authors can reorient the camera to present a maximal view of the desired object. The degrees of freedom are therefore restricted and the user can concentrate more on the task of navigating through the environment.

Brooks [1, 2] developed several different methods for moving around architectural simulations including steerable treadmills or shopping carts with devices to measure the direction and speed of movement.

The above work shows that different interfaces are appropriate for different application requirements. In our view, no one interface is ideally suited for all tasks, and a common underlying structure on top of which several different metaphors can be implemented would give the user a powerful tool to interact with 3D environments.

An important ability is to allow the user to select an object of interest within the environment. We have expanded on this by allowing the user to make general queries about the visibility and orientation of objects within the environment. This allows the user to manipulate camera motion based on the actions within the environment.

Furthermore, while direct manipulation has certain advantages in interactive systems, there are several deficiencies. It is not necessarily good for repetitive actions, and any action that requires a great deal of accuracy, such as smooth movement for cameras, is not necessarily suited to input using one of the metaphors suggested in the preceding paragraphs. Some of the problems inherent in using 6 DOF input devices presently available are noise which is inherent in user movements and the number of degrees of freedom which must be simultaneously controlled. Textual systems, with interaction built on top of them, allow both a high level input device interface, and an underlying language through which commands can be specified directly or generated through other rule bases.

An expert system for presentation, including the selection of proper camera movements, is discussed in some detail by Karp and Feiner [6]. In their Esplanade system (Expert System for PLANning Animation Design and Editing), they emphasize the ability to incorporate cinematic knowledge for the construction of coherent descriptions of a scene. To do so, they need to have representations of a database of objects and explicit events, along with a notion of how frames, shots, scenes and sequences can be put together to make an effective narrative. Their work emphasizes using a knowledge based system for automatically selecting camera placement and for choosing appropriate camera movements based on cinematic considerations. Currently, they do not concentrate on the movements themselves, but more on the initial placement of the camera for shots and how to make transitions to other shots.

3. The CINEMA System

We have developed the CINEMA system to address the problem of combining different paradigms for controlling camera movements into one system. The CINEMA system is extensible, permitting the user to build higher level procedures from simpler primitives. It also provides the very important ability to make inquiries into a database which contains information describing the state of objects within a 3D environment. After the system was developed, it was used by a dozen students in a course entitled "Synthetic Cinematic and Cinematic Knowledge.[1]" In this course the students used this system to explore alternative ways of animating one of several scenes. Although this system has mainly been used for a synthetic narrative application, we feel that what was learned is applicable to the other domains such as the applications mentioned above.

The CINEMA system is divided up into two major parts. The first is a database which contains information about objects, their positions over time, and events over time. The second part is a parser that accepts and interprets user commands. The user commands are restricted to inquiries about the state of the database and commands which query or affect the state of the camera.

---

1 The course has been taught at the MIT Media Lab by Professors David Zeltzer and Glorianna Davenport – two short versions in January 1989 and 1990, and two full semester courses in the Spring of 1991 and 1992.

3.1 Support structure for CINEMA

To produce CINEMA's procedural interface it was necessary to develop a set of primitive functions. There are three parts to this support structure. First, there is a set of commands for moving the camera or inquiring about the current camera state. Second is a set of commands for inquiring about the state of the 3D world. Last is a set of mathematical routines for manipulating the values returned from the other functions.

There are two sets of primitive functions for changing the camera position and orientation. The lower level of these are the commands that directly set the x, y, and z positions and the *from*, *up*, and *at* vectors that are so commonly used in computer graphics. The slightly higher level primitives (but still part of the support structure) perform simple camera moves like *pan*, *tilt*, *roll*, *truck*, *dolly*, and *crane* [7]. In the film industry terms such as dolly and truck are loosely used. For example, truck may be used to mean a move in or out, or a move from side to side. In this implementation we have chosen one of the possible definitions for these terms to avoid confusion. The conversion between the computer graphics vectors and the film standards is straightforward.

Many descriptions of how to film, frame, and navigate the scene (by both screenwriter and layperson) are with respect to the objects in the world. For example one might ask for the camera to move alongside object A while looking at object B. An interface that supports these descriptions must provide information about events, geometric and spatial relationships such as position, relative occlusion, direction of glance, and distances. For example, functions like *obj_visibility()*, *obj_obj_visibility()* find visibility information between the camera and an object or between two particular objects. Currently this is implemented by using simple ray casting with bounding box intersection. More sophisticated techniques can be used to provide a more precise notion of visibility. However, this implementation has proven adequate for this preliminary research. Other functions (like *frame_events()*) are provided to support inquiry into discrete events which might take place during an animation.

In addition to the commands described above, the system provides a set of supporting mathematical commands, including both scalar and vector calculations. These commands are needed to manipulate the output of the inquiry commands. With these functions, an inquiry about the state of the scene can be manipulated to calculate new camera parameters (such as position, from, at and up vectors). With combinations of these basic tools higher level procedures can be built.

3.2 Implementation

The entire system is currently implemented on 2 platforms: an HP9000-835 turbo SRX in C using a public domain front end language called Tcl [10], and on an Apple Macintosh. The Macintosh platform can not provide interactive update rates for rendered images, but is successfully used for wireframe images.

3.3 Examples

The following examples are representative of how the CINEMA System was used in several different situations. The first example shows how the CINEMA system is interfaced to a 3D environment, and implements one of Ware et al's movement metaphors. The second example shows how higher level camera move-

ments can be built from lower level primitives and inquiry functions. Finally, example 3 shows the cinematic power of the system in filming a simple animation.

Example 1: CAMERA MOVEMENT METAPHOR: This example shows how a 3D input device such as the Isotrack Polhemus or Spatial Systems Spaceball can be used to change the view in a scene. In the accompanying video, we use an Ascension Technologies Bird to control the x, y, and z position of the camera while always looking at the object called "joe." This is very similar to the "eyeball in hand" movement metaphor discussed by Ware et al.

The following pseudocode shows how this function is implemented using the CINEMA system. The function consists of an inquiry to the 6 DOF input device and then translating the camera based upon the translation returned by the input device.

```
proc eyeball_in_hand(object) {
  (x,y,z) := get_input_from_device();
  cam_set_point(x,y,z);
  lookat(object);
}
```

Example 2: EXTENSIBLE LANGUAGE: The procedure "vertigo shot" simulates Hitchcock's classic shot in the film "Vertigo" where the camera moves outwards while the field of view grows narrower keeping the object a constant size at the center of the frame. This effect makes viewers feel as if they are moving closer and closer to an unattainable goal. In only a few minutes we constructed the following procedure to make a vertigo shot.

```
proc vertigo_shot(obj, rate, no_frames) {
 /* get the angle subtended by the object */
 angle := get_angle_height(obj);
 /* get the camera's field of view */
 fov := cam_fov();
 /* compute the percentage of the fov */
 /* which the object subtends */
 percent := angle/fov;
 for (i=0;i<no_frames;i++) {
        /* truck in the specified direction */
        /*    at the specified rate */
        cam_truck(rate);
        /* set the field of view so that */
        /*    the object subtends the same */
        /*    percentage as before */
        frame_it(obj, percent);
 }
}
```

Example 3: SYNTHETIC NARRATIVE: The last example shows that the system can be used for simple cinematic teaching purposes. An animation of a figure sitting down is filmed. A cut in the middle of the animation changes the viewpoint from an oblique view to a head on view. The views are selected so that a "match" cut [5] is achieved. See sequence of frames at the end of the paper.

4. Future Work

The CINEMA system needs to be extended to provide a mechanism to easily combine and constrain multiple procedures. For example, suppose a user would like to track the motion of a walking figure while preventing the camera from moving through walls. Ideally, one would like to have these procedures (one for tracking and one for avoidance) automatically combined to achieve the desired performance. Currently, it would be necessary to construct a new procedure meeting both constraints.

The ability to combine procedures would allow user input to be treated as another procedure that can be combined with other constraints. Camera movements could then be interactively adjusted to achieve a desired result.

To address some of these problems, we have already begun exploration into constraint satisfaction techniques for camera placement and movement. By specifying the camera's relationship to other objects via weighted constraints, the system can find the best position that satisfies certain criterion. These constraints are maintained as the objects, and the camera moves throughout the environment. Additional constraints can be placed on the movement of the camera, so that the camera can have attributes of a simulated physical object such as a fluid head.

5. Conclusion

The CINEMA system provides users with the ability to rapidly experiment with various camera movement paradigms. Users can create new camera metaphors or extend existing ones. The ability to inquire about the state of objects in the environment provides support for more powerful camera movement procedures.

The CINEMA system has already proven quite useful in the teaching domain. Students were able to use the CINEMA system to explore different ways to film and present a simple animation, and to plan a real camera shoot. The constraint satisfaction methodology described above is an ongoing area of research. There are many other areas to explore in camera movement systems including rule based generations systems, codifying stylistic attributes, examining cuts, and interfacing with task oriented applications to name just a few. The hope is that once a strong support base for camera positioning and movement is produced, further research in these areas will be easier.

The CINEMA system makes it possible to experiment with camera paradigms quickly and conveniently. We intend to continue evolving the CINEMA system with an eye toward different application domains including telerobotics/virtual environments and synthetic narratives.

Acknowledgements

The authors wish to thank Glorianna Davenport, David Sturman, Mike McKenna, Steve Pieper, and David Chen for their comments and assistance. Hong Tan was invaluable for her help with the implementation on the Macintosh. The students in the Synthetic Cinema course also provided many useful suggestions. This work was sponsored in part by NHK (Japan Broadcasting Corporation), DARPA/Rome Air Development Center Contract F30602-89-C-022, and equipment grants from Apple Computer and Hewlett-Packard.

References

1 Brooks, F.P. (1986). Walkthrough - A Dynamic Graphics System for Simulating Virtual Buildings. *Proceedings of 1986 Workshop on Interactive 3D Graphics* (Chapel Hill, North Carolina). In *Computer Graphics*, 9-21.

2 Brooks, F.P. (1988). Grasping Reality Through Illusion: Interactive Graphics Serving Science. *SIGCHI '88* 1-11.

3 Chen, M., S.J. Mountford, A. Sellen. (1988). A Study of Interactive 3D Rotation Using 2D Control Devices. *Proceedings of SIGGRAPH '88* (Atlanta, Georgia). In *Computer Graphics* 22(4):121-129.

4 Davenport, G., T.A.Smith., N.Pincever (1991). Cinematic Primitives for Multimedia. IEEE Computer Graphics & Applications. July. 67-74.

5 Hochberg, J. and V. Brook. (1978). The perception of motion pictures. in Handbook of Perception Vol X. eds. Carterette and Friedman. Academic Press: New York. Chapter 11.

6 Karp, P., S.Feiner. (1990). Issues in the Automated Generation of Animated Presentations. *Graphics Interface '90* (Halifax, Nova Scotia). 39-48.

7 Katz, E. (1979). *The Film Encyclopedia*. Perigree Books: New York.

8 Kochanek, D.H.U. (1984). Interpolating Splines with Local Tension, Continuity, and Bias Control. *Proceedings of SIGGRAPH '84* (Minneapolis, Minnesota). *Computer Graphics*.18(3):33-42.

9 Mackinlay, J.D., S. Card, G. Robertson. (1990). Rapid Controlled Movement Through a Virtual 3D Workspace. *Proceedings of SIGGRAPH '90* (Dallas, Texas). In *Computer Graphics* 24(4):171-176.

10 Ousterhout, J. (1990). Tcl: An Embeddable Command Language. Proceedings of USENIX Winter Conference. 133-146.

11 Shoemake, K. (1985). Animating Rotation with Quaternion Curves. *Proceedings of SIGGRAPH '85* (San Francisco, CA). In *Computer Graphics* 19(3):245-254.

12 Ware, C., S. Osborne. (1990). Exploration and Virtual Camera Control in Virtual Three Dimensional Environments. *Proceedings of the 1990 Symposium on Interactive 3D Graphics* (Snowbird, Utah).In *Computer Graphics* 24(2):175-184.

13 Zeltzer, D. (1991). Task-level Graphical Simulation: Abstraction, Representation, and Control, *Making Them Move*, eds. Badler, Barskey and Zeltzer. Morgan Kaufmann Publishers: California. 3-33.

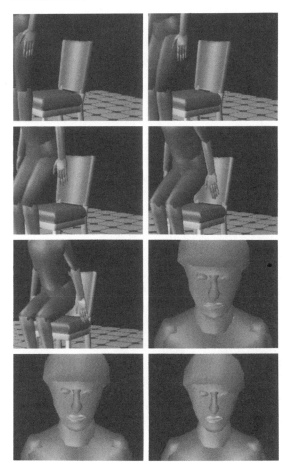

Automatic Viewing Control for 3D Direct Manipulation

Cary B. Phillips[†]
Norman I. Badler
John Granieri

Computer Graphics Research Laboratory
Department of Computer and Information Science
University of Pennsylvania
Philadelphia, Pennsylvania 19104-6389

Abstract

This paper describes a technique for augmenting the process of 3D direct manipulation by automatically finding an effective placement for the virtual camera. Many of the best techniques for direct manipulation of 3D geometric objects are sensitive to the angle of view, and can thus require that the user coordinate the placement of the viewpoint during the manipulation process. In some cases, this process can be automated. This means that the system can automatically avoid degenerate situations in which translations and rotations are difficult to perform. The system can also select viewpoints and viewing angles which make the object being manipulated visible, ensuring that it is not obstructed by other objects.

Introduction

3D direct manipulation is a technique for controlling positions and orientations of geometric objects in a 3D environment in a non-numerical, visual way. Although much research has been devoted to 3D direct manipulation of geometric objects, no existing system has adequately integrated the controls for viewing into the direct manipulation process. Evans, Tanner, and Wein [3], Nielson and Olson[6], and Chen et al [1] all discuss techniques for manipulation that are sensitive to the viewing direction, but they do not address how the view can be manipulated. Ware and Osborne[10] discuss the viewing process in general, in terms of metaphors that it suggests, and Mackinlay et al [5] discuss an effective technique for manipulating the viewpoint, both in proximity to other objects and through large distances. Neither of these relate the viewing process to direct manipulation.

Our direct manipulation system includes a mechanism for automatically placing the virtual camera at a viewpoint which avoids the problems with degenerate axes suffered by most direct manipulation schemes. The basic idea is to rotate the camera through small angles to achieve a better view. Our system also rotates the camera to avoid viewing obstructions. This viewing operation is an integral part of the manipulation system, not a separate viewing facility which the user must explicitly invoke.

The problem of automatic viewing placement for manipulation is different from that of automatic camera control in animation. Karp and Feiner[4] describe a system called ESPLANADE that automatically visualizes simulations. It automatically finds camera placements which provide a good view of movement during an animation. This is an adjunct to the process of animation, not an interactive technique.

3D Direct Manipulation

Several techniques have been developed for describing three dimensional transformations with a two dimensional input device such as a mouse or tablet. Nielson and Olson [6] describe a technique for mapping the motion of a two dimensional mouse cursor to three dimensional translations based on the orientation of the projection of a world space coordinate triad onto the screen. This mapping makes it difficult to translate along an axis parallel to the line of sight, because the

[†]Cary Phillips' current address: Pacific Data Images, 1111 Karlstad Dr, Sunnyvale, CA 94089

axis projects onto a point on the screen instead of a direction.

Rotations are considerably more complex, but several techniques have been developed, with varying degrees of success. The most naive technique is to simply use horizontal and vertical mouse movements to control the world space euler angles which define the orientation of an object. This technique provides little kinesthetic feedback because there is no natural correspondence between the movements of the mouse and the rotation of the object. A better approach, described by Chen et al [1], is to make the rotation angles either parallel or perpendicular to the viewing direction. This makes the object rotate relative to the graphics window, providing much greater kinesthetic feedback, but it also makes the available rotation axes highly dependent on the viewing direction.

3D Manipulation in *Jack*

Our interactive system is called *Jack*™[†], and it is designed for modeling, manipulating, animating, and analyzing human figures, principally for human factors analysis. The 3D direct manipulation facility in *Jack* allows the user to interactively manipulate figure positions and orientations, and joint angles subject to limits[7]. *Jack* also has a sophisticated system of manipulating postures through inverse kinematics and behavior functions [8, 9]. *Jack* runs on Silicon Graphics IRIS workstations, and it uses a three button mouse to control translation and rotation. Within the direct manipulation process, the user can toggle between rotation and translation, and between the local and global coordinate axes, by holding down the CONTROL and SHIFT keys, respectively.

With translation, the user controls the movement by moving the mouse cursor along the line which the selected axis makes on the screen. This is similar to the projected triad scheme of Nielson and Olson[6], and it ensures good kinesthetic correspondence. Pairs of buttons select pairs of axes and translate in a plane. A 3D graphical translation icon located at the origin of the object being manipulated illustrates the selected axes and the enabled directions of motion.

The user can control rotation around the x, y, and z axes, in either local or global coordinates. Only one axis can be selected at a time. A graphical wheel icon illustrates the origin and direction of the axis. The user controls the rotation by moving the cursor around the perimeter of the rotation wheel, causing the object to rotate around the axis. This is analogous to turning a crank by grabbing the perimeter and dragging it in circles. This is somewhat similar to Evans, Tanner and

---

[†] *Jack* is a trademark of the University of Pennsylvania.

Wein's turntable technique[3], but it provides greater graphical feedback.

Drawbacks

A drawback of the manipulation technique in *Jack* is the inability to translate an object along an axis parallel to the line of sight, or to rotate around an axis perpendicular to the line of sight. In these cases, small differences in the screen coordinates of the mouse correspond to large distances in world coordinates, which means that the object may spin suddenly or zoom off to infinity. This is an intrinsic problem with viewing through a 2D projection: kinesthetic correspondence dictates that the object's image moves in coordination with the input device, but if the object's movement is parallel to the line of projection, the image doesn't actually move, it only shrinks or expands in perspective.

In the past, we adopted the view that the first prerequisite for manipulating a figure is to position the camera in a convenient view. Although the viewpoint manipulation techniques in *Jack* are quite easy to use, this forced the user through additional step in the manipulation process, and the user frequently moved back and forth between manipulating the object and camera.

3D Viewing

The computer graphics workstation provides a view into a virtual 3D world. It is natural to think of a graphics window as the lens of a camera, so the process of manipulating the viewpoint is analogous to moving a camera through space. Evans, Tanner, and Wein describe viewing rotation as the single most effective depth cue, even better than stereoscopy [3]. In order for an interactive modeling system to give the user a good sense of the three-dimensionality of the objects, it is essential that the system provide a good means of controlling the viewpoint.

Control over the viewpoint is especially important during the direct manipulation process, because of the need to "see what you are doing." The whole notion of direct manipulation requires that the user see what is happening, and feel the relationship to the movement of the input devices. If the user can't see the object, then he or she certainly can't manipulate it properly.

Jack uses Ware and Osborne's *camera in hand* metaphor[10] for the view. The geometric environment in problems in human factors analysis usually involve models of human figures in a simulated workspace. The most appropriate cognitive model to promote is one of looking in on a real person interacting with real, life-size objects. Therefore, *Jack* suggests that the controls on the viewing mechanism more or less match the controls we have as real observers: move side to side and up and down while staying focused on the same point.

The viewing adjustments in *Jack* are easy to invoke from within the direct manipulation process, and this is a very common thing to do. The typical way of performing a manipulation is to intersperse translations and rotations with viewing adjustments, in order to achieve a better view during the process. The context switch between viewing and manipulation is very easy to make.

Automatic Viewing Adjustments

Much of this viewing adjustment as an aid to manipulation can be automated, in which case the system automatically places the camera in a view which avoids the problems of degenerate axes. This can usually be done with a small rotation to move the camera away from the offending axis. This automatic camera rotation can even be helpful by itself, because it provides a kind of depth cue.

To prevent degenerate movement axes from causing problems during direct manipulation, *Jack* uses a threshold between the movement axis and the line of sight, beyond which it will not allow the user to manipulate an object. To do so would mean that small movements of the mouse would result in huge translations or rotations of the object. This value is usually 20°, implying that if the user tries to translate along an axis which is closer than 20° to the line of sight, *Jack* will respond with a message saying "can't translate along that axis from this view," and it will not allow the user to do it. The same applies to rotation around axes perpendicular to the line of sight. In these cases, the rotation wheel projects onto a line, so the user has no leverage to rotate it.

The automatic viewing adjustment invokes itself if the user selects the same axis again after getting the warning message. *Jack* will automatically rotate the camera so that its line of sight is away from the transformation axis. To do this, it orients the camera so that it focuses on the object's origin, and then rotates the camera around both a horizontal and a vertical axis, both of which pass through the object's origin. The angles of rotation are computed so that the angular distance away from the offending axis is at least 20°.

This technique maintains the same distance between the camera and the object being manipulated. In general, this "zoom factor" is much more subjective and is difficult for the system to predict. In practice, we have found it best to require the user to control this quantity explicitly.

The reason for the repeated axis selection is to ensure that the user didn't select the axis by mistake. It is common to position the view parallel to a coordinate axis to get a 2D view of an object. If the user likes this view, then it would be wrong to disturb it. For example,

if the user positions the view parallel to the z axis to get a view of the xy plane, and then accidentally hits the right mouse button, the view will not automatically change unless the user confirms that this is what he or she wants to do.

Automatic view positioning also takes place when the object is not visible. This may mean that the object is not visible at all, or only that its origin is not visible. For example, a human figure may be mostly visible but with its foot off the bottom of the screen. In this case, a command to move the foot will automatically reposition the view so that the foot is visible.

Smooth Viewing Transitions

Both the horizontal and vertical automatic viewing rotations occur simultaneously, and *Jack* applies them incrementally using a number of intermediate views so the user sees a smooth transition from the original view to the new. This avoids a disconcerting snap in the view. *Jack* applies the angular changes using an ease in/ease out function which ensures that the transition is smooth.

The procedure for rotating the camera is sensitive to the interactive frame rate so that it provides relatively constant response time. If the camera adjustment were to use a constant number of intermediate frames, the response time would be either too short if the rate is fast or too long if the rate is slow. *Jack* keeps track of the frame rate using timing information available from the operating system in 1/60th's of seconds. We compute the number of necessary intermediate frames so that the automatic viewing adjustment takes about 1 second of real time.

Avoiding Viewing Obstructions

When manipulating an object using solid shaded graphics, it can be especially difficult to see what your are doing because of the inability to see through other objects. In some situations, this may be impossible to avoid, in which case the only alternative is either to proceed without good visibility or revert to a wireframe image. Frequently however, it may be possible to automatically change the view slightly so that the object is less obstructed. To do this, we borrow an approach from radiosity, the *hemicube* [2].

The hemicube determines the visibility of an entire geometric environment from a particular reference point, and we can use this information to find an unobstructed location for the camera if one exists. We perform the hemicube computation centered around the origin of the object being manipulated, but oriented towards the current camera location. This yields a visibility map of the entire environment, or what we would see through a fish-eye lens looking from the object's origin towards the camera. If the camera is obstructed in the visibility map, we look in the neighborhood of the direction of the camera for an empty area in the hemicube map. This area suggests a location of the camera from which the object will be visible. From this, we compute the angles through which the camera should be rotated. We generate the hemicube map using the hardware shading and z-buffer, so its computation is quite efficient.

This type of hemicube is somewhat different from the type used radiosity because it is not necessarily centered around the surface of an object. In fact, it need not be associated with a surface at all, as when the direct manipulation operation is applied to a shapeless entity like a 3D control point or a goal point for an inverse kinematics operation. Therefore, our hemi-cube is actually not "hemi" at all, since we use all six sides of the cube. In cases when the direct manipulation operation is moving a geometric object, it is convenient to omit the object from the hemicube visibility computation altogether. Otherwise, most of the visibility map will be filled up with the object itself, even though it is usually quite acceptable to manipulate an object from a view opposite its coordinate origin.

In our current implementation, the hemicube maintains only occlusion information, not depth information. Therefore, it will fail to find suitable camera locations in an enclosed environment. In such cases, there are no holes in the visibility map at all, although there may be regions only occluded by very distance objects. These very distant objects don't matter unless we were considering placing the camera very far away. A better approach would be to retain depth information in the hemicube and search for a camera position which is unobstructed only between the camera and the object, allowing the distance between the object and the camera change as necessary, possibly causing the camera to move in front of other objects.

Conclusion

The control of a virtual camera is vitally important to many techniques for 3D direct manipulation system, although no one has previously addressed the two issues in an integrated manner. Our technique for automatically adjusting the view in conjunction with direct manipulation has been implemented, and it is an effective addition to the manipulation process. The automatic viewing rotations are usually very small so they do not interject large changes to the user's view of the geometric environment. Since the viewing adjustments are only activated on the second attempt at movement along a degenerate axis, the adjustments are seldomly invoked

accidentally, minimizing the degree to which the adjustments are inappropriate.

References

[1] Michael Chen, S. Joy Mountford, and Abigail Sellen. A Study in Interactive 3-D Rotation Using 2-D Control Devices. *Computer Graphics*, 22(4), 1988.

[2] Michael F. Cohen and Donald P. Greenberg. The Hemi-Cube: A Radiosity Solution for Complex Environments. *Computer Graphics*, 19(3), 1985.

[3] Kenneth B. Evans, Peter Tanner, and Marceli Wein. Tablet Based Valuators That Provide One, Two or Three Degrees of Freedom. *Computer Graphics*, 15(3), 1981.

[4] P. Karp and S. Feiner. Issues in the Automated Generation of Animated Presentations. In *Proceedings of Graphics Interface '90*, 1990.

[5] Jock D. Mackinlay, Stuart K. Card, and George G. Robinson. Rapid and Controlled Movement Through a Virtual 3D Workspace. *Computer Graphics*, 24(4), 1990.

[6] Gregory Nielson and Dan Olsen Jr. Direct Manipulation Techniques for 3D Objects Using 2D Locator Devices. In *Proceedings of 1986 Workshop on Interactive 3D Graphics*, Chapel Hill, NC, October 1987. ACM.

[7] Cary B. Phillips and Norman I. Badler. Jack: A Toolkit for Manipulating Articulated Figures. In *Proceedings of ACM SIGGRAPH Symposium on User Interface Software*, Banff, Alberta, Canada, 1988.

[8] Cary B. Phillips and Norman I. Badler. Interactive Behaviors for Bipedal Articulated Figures. *Computer Graphics*, 25(4), 1991.

[9] Cary B. Phillips, Jianmin Zhao, and Norman I. Badler. Interactive Real-Time Articulated Figure Manipulation Using Multiple Kinematic Constraints. *Computer Graphics*, 24(2), 1990.

[10] Colin Ware and Steven Osborne. Exploration and Virtual Camera Control in Virtual Three Dimensional Environments. *Computer Graphics*, 24(4), 1990.

Hardware Antialiasing of Lines and Polygons

Walter Gish and Allen Tanner

Terabit Computer Engineering

ABSTRACT

This paper describes a hardware design for antialiasing both lines and polygons. The hardware prefilters lines and polygons defined on a high resolution grid at one-eighth the pixel spacing. The resolution of this sub-pixel grid is based on the limits of human visual perception. The antialiasing filters can extend over a 1-by-1 or 2-by-2 pixel domain for polygons and a 3-by-3 pixel domain for lines. The design uses regular decomposition and the symmetry of antialiasing filters to minimize the size of the filter tables. The resulting hardware is surprisingly small and very efficient (typically one cycle per output pixel). It is therefore suitable for antialiasing lines and polygons at real-time or interactive rates.

CR CATEGORIES AND SUBJECT DESCRIPTORS:
I.3.1 [Computer Graphics]: Hardware Architecture - Raster display devices; I.3.3 [Computer Graphics]: Picture/Image Generation - display algorithms.

ADDITIONAL KEYWORDS AND PHRASES:
Antialiasing, prefiltering, real-time graphics.

1 INTRODUCTION

Antialiasing is a desirable feature for interactive graphics, but it is not currently available without cost or performance compromises. Although today's workstations can draw antialiased vectors at high speed, rendering antialiased polygons with workstations imposes a performance degradation proportional to the number of samples per pixel calculated for antialiasing (supersampling). Antialiased polygons at real-time rates are available only on flight simulators, but flight simulators have their drawbacks. Flight simulators are much more expensive than workstations and they are not general purpose platforms.

We begin with a review of existing prefiltering techniques with an emphasis on those techniques potentially suitable for

Authors' current addresses: W. Gish, Terabit Computer Engineering, 1891 Calle Borrego, Thousand Oaks, CA 91360. A. Tanner, Terabit Computer Engineering, 224 Cottage Ave., Salt Lake City, UT 84070.

© 1992 ACM 0-89791-471-6/92/0003/0075...$1.50

hardware. We then describe our approach in detail. Finally, we present some thoughts on how this approach to antialiasing can be integrated with hidden surface removal.

2 EXISTING METHODS FOR ANTIALIASING

2.1 Lines

A common technique for antialiasing lines models the geometry of a finite width line and pixel by a single parameter - the distance from the center of the pixel to the center of the line [13]. This single parameter is then used as the index into a precomputed table of filter results (i.e., precomputed convolutions). While this single parameter model is exact sufficiently far from the endpoints, it requires a correction near the endpoints. Furthermore, modeling lines as finite width entities causes other problems near endpoints. When lines are connected end-to-end, overlapping can cause intensity errors at endpoints (see Fig. 1).

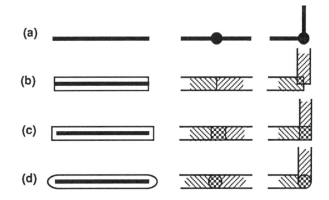

Fig. 1. Overlapping with different line endpoint shapes - the original line (a), with cut-off (b), rectangular (c), and rounded (d) endpoints.

One solution to these overlapping effects is to solve the hidden surface problem for finite width lines [28]. Alternatively lines can be modeled as infinitely thin, so that the antialiasing filter itself gives thickness to the line and "shape" to the endpoints. Accurate handling of endpoints is crucial for rendering curves using a sequence of short line segments [19].

2.2 Polygons

Polygons are commonly antialiased using supersampling [8]. Unfortunately, with supersampling the number of samples required to eliminate aliasing artifacts is significant. Although non-uniform sampling requires fewer samples than regular sampling, even with optimized non-uniform sampling the number of samples per pixel necessary for high quality is on the order of 25 ([17]) to 40 ([14]). This forces either a performance degradation with respect to aliased rendering (as with workstations) or more hardware (as in flight simulators).

The alternative to supersampling is prefiltering. To place the technique described here in perspective, we review several prefiltering methods published in the literature.

Catmull [4] introduced the technique of calculating visible area as a method of antialiasing. This area calculation is straightforward and relatively fast. Unfortunately, using visible area for antialiasing is equivalent to using an unweighted filter, and unweighted filters are far from the optimal filter shape. [16]

Feibush, Levoy and Cook [7] described a method for prefiltering polygon edges. Their method begins by clipping a polygon to the filter domain surrounding each pixel. The resulting clipped polygon is decomposed into several right triangles, two for each edge in the clipped polygon. The filtered contribution for each of these triangles is obtained from a small table, and the individual contributions are accumulated (with sign) to yield the final filter result. They mention two extensions: one for filters that are not circularly symmetric (a three parameter table), and one that uses the coordinates of edge endpoints to look-up the filter result with one table access per edge instead of two (a four parameter table). The drawbacks of this approach are that it is oriented toward circularly symmetric filters and that it is slow. For the basic two parameter table, it requires calculations to determine the base and height of the right triangles into which the clipped polygon is decomposed followed by several table look-ups (at least six). The four parameter table would require a table as large as that used in our method, yet there are still several table look-ups per pixel. In contrast, the method we propose requires only simple reflections on the clipped polygon fragments and typically only one table look-up per pixel.

Abram, Westover, and Whitted [1] proposed a method requiring only one look-up for many cases. After clipping the visible portion of a polygon to the filter domain surrounding a pixel, they directly look-up the result for cases where no edge endpoint is within the filter domain. When one or more vertices lie within the filter domain, the method reverts to using sub-pixel bit masks. While it is claimed that this causes only an "unnoticeable degradation" at 64 sub-pixel mask bits per pixel, it does require perturbing the table values and using sub-pixel bit masks. In contrast our method decomposes polygons into fragments whose shape is well-constrained (so there are no special cases) and it explicitly allows vertices to lie within the filter domain.

Lobb [15] described a method for prefiltering, restricted again to filters possessing circular symmetry. His method is much like line antialiasing in that it is simple and exact sufficiently far from vertices. The filter response near a vertex is approximated with a claimed error of less than 4%.

Duff [6] extended the trapezoidal decomposition generally used to calculate area for antialiasing to a method for computing the exact (to floating point accuracy) convolution for non-uniform filters (particularly polynomial splines). He mentions the possibility of storing convolution results in tables. This would require one to three table look-ups while our approach requires only one. Still, his method is very efficient as a software algorithm.

Schilling [25] described a method which uses tables to determine sub-pixel masks. Schilling bases his table look-up upon edge slope and distance from pixel center, although other parameters such as intersection location along the filter domain boundary (as [1] used) are equivalent. The unique feature of Schilling's method is that the table turns on sub-pixel bits according to polygon area rather than explicit geometric coverage of the sub-pixel sampling point. Consequently, some of the bits turned on are outside the polygon! The mask for a convex polygon is the logical AND of the masks for each of its edges. The effect of ANDing masks that have samples outside the polygon was not discussed. This method is similar to a technique used in some flight simulators, in which edge parameters are used to look-up the sub-pixel mask for non-uniform sampling. Fig. 2 diagrams this technique. Any two of the four parameters (slope, distance to pixel center, x-intercept, y-intercept) can serve as the index into a table containing the mask for an edge.

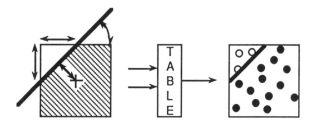

Fig. 2. Table look-up of sub-pixel mask bits

Overall, none of the existing methods is entirely satisfactory. Each has one or more drawbacks:
- Filter shape is restricted to unweighted or circularly symmetric functions ([4], [7], [15], [25]).
- The method is slow, requiring several look-ups per pixel or other calculations ([4], [7], [15], [6]).
- The method is approximate near vertices ([1], [15], [25]).
- The method is simply a way to maintain sub-pixel masks ([1], [25]).

The first drawback is important because an unweighted filter leaves too many residual artifacts, and a circularly symmetric filter can't provide uniform total field response [17] (also called the constant energy criteria [29] or zero sampling frequency ripple [16]). The last drawback is important because the number of bits needed in a sub-pixel mask is at least 32 for high quality antialiasing. To store an arbitrary filter function in a table that can be indexed by sub-pixel mask becomes difficult for high resolution masks because the table size grows exponentially with the number of sub-pixel masks bits (16 bits require a 64K word table, but 32 bits require a 4 Giga-word table!). Furthermore, since prefiltering must be used for lines, resorting to sub-pixel masks forces line and polygon antialiasing to be somewhat inconsistent. In contrast the method proposed here offers:

- Arbitrary filters defined over large domains.
- High image quality (from the 1/8 pixel grid resolution).
- Hardware speed (one table look-up per output pixel).
- Hardware simplicity.
- Uniform antialiasing of both lines and polygons.

3 HARDWARE FOR PREFILTERING

Our hardware implementation of prefiltering allows arbitrary filters defined over a 1-by-1 or 2-by-2 pixel domain for polygons and a 3-by-3 domain for vectors (Fig. 3). Input primitives are described by the polygon vertices or line endpoints. These points are specified to a resolution of 1/8 the pixel spacing. Intersections (for clipping) of lines or polygon edges with the boundaries of filter domains are calculated to the same accuracy. The high resolution of this grid is important. At lower resolutions many implementations are possible but they can't result in high quality antialiasing. This resolution was chosen because it matches the ability of human visual perception to infer sub-pixel position from greyscale (i.e., antialiasing) information [18]. By comparison, prefiltering at a resolution of 1/8 pixel is more accurate than supersampling on an 8-by-8 regular grid (64 samples per pixel). The consequences of using a coarser grid (or fewer samples per pixel) have been discussed in a previous paper [11].

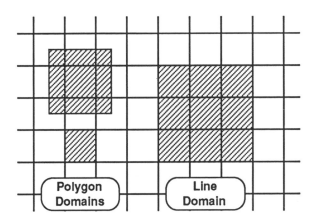

Fig. 3. Filter domains for lines and polygons.

To use tables for prefiltering requires transforming input primitives into a form simple enough to allow the filter table to be of reasonable size. Our approach is comprised of three steps for both lines and polygons:

(1) Regular decomposition.
(2) Efficient clipping to the filter domains.

(3) Encoding of intersection shape.

For lines, the decomposition stage simply orders the endpoints in top-to-bottom order. For polygons the decomposition is a conventional trapezoidal decomposition of input polygons. The second step clips the input line or trapezoids from the polygon decomposition to the filter domain at each pixel. It organizes the process of intersection calculation as a sequence of interpolations along edges. Interpolations are calculated only once and shared between neighboring filter domains. The third step reduces the plethora of clipped line segments and polygon fragments into a set small enough for direct table look-up. It uses the horizontal and vertical symmetry of antialiasing filters to reflect clipped fragments into a canonical form. This reduces the table size for lines by a factor of 8, and for polygons by a factor of 4.

3.1 Decomposition and Clipping of Lines

The decomposition stage for lines simply orders the endpoints in top-to-bottom order. Chained lines are broken up into groups of line segments that can be processed in top-to-bottom order.

The result of clipping a line to a filter domain is clearly a segment of the original line. If the filter domains were single pixels, the clipping would consist of simply slicing the line up into pieces, each of which lies on a single scanline, and then slicing those pieces horizontally for each pixel. However, the filter domain for antialiased lines is larger than a single pixel so that the filter domains overlap. Therefore, the clipping process must take this into account. Fig. 4 shows how the clipping in the y-direction works for the 3-by-3 pixel domain for antialiased lines.

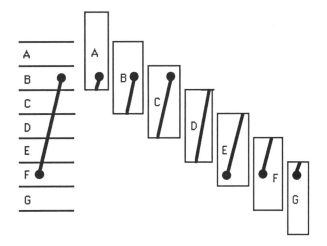

Fig. 4. Vertical clipping for lines.

Fig. 4 shows a line from a sub-pixel location in scanline B to one in scanline F. The x and color parameters of the original line are interpolated (as a function of y) at the boundaries between scanlines B through F. Then a series of line segments is created from the original line endpoints and the interpolated points. One segment is created for all the filter domains on each scanline (as shown at the right of the Fig. 4). This construction is equivalent to sliding a horizontal band 3 scanlines high down over the original line and noting the intersection when the band is centered on a scanline.

Operationally, the hardware creates a stream of points in the following order: the top point of a line segment, an interpolated point at the boundary between the topmost scanlines (B and C for the example in Fig. 4), ..., an interpolated point at the boundary between the bottom-most scanlines (E and F), and the bottom point. This stream of points flows through a register followed by a variable depth pipeline that together reconstruct the clipped segments. The output of the register is the bottom point for the filter domain on a scanline while the output of the variable depth pipeline is the corresponding top point (Fig. 5).

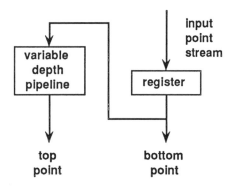

Fig. 5. Reconstruction of overlapping segments.

The clipping process in the x-direction operates on these new segments in an analogous fashion (y and color interpolated as a function of x). The final result is the intersection of the original line with its occupied filter domains.

3.2 Decomposition and Clipping of Polygons

Conventional (aliased) polygon scan conversion interpolates polygon edges in one direction to produce a set of imbedded lines and then interpolates along these lines (in the perpendicular direction) at the center of each pixel [2]. This generates the set of points that lie within the original polygon (left of Fig. 9). In contrast, the antialiased scan conversion method presented here retains the shape of the original polygon within each filter domain. That is, it clips polygons (actually trapezoidal slices of polygons) to the filter domain surrounding each pixel. This decomposition and clipping is nonetheless similar to conventional scan conversion. As we saw with lines, this process is a sequence of interpolations on the point data (x, y, color, opacity, texture co-ordnates, etc.) that defines the original line or polygon.

Polygon decomposition and clipping occurs in three stages. First arbitrary polygons (any number of sides, convex or concave, and with or without holes) are decomposed into

horizontally aligned trapezoids. Secondly, these trapezoids are clipped in the y-direction into smaller trapezoids within the filter domains on only a single scanline. This clipping is, like the edge clipping, a series of interpolations followed by reconstruction using hardwired registers. Then a similar clipping occurs in the x-direction. Usually this clipping results in a piece with just one edge per filter domain. If there are two edges in the filter domain, the piece is represented as the difference of two single-edged pieces.

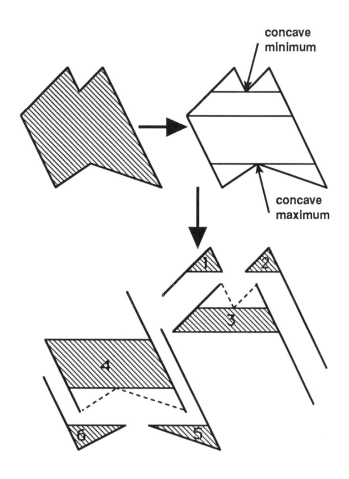

Fig. 6. Trapezoidal decomposition example.

Fig. 6 shows an example of the decomposition of a polygon into a set of horizontally aligned trapezoids (which can degenerate into triangles). The resulting trapezoids are defined by:
   (1) Left and right edges
   (2) A vertical extent determined by the endpoints of the left and right edges and possibly a concave minimum (at the top of region 3 in Fig. 6) or a concave maximum (at the bottom of region 4 in Fig 6):

$$y_{max} = \min \{ y_{left\text{-}top}, y_{right\text{-}top}, y_{concave\text{-}min} \}$$
$$y_{min} = \max \{ y_{left\text{-}bottom}, y_{right\text{-}bottom}, y_{concave\text{-}max} \}$$

Operationally, this trapezoidal decomposition creates two sequences of points, one for the left bounding edges and one for the right. Note that the top and bottom horizontal edges are implicitly defined. The actual vertices of the trapezoid are not calculated until the clipping in y takes place. Algorithms for performing this decomposition on arbitrary polygons (including concave and with holes) are known [3].

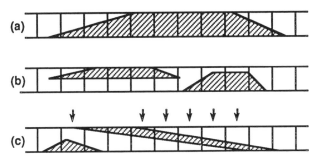

Fig. 7. Types of polygon spans.

Once a polygon is decomposed into trapezoids, the left and right edges are clipped in y (analogously to the line clipping described earlier) producing a set of smaller (vertically) trapezoids. These smaller trapezoids are called spans. For polygons, the size of the filter domain is either a single pixel or 2 pixels high (in which case the interpolation points are at the middle of a scanline instead of the boundary between scanlines). Fig. 7 shows the types of spans that can result from clipping in y (with the single pixel filter domain shown for clarity). A polygon span often has its left and right edges separated in x while the extent of the span y covers the entire filter domain (Fig. 7a). The left portion of the span just contains the left edge, the middle has no edges and the right portion has just the right edge. At the top or bottom of a trapezoid from the polygon decomposition, the extent in y doesn't necessarily cover the whole filter domain (Fig. 7b). Lastly, a filter domain can contain two edges near vertices or for very thin polygons (Fig. 7c). When two edges are present (which occurs only a small percentage of the time) the filter result is computed as the difference for each individual edge (Fig. 8). The case of two edges per pixel is the only shape that is not handled in a single cycle.

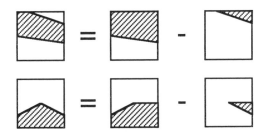

Fig. 8. Handling domains with 2 edges.

Fig.9 compares conventional scan conversion (left) and the antialiasing decomposition and clipping (right) for the single pixel domain (again, for clarity). In the y-direction, both require 5 interpolations - the only difference is that in conventional scan conversion the interpolations are at the middle of scanlines, while in the antialiasing case they are

between scanlines and opposite every encountered vertex (e.g., vertex 1 in Fig. 9). Because interpolations are shared between neighboring scanlines, the number of y-interpolations is, to first order, the same in either case. Thus no additional calculation is needed for the clipping in y required for antialiasing. The final stage, clipping in the x-direction, is performed only on color in the conventional case, while in the antialiasing case, y also needs to be interpolated at the vertical boundaries between filter domains (the 4 points indicated by the small arrows in Fig. 9). This interpolation needs to be accurate to only 5 bits since y is within a filter domain. In summary, the antialiasing decomposition and clipping is of about the same difficulty as the simpler interpolations for aliased scan conversion. Antialiasing additionally requires only a low-resolution interpolation of y as a function of x, and registers for reconstructing the data describing the clipping result.

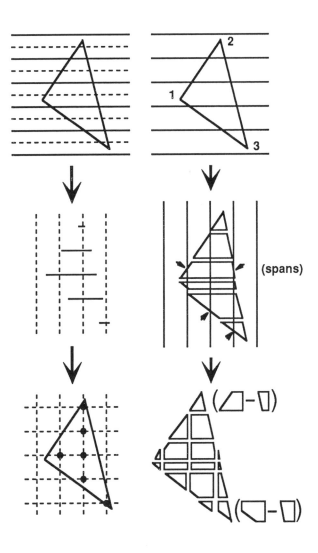

Fig. 9. Conventional (left) and antialiasing (right) decomposition.

3.3 Line Encoding

Clipping a line to the 3-by-3 pixel filter domain yields a (usually shorter) line segment. Direct addressing of a filter table using the coordinates of the endpoints of this clipped line would require a table whose size is much too large. The x and y coordinates of each endpoint take on a possible 25 values (3 pixels at 1/8 pixel resolution). A straightforward translation from geometry to table address, i.e.,

$$\text{ADDR} = x_1 + 25\, y_1 + (25)^2\, x_2 + (25)^3\, y_2$$

requires $25^4 = 380{,}625$ table entries or a half-megaword table!

Our solution is to encode these endpoints using conditional reflections and followed by bit-packing. The reflections assume only that the antialiasing filter possesses x- and y-symmetry. Given the result of clipping a line to a filter domain, the endpoints are conditionally reflected about filter symmetry axes so that one of the endpoints always lies in a small region. In particular, given two endpoints (x_1,y_1) and (x_2,y_2), the reflected line always has point (x_1,y_1) lying in a particular octant. The reflections are done in two stages as shown in Fig. 10. First both points are reflected across the y-axis if $x_1 > 0$, and simultaneously the x-axis if $y_1 > 0$. The second stage reflects the result across the line $x = y$ if the reflected $x_1 < y_1$. This sequence of conditional reflections forces point 1 to end up in the shaded region shown in Fig. 10. For the 3-by-3 pixel domain at 1/8-pixel resolution this encoding yields 91 possible values for (x_1,y_1) and 625 values for (x_2,y_2) for a total of 56,875 possible cases (a reduction by almost a factor of eight).

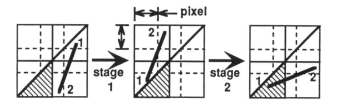

Fig. 10. Two-stage reflections for line encoding.

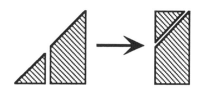

Fig. 11. Bit-packing point 1.

After the conditional reflection, the co-ordinates for point 1 are packed into a 7-by-13 rectangle (Fig. 11). The conditional reflections and packing of point 1's coordinates are easily done in small PALs. The table address could be computed as

$$\text{ADDR} = x_1 + 7\, y_1 + 7(13)\, x_2 + 7(13)(25)\, y_2$$

for look-up in a 64K word table. However, we prefer to simply concatenate the co-ordinates (3 bits for x_1, 4 bits for y_1, 5 bits

for x_2 and 5 bits for y_2) for direct addressing of a 128K-word table.

3.4 Polygon Encoding

Analogous to line encoding, polygon encoding consists of conditional reflections followed by bit-packing. Note that the material of a polygon lies to the right of a left edge, and to the left of a right edge. Thus if the antialiasing filter is symmetric about the y-axis, a right bounding edge can be reflected into a left edge (Fig.12a). Likewise, y-symmetry allows reflection across the filter domain's x-axis so that the slope of an edge is always positive (Fig. 12b).

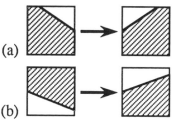

Fig. 12. Conditional reflections on edge-domain intersections.

These positive-sloped left-edge regions of a filter domain are called **fragments**. A fragment is primarily defined by the two endpoints of the edge inside or on the boundary of the filter domain. In addition, a fragment can posses an optional third y value, Y_g (Fig. 13), which arises when the span doesn't cover the entire vertical extent of the filtering domain (recall Fig. 7b). Because of the reflections, Y_g for a fragment will always be below the main edge.

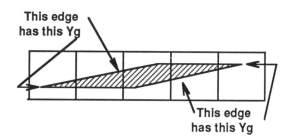

Fig. 13. Optional y-values associated with an edge.

Our concept of fragment differs from that of others in that we explicitly allow edge endpoints to lie within the filter domain. In addition, we include the global y-value for efficiency in scan conversion (otherwise these cases would take two cycles, and they occur a significant percentage of the time).

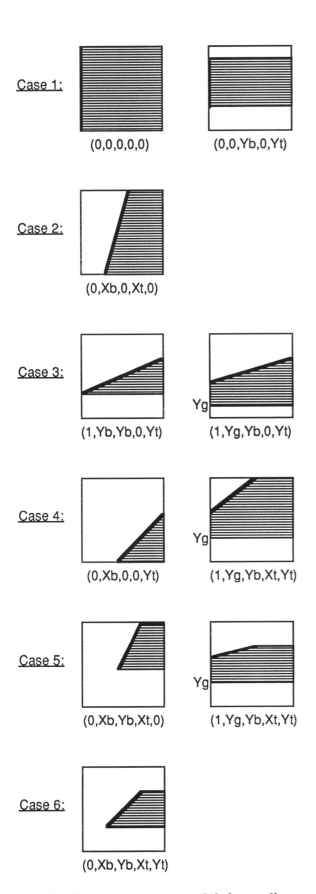

Fig. 14. Fragment taxonomy and their encodings.

A taxonomy of fragment geometry (with the final address from bit-packing) can be organized into six cases as shown in Fig. 14:

Case 1. Edge at left or no edge in domain.
Case 2. Edge crossing (top-to-bottom).
Case 3. Edge crossing (left-to-right).
Case 4. Edge crossing (corner).
Case 5. One point inside.
Case 6. Both points inside.

These cases are presented primarily for comparison with previous methods. The bit-packing follows directly from the definition of a fragment, not from the explicit consideration of each of these cases.

For a resolution of 1/8 the pixel spacing, all possible fragments are encoded into 13 bits for a single pixel filter domain or 17 bits for the 2-by-2 pixel domain. The following description is for the single pixel case, the 2-by-2 pixel case differs only in that 4 bits are allocated for coordinates instead of 3 bits.

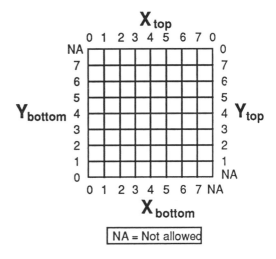

Fig. 15. Allowable values for fragment coordinates.

The fragment encoding is given the top and bottom points of the fragment's edge, (X_{top}, Y_{top}) and (X_{bot}, Y_{bot}), and possibly Y_g. Initially, these coordinates are defined on a grid and can take on the values 0 through 8 for the 1-by-1 domain (or values 0 through 16 for the 2-by-2 domain). The constraints that allow efficient bit packing are:

(1) Since Y_{top} cannot be 0 (Fig. 16b) and Y_{bot} cannot be 8 (Fig. 16a), Y_{bot} and Y_{top} are encoded in 3 bits by having 0 signify different positions for the top and bottom y (Fig. 15).

(2) Similarly, since edge slope is positive X_{bot} cannot be 8 (Fig. 16c), and so X_{bot} also requires only 3 bits (Fig. 15).

(3) Because the edge slope is positive, then $X_{top} > X_{bot}$. Thus when $X_{bot} > 0$, $X_{top} = 8$ can be represented by the value 0.

81

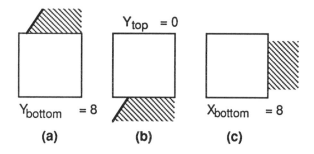

Fig. 16. Polygon bit-packing constraints.

All that remains is to encode Y_g (if present) and the case X_{top} = 8 with X_{bot} = 0. This requires one additional signal bit. When Y_g occurs, we must have X_{bot} = 0. Thus in either case (X_{top} = 8 and X_{bot} = 0, or Y_g present), the signal bit implies that X_{bot} is zero. This frees up the bits normally used for X_{bot}. Since $Y_g < Y_{bot}$, this allows substituting Y_g for X_{bot} when Y_g is necessary, or substituting Y_{bot} for X_{bot} for the case X_{top} = 8 with X_{bot} = 0. This bit-packing can be summarized in the C programming language as follows:

```
Xtop = Xtop % 8;
Ytop = Ytop % 8;
if (Yg is not needed) {
  if (Xtop == 8 && Xbot == 0 )
    ADR = (1,Ybot,Ybot,0,Ytop);
  else
    ADR = (0,Xbot,Ybot,Xtop,Ytop);
} else
    ADR = (1,Yg,Ybot,Xtop,Ytop);
```

When there is no edge in the domain, the encoding defaults to $(0, 0, Y_{bot}, 0, Y_{top})$. This bit-packing requires a total of $1 + 3 + 3 + 3 + 3 = 13$ bits for the signal pixel filter domain, and similarly 17 bits for the 2-by-2 pixel domain. This is not the most compact packing possible (there are 69,632 cases for the 2-by-2 pixel domain), but for memory sizes in powers of two it's good enough.

3.5 Alpha-Blending in the Frame Buffer

For both lines and polygons the filter weight obtained from the table is multiplied by the opacity (opacity = 1 - transparency) of the polygon or line, and the result is called α. This α controls the blending of the new color with the existing color (or the background color) in the frame buffer. Color can be blended according to the rules of compositing [22]:

$$C_{FB} = \alpha_{IN} * C_{IN} + (1-\alpha_{IN}) * C_{FB}$$
$$\alpha_{FB} = \alpha_{IN} * \alpha_{IN} + (1-\alpha_{IN}) * \alpha_{FB}$$

where C stands for any color component, and the subscripts FB and IN designate the current frame buffer contents and the input values coming into the frame buffer respectively. This is used primarily for rendering transparent surfaces in back-to-front order and for lines. There is also a mode where the pixel can be "filled" until it is "full":

$$\alpha = min(\alpha_{IN}, 1-\alpha_{FB})$$
$$C_{FB} = \alpha * C_{IN} + (1-\alpha) * C_{FB}$$
$$\alpha_{FB} = \alpha_{FB} + \alpha$$

This is called the image accumulation mode, and it is primarily used for rendering polygons in front-to-back order.

3.6 Hardware Details

The system as a whole consists of three 9U-sized VME circuit boards built with off-the-shelf TTL and CMOS parts. At present no ASICs are used. The first board performs the decomposition and clipping in the y-direction. The second board does the clipping in the x-direction, Gouraud shading, symmetry encoding, filter table access, and alpha calculation. The third board contains the frame buffer, alpha blending, and video output.

All encoding is done in a layer of PAL logic, and the resulting tables fit in a 1 Mbit RAM for either lines or polygons. The required hardware is surprisingly small. Fig. 17 compares the module that implements the encoding logic and filter tables with a similar module for Gouraud shading. While both modules are about the same size, the Gouraud module is double-sided while the encoding-filter module is only single-sided.

The system runs at 20 MHz and fills up to 4 pixels in every clock cycle. This results in a polygon throughput (when used with a front-end performing hidden surface removal) of 600 thousand antialiased polygons per second (interlaced) or 300 thousand polygons (non-interlaced) for a 1-megapixel display. The line throughput (averaged over all orientations) is 2 million antialiased 10-pixel vectors per second. This performance is competitive with larger systems requiring custom VLSI.

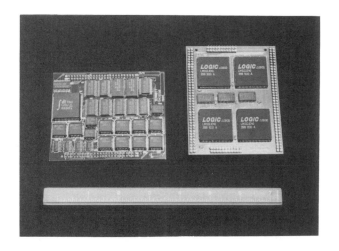

Fig. 17. Encoding-filter and Gouraud modules.

4 HIDDEN SURFACE REMOVAL

Supersampling has the advantage that it integrates easily with point sampling methods for hidden surface removal such as z-buffering or ray tracing. Because antialiasing requires hidden surface removal, we must address just how the hidden surface problem might be solved given that the point sampling paradigm (z-buffer or ray tracing) has been abandoned. A full consideration of this issue is beyond the scope of this paper. Our goal here is simply to suggest that useful hidden surface techniques already exist, and there is room for even better ones. We will briefly consider two approaches: priority based rendering and a hardware implementation of a scan-line hidden surface algorithm.

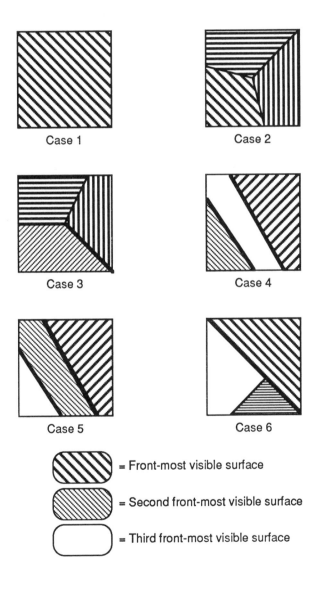

Case 1

Case 2

Case 3

Case 4

Case 5

Case 6

= Front-most visible surface

= Second front-most visible surface

= Third front-most visible surface

Fig. 18. Priority rendering cases.

4.1 Priority Methods

One way to employ this antialiasing method is to render front-facing polygons in front-to-back order using the image accumulation mode described in Section 3.5. The resulting image is correctly rendered at all pixels except those that contain contours from three or more overlapping relevant surfaces [26] (a relevant surface is a forward-facing connected set of polygons or other surface elements). Let's explicitly consider several cases to uderstand where it's exact and where it errs (Fig. 18).

Case 1, where there is one polygon in the domain, is trivially seen to be correctly filled. Case 2, where there are no visible contour edges in the domain, is also correctly filled because all the pieces will simply add up to unity. Case 3, where there is only one contour (which may consist of more than one edge) and therefore only two visible relevant surfaces, is also correctly rendered. The front-most surface is accumulated in the pixel and the back-most surface "fills" the remainder of the pixel. This assumes that the shading gradients for the back-most surface are small, but the error in shading is inversely proportional to the visible area of the backmost surface. Thus, the shading error can be large only when the total contribution of the backmost surface is small. Case 4, where there are two non-intersecting contours, and the two front-most surfaces do not overlap is also rendered correctly by the same logic. The only errors occur for Cases 5 and 6, where there are three or more visible surfaces and the first two overlap. Clearly these two cases occur only for a few pixels in most scenes. Furthermore, the front-most surface is always weighted correctly. This has led Crow to conclude that the errors in this approach have "not proven to be noticeable in practice" [5].

Plate 1 shows an example of front-to-back rendering at a resolution of 1024 by 768 pixels. Methods for determining polygon priority either a priori [10] or on-the-fly are well known. The advantage of priority methods is that the time to input polygonal data is proportional to the number of polygon vertices and the time to render is proportional to the total area (visible or not) of all polygons within the viewport. The disadvantage is that the rendering time is also proportional to the average depth complexity of the scene.

4.2 A Scan-Line Algorithm

It is intriguing that, despite the significant literature on hidden surface removal, almost all hardware systems use the z-buffer, what Sutherland aptly called "brute-force image space" [26]. Furthermore, most proposals for future hardware systems employ either the z-buffer or ray tracing [12]. What's happened to analytic and optimal hidden surface removal? Is the hidden surface problem simply an academic exercise? We don't think so. We believe that there are simple reasons why analytic hidden surface methods are not common in hardware. Three of these reasons are:
  (1) Numerical problems
  (2) Absence of optimized programmable hardware
  (3) Asymptotic efficiency is not linear.

Let's consider numerical issues first. All efficient hidden surface algorithms make extensive use of calculated edge intersections. Unfortunately, the edge (or line) intersection calculation is not numerically stable. This calculation requires the quotient of two cross products of endpoint co-ordinates. The problem is that the denominator of this quotient approaches zero as the two line segments being tested for intersection approach parallel. Near zero, round-off errors in computing the denominator can result in a completely erroneous answer - a misplaced intersection location or even no intersection where there is one and vice-versa. The solution to this problem is either to use fixed point co-ordinates with extended precision or use accurate dot product calculations for floating point co-ordinates [21] [27].

The second issue is the absence of optimized hardware architectures for running graphics algorithms. Historically, the widespread use of Z-buffers was coincident with the advent of VLSI powerful enough to imbed the z-buffer algorithm in silicon. Software Z-buffers were too slow. Is this the general purpose graphics processor? In comparison, digital signal processing (DSP) has its genre of architectures and chips. DSP chips are optimized for FFTs and filtering (fast address calculations and multiply-add instructions). Also, today's workstations have architectures optimized for performance with compilers (and Unix), i.e., RISC. There are no corresponding programmable architectures optimized for geometric calculations. In practice manufacturers use DSP chips or RISC chips for graphics. We think an optimized graphics architecture exists and offers significant performance improvement over using existing DSP or RISC processors as graphics substitutes. One possible architecture is described below. While it has much in common with DSP chips or RISC chips, the difference is in how the major functional blocks are organized and optimized.

First, we observe that graphics algorithms have two components - a topological component and a geometric component. The topological component deals with list-like relationships

while the geometric component deals with calculations on geometric entities such as points, lines, plane equations, etc. We propose handling these two components in separate processors with separate data memories. We call this arrangement a topology-geometry processor (TGP). It has the generic structure shown in Fig. 19.

The topology processor is optimized for manipulating lists and pointers. For example, in a single cycle it can select a base address (like a "C" structure address), calculate an offset address (an item within that structure), and read or write the corresponding memory location. Calculating these addresses in a RISC processor would take several additional cycles. Such address calculation units are more common in DSP chips. The geometry processor is a floating-point or fixed point arithmetic unit. It receives macro commands from the topology processor (e.g., "do these two lines intersect?"). By running it as a separate processor with separate datapaths, simultaneous operation of both processors is more easily handled than on chips that require complex interleaved software in order to dispatch integer and floating-point operations in the same cycle. Clearly, this is more or less the same amount of hardware as exists in current RISC processors, it's just organized and optimized a little differently. Lastly, the data and instruction memories are small enough to be implemented in SRAM, eliminating caches.

We have performed a preliminary assessment of one possible implementation of this architecture. The implementation uses two TGPs in series. The first TGP takes the world data base, transforms it and discards polygons which are back-facing or outside the field of view. Its output is a topologically-connected screen-space database of potentially visible polygons. The second TGP has two topology processors and two geometry processors. It executes a scanline hidden surface algorithm and decomposes the visible pieces of polygons into trapezoids (as in Section 3.2). This scan-line algorithm uses the plane-sweep [20] paradigm at the highest level, with pointers to distinguish internal and contour edges [24]. The algorithm processes each polygon vertex and well as intersections between contour edges and intersections between visible contour edges and visible internal edges. Each of these cases is processed in 30-50 machine cycles. Thus a 25 MHz implementation results in polygon throughputs of 300K-600K polygons per second for all but the most pathological cases. Extending this algorithm to multiple processors for parallelism (in screen space) is straightforward.

Although this scanline algorithm is adequate for real-time (30Hz-60Hz) scenes of moderate complexity (5k-10K potentially visible polygons per frame), there is still the question of how effective is such an approach for more complex scenes. It is known that the asymptotic performance of analytic hidden surface algorithms is not linear. In particular
  • Intersections can be $O(n^2)$
  • Sorting is $O(n \log(n))$
These problems are topics of current research. One obvious approach is some degree of parallel processing for hidden surface removal [9]. Other possible approaches are
  • Hybrid algorithms
  • Content-addressable and associate memories

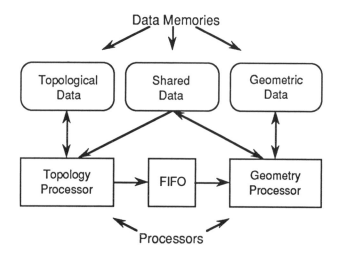

Fig. 19. Topology-geometry processor (TGP).

Hybrid algorithms use some combination of priority and full hidden surface removal. In areas with many intersections, priority can be more efficient (trading intersections against depth complexity). The non-linear efficiency of sorting can be ameliorated by noting that the n log(n) complexity is for traditional algorithms running on traditional machines. In contrast, content addressable and associative memories can sort in linear time. Very efficient CAM cells (in terms of silicon area) have been reported in the literature and the use of such innovative memory architectures holds interesting possibilities.

5 SUMMARY AND CONCLUSIONS

We have described a straightforward and comprehensive implementation of prefiltering. Our design leverages the availability of large (1 M-bit) semiconductor memory to provide an efficient system, both in hardware complexity and speed. The high-resolution one-eighth pixel grid provides excellent image quality and smooth motion for both lines and polygons. The antialiasing filters themselves can be arbitrary symmetric functions over a 2-by-2 pixel domain for polygons and a 3-by-3 domain for lines.

This antialiasing approach is used in commercially available hardware. We believe it encourages the development of algorithms and special hardware for priority or full hidden surface removal. Such systems would combine real-time performance with image quality not possible with z-buffer or ray tracing architectures.

REFERENCES

1. Abram, G., L. Westover, and T. Whitted. Efficient Alias-free Rendering Using Bit-masks and Look-up Tables. SIGGRAPH '85 Proceedings, Computer Graphics, V. 19, No. 3, July 1985, pp. 53-59.

2. Akeley, K, and T. Jermoluk. High-Performance Polygon Rendering. SIGGRAPH '88 Proceedings, Computer Graphics, V. 22, No. 4, August 1988, pp 239-246.

3. Brassel, K. E. and R. Fegas. An Algorithm for Shading of Regions on Vector Display Devices. SIGGRAPH '79 Proceedings, Computer Graphics, V. 13, No. 2, August 1979, pp 126-133.

4. Catmull, E. C. A Subdivision Algorithm for Computer Display of Curved Surfaces. Technical Report UTEC-CSc-74-133, Department of Computer Science, University of Utah, December 1974.

5. Crow, F.C. Antialiasing. In Computer Graphics Techniques - Theory and Practice, D. F. Rodgers and R. A. Earnshaw, Eds. Springer-Verlag, New York, 1990.

6. Duff, T. Polygon Scan Conversion by Exact Convolution. Proceedings of the International Conference on Raster Imaging and Digital Typography, J. André and R. D. Hersch, Cambridge University Press, 1989.

7. Feibush, E. A., M. Levoy, and R. L. Cook. Synthetic Texturing Using Digital Filters. SIGGRAPH '80 Proceedings, V. 14, No. 3, July 1980, pp 294-301.

8. Foley, J. D., A. van Dam. S. K. Feiner, J. F. Hughes. Computer Graphics - Principles and Practice, Addison-Wesley, 1990.

9. Franklin, W. R., and M. S. Kankanhalli. Parallel Object-Space Hidden Surface Removal. SIGGRAPH '90 Proceedings, Computer Graphics, V. 24, No. 4, August 1990, pp. 87-94.

10. Fuchs, H., G. D. Abram, and E. D. Grant. Near Real-Time Shaded Display of Rigid Objects. SIGGRAPH '83 Proceedings, Computer Graphics, V. 17, No. 3, July 1983, pp 65-72.

11. Gish, W. and A. Tanner. Antialiasing Without Supersampling. Proceedings of the 13th Interservice/Industry Training Systems Conference, December 1991, pp. 262-270.

12. Green, S. Parallel Processing for Computer Graphics, MIT Press, 1991.

13. Gupta, S. and R. F. Sproull. Filtering Edges for Grey-Scale Displays. SIGGRAPH '81 Proceedings, Computer Graphics, V. 15, No. 3, August 1981, pp. 1-7.

14. Kajiya, J. T. The Rendering Equation. SIGGRAPH '86 Proceedings, Computer Graphics, V. 20, No. 4, August 1986, pp. 143-150.

15. Lobb, R. J. Antialiasing of Polygons with a Weighted Filter. In Computer Graphics 87, T. L. Kunii Ed., Springer-Verlag 1987.

16. Mitchell, D. P. and A. N. Netravali. Reconstruction Filters in Computer Graphics. SIGGRAPH '88 Proceedings, Computer Graphics, V. 22, No. 4, August 1988, pp 221-227.

17. Molnar, S. Efficient Supersampling Antialiasing for High-Performance Architectures. Technical Report 91-023, Dept. of Computer Science, University of North Carolina at Chapel Hill, April 1991.

18. Naiman, A. C. and W. Makous. Information Transmission for Greyscale Edges. Soc. for Information Display 91 Digest, pp. 109-112.

19. Nelson, Scott R. Wireframe Image Quality. SIGGRAPH '91 course on the Technical Evaluation of 3D Graphics Workstations.

20. Nievergelt, J. and F. P. Preparata. Plane Sweep Algorithms for Intersecting Geometric Figures. Communications of the ACM, Vol. 25, No. 10, Oct. 1982, pp 739-747.

21. Ottman, T., G. Thiemt, and C. Ullrich. Numerical Stability of Geometric Algorithms. Proceeding of the Third Annual Symposium on Computational Geometry, June 1987, pp 119-125.

22. Porter, T. and T. Duff. Compositing Digital Images. SIGGRAPH '84 Proceedings, Computer Graphics, V. 18, No. 3, July 1984, pp 253-259.

23. Reif, J. and S. Sen. An Efficient Output-Sensitive Hidden-Surface Removal Algorithms and Its Parallelization. Proceedings of the Fourth Annual Symposium on Computational Geometry, June 1988, pp 193-200.

24. Séquin, C. H. and P. R. Wensley. Visible Feature Return at Object Resolution. IEEE Computer Graphics and Applications, Vol. 5, No. 5, May 1985, pp 37-50.

25. Schilling, A. A New Simple and Efficient Antialiasing with Subpixel Masks. SIGGRAPH '91 Proceedings, Computer Graphics, V. 25, No. 4, July 1991, pp. 133-141.

26. Sutherland, I.E., R. F. Sproull, and R. A. Schumacker. A Characterization of Ten Hidden Surface Algorithms. Computing Surveys, Vol. 6, No. 1, March 1974, pp 1-56.

27. Ullrich, C., Editor. Computer Arithmetic and Self-Validating Numerical Methods, Academic Press, 1990.

28. Whitted, T. Anti-Aliased Line Drawing Using Brush Extrusion. SIGGRAPH '83 Proceedings, Computer Graphics, V. 17, No. 3, July 1983, pp. 151-156.

29. Yan, Johnson K. Advances in Computer-Generated Imagery for Flight Simulation. IEEE Computer Graphics and Applications, Vol. 5, No. 8, August 1985, pp 37-51.

Interactive Volume Rendering on a Multicomputer

Ulrich Neumann

Department of Computer Science
University of North Carolina at Chapel Hill

Abstract

Direct volume rendering is a computationally intensive operation that has become a valued and often preferred visualization tool. For maximal data comprehension, interactive manipulation of the rendering parameters is desirable. To this end, a reasonable target would be a system capable of displaying 128^3 voxel data sets at multiple frames per second. Although the computing resources required to attain this performance are beyond those available in current uniprocessor workstations, multicomputers and VLSI rendering hardware offer a solution. This paper describes a volume rendering algorithm for MIMD message passing multicomputers. This algorithm addresses the issues of distributed rendering, data set distribution, load balancing, and contention for the routing network. An implementation on a multicomputer with a 1D ring network is analyzed, and extension of the algorithm to a 2D mesh topology is described. In addition, the paper presents a method of exploiting screen coherence through the use of VLSI pixel processor arrays. Though not critical to the general algorithm, this rendering approach is demonstrated in the example implementation where it serves as a hardware accelerator of the rendering process. Commercial graphics workstations use pixel processors to accelerate polygon rendering; this paper proposes a new use of this hardware for accelerating volume rendering.

1. Introduction

Direct volume rendering is the common name that describes the viewing of volume data as a semi-transparent cloudy material. Its advantages are that much or all of the volume may be visible to the observer at one time; there is no need to introduce intermediate geometry that doesn't really exist in the data. We assume the input data is a scalar field sampled at the vertices of a 3D rectilinear lattice - a situation often encountered in medical and simulation data. Plate 1 is an image of a representative medical data set of dimensions 128×128×124. The following 3-step conceptual model of the volume rendering process is based on previously published derivations [Blinn82] [Kajiya+84]. Much of this example comes from Wilhelms and Gelder [Wilhelms+91].

1 - Reconstruct the continuous 3D scalar function $\mathbf{F}$ by convolving each sample point $\mathbf{f}$ with a reconstruction filter kernel $\mathbf{K}$.

$$\mathbf{F}(x,y,z) = \sum_{x,y,z} \mathbf{f}_{x,y,z} * \mathbf{K}$$

2 - Apply an opacity $\mathbf{O}$ and shading $\mathbf{S}$ function to the continuous scalar field. These user definable transfer functions yield a differential opacity $\Omega = \mathbf{O}(\mathbf{F})$ and color emittance $\mathbf{E} = \mathbf{S}(\mathbf{F})$ at each point in the volume as a function of the scalar field properties at that point. The Ω and $\mathbf{E}$ fields should then be low-pass filtered for resampling in the next step.

3 - Integrate an intensity and transparency function along sample view-ray paths through the volume. The integrals may be taken toward or away from the viewer. When taken towards the viewer, the accumulated intensity $\mathbf{I}$ and transparency $\mathbf{T}$ along the sample ray is

$$\mathbf{I}(p) = \mathbf{T}(p)\int_0^p \frac{\mathbf{E}(v)}{\mathbf{T}(v)} dv, \quad \text{where } \mathbf{T}(p) = e^{-\int_0^p \Omega(v)\, dv}$$

The intensity equation has an analytic solution if we assume $\mathbf{T}$ and $\mathbf{E}$ constant over the interval $[0,p]$. By applying this constraint over limited size intervals, we may approximate the intensity and transparency of any interval. Successive intervals are composited to obtain the cumulative intensity or color reaching the viewer along the ray.

There are four common algorithmic approaches to approximating the above three step process in actual implementations.

1.1. Ray-casting - The volume is resampled along view rays [Levoy88] [Sabella88] [Upson+88]. The Ω and $\mathbf{E}$ functions must be reconstructed at the new sample points along the rays. Typically, 3D reconstruction is done by trilinear interpolation of the Ω and $\mathbf{E}$ function values evaluated at the lattice vertices. Successive samples along a ray are composited to produce the final ray color.

1.2. Serial Transformations - An affine view transformation is decomposed into three sequential 3D shear operations. Each shear is affected by a 1D transformation of the form $x' = Ax + B$ [Drebin+88] [Hanrahan90]. Since these transformations require only a 1D reconstruction filter, cubic splines are commonly used to facilitate the resampling. The resampled volume is screen-aligned and ready for integration and compositing.

1.3. Splatting - This approach computes the effect of each voxel on the pixels near the point to which it projects. Slices of voxels are sorted by depth order and reconstructed by convolution with a 2D filter kernel. The reconstructed function is resampled and accumulated on a screen-aligned grid. Successive slices are composited to produce the final image. Since the filter is position-invariant for affine transformations, software table methods are often used to quickly approximate it [Westover89].

1.4. Cell Projection - Volumes are decomposed into polyhedra whose vertices are derived from the sampled data lattice [Shirley+90] [Max+90] Wilhelms+91]. The polyhedra are converted to polygons by projecting them under the view transformation. Reconstruction is done to obtain each polygon's vertex values for the opacity and emission functions. The resulting polygons are rendered by conventional means using a painter's algorithm and alpha compositing. These methods make effective use of existing polygon rendering hardware. The reconstruction functions are usually linear since most rendering hardware does linear interpolation of the polygon vertex values.

2. Rendering Hardware

The rendering method proposed here is a parallelized splatting approach. Using multiple processors with parallel frame buffer access, a splat kernel is produced and merged into an image at many pixels simultaneously. Current graphics workstations [SGI] use multiple processors to allow parallel access of pixel values in a frame buffer. Such groups of processors with parallel frame buffer access are what we refer to with the term *pixel processors*.

This idea of using pixel processors to accelerate volume rendering is not totally new. Cell projection methods were created to make use of it. Laur and Hanrahan approximate splat filter kernels with groups of polygons rendered by dedicated hardware [Laur+91]. The new aspect of the method proposed here is that of coercing the hardware to render a splat filter kernel directly as a single graphic primitive. The next sections describe two methods whereby pixel processor arrays create splat kernels for convolution with voxels.

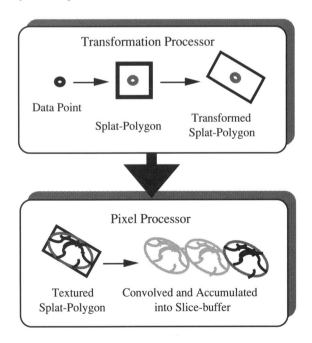

Fig.1. Splatting with hardware for textured polygons

2.1. Textured Kernel - The kernel primitive can be thought of as a polygon with a nonlinear interpolation function. Arbitrary interpolation functions may be defined as textures. Given an array of pixel processors capable of texture lookup and multiplication, the screen coherence of each splat can be exploited. Current generation graphics workstations have this capability, although they may not yet offer the firmware needed to exploit it [SGI]. The splat-polygon's color and opacity are those of the voxel it represents. The splat-polygon with its texture coordinates is transformed and rendered normally except for the additional processing required by the pixel processors (Fig. 1). The pixel processors compute the texture value based on the texture coordinates at each pixel. This texture is the kernel function which is used to weight the polygon color and opacity. The convolution results at each pixel are accumulated in a slice buffer [Westover89]. When a complete slice of voxels is splatted, the pixel processors composite the slice buffer into the image.

In lieu of texture lookup capability, a kernel may be computed. This latter approach is most appropriate for Pixel-Planes 5, the target machine for the implementation described here. Before detailing the kernel computation algorithm, the next section briefly describes some essential aspects of this machine.

2.2. Pixel-Planes 5 Overview - This machine has multiple i860-based Graphics Processors (GPs), and multiple SIMD pixel processor arrays called Renderers (Fig. 2). Each Renderer is a 128x128 array of pixel processors capable of executing a general purpose instruction set. GPs send Renderers opcode streams which are executed in SIMD fashion. Renderers also have a Quadratic Expression Evaluator (QEE) that may be configured to occupy any screen position [Fuchs+89]. Special QEE opcodes evaluate the function

$$Q = Ax + By + C + Dx^2 + Exy + Fy^2$$

at each processor in the Renderer for its unique x,y location. Configuring a Renderer to a new screen position is accomplished by offsetting the QEE so that each pixel processor's QEE result is based on its offset x,y location. The coefficients A - F are part of the instruction stream from the GPs. Renderers also have ports that allow data movement in and out of the processor array under GP control. The GPs, Renderers, a Frame Buffer, and workstation host all communicate over an eight-channel 1D ring-network whose aggregate bandwidth is 160 Mwords per second.

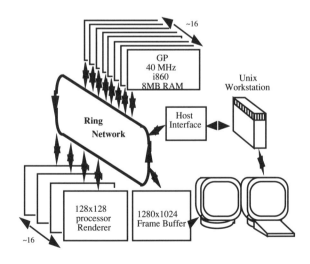

Fig. 2. Pixel-Planes 5 system components

2.3. Computed Kernel and Slice Splatting

2.3. Computed Kernel and Slice Splatting - Polynomials are reasonable approximations to a gaussian filter kernel and easily computed. The function

$$2r^3 - 3r^2 + 1 \quad \text{where} \quad 0 < r < 1$$

is a low order gaussian approximation, but is somewhat awkward to compute directly. A quartic

$$Q^2 = (1 - r^2)^2$$

is a more practical solution since a quadratic term $Q = (1-r^2)$ may be computed directly by the QEE and later squared at all pixels in parallel. The kernel value (Q^2) at each pixel scales a voxel's color and opacity. Volumes are splatted a slice at a time by summing the scaled color and opacity values into a slice buffer and then compositing the slice buffer into the accumulated image. The squaring and scaling operations are expensive and should be factored out of the per-voxel inner loop. The kernels of adjacent voxels, however, typically overlap so we must square and scale more than once per data slice. By limiting the kernel radius to two inter-voxel distances, every fourth voxel in x and y will affect a disjoint set of pixels (Fig. 4). Therefore, in one pass we can splat one-sixteenth of the voxels in a slice before squaring, scaling, and accumulation into the slice buffer must be done. (A kernel radius of about 1.6 seems to yield the best overall image.) Pseudocode to implement the slice splatting process on Pixel-Planes 5 is given in figure 3.

```
for (xs = 0; xs < 4; xs++) {          /* cycle all 16 passes */
 for (ys = 0; ys < 4; ys++) {
  for (x = xs; x < slice_xsize; x += 4) {
   for (y = yz; y < slice_ysize; y += 4) {
    /* take every fourth voxel in x and y */
    GP computes QEE coefficients needed to produce Q at
                 position S in the Renderer array;
    GP sends opcode and coefficients to Renderer which
                 computes Q values in the pixel array;
   Renderer enables pixels with Q > 0;
   /* only enabled pixels participate in the next instruction */
   Renderer pixels save Q and load voxel color and
                 opacity sent by GP;
  } }          /* end of pass */
  GP instructs Renderer to square the saved Q values at
                 ALL pixels;                    /* one mult */
  GP instructs Renderer to scale the color and opacity
                 by Q2;                          /* two mults */
  GP instructs Renderer to accumulate scaled color and
                 opacity into slice buffer;      /* two adds */
 } }          /* end of slice */
 GP instructs Renderer to composite slice buffer into image;
```

Fig.3. Pseudocode for splatting one slice using Pixel-Planes 5 Renderers

When all the voxels in slice i are splatted, the accumulated slice color and opacity at each pixel are composited behind the current image of i-1 slices to produce an image of i slices. The compositing operation is efficiently done in parallel for each pixel of the array.

$$\text{Alphai} := \text{Alphai-1} + \text{Alphaslice} * (1 - \text{Alphai-1})$$
$$\text{Colori} := \text{Colori-1} + \text{Colorslice} * (1 - \text{Alphai-1})$$

For arbitrary rotations, different slice orientations are used and the kernels are made elliptical to preserve the independence of pixels during each pass (Fig. 4). For affine projections, the elliptical shape is constant for all voxels making the D, E, and F quadratic coefficients constant over the whole frame. In this case, a linear expression evaluator (LEE) is all that is needed on the pixel processor since the D, E, and F terms may be computed once per frame at each pixel and added to each data point's linear term. This, however, exacts a small

Fig.4. Elliptical kernel extents for one pass showing independence of every fourth voxel in x and y

performance penalty, so in this implementation the available QEE was used.

The elliptical kernel coefficients are computed from the scaling and rotation portions of the view transformation **V**. We first scale **V** to account for the kernel radius T, specified as the number of inter-voxel distances.

$$[M] = T[V]$$

Now the pixel coordinates $\langle x, y, z \rangle$ must be transformed back to the data space coordinates $\langle i, j, k \rangle$ where the computed kernels are always radially symmetric, of unit radius, and therefore, the kernels

$$[M^{-1}] \begin{bmatrix} x \\ y \\ z \end{bmatrix} = \begin{bmatrix} i \\ j \\ k \end{bmatrix}$$

of each pass are non-overlapping.

$$a = -\frac{M_{31}}{M_{33}} \quad \text{and} \quad b = -\frac{M_{32}}{M_{33}}$$

Let k = 0 always. Solving for z produces $z = ax + by$ where Now we can express data coordinates $\langle i, j \rangle$ in terms of pixel

$$[P] \begin{bmatrix} x \\ y \end{bmatrix} = \begin{bmatrix} i \\ j \end{bmatrix}$$

$$\text{where} \quad [P] = \begin{bmatrix} M_{11} + a\,M_{13} & M_{21} + a\,M_{23} \\ M_{12} + b\,M_{13} & M_{22} + b\,M_{23} \end{bmatrix}$$

coordinate $\langle x, y \rangle$.
The kernel function is $Q^2 = (1 - r^2)^2$, but we render

$$Q = (1 - r^2) = 1 - [(i - i_0)^2 + (j - j_0)^2]$$

where i_0 and j_0 define the center of the kernel. Using **P**, we transform Q into a function of pixel coordinates $\langle x, y \rangle$, and after some algebra we obtain the coefficients that allow the QEE to directly evaluate Q in the Renderer.

$$A = 2[x_0 (P_{11}^2 + P_{21}^2) + y_0 (P_{11}P_{12} + P_{21}P_{22})]$$

$$B = 2[y_0 (P_{12}^2 + P_{22}^2) + x_0 (P_{11}P_{12} + P_{21}P_{22})]$$

$$C = 1 - x_0 (P_{11} + P_{21}) - y_0 (P_{12} + P_{22})$$

$$D = - P_{11}^2 - P_{21}^2$$

$$E = -2(P_{11}P_{12} + P_{21}P_{22})$$

$$F = - P_{12}^2 - P_{22}^2$$

Note that D, E, and F do not depend on the kernel position $<x_0, y_0>$. Given any kernel position and allowing for precomputation of the view dependent terms, computing A or B requires only two multiplications and one addition. Computing the C coefficient requires two multiplications and two additions.

3. Multicomputer Rendering Algorithm

Parallel volume rendering algorithms must cope with potentially moving massive amounts of data every frame. For this reason, optimizing the distribution of data among the memory spaces in the machine is important. Full data replication is a trivial option deemed too expensive for most cases. Partial replication is often necessary or desirable. Data subsets may be *slabs* or *blocks*, *packed* or *interleaved*, and *static* or *dynamic*. The proposed algorithm makes use of a static, interleaved, slab distribution. It is static because each voxel is assigned a home node (or nodes) where it remains. It is interleaved since each node has several subvolumes of data, slices to be exact, that are not adjacent to each other. Slices are identified as slabs since they extend to the volume boundaries in two dimensions. This distribution is simply achieved by assigning slices to nodes in a round-robin fashion. It was chosen for load balancing and memory limitation reasons. If packed slices (a single slab) were used, there exists a strong possibility of the outer slice sets having less non-zero data to render than the inner slice sets. By interleaving slices, the spatial distribution of data at each node is similar.

The memory space issue arises from the need to buffer an entire slice's Renderer instruction stream as well as store three sets of slice data. This distribution stores three copies of the data set since we need slice sets oriented perpendicular to each of the data axes i, j, and k. The set of slices most parallel to the view plane are used when traversing the data set.

The proposed algorithm attempts to maximize the utilization of Renderers and GPs without requiring an executive processor. Although this implementation uses special hardware Renderer nodes, rendering could be performed by general purpose processors. In fact, the latter would offer freedom in allocating GP or Renderer tasks as necessary to achieve optimal performance. The algorithm makes use of image parallelism by assigning each Renderer to a unique 128×128 pixel screen region. Renderers receive splatting instructions only for voxels that project to their region. Voxels near region boundaries are splatted at two or four Renderers to eliminate seams in the image. Since compositing must proceed in front-to-back or back-to-front order, Renderers must receive slices in sequence.

Figure 5 illustrates three GPs and two Renderers computing a frame of a six slice data set. At the start of a frame, each GP shades and transforms their front-most slice. Phong shading is accomplished via a lookup table indexed by the voxel's gradient vector. An affine transformation is performed by DDA methods requiring only three adds per point after setup. Renderer instructions for splatting the shaded and transformed voxels are sorted by screen regions and

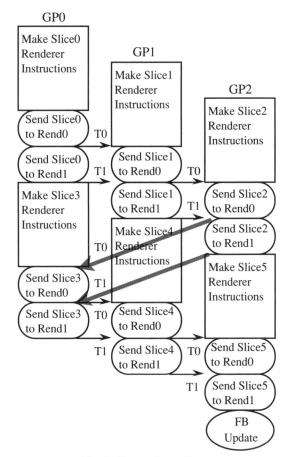

Fig.5. Rendering a Frame

placed into separate buffers. A token for each Renderer is circulated among the GPs to indicate permission to send splat instructions to that Renderer. Initially, all renderer tokens originate at the GP with the front-most slice. The T0 and T1 arcs in figure 5 represent the tokens for Renderer0 and Renderer1 respectively. Upon receipt of a token, a GP transmits the splat instructions for that Renderer's region. The token is then passed to the GP with the next slice. The circulating tokens ensure that Renderers receive slices in front-to-back sequence. The tokens also allow multiple GPs to simultaneously transmit instructions to different Renderers. When all the tokens have passed through a GP, it computes the Renderer instructions for its next slice. The GP with the last slice is responsible for instructing the Renderers to transmit their final color values to the frame buffer.

3.1. Mesh Topology Extension - Since large mesh topology machines are being built and commercially offered, it is of interest to note that this general approach does extend to them. Extension to square N × N mesh topologies requires that at least one edge of the mesh be connected to N Renderers. The data slices are assigned to mesh nodes sequentially row by row (Fig. 6). Tokens (N of them) are circulated through the nodes as before. To avoid contention, we specify that manhattan-style routing is performed for all Renderer messages; messages travel as far as possible in the direction sent, and then, if needed, with one turn they head to their destination. In effect, we utilize the mesh as a cross-bar interconnect. With some inspection it should become apparent that, if tokens move in-step, Renderer splat instructions will never compete for a communication link; routing hardware will always be able to forward messages.

It should be noted that although the number of nodes increases as $O(N^2)$, the number of Renderers increases only as $O(N)$. A scheme

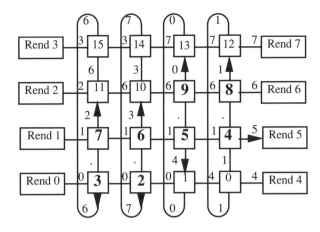

Fig.6. Data distribution, Renderer region assignment, and message paths for a mesh topology

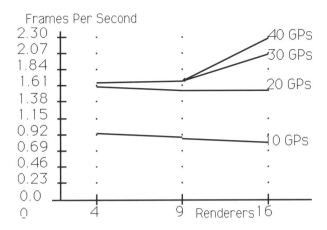

Fig.7. Renderer-Bound Performance

that accommodates a limited N range is to place Renderers along both sides of the array and allow 2N tokens to circulate. In a vertically wrapped mesh, all 2N Renderers can receive instructions simultaneously without incurring contention for the network. Figure 6 shows sixteen nodes and eight renderers with eight tokens in circulation. Nodes with arrow arcs leaving them (nodes 2 - 9) have tokens and are transmitting Renderer instructions. Utilized paths are marked with the message's destination Renderer number.

A practical issue inhibiting this and other implementations of this sort, is the general difficulty of constructing distributed frame buffers and their consequent commercial unavailability.

4. Performance

To understand the behavior of this system, we first analyze the performance of each system element. Then we look at the load balance between the elements and how that affects the overall system performance.

4.1. Renderer Performance - The Renderers digest six instruction words per splat point and compute Q to ten bit precision in 77 cycles of a 40 MHz clock. The squaring and scaling operations use about 900 cycles per pass. Compositing at the end of each slice requires about 700 cycles. For a 128^3 data set, the pass and slice overhead totals 1,932,800 cycles for each Renderer, or about 50 ms. Based on these cycle counts, splatting 128^3 voxels on one Renderer should take 4.09 seconds including the 50 ms overhead. Experimental data correlates well with this predicted Renderer performance. Using twenty GPs and one Renderer, a 128^3 cube of voxels is splatted in 4.38 seconds. This corresponds to a Renderer throughput of about 478,000 voxels per second. Use of multiple Renderers distributes the voxel load while increasing only the GP token passing overhead. With four Renderers, the same 128^3 voxels are splatted in 1.29 seconds, or equivalently, a combined Renderer throughput of 1.622 Mvoxels per second.

4.2. GP Performance - The GP cost of splatting a voxel is the view transformation followed by four additions and six multiplies to compute the QEE coefficients. The transformed voxel must also be sorted by screen region so that the six instruction words to splat it are placed in the proper Renderer's buffer. For a 128^2 slice, a GP processes 16,384 voxels into 98,304 buffered instruction words in 0.16 seconds, achieving a computation throughput of about 102,000 voxels per second. As tokens arrive, the buffered instructions are transmitted to the Renderers. Pixel-Planes 5 GPs use specially addressed read cycles to move data to the ring. This scheme achieves >30 Mword per second peak throughput into the transmit FIFO. The

ring requires about 5 milliseconds to transmit this data. Message software overhead adds roughly 4 milliseconds for the 192 message packets transmitted, hence a GP is able to transmit a slice's buffered Renderer instructions in under 10 milliseconds assuming no ring or Renderer contention.

In most volume data sets, many voxels are transparent and therefore no Renderer splat instructions are generated for them. Passes or slices that contain only transparent voxels produce no Renderer instructions for splatting or overhead operations. Figure 7 shows performance statistics for the 128×128×124 data set shown in Plate 2. About 32% of the voxels (664,486) are non-transparent and actually rendered. The image size is determined by the number of Renderers. Four Renderers produce a 256×256 image while nine and sixteen Renderers produce 384×384 and 512×512 images respectively. It is unusual, but with this sort of hardware larger images render faster because of the increased Renderer parallelism.

4.3. Load Balance - In heterogeneous systems load balancing is difficult. Computing resources are not interchangeable and therefore can not be shifted (without swapping boards) as needed to the task most burdening the system. In this implementation, either Renderers or GPs can limit system performance.

Figure 7 illustrates the case where performance is limited by the number of Renderers. This is often the case if there are many non-transparent voxels to be splatted. Adding more than twenty GPs has minimal effect unless the number of Renderers is increased above nine. In the case of thirty GPs and four Renderers, GPs are waiting over 0.5 seconds total for their first Renderer tokens after they have finished processing slices. Figure 8 illustrates a Renderer-bound frame with three GPs, two Renderers, and a six slice data set. The shaded areas are wasted GP waiting time. Circulating tokens are shown as arcs and marked T0 and T1 for their respective Renderers.

When a very high percentage of voxels are transparent, the system behavior changes. This occurs in the case of isosurface extraction. Figure 9 shows performance statistics for a 128×128×128 data set where about 11% of the voxels (238,637) are non-transparent and actually rendered. Here, the GP slice traversal time dominates the system performance. With so few voxels actually getting splatted, using more than nine Renderers has no appreciable benefit. Figure 5 illustrates a GP-bound frame with three GPs, two Renderers, and a six slice data set. The shaded arcs represent idle Renderer time. Tokens have been sent to GP0 where they must wait for the traversal of the next slice to complete before Renderer instructions can be sent.

91

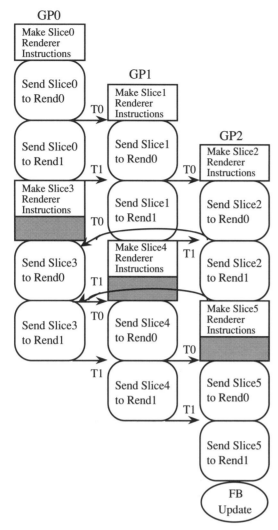

Fig.8. Renderer-Bound Frame

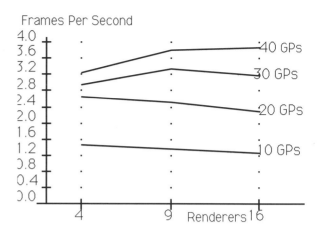

Fig.9. GP-Bound Performance

The latter is simple to implement by rendering every other voxel in all directions of the data set. A 128^3 data set is, for example, effectively rendered as 64^3. While the speed up varies due to load balance issues and relative frame overhead, this technique usually yields at least a factor of five. As an example, consider the small system of ten GPs and four Renderers that produces the image in Plate 2 at 0.93 Hz. Undersampling the volume as a 64×64×62 data set produces a sightly blurred image at a rate of 6.15 Hz; a speed up of over 660%. Undersampled image quality can be improved by rendering a separate prefiltered data set instead of simply skipping voxels.

5. Summary and Discussion

This paper presented a distributed algorithm for volume rendering on multicomputers along with two methods for using a pixel processor array to accelerate splatting. The algorithm was implemented on a 1D ring topology and its extension to a 2D mesh topology was outlined. The splat acceleration technique was demonstrated on a processor array with QEE capability. An alternative approach using texture table lookup was proposed for other pixel processor array architectures.

This implementation is not presented as the fastest or best way of doing volume rendering, but as a promising alternative approach whose merits are system and application dependent. The algorithm was implemented on Pixel-Planes 5 since that machine was available and was the inspiration of the pixel processor rendering idea to begin with. This system has no less than five different parallel volume rendering approaches implemented on it at this time. It is a credit to its designers that this is so, since volume rendering was never an explicit design consideration. The algorithm is implemented in C; some of the low level communications library routines were crafted in i860 assembly code.

Many issues remain for consideration in future work. The errors produced by view-dependent filter kernels need further analysis. Faster pixel processor arrays are desirable, perhaps with nibble or byte-wide data paths. The textured filter kernel method should be explored on a suitable machine. Other parallel algorithms that cope with load imbalance and offer adaptive processing savings should be investigated. The algorithmic impact of different data distributions should also be studied - particularly dynamic distributions in which data migrates among the GPs as the view changes [Neumann91].

Finally, it should be observed that the limiting resource utilization does not approach 100% in either the GP-bound or Renderer-bound test case. Utilization peaks only in the unlikely situation where each GP's slices are an identical workload and the Renderers are each hit by the same number of voxels every slice. Since the system resynchronizes every slice due to the token passing, each slice has it's own load balance. The overall behavior of the system could resemble GP-bound, yet a number of slices in a frame may actually be Renderer-bound, thereby lowering the GP utilization. In most cases then, neither the GPs nor Renderers are fully utilized. This is unfortunately symptomatic or many parallel algorithms - computing resource utilization often decreases as parallelism increases.

4.4. Progressive Refinement - The interactive response of a system can often be increased at the expense of image quality. Usually this is done by undersampling somewhere during the rendering process. Using the pixel processor approach, there is no advantage to undersampling in screen space and then interpolating the remaining pixels; in fact, as pointed out before, frame rate often increases as the number of Renderers, and therefore screen pixels, increases. Instead we may undersample the volume itself. The undersampling may be adaptive [Laur+91] or a regular skipping of some fraction of voxels.

6. Acknowledgements

John Eyles provided a special Renderer splat instruction which is appreciated. Many persons at UNC participated in useful discussions that influenced this work. Tim Cullip's ideas about parallel algorithms were particularly inspiring. The following agencies helped support this work:

NSF, DARPA/ISTO: NSF Grant # MIP-860 1552. DARPA order #6090. "Curved Surfaces and Enhanced Parallelism in Pixel-Planes".

Corporation for National Research Initiatives: "VISTAnet: A Very High Bandwidth Prototype Network for Interactive 3D Medical Imaging", A collaborative project among BellSouth, GTE, Microelectronics Center of NC, and UNC at Chapel Hill.

National Cancer Institute: NIH grant #1 PO1 CA47982-01. "Medical Image Presentation".

7. References

[Blinn82] Jim Blinn "Light Reflection Functions for Simulation for Clouds and Dusty Surfaces". Proceedings of SIGGRAPH '82, Computer Graphics 16, 3. July 1982, pp. 21 - 29.

[Drebin+88] Robert A. Drebin, Loren Carpenter, and Pat Hanrahan. "Volume Rendering". Proceedings of SIGGRAPH '88, Computer Graphics 22, 4. August 1988, pp. 65 - 74.

[Fuchs+89] Henry Fuchs, John Poulton, John Eyles, Trey Greer, Jack Goldfeather, David Ellsworth, Steve Molnar, Greg Turk, Brice Tebbs, Laura Israel. "A Heterogeneous Multiprocessor Graphics System Using Processor Enhanced Memories". Proceedings of SIGGRAPH '89, Computer Graphics 23, 4. August 1989, pp. 79 - 88.

[Hanrahan90] Pat Hanrahan. "Three-Pass Affine Transforms for Volume Rendering". Proceedings of the San Diego Workshop on Volume Visualization, Computer Graphics 24, 5. November 1990, pp. 71 - 78.

[Kajiya+84] Jim Kajiya and Brian Herzen. "Ray Tracing Volume Densities". Proceedings of SIGGRAPH '84, Computer Graphics 18, 3. July 1984, pp. 165 - 174.

[Laur+91] David Laur and Pat Hanrahan. "Hierarchical Splatting: A Progressive Refinement Algorithm for Volume Rendering". Proceedings of SIGGRAPH '91, Computer Graphics 25, 4. July 1991, pp. 285 - 288.

[Levoy88] Marc Levoy. "Display of Surfaces From Volume Data". IEEE Computer Graphics and Applications 8, 3. March 1988, pp. 29 - 37.

[Max+90] Nelson Max, Pat Hanrahan, and Roger Crawfis. "Area and Volume Coherence for Efficient Visualization of 3D Scalar Functions". Conference Proceedings, San Diego Workshop on Volume Visualization. Computer Graphics 24, 5. November 1990, pp. 27 - 33.

[Neumann91] Ulrich Neumann. "Taxonomy and Algorithms for Volume Rendering on Multicomputers". Tech Report TR91-015, Dept. of Computer Science, UNC at Chapel Hill, January 1991.

[Sabella88] Paolo Sabella. "A Rendering Algorithm for Visualizing 3D Scalar Fields". Proceedings of SIGGRAPH '88, Computer Graphics 22, 4. August 1988, pp. 51 - 58.

[SGI] Silicon Graphics. "Power Series Technical Report". Document # 1000027.

[Shirley+90] Peter Shirley and Allen Tuchman. "A Polygonal Approximation to Direct Scalar Volume Rendering". Conference Proceedings, San Diego Workshop on Volume Visualization. Computer Graphics 24, 5. November 1990, pp. 63 - 70.

[Shroder+91] Peter Shroder and James B. Salem. "Fast Rotation of Volume Data on Data Parallel Architectures". IEEE Visualization '91. pp. 50 - 57.

[[Upson+88] Craig Upson and Michael Keeler. "V-Buffer: Visible Volume Rendering". Proceedings of SIGGRAPH '88, Computer Graphics 22, 4. August 1988, pp. 59 - 64.

[Westover89] Lee Westover. "Interactive Volume Rendering". Conference Proceedings, Chapel Hill Workshop on Volume Visualization. May 1989, pp. 9 - 16.

[Westover91] Lee Westover. "Splatting: a Parallel, Feed-Forward Volume Rendering Algorithm". Ph.D. Dissertation. Dept. of Computer Science, UNC at Chapel Hill. TR91-029 July 1991.

[Wilhelms+91] Jane Wilhelms and Alan Van Gelder. "A Coherent Projection Approach for Direct Volume Rendering". Proceedings of SIGGRAPH '91, Computer Graphics 25, 4. July 1991, pp. 275 - 284.

Real-Time Procedural Textures

John Rhoades, Greg Turk, Andrew Bell, Andrei State,
Ulrich Neumann and Amitabh Varshney

Department of Computer Science
University of North Carolina at Chapel Hill

Abstract

We describe a software system on the Pixel-Planes 5 graphics engine that displays user-defined antialiased procedural textures at rates of about 30 frames per second for use in real-time graphics applications. Our system allows a user to create textures that can modulate both diffuse and specular color, the sharpness of specular highlights, the amount of transparency and the surface normals of an object. We describe a texture editor that allows a user to interactively create and edit procedural textures. Antialiasing is essential for real-time textures, and in this paper we present some techniques for antialiasing procedural textures. Another direction we are exploring is the use of dynamic textures, which are functions of time or orientation. Examples of textures we have generated include a translucent fire texture that waves and flickers and an animated water texture that shows the use of both environment mapping and normal perturbation (bump mapping).

Introduction

The current trend in graphics libraries is to give users complete control of an object's surface properties by providing a language specifically for shading [Hanrahan & Lawson 90]. There are two lines of research that have come together to form modern shading languages. One line of research is the notion of programmable shaders, which has its roots in the flexibility of the shader dispatcher [Whitted & Weimer 82] and which was expanded to fully programmable shaders in [Cook 84]. The other research track is the use of mathematical function composition to create textures [Schachter 80] [Gardner 84]. These two lines of research were dramatically brought together to produce a mature shading language in the work of Ken Perlin [Perlin 85]. There are now several graphics machines fast enough to bring some of this flexibility to real-time graphics applications [Apgar 88] [Potmesil & Hoffert 89] [Fuchs 89]. This is the point of departure for our research.

The organization of this paper is as follows: a discussion of the pros and cons of procedural textures; an overview of the Pixel-Planes 5 hardware and software; a brief description of our

language for composing textures; an outline of the algorithms involved in displaying such textures on Pixel-Planes 5; a description of an interactive texture editor that dynamically displays a texture as the user changes its parameters; examples of dynamic textures; examples of applications that make use of the texture capabilities of our system; and future directions for this research.

Why Use Procedural Textures?

Procedural textures provide an alternative to the choice of image-based textures. The central tradeoff between image and procedural textures is between memory cost and execution time.

Graphics architectures that are well-suited for displaying image textures typically have large amounts of memory associated with a handful of fast processors. Each processor retains a copy of every image texture for a given scene so that any processor can perform the texture look-up at any given pixel in the scene. Texture evaluation thus has a small, fixed computational cost, at the expense of using large amounts of memory to store the texture copies. The Silicon Graphics Skywriter and the Star Graphicon 2000 are two commercial graphics engines that use this approach with impressive results.

Our implementation of procedural textures on Pixel-Planes 5 provides a look at the opposite end of this spectrum. Each pixel processor has only 208 bits of memory, but the graphics machine may be configured to have on the order of 256,000 pixel processors, giving the ability to perform several billion instructions per second. Their very small memory makes the pixel processors poor for rendering image-based textures but their computational power makes them ideal for generating procedural textures on-the-fly.

It is clear that any procedural texture can be computed once, saved as an image, and used in a scene like any other image texture. In this sense, it can be argued that image-based textures offer everything that procedural textures can provide, with the only additional cost being the use of more memory. Also, it is clear that procedural textures are a poor choice when the scene requires a picture hanging on the wall or an image on the cover of a book. Nevertheless, procedural textures do have benefits of their own. One benefit is that the texture can be arbitrarily detailed, provided that the texture coordinates are represented with enough bits. Each additional bit added to computation of a function of two variables is reflected by a factor of four in memory cost to mimic the texture with a stored image. A more dramatic benefit is the ability to define textures which are functions of many variables, such as animated textures and solid textures. The memory capacity of graphics systems that we are familiar with is not large enough to explicitly store such textures. Pixel-Planes 5 offers us the alternative of evaluating on demand the values from textures of several variables.

Pixel-Planes 5 Overview

Hardware - The Pixel-Planes 5 machine has multiple Intel i860-based Graphics Processors (GPs) and multiple SIMD pixel processor arrays called Renderers. A Renderer is a 128×128 array of bit-serial pixel processors, each with 208 bits of local memory, called *pixel memory*, and 128×32 bits of off-chip backing store memory. Each Renderer can be mapped to any 128×128 pixel region of an image. The Renderer processors are capable of general arithmetic and logical operations and operate in SIMD mode. Each processor has an enable bit that regulates its participation in instructions. Graphics Processors, Renderers, Frame Buffers, and workstation host communicate over a shared 640 Mb/sec ring network.

Software - Generating images with textured polygons on Pixel-Planes 5 is a multi-stage process which can be viewed as a graphics pipeline [Fuchs 89] as shown in Figure 1. Transparent polygons are handled by making multiple passes through the pipeline. In the first stage of the graphics pipeline, the Graphics Processors transform the polygon vertices from model space to perspective screen space and create SIMD instruction streams (*Image Generation Controller* or *IGC commands*) for the Renderers to rasterize the polygons. A Z-buffer algorithm is executed in parallel for all pixels within a polygon. During rasterization, intrinsic color components, surface normals, texture u,v coordinates, texture scale factor (used for antialiasing), texture-id, etc., are stored in the pixels. After rasterization of all polygons, each pixel processor has the parameters of its front-most polygon. These parameters are then used in the next two stages of the pipeline: texture program interpretation and lighting model computation. At the beginning of texture program interpretation, some initialization is performed. The rasterization phase actually

stores u•z and v•z rather than u and v in pixel memory (since u•z and v•z are linear in screen space), so a z division is needed. Also a time value is stored in pixel memory for use in animated textures. The lighting model currently used is Phong shading. Since all pixels are handled concurrently after all rasterization, we call this approach *deferred shading*. Because of the high degree of parallelism achieved during deferred shading, we can afford to have quite elaborate procedural textures and lighting models while maintaining high frame rates.

Texture Programs

Programming Model - Procedural textures are implemented via a simple virtual machine. This texture machine comprises an assembly language-like instruction set called *T-codes*, a set of registers in pixel memory, and a set of parameters in the Graphics Processor memory. The pixel parameters, such as intrinsic color, u,v coordinates, etc., are accessible to the texture machine via its pixel memory registers. The Graphics Processors execute the T-codes interpretively, modifying the pixel variables that affect shading. More exactly, interpretation of a T-code program produces an IGC command instruction stream, which is routed to the appropriate Renderers for SIMD execution.

T-Codes - There are three kinds of T-codes: generators, which produce several basic texture patterns, operators, which perform simple arithmetic operations on texture patterns, and conditionals which permit selected pixels to be included or excluded in a computation. Generators include Perlin's band-limited noise function [Perlin 85], Gardner's sum-of-sines [Gardner 84], antialiased square waves, and a Julia set. Examples of operators include add, scale, max, square root, splines, and color table lookup. These operators can be cascaded to implement arbitrary functional composition. There are T-codes for conditional execution (by having selected pixel processors conditionally disable themselves), but no T-codes for looping. Adding a new T-code to our system is a straightforward task. Besides coding and testing of the T-code subroutine in C, the programmer needs only to update the T-code assembler parse table and the T-code subroutine dispatch table.

Sample Texture Program - The following T-code fragment computes an antialiased black and white checkerboard pattern. The U and V registers contain the texture coordinates, and the D register contains the texture scale factor. Output is to the diffuse color components D_Red, D_Green and D_Blue. The swave generator produces antialiased square waves in one dimension. Note how the outputs of the generators are combined by continuous operators for antialiasing, rather than using bitwise exclusive-OR.

```
# make antialiased square wave in U direction
     swave  R,U,D; swave_params
# make antialiased square wave in V direction
     swave  S,V,D; swave_params
# R and S registers now contain stripes
     mul    T,R,S
     add    W,R,S
     sub    W,W,T
     sub    W,W,T
# W := R+S-2*R*S, countinuous exclusive OR
# set diffuse colors from W
     copy   D_Red,W
     copy   D_Green,W
     copy   D_Blue,W
```

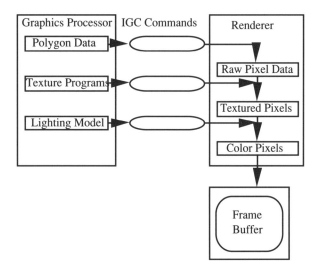

Figure 1: Pixel-Planes 5 Graphics Pipeline

Certainly, our texture programming language is hardly state-of-the-art with respect to programming ease. This is compensated to some extent by the fact that texture programs tend to be rather short - typically 20-40 instructions. The programs are short because the built-in generators and some of the operators (such as spline and color table lookup) are fairly powerful. The main job of the texture programmer is producing the appropriate "glue" code to tie these together. In addition, as discussed later, programming is facilitated by an interactive texture editor program which allows the use of macros.

Texture Procedure Evaluation Details

Pixel Memory Management - The Pixel-Planes 5 Renderers contain 208 bits of on-chip memory and 4096 bits of off-chip backing store memory per pixel. Backing store memory cannot be directly addressed by IGC instructions, but must be swapped in and out by special instructions. Because texture programs usually require the use of scratch memory space and because a rather large number of pixel variables are needed to support deferred shading, there is not enough pixel memory to statically allocate it for the worst case. Therefore, a pixel memory manager keeps track of the locations of the variables and to perform memory movement and backing store swapping to make available required amounts of scratch memory space.

Caching of IGC Commands - For static texture programs, the IGC commands do not change from frame to frame, and thus the T-code translation step need occur only once. Note that static texture programs do not imply static textures; the result of executing a texture program may vary with time, if time is an input variable. During texture parameter editing, the T-code program must be reinterpreted each time it is changed. The Graphics Processors cache the IGC commands resulting from texture interpretation to avoid generating them repeatedly.

Region-Hit Flags - Since each Renderer covers a small (128×128 pixel) region of the screen, it is likely that only a small subset of the textures will be represented in a given region. The Graphics Processors flag each region that any textured polygon intersects as needing that particular texture. The Graphics Processor that creates the texturing commands for a particular region checks the OR'ed flags from all Graphics Processors for that region, and creates and sends the texture programs for only those textures that might be visible.

Obtaining Real-Time Performance

Our goal for real-time procedural textures was to deliver at least 15 frames-per-second to real applications in research projects at UNC. This goal has been met, and these applications are described in a later section.

There are two crucial issues for rapid texture evaluation. The first issue is to maximize utilization of the pixel processors. This is achieved by waiting to execute the texture programs until all polygons have been rasterized, so parallelism of the texture programs can be maximized. In addition, by use of region-hit flags, we avoid processing texture programs for screen regions that don't have the texture. The second issue is enabling the Graphics Processors to keep up with the Renderers. This is accomplished by the IGC instruction caching. We increased the performance of the Walkthrough application from 2 to 20 frames/sec by the use of region-hit flags and the IGC instruction caching.

Antialiasing Techniques

Antialiasing of procedural textures is a difficult problem to which we have not found a general solution; instead we have developed a few techniques which work fairly well for many texture programs. The theoretically proper method is to convolve the texture with a filter kernel of an appropriate shape, centered at the pixel. In principle, this is possible since each pixel processor knows the entire texture, but in practice, this can be done only for the simplest textures, because integrating arbitrary functions of two variables is difficult.

In order to do antialiasing, we need some estimate at each pixel of how an area element in screen space maps into texture space. Ideally, we would use the derivatives of u and v with respect to screen space x and y. However because of limited pixel memory, we decided to record this estimate using a single number, called the *texture scale factor*. This number is intended to represent the maximum magnification factor that can occur when a unit vector in screen space is mapped to texture space. The texture scale factor is available in a pixel memory register for use in T-code programs. The approximation we use is $\max(|u_x|+|u_y|,|v_x|+|v_y|)$, which is within a factor of 1.42 of the commonly used formula $\max((u_x^2+u_y^2)^{1/2}, (v_x^2+v_y^2)^{1/2})$ for MIPmaps [Williams 83]. Because of this, our textures are over-blurred when viewed at certain angles, just like MIPmaps. Texture scale factor is computed for polygons as follows. When the polygon is rasterized, the u and v coordinates at the middle of the polygon, u_{mid} and v_{mid} are computed. The linear expression for $uz = ax+by+c$, is differentiated to give $u_xz+uz_x = a$, which is solved for the constant $u_x = a-u_{mid}z_x$. Similarly u_y, v_xz, and v_yz are computed. From these $\max(|u_xz|+|u_yz|,|v_xz|+|v_yz|)$ is computed and stored in pixel memory. Finally, just before texture program evaluation, a parallel z divide is performed for all pixels. This is, of course, an approximation due to the substitution of u_{mid} for u. The approximation error manifests itself as a difference in the amount of blurring at the corners of a polygon that is being viewed at a very oblique angle (large z_x). We found that the error is not noticeable in ordinary scenes, although it can be seen in contrived test cases.

The antialiased square wave generator produces an antialiased stripe pattern with a specified phase, frequency, and duty cycle. The generator analytically computes the convolution integral of a box filter kernel with a square wave function of its input parameter in one dimension. The width of the box filter is the texture scale factor. Initially we implemented a triangular filter kernel, but found that it required too much scratch pixel memory.

A method that works for some textures is to antialias the final color table lookup. The idea is to return a final color that is the integral over some finite interval in the color table, rather than a point sample. The width of the integration interval is proportional to the texture scale factor times the maximum gradient magnitude of color with respect to u and v. This integral is simple enough to be computed analytically in the pixel processors. If the gradient magnitude of the texture value input to the color table is reasonably smooth, this roughly approximates the correct convolution integral, and does a fairly good job in practice for many textures. It fails utterly for textures that are discontinuous functions of u and v. This kind of texture gradually loses contrast as the texture scale factor increases, but before the texture fades to a uniform color, there is severe aliasing.

Another method works in the frequency domain. Some of our texture programs "roll off" the amplitude of the band-limited noise based on the texture scale factor. The result is that the noise fades to a uniform value at scales where aliasing would be a problem.

Interactive Editing of Texture Procedures

An interactive texture editor eliminates the need for an edit-compile-link-test cycle. Since T-code programs are executed interpretively at run time, texture procedures can be changed without recompilation. Furthermore, the interpretation phase is fast enough so that literal values (Graphics Processor parameters) in T-code instructions can be updated in a single frame time, at frame rates of more than 30 frames per second. The texture editor displays the T-code instructions of a selected procedural texture in a text window. The user can position a movable cursor on any literal value in a T-code instruction, and then smoothly vary this value via a joystick. The dynamically updated texture pattern is displayed on the graphics system with a two-frame lag (the graphics pipeline overlaps two frames). At over 30 frames per second this lag time is hardly noticeable. Hence the user can explore the parameter space of a texture procedure continuously in real time.

More drastic changes to texture programs can be made by interactively editing the text of the program in another window via a conventional text editor. T-code instructions can be added, rearranged, and deleted, producing a new program. Then with a couple of commands, the user can save the updated texture program and reload it into the texture editor for immediate display. This process takes from one to five seconds, which due to the more discrete nature of such changes, can still be viewed as interactive editing.

What the user sees on the graphics system is a complete scene with possibly many graphics primitives and texture procedures, not just a single isolated texture pattern. The texture editor provides a complete set of commands to access the facilities of our graphics library. Thus the user can change the viewpoint, move objects around, change the locations and parameters of light sources, etc. This is important, because the appearance of a texture is dependent on its visual context.

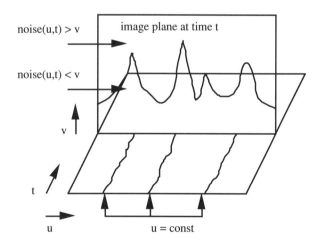

Figure 2: Generating Flames

Dynamic Textures

Textures have been traditionally considered to be functions of spatial coordinates u and v. A generalized texture, however, need not be restricted to just mappings from the spatial coordinates. One could consider a texture to be a function of several other parameters as well - time and surface normal, to mention just a couple. Procedural textures permit us to create these generalized textures without the memory overheads that would be required with image textures. Since these textures change spatially based on input parameters that need not be restricted to just those that define the mapping, we prefer to call them *dynamic* textures.

If we consider a textures to be a function of u, v, and t, where t is a time variable, we can produce time-varying *animated* procedural textures such as a fire texture that flickers and water waves that ripple. If we consider textures as functions of u, v and n where n is the normal to the surface that has been textured, then it is possible to do environment mapping by defining an appropriate procedural texture. Dynamic textures implemented this way can still be precomputed because the program text for the texture doesn't change. Another way to produce dynamic textures is to edit the texture programs after each frame, but then there is some loss of performance since precomputation of IGC commands isn't possible. In the following sections we describe how we implemented several dynamic textures.

Fire - An example of an animated texture is a flickering flame. We implement a fire texture as follows (Figure 2): First perturb u by adding to it a 2D noise function of u and t. Then generate a height field h by applying a 2D noise generator to u and t. Compute flame intensity $f = 1-v/h$. If $f < 0$ set f to 0. This creates a moving outline of the flame. Because of the noise perturbation of u, the outline moves both vertically and horizontally. Finally we copy f to opacity and use a color table with input f to produce color. We use two layers of transparent fire texture to produce the fireplace shown in Photo 3.

Environment Mapping - The next example is a dynamic texture depending on object orientation instead of time. It implements environment mapping of a simple checkerboard pattern onto a teapot. The textured teapot appears to be located inside a room with checkerboard walls, as shown in Photo 5. Rotating the object lets the reflections move across the surface in a realistic way. We accomplish this by performing typical environment mapping computations [Blinn & Newell 76] (determine reflected eye vector, compute indices, compute procedural texture as function of indices) in a T-code program for each pixel.

Our current system has two limitations for environment mapping. First, because the normal vector is only available in eye space coordinates, the (infinitely distant) reflective environment appears to be attached to the camera. Thus, whenever the camera is rotated (panned, tilted or rolled), the reflections move across the object's surface in an erroneous way. If we had enough pixel memory to store world space normals this restriction could be removed. Second, we cannot perform antialiasing properly, since we do not have surface curvature information available in pixel memory.

Water - The final example, shown in Photo 6, is an animated texture approximating water waves by means of an animated procedural bump map. This dynamic texture is a function of both time and spatial orientation. The pixel normals are perturbed on the basis of a height field whose value is computed at each pixel. The derivatives required for the normal perturbation are computed by finite differences. The height field consists of superimposed circular and parallel moving sinusoidal waves generated by a number of sources distributed across the water-textured surface, a common approach for this problem. The surface characteristics are such that the water surface appears highly specular. In addition, the normals are used to compute a simple one-dimensional color scale environment map, which is used to create a more natural appearance. The map has rotational symmetry about a vertical axis, so that the camera can be arbitrarily panned. However, tilting or rolling the camera would generate erroneous results, for the reasons mentioned in connection with the environment mapping texture. As mentioned, this restriction could be removed by storing world space normals at each pixel. We also have a problem with determining which way to perturb the surface normals, since we do not have the surface tangent vectors in the u and v directions available in pixel memory. We can circumvent this problem for horizontal polygons (like water surfaces) by broadcasting the current transformation matrix to the pixel processors during the texturing phase of each end-of-frame calculation. The scene in Photo 6 was rendered in 33 milliseconds, low resolution, with 24 GPs and 12 Renderers.

Applications Using Procedural Textures

Pixel-Planes 5, besides being a research project in its own right, is also an important resource for several other research projects at UNC. Two of those for which textures are important are the Building Walkthrough project and the Head-Mounted Display project. Both of these use a stereo head-mounted display and head tracking, so high frame rates are necessary to maintain the illusion of the virtual environment.

Walkthrough - The UNC Walkthrough Project aims at the development of a system for creating virtual building environments [Brooks 86]. This is intended to help architects and their clients explore a proposed building design prior to its construction, correcting problems on the computer instead of in concrete. Texturing plays an important role in enhancing image realism. Having textures for bricks, wood, ceiling tiles, etc., adds to the richness of the virtual building environment and gives an illusion of greater scene complexity. The radiosity illumination model is used in the Walkthrough project. We can display a model of a house that contains about 34,000 polygons and 20 procedural textures at 15-20 frames/sec on 24 Graphics Processors and 12 Renderers at 640×512 resolution. Photo 1 shows a view of the living room of the house, and Photo 2 shows a view of the kitchen.

For enhanced realism, textures have been integrated with radiosity in Walkthrough. There are two stages in this integration. The first stage is to calculate radiosity values for a textured polygon, such that the radiosity effects such as color bleeding are correctly simulated for the polygons near this textured polygon. The second stage is to shade the textured polygon itself by the radiosity values at its vertices. To effect the first step, the color of a textured polygon is assigned to be the average color of its texture. This color is then used in the radiosity process as usual. After the radiosity values at the vertices of a polygon have been computed, they are passed as input parameters to the procedural texture for this polygon along with other input parameters such as the u and v coordinates. These shading values are linearly interpolated across the polygon. The procedural texture is computed as before and a post-multiplication of the interpolated radiosity shading values with the computed texture colors at each pixel gives a smooth shading effect over the textured polygon.

Another application which textures find in the Walkthrough project is that they offer one way to switch lights in a virtual building. The total radiosity illumination of a polygon is determined by the dot-product of the vector of light values and the radiosity vector specifying the contribution of each light source to the illumination of the polygon. This then means that given the latter, the user can vary the intensity of a light source and observe the same building model under different light scales (but same light positions), by just computing the dot product as described before [Airey90]. This however takes roughly 3 - 5 seconds for a dataset of roughly 30,000 polygons and 20 light sources if done sequentially on the host workstation and fails to provide the effect of instantaneous light switching. One possibility to do this fast enough to provide an instantaneous effect (under a tenth of a second) is to do this in parallel by using T-codes. The idea is to pass the intensity value of a light source as an input parameter to a T-code program (along with the polygon colors) which computes the dot-product of the input parameter with the value of the interpolated radiosity (as described in the preceding paragraph) and uses the resulting value to shade the polygon. Changing the intensity of a light source can then be done by editing the T-code program and changing this input parameter. This is essentially using the T-code commands as a shading language.

Head-Mounted Display - In the Head-Mounted Display project, the primary use of textures has so far been in a mountain bike simulation, where the user rides a stationary bicycle and views simulated terrain through the head-mounted display. Textures are used to increase the apparent scene complexity and to improve the user's perception of motion through the environment. This application features relatively few textures (grass, road, and cloudy sky), each of which covers a fairly large area of the images. A scene from this application is shown in Photo 4. The cloudy sky texture makes use of the Gardner texture generator. The grass and road texture make use of band-limited 2-D noise, and are antialiased by decreasing the noise amplitude as the texture scale factor increases. Several frequencies of noise are used, each with its own threshold for rolloff. This simulation runs at 20-25 frames per second in low resolution (640×512) stereo mode using 32 Graphics Processors and 20 Renderers.

Future Work

The logical next step to our simple texture language is to implement a full-fledged shading language that can be executed on-the-fly. Using the deferred shading paradigm on a high-end graphics machine, real-time execution of a shading language such as Renderman [Hanrahan & Lawson 90] seems to be a very real possibility. Unfortunately, this is impractical on the current Pixel-Planes system due to the small amount of memory available to the pixel processors. However, it is likely that the Pixel-Flow machine [Molnar 91], now being designed at UNC Chapel Hill, will have sufficient pixel memory to make this idea viable.

Acknowledgements

We would like to acknowledge the support and cooperation of Pixel-Planes 5, Walkthrough, and Head-Mounted Display research project teams at UNC. In particular, we would like to thank the following individuals: David Ellsworth, Trey Greer, and Brice Tebbs for their help on the initial stages of the design of texture algorithms, Eric Erikson for his work on the virtual bike, John Alspaugh for modeling the house model in Walkthrough and Carl Mueller for the Pixel-Planes frame-saving facility. We would also like to acknowledge Professors Henry Fuchs, Frederick Brooks, and John Poulton for their encouragement and support.

This work has been supported in part by the following grants: NSF MIP-9000894 DARPA order No 7510, DARPA Grant No: DAEA 18-90-C-0044, NSF Cooperative Agreement No ASC 8920219, NSF Walkthrough Grant No: CCR 8609588, ONR Grant No N00014-86-K-0680.

References

[Airey 90] Airey, J.M., J.H. Rohlf and F.P. Brooks, Jr. "Towards Image Realism with Interactive Update Rates in Complex Virtual Building Environments" *ACM Computer Graphics* (Proceedings 1990 Symposium on Interactive 3D Graphics), Vol. 24, No. 2, pp 41-50.

[Apgar 88] Apgar, Brian, Bret Bersack and Abraham Mammen, "A Display System for the Stellar Graphics Supercomputer Model GS1000," *Computer Graphics*, Vol. 22, No. 4, (SIGGRAPH '88), pp. 255–262.

[Blinn & Newell 76] Blinn, J. F. and M. E. Newell, "Texture and Reflection for Computer Synthesized Pictures," *Communications of the ACM*, Vol. 19, No. 10, pp. 542–547.

[Brooks 86] Brooks, F. P., Jr., "Walkthrough– A Dynamic Graphics System for Simulating Virtual Buildings," *Proceedings of the 1986 Workshop on Interactive 3D Computer Graphics*, pp. 9–21.

[Cook 84] Cook, Robert L., "Shade Trees," *Computer Graphics*, Vol. 18, No. 3, (SIGGRAPH '84), pp. 223–231.

[Fuchs 89] Fuchs, Henry, John Poulton, John Eyles, Trey Greer, Jack Goldfeather, David Ellsworth, Steve Molnar, Greg Turk, Brice Tebbs and Laura Israel, "Pixel-Planes 5: A Heterogeneous Multiprocessor Graphics System Using Processor-Enhanced Memories," *Computer Graphics*, Vol. 23, No. 3, (SIGGRAPH '89), pp. 79–88.

[Gardner 84] Gardner, Geoffery Y., "Simulation of Natural Scenes Using Textured Quadric Surfaces," *Computer Graphics*, Vol. 18, No. 3, (SIGGRAPH '84), pp. 11–20.

[Hanrahan & Lawson 90] Hanrahan, Pat and Jim Lawson, "A Language for Shading and Lighting Calculations," *Computer Graphics*, Vol. 24, No. 4, (SIGGRAPH '90), pp. 289–298.

[Molnar 91] Molnar, Steve, "Image Composition Architectures for Real-Time Image Generation," Ph.D. thesis, Computer Science Department, University of North Carolina at Chapel Hill, 1991.

[Perlin 85] Perlin, Ken, "An Image Synthesizer," *Computer Graphics*, Vol. 19, No. 3, (SIGGRAPH '85), pp. 287–296.

[Potmesil & Hoffert 89] Potmesil, Michael and Eric M. Hoffert, "The Pixel Machine: A Parallel Image Computer," *Computer Graphics*, Vol. 23, No. 3, (SIGGRAPH '89), pp. 69–78.

[Schachter 80] Schachter, B. J., "Long-crested Wave Models," *Computer Graphics and Image Processing*, Vol. 12, pp. 187–201.

[Whitted & Weimer 82] Whitted, Turner and David M. Weimer, "A Software Testbed for the Development of 3D Raster Graphics Systems," *ACM Transactions on Graphics*, Vol. 1, No. 1, pp. 44–58.

[Williams 83] Williams, Lance, "Pyramidal Parametrics," *Computer Graphics*, Vol. 17, No. 3, (SIGGRAPH '83), pp. 1-11.

Geometric Manipulation of Tensor Product Surfaces

Barry Fowler

Royal Melbourne Institute of Technology
Advanced Computer Graphics Centre [1]

Abstract

Tensor product surfaces are now widely used in application areas such as industrial design and computer animation and thus the quest for more effective design methods continues. Although several methods exist for applying high-level operators such as bends, twists and free-form deformations (FFD's), much less effort has been applied to improving direct and precise free-form shaping which is often desired. The dominant form of free-form manipulation has been control-point based. Here we offer a manipulative method that presents geometric properties (e.g. points on the surface, normal vectors, etc.), rather than control vertices or deformation lattices, and allows direct manipulation of these properties at any selected point on the surface. The difficulties of interacting with these three-dimensional geometric entities using both two- and three-dimensional input devices are discussed, as are possible interactive schemes using several such devices.

CR Categories: I.3.5 [Computer Graphics]: Computational Geometry and Object Modelling - parametric surfaces; I.3.6 [Computer Graphics]: Methodology and Techniques - interactive techniques, direct manipulation, constraints; J.6 [Computer-Aided Engineering]: Computer-Aided Design (CAD).

Keywords: Computer-aided geometric design, B-spline surfaces, interactive sculpting, three-dimensional interaction.

1 Introduction

Tensor product surfaces are a widely used primitive in many geometric modelling systems. The majority of recent work in the interactive aspects of modelling these surfaces has been in providing high-level deformation tools [6, 12, 7]. In many applications, however, free-form shaping is required that is not easily expressed in terms of regular shape operators. Control point manipulation is generally inappropriate in such cases, and construction of deformation lattices for tool-based deformation is an indirect, often unnecessarily tedious, solution. When specific geometric properties are required, a designer should be able to select a point or region of a surface and specify these target properties. Such direct manipulation can be achieved for curves [10] and recent work on differential manipulation [14] points to constraint based methods for surfaces.

Meanwhile, there is a constant drive to develop new geometric forms that overcome these and other limitations of tensor product surfaces. Triangular surface patches have long been available (see [8]) as a blending primitive to help alleviate the topological restrictions of tensor product surfaces. Meanwhile Loop and DeRose [11] are two of many who have pursued multi-sided patches. More recently a new modelling paradigm, based on triangular patches, has been presented [3] that combines geometric constraints with sculpting operations based on forces and loads that yield very fair shapes, hence addressing both the topological restrictions and geometric constraints. Although this method shows definite promise for the engineering community, its suitability for non-technical users is unclear as the interactive issues in dealing with forces and loads are still being explored. Regardless of the promise of these new forms, there is still a large investment in tensor product surfaces, and developers would rather find ways to improve their current technology than pursue a new approach.

There has been little attention paid to the problems of interactively designing free-form geometric shapes in three dimensions, not from the view of algorithms or tools, but in terms of direct interaction with surface geometry in three dimensions. Clark [5] used a hand held wand to select and reposition B-spline control vertices as early as 1976, but not much has happened since that time. More contemporary work in 3D interaction, including Bier [2], relies on the use of construction aides that affect attributes being manipulated, but in the case of surfaces, those attributes are almost always the control points. More recently, Weimer and Ganapathy [13] have used a VPL DataGlove to manipulate surfaces in an experimental modelling environment. Although their system is far in advance of Clarke's work (incorporating voice and hand gestures for input) their methods of manipulating curves and surfaces consist primarily of free-hand sketching and direct control point manipulation in space – methods that have long been achievable (albeit more awkward) with a mouse or tablet. One of our goals is to use a pair of "virtual hands" (at this point a pair of VPL DataGloves) that will allow direct "hands-on" interaction with the surface itself, and *not* it's mathematical attributes, i.e. it's control points. To this end, we discuss a few methods we have implemented to provide more intuitive shaping of the surface with a single DataGlove.

Accepting the fact that tensor product surfaces are widely used and that their full potential has not yet been realised, we propose methods of improving interaction with these surfaces. In Section 2 we illustrate how to efficiently solve and apply systems of differential constraints to tensor product surfaces. In Section 3, the formulation of geometric constraints in terms of differential constraints is given, along with a discussion of additional degrees of freedom that have intuitive geometric effects (which we refer to as uniform and

[1]RMIT Advanced Computer Graphics Centre, 723 Swanston Street, Melbourne, Victoria, AUSTRALIA 3053, +61-3-282-2461, bmfowler@godzilla.cgl.citri.edu.au

directional tension). We limit ourself in this paper to the manipulation of properties dependent solely upon first-order derivatives, deferring a more analytical study of surface curvature to a later date. In Section 4, we suggest possible ways of interacting with these geometric properties and degrees of freedom with conventional 2D input devices (a mouse or tablet), a Polhemus 3Space Isotrak [2] and a VPL DataGlove.[3] We close with a summary and description of related work in progress.

2 Differential Constraints

Recent work on interactive techniques for curves has led to the development of direct manipulation interfaces that do not rely on user interaction with control points. The direct manipulation technique described in [1] was generalized in [10] to manipulate higher order properties including tangency and curvature. Here we extend this work to tensor product surfaces.

For parametric curves, direct manipulation of geometric properties was achieved by coordinating the parametric derivatives (to achieve a specified geometry) and solving a linear system of equations that enforced the required changes to these derivatives. We refer to such specifications of derivatives as *differential constraints* whereas a set of differential constraints that achieve a specified geometric property are referred to as a single *geometric constraint*. Other sets of differential constraints that are significant, but not necessarily geometrically intuitive, may be referred to loosely as a *parametric constraint*.

Since a geometric constraint at a particular point on the curve is determined by its parametric derivatives at that parametric point, a geometric constraint will generally consist of an underdetermined (in a minority of cases, well-determined) system of equations. This statement, however, assumes that the degree of the curve supports the degree of the properties to be manipulated, e.g. specifying a change in curvature for a curve that is a straight line (a linear polynomial) would result in an overdetermined system, requiring the degree of the curve to be raised. Overdetermined systems may also occur when combining multiple geometric constraints at different (but nearby) points on the curve. Such a system can always be made underdetermined by suitable refinement.

The solutions obtained for these underdetermined systems was that which minimized the combined movement of the control vertices involved. This method is briefly summarized here. Its applicability to tensor product surfaces is then illustrated.

2.1 Constraints for Curves

A parametric curve segment of degree n (both non-rational and rational) may be expressed as

$$\sum_{i=0}^{n} V_i B_i(u) = Q(u)$$

and thus its derivatives as

$$\sum_{i=0}^{n} V_i B_i^{(k)}(u) = Q^{(k)}(u).$$

A change to a derivative of the curve is similarly represented as

$$\sum_{i=0}^{n} \Delta V_i B_i^{(k)}(u) = \Delta Q^{(k)}(u)$$

which is referred to in matrix form as

$$B^{(k)}(u)\Delta V^T = \Delta Q^{(k)}(u). \tag{1}$$

When shaping a curve in a design application, a user typically has some target geometry in mind, e.g. a point to be interpolated, a tangent line to be met, etc. Such targets can be expressed in terms of changes to the derivatives of the curve at some chosen parametric point. A system of equations containing these changes to the derivatives is given as

$$B(\overline{u})\Delta V^T = \Delta Q^T(\overline{u}) \tag{2}$$

where each row of the matrix $B(\overline{u})$ and vector $\Delta Q^T(\overline{u})$ represents a differential constraint, recall (1), applied at $\overline{u}$.

Note that we select $\overline{u}$ at which to apply the constraints. Although we might allow the parametric point to vary in satisfying the constraints, we select $\overline{u}$ to preserve the linearity of the system, which allows extremely efficient interactive updates. The actual determination of $\overline{u}$ can be performed geometrically by the user by either selecting the curve itself, or by specifying a nearby point to be interpolated, in which case the closest parametric point on the curve can be determined. In both of these cases, $\overline{u}$ is chosen *implicitly* by a *geometric* specification on the user's part.

Conventional control point based manipulations require the user to specify the left hand side of (2), i.e. the ΔV^T, in order to achieve a desired change to the shape of the curve reflected in the resulting ΔQ^T. The assessment of the success of this change is usually performed visually, and is thus often inadequate (exact positioning of control points or endpoints of the curve is often permitted, but not an arbitrary point on the curve). Instead, we derive a suitable solution for ΔV^T given a specification of the right hand side, ΔQ^T, i.e. given one or more geometric constraints.

The solution to the system in (2) is given in [10] as

$$\Delta V^T = B^T (BB^T)^{-1} \Delta Q^T \tag{3}$$

which turns out to be the right-inverse of B when the rows of B are linearly independent (as is most often the case). For the sake of notational convenience, when we refer to the inverse of a matrix, if it is non-square, this will imply the right-inverse. Note that since B^{-1} is independent of ΔQ^T (which changes in each iteration of an intercive loop), the solution can be applied efficiently by precomputing B^{-1} for a given $\overline{u}$ (or set of $\overline{u}$'s at which constraints are applied). This solution becomes particularly efficient when only one element of ΔQ is nonzero (a common occurrence) in which case only one column of B^{-1} need be computed.

One issue that arose with direct manipulation of curves was how many and which control vertices to incorporate into the systems of constraints. We found that the control vertex with maximal positional influence on the curve at $\overline{u}$ should definitely be used, and that one additional degree of freedom (control vertex) should be included, i.e. if we have two constraints, then three control vertices should be included in the system. Including this additional degree of freedom reduced undesirable asymmetry that can result when the solution is unique. The control vertices discarded from the system should be those with the least influence on the curve at $\overline{u}$.

2.2 Constraints for Surfaces

The solution method described for curves can be applied to any underdetermined system of linear equations. Tensor product surfaces are merely bivariate polynomials that are expressed conveniently in terms of univariate basis functions:

$$\sum_{i=0}^{n-1} \sum_{j=0}^{m-1} V_{i,j} B_j(v) B_i(u) = S(u,v).$$

---

[2]3Space IsoTrak is a trademark of Polhemus Navigation Sciences.
[3]DataGlove is a trademark of VPL Research Inc.

When we re-express this as a linear combination of control vertices and bivariate basis functions

$$\sum_{i,j} \mathbf{V}_{i,j} B_{i,j}(u, v) = S(u, v) \qquad (4)$$

where

$$B_{i,j}(u, v) = B_i(u)\, B_j(v)$$

we can apply the methods described in Section 2.1.

In keeping with the notation of Section 2.1 we use matrix notation for our differential constraints. A system of constraints at some parametric point $(\overline{u}, \overline{v})$ will then be represented as:

$$\mathbf{B}(\overline{u}, \overline{v})\, \Delta \mathbf{V}^T = \Delta S^T(\overline{u}, \overline{v}) \qquad (5)$$

where $\Delta \mathbf{V}$ is now indexed as a vector, rather than a matrix. At $(\overline{u}, \overline{v})$ we may now constrain any subset of partial derivatives by selecting appropriate values for the right hand side. By applying changes to appropriate partial derivatives in a controlled manner, we can obtain direct control of the surface geometry at $(\overline{u}, \overline{v})$.

An alternate solution method can be applied in certain instances. Recalling the matrix representation of a tensor product surface

$$\mathbf{B}_0(u)\, \mathbf{V}\, \mathbf{B}_0(v)^T = S(u, v) \qquad (6)$$

we can express a set of changes to the derivatives of the surface as follows

$$\begin{bmatrix} \mathbf{B}_0 \\ \mathbf{B}_u \\ \vdots \end{bmatrix} \Delta \mathbf{V} \begin{bmatrix} \mathbf{B}_0 \\ \mathbf{B}_v \\ \vdots \end{bmatrix}^T = \begin{bmatrix} \Delta S_0 & \Delta S_v & \cdots \\ \Delta S_u & \Delta S_{uv} & \\ \vdots & & \ddots \end{bmatrix} \qquad (7)$$

where we have omitted the (u, v) for brevity. When a chosen submatrix of the right hand side of (7) is fully specified we can apply the curve solution to the rows and columns of $\Delta \mathbf{V}$ to yield the solution

$$\Delta \mathbf{V} = \mathbf{B}(\overline{u})^{-1}\, \Delta S(\overline{u}, \overline{v})\, (\mathbf{B}(\overline{v})^{-1})^T. \qquad (8)$$

Here we precompute $\mathbf{B}(\overline{u})^{-1}$ and $\mathbf{B}(\overline{v})^{-1}$. The cost of applying these two matrices to each ΔS is no greater than the cost of applying the single matrix that would result using the bivariate vector solution (5). The savings in (8) is in computing the right inverses of two basis matrices with low row dimension (one or two in the cases to be discussed), rather than one matrix whose row dimension is the product of the row dimensions of these two matrices. When partial derivatives in the right hand side submatrix are not specified, i.e. are left free to vary, we use the vector solution (3).

Based on our experience with curves, we generally choose not to incorporate all control vertices defining the patch containing $(\overline{u}, \overline{v})$. Instead, we use the control vertex of maximal influence and an additional degree of freedom *in each parametric direction*. This amounts to introducing zeroes into the least significant columns of $\mathbf{B}(u)$ and $\mathbf{B}(v)$. The resulting control vertices that are affected typically belong to a rectangular subset of the control point mesh. This has produced good results for most systems of constraints, although in some cases the area of effect can be further reduced. In order to involve a non-rectangular subset of control vertices, however, the vector solution (3) must be used.

3 Geometric Constraints

Here we describe how appropriate systems of differential constraints are formulated to achieve certain geometric properties, i.e. how to construct geometric constraints. The details of how one might interact graphically with the surface to control these properties are deferred to Section 4. For this paper we restrict our discussion to geometric properties that can be specified in terms of of the first derivatives of the basis functions

$$\begin{bmatrix} \mathbf{B}_0(\overline{u}) \\ \mathbf{B}_u(\overline{u}) \end{bmatrix} \Delta \mathbf{V} \begin{bmatrix} \mathbf{B}_0(\overline{v}) \\ \mathbf{B}_v(\overline{v}) \end{bmatrix}^T = \begin{bmatrix} \Delta S_0(\overline{u}, \overline{v}) & \Delta S_v(\overline{u}, \overline{v}) \\ \Delta S_u(\overline{u}, \overline{v}) & \Delta S_{uv}(\overline{u}, \overline{v}) \end{bmatrix}$$

which actually includes the mixed partial (a second derivative) commonly referred to as the "twist" vector. We assume that we are dealing with a regular surface and that the derivatives we are interested in (not necessarily all of the above) do not vanish at the parametric points of interest. The examples in all illustrations are of bicubic non-uniform B-spline surfaces.

3.1 Position

Controlling the position of a point on the surface is a straightforward process. If a desired point is to be interpolated, a designer can select a nearby point on the surface (for which we determine $(\overline{u}, \overline{v})$) and relocate the point to the target location. This is done by applying a change in position to the surface at $(\overline{u}, \overline{v})$ using the single differential constraint

$$\begin{bmatrix} \mathbf{B}_0(\overline{u}) \end{bmatrix} \Delta \mathbf{V} \begin{bmatrix} \mathbf{B}_0(\overline{v}) \end{bmatrix}^T = \begin{bmatrix} \Delta S_0(\overline{u}, \overline{v}) \end{bmatrix}.$$

Figures 1 and 2 illustrate examples of positional displacement

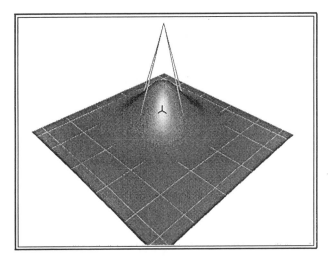

Figure 1: Positional displacement of a point near the centre of flat sheet. One control vertex is involved, hence the asymmetry.

incorporating varying degrees of freedom. The gross asymmetry in the former is absorbed by the inclusion of an extra degree of freedom in each parameter. This extra degree of freedom involves four control vertices and has produced good results in our current B-spline modeller.

3.2 Tangent Plane Orientation

Controlling tangency for surfaces is a much less well-defined task than was the case for curves. For a regular parametric surface, the equation for the normal vector is given by

$$N(\overline{u}, \overline{v}) = \frac{S_u(\overline{u}, \overline{v}) \times S_v(\overline{u}, \overline{v})}{\| S_u(\overline{u}, \overline{v}) \times S_v(\overline{u}, \overline{v}) \|}$$

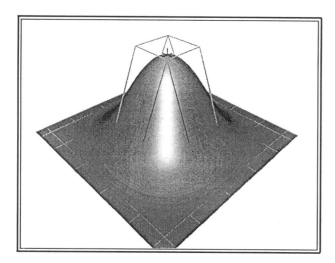

Figure 2: Positional displacement as in Figure 1 using an extra degree of freedom in each parametric direction. The previous asymmetry is absorbed.

which in turn defines the tangent plane at $(\overline{u}, \overline{v})$. To control the tangent plane at $(\overline{u}, \overline{v})$, while preserving $\mathbf{S}(\overline{u}, \overline{v})$, we use the following system of differential constraints

$$\begin{bmatrix} \mathbf{B}_0(\overline{u}, \overline{v}) \\ \mathbf{B}_{\mathbf{u}}(\overline{u}, \overline{v}) \\ \mathbf{B}_{\mathbf{v}}(\overline{u}, \overline{v}) \end{bmatrix} \Delta \mathbf{V}^T = \begin{bmatrix} 0 \\ \Delta \mathbf{S}_{\mathbf{u}}(\overline{u}, \overline{v}) \\ \Delta \mathbf{S}_{\mathbf{v}}(\overline{u}, \overline{v}) \end{bmatrix} \quad (9)$$

and apply coordinated changes to $\Delta \mathbf{S}_{\mathbf{u}}$ and $\Delta \mathbf{S}_{\mathbf{v}}$.

If we wish to change the normal vector (and hence the tangent plane), we can do so by rotating the entire frame defined by $\mathbf{N}$, $\mathbf{S}_{\mathbf{u}}(\overline{u}, \overline{v})$ and $\mathbf{S}_{\mathbf{v}}(\overline{u}, \overline{v})$. Once a desired normal is obtained, both $\mathbf{S}_{\mathbf{u}}(\overline{u}, \overline{v})$ and $\mathbf{S}_{\mathbf{v}}(\overline{u}, \overline{v})$ can be further manipulated *within* the tangent plane for additional shaping freedom. When rotated about the normal vector, a twisting effect results without affecting tangency. In cases where one partial is to be manipulated while the other is fixed, another of the right hand side entries will become zero.

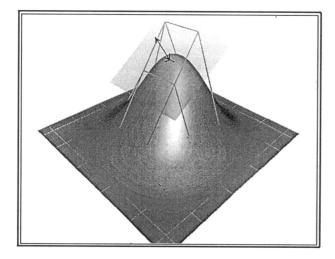

Figure 3: Normal orientation by rotating the frame about one of the coordinate axis.

Figures 3 through 5 illustrates three examples of tangent plane

orientation by rotation of the partial derivative frame. Adding an extra degree of freedom here incorporates nine control vertices, which distributes the effects well, but over a potentially significant area of the surface. Using bicubic B-splines, this results in 36 patches affected by the change. In cases where one or both partials do not change significantly, a degree of freedom can be dropped in one or both directions reducing the area of effect without introducing any "unbalanced" effects.

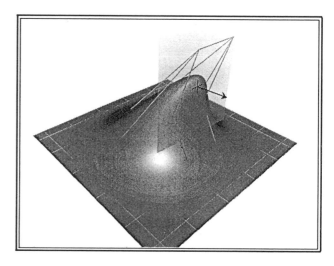

Figure 4: Alignment of the tangent plane with a vertical plane.

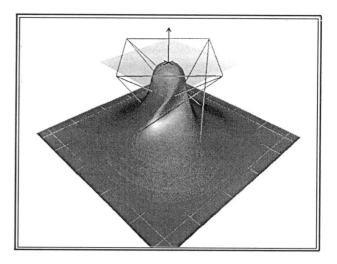

Figure 5: The "twisting" effect produced by rotation of the partial derivative frame about the normal.

3.3 Tension

In the case of curves, changing the magnitude of the first derivative produced a "tension-like" effect (a marked change in curvature) similar to that produced by changing the tension parameter of β-splines or the weights of a rational curve. An analogous effect can be created by changing the magnitudes of the partial derivatives at a point on a surface. We apply two styles of this tension-like effect while preserving the orientation of the tangent plane. Both styles involve changes to (in general) both partial derivatives, thus we use the same set of differential constraints in (9).

We refer to *uniform tension* as the effect created by scaling both partial derivatives uniformly. Figures 6 and 7 illustrate uniform tension applied while preserving position and tangent plane.

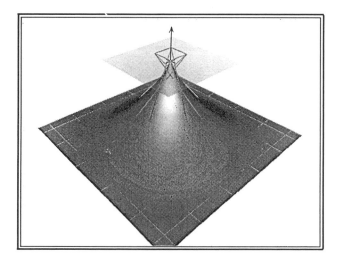

Figure 6: Uniform tension applied to the example in Figure 2. Magnitudes of the partial derivatives are decreased.

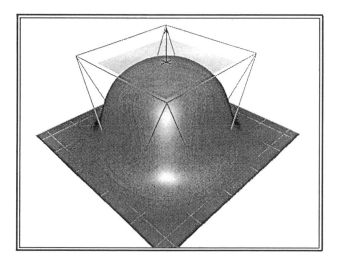

Figure 7: Uniform tension applied to the example in Figure 2. Magnitudes of the partial derivatives are increased.

We could also scale the partial derivatives individually, but this restricts us to two directions of effect – directions which are parametrically dependent. Instead, we allow application of tension in a user-specified direction in the tangent plane, hence the term *directional tension*. This directional tension is achieved by defining an axis in the tangent plane (through the origin) and scaling the perpendicular components of the partial derivatives relative to this axis. Figures 8 and 9 give two examples of directional tension applied along varying axes oblique to the partial derivatives.

We apply directional tension by mapping the tangent plane to the XY-plane and aligning the axis of interest with the X-axis. We then apply the resulting transformation to the partial derivatives, scale

their resulting Y component, then apply the inverse transformation. This works well for the vast majority of cases. When extreme directional tension is applied in one direction and then a second direction is chosen, the effect of the second deformation is sometimes not as marked as expected. This can often be remedied by undoing the effects of the previous deformation by rotating the partials so that they "straddle" the deformation axis prior to performing the scaling transformation.

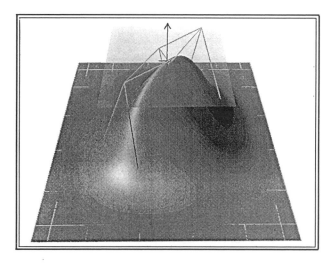

Figure 8: Directional tension applied to example in Figure 7 along a parametrically independent axis.

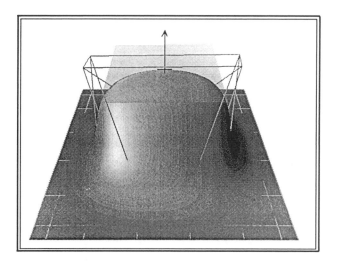

Figure 9: Directional tension applied in the direction of one of the partial derivatives.

3.4 Other Parametric Constraints

There are other sets of differential constraints that may be of interest, but that we choose not to include as geometric constraints, as their effect on the surface in not necessarily geometrically intuitive. We include them here as they may be useful in certain applications.

3.4.1 Direction Vectors

Although useful for curves, we have not found manipulation of a single partial derivative at $(\overline{u}, \overline{v})$ particularly useful for surfaces. For curves the first derivative has a close association to the unit tangent, so the parametric and geometric properties are closely linked. For surfaces, the directions of parametric derivatives have a lesser significance when considering the entire surface about a particular point.

A partial derivative may be set simply by applying the required change to the existing derivative. For example, in order to alter the tangency of the curve through $(\overline{u}, \overline{v})$ traveling in the u or v direction, systems of the form

$$\left[\begin{array}{c} \mathbf{B}_0(\overline{u}) \\ \mathbf{B}_u(\overline{u}) \end{array} \right] \Delta \mathbf{V} \left[\begin{array}{c} \mathbf{B}_0(\overline{v}) \end{array} \right]^T = \left[\begin{array}{c} 0 \\ \Delta \mathbf{S}_u(\overline{u}, \overline{v}) \end{array} \right]$$

$$\left[\begin{array}{c} \mathbf{B}_0(\overline{u}) \end{array} \right] \Delta \mathbf{V} \left[\begin{array}{c} \mathbf{B}_0(\overline{v}) \\ \mathbf{B}_v(\overline{v}) \end{array} \right]^T = \left[\begin{array}{cc} 0 & \Delta \mathbf{S}_u(\overline{u}, \overline{v}) \end{array} \right]$$

should be solved. If we incorporate the second derivative in the same parametric direction, we can control curvature in that direction, as described in [10].

3.4.2 The "Twist" Vector

The mixed partial, $\mathbf{S}_{uv}(u, v)$, is often referred to as the "twist" vector and has a long history in the construction of composite surfaces [8]. If desired, the twist vector can be manipulated while the normal to the surface is left free to vary using the following:

$$\left[\begin{array}{c} \mathbf{B}_0(\overline{u}, \overline{v}) \\ \mathbf{B}_{uv}(\overline{u}, \overline{v}) \end{array} \right] \Delta \mathbf{V}^T = \left[\begin{array}{c} 0 \\ \Delta \mathbf{S}_{uv}(\overline{u}, \overline{v}) \end{array} \right].$$

The twist vector may also provide an added shaping handle while the tangent plane is fixed at a point. This is achieved by augmenting (9) with a differential constraint for the twist vector (which then permits us to use the more efficient matrix solution) while setting the change to the other partials to zero:

$$\left[\begin{array}{c} \mathbf{B}_0(\overline{u}) \\ \mathbf{B}_u(\overline{u}) \end{array} \right] \Delta \mathbf{V} \left[\begin{array}{c} \mathbf{B}_0(\overline{v}) \\ \mathbf{B}_v(\overline{v}) \end{array} \right]^T = \left[\begin{array}{cc} 0 & 0 \\ 0 & \Delta \mathbf{S}_{uv}(\overline{u}, \overline{v}) \end{array} \right]$$

The twist vector can then be arbitrarily rotated or scaled to adjust the surface. The partials may also be manipulated within the tangent plane while changing the twist vector. We have not yet found any geometrically intuitive methods for controlling the twist vector at this point.

4 Interactive Issues

Now that we can express geometric properties in terms of differential constraints, we require visual and interactive mechanisms to present and manipulate these properties. This section describes numerous methods that we have tried with varying levels of success. This work is still in progress (particularly three-dimensional input) and we will no doubt come across more possibilities.

One aspect that needs to be addressed before discussing input devices is the visual representation of the surface. Our favoured display representation is a shaded tesselated surface. Unfortunately, few machines are capable of displaying complex shaded surfaces at interactive rates. For such machines a wireframe rendering is usually all that can be supported at such a rate. Aside from resolving the ambiguity present in wireframe models, a shaded representation gives a visual representation of the surface over the entire parametric range. This is in contrast to renderings of isoparametric curves where the gaps present in the display make selection awkward. The combination of direct manipulation methods with an interactive shaded display has been extremely effective.

4.1 Two-dimensional Input

Two-dimensional input devices will generally be less expensive to manufacture than their three-dimensional counterparts. As a result, we must consider reasonable methods of controlling surface geometry with the ever-present mouse if our techniques are to be usable on conventional workstations and personal computers. There are a variety of effective two-dimensional input methods and interactive techniques that are useful, notably [2] and [4]. Our first application of geometric constraints was naturally tested and debugged using a simple mouse for input.

Our first issue to be resolved was that of selecting the point on the surface. What was originally intended as a "quick hack" to get something working for demonstration purposes has turned out to be much more useful than expected. This method was to select the parametric point on the surface by mapping screen space to the parametric domain of the surface. As the user moves the mouse on the screen, while pressing a particular mouse button, a position marker is moved across the surface. This guarantees that a valid parametric point is always available. When just the position marker for the point was displayed, this method was not visually interesting and the presence of poor mapping when the orientation of the object changed was prevalent. However, once we displayed the normal vector and tangent plane (either a wire-frame mesh or a transparent polygon), this method turned into a useful evaluation tool. The undulating tangent plane gave a good feel for the curvature of the surface, and sometimes barely visible changes were made obvious. Prior awkwardness felt in the absence of the tangent plane was tolerated and virtually ignored as the visual feedback became much more valuable.

In order to experiment with the effects of applying the numerous systems of differential constraints described, a series of interaction panels were created, each with a variety of buttons, valuators and positioners. These were created for us to explore the various constraint systems described, rather than as intuitive tools for a designer. Since our primary interest is in three-dimensional input, we did not go to great effort to pursuing any radical new methods, but this experimentation did give us the opportunity to compare a few ideas.

Functionality was grouped into four panels that controlled position, normal orientation, partial derivative manipulation in the tangent plane, and the twist vector. Much of the functionality of these panels involved simple scaling and rotation of vectors, which could be performed in numerous ways. Separate sliders for rotation about the three coordinate axes proved awkward (as expected) for arbitrary vector orientation. A separate 2D positioner for azimuth and inclination was more successful when the extremities of the panel were avoided. Chen et al's "virtual sphere" [4] provided a much more intuitive feel than both.

The position panel contained several functions. Displacement could be applied along any of the coordinate axes, along the normal or partial derivative vectors, or along a vector whose direction could be set arbitrarily. The tangent plane could also be either fixed or free to vary during the displacement. The normal and twist orientation panels provided simple orientation of their representative vector. The panel of most interest to us was that which provided control of the partial derivatives in the current tangent plane, and hence controlled uniform and directional tension. This panel is illustrated in Figure 10.· Again, although it is not suggested as tool for a designer, it did provided us with flexible control of the parameters at our disposal.

A more intuitive panel for tension control was designed to presents a projection of the tangent plane onto a small window, along with a few additional controls, as illustrated in Figure 11. The window contains a vector for the application of directional tension along its orthogonal counterpart. These vectors may be selected

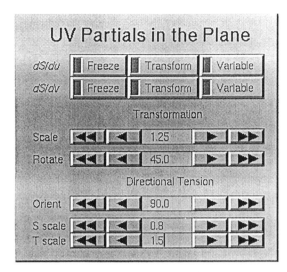

Figure 10: Illustration of a panel used to experiment with manipulation of the partial derivatives in the tangent plane – *not* suggested as geometrically intuitive.

and scaled individually, or coupled to apply uniform tension. They may also be rotated in two modes: one which simply re-orients the axes for directional tension, another which actually results in the rotation of the partial derivatives to achieve the twisting effect previously described. The vectors are simultaneously displayed with the tangent plane on the three-dimensional view of the surface. When

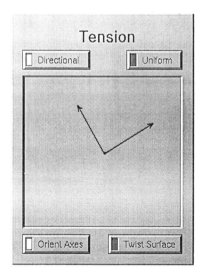

Figure 11: A more useful panel to control tension and twist.

selecting a vector with the left mouse button, subsequent movement of the mouse was used to apply tension (set to either directional or uniform). The scale factor was measured proportional to the distance of the mouse to the centre of the window. Similarly, selection and movement with the right mouse button would applied rotation (set to either orient the axes or actually twist the surface) to these axes. We will soon be using this window to actually view the surface beneath the tangent plane as these operations are performed.

4.2 Spatial Input

Devices offering spatial input have been available for years now, but have failed to become widely accepted. This may be due to a combination of both high cost and poor utilization of the technology.

One such device, the Polhemus 3Space IsoTrak, is "a full six deggree-of-freedom" device, providing information on both position and orientation. The IsoTrak is a magnetic field device consisting of a fixed "source" and a movable "sensor." The sensor has a working volume consisting of a 30 inch hemisphere. Accuracy degrades significantly outside this range, or in the presence of other magnetic devices, e.g. workstation monitors.

A three-dimensional locator allows the space in which a surface is defined to be mapped into the space about the user's hand. The IsoTrak can be hand-held, is also available as part of a digitizing stylus, and also may be mounted on the back of a VPL DataGlove. This can permit a designer to move a 3D cursor freely in space and thus approach the surface from either side. An obvious method for selecting a point on the surface is to detect intersection of the cursor with the surface. We have not yet implemented such selection, and still rely on selection by the surface scanning method previously described. Rather than use the mouse, though, we use the IsoTrak as a 2D device, i.e. a tablet, and map the table top of the user's work space to the parametric domain of the surface. The height and orientation data is ignored. Since there is no button of any kind on the IsoTrak, any character on the keyboard is used to indicate selection.

Once selected, the position of the surface is naturally displaced by mapping the coordinate system of the IsoTrak to correspond with the current view (or a selected view, if more than one are present) of the surface (thus left-to-right movement of the hand corresponds to left-to-right displacement of the surface). The change to the orientation vector maps naturally to a change in normal vector. Note that if the user intends to displace the surface downward in the current view, selection must be done while the hand is at a sufficient height above the table top to allow specification of the desired displacement. The user's work space may also be mapped to the local coordinate system of a desired surface if desired. The advantage here is that the changes are relative to the surface. The IsoTrak can thus be laid to rest on a table top, oriented at an angle that allows most comfortable application of the desired change.

We control the twisting of the partial derivatives about the tangent plane is controlled by simply rotating the IsoTrak while maintaining its "up-vector." We do not provide any control of tension in this "mode" of operation as yet.

This relative method has proven to be much easier than maintaining absolute position and orientation at the selected point, as originally attempted. The freedom to rest and rotate the hand comfortably is much preferable to reaching out into space with the hand at awkward angles. Due to the limited accuracy of the IsoTrak, it is best to map only a local area about the point of deformation into the sensor's work space so that noise does not cause large unexpected perturbations of the surface.

4.3 A "Virtual Hand"

Our primary goal is to develop a direct manipulation sculpting environment utilizing three-dimensional display and a pair of "virtual hands." We are currently using one of a pair of VPL Data-Gloves with our direct surface manipulation methods. Each Data-Glove consists of a thin glove mounted with a 3Space IsoTrak and a set of optical fibers (referred to as flex sensors) measuring two joint angles for each finger and the thumb. The angles of abduction between the fingers (and the thumb) are not measured by the DataGlove.

Although the Datagloves are still a long way from providing the full flexibility of the human hand, the joint sensors have provided us with additional shaping methods to those described for the Iso-Trak. The vast majority of work with these gloves, including [13], is through the use of gestures. We prefer to use the right hand purely as a shaping tool – free of the burden of making gestures – and use the keyboard (eventually gestures from a glove on the left hand) to initiate and terminate actions. Voice recognition, as used in [13], would be even more preferable mechanism, freeing both hands for shaping.

Since the DataGlove is mounted with an IsoTrak, we inherit the functionality described in Section 4.2. What we lacked with the IsoTrak was a means of applying uniform and directional tension. We can employ the flex sensors of the DataGlove for this purpose. We use the flex sensors of the four fingers to apply tension along one axis, and the flex sensors of the thumb to apply tension along the orthogonal axis. A clenching of the fist flexes all joints simultaneously and thus results in the application of (approximate) uniform tension. We eliminate the twisting of the surface about the normal, and instead use that degree of freedom from the IsoTrak to alter these axes of directional tension. In practice, the thumb is rarely used independently of the fingers – it seems more natural to rotate the hand to re-orient the required axis along the fingers.

Currently the values of the joint angles involved are simply averaged to determine the scale factors to be applied. This helps to smooth out some of the noise present in the flex sensors, which at times can be extreme.. The inner sensors control a greater rate of "squeezing" while we attempt to gain finer control from the flex sensors of the outer joints, although the noise and non-linearity of these sensors makes this difficult to achieve.

The keyboard must currently be used to control modes of operation. When the hand is fully clenched and more tension is desired, a "clutch" must be used to release the hand from the surface so that it can be reclenched to apply further tension. We suggest that the hand be loosely clenched when selection takes place so that tension can be both increased and decreased by moderate amounts.

This technique at times shows great promise, but at other times poor calibration of the glove and the instability of the flex sensors make it difficult to gain fine control of the tension. We feel that the approach is sound and that given a more accurate and stable device will be very useful. Noise is present in both the IsoTrak and the flex sensors of the DataGlove. The noise in the flex sensors makes accurate "moulding" virtually impossible

5 Future Work

The current direct manipulation B-spline modeler runs on an SGI IRIS 4D340/VGX. We are capable of direct surface manipulation with shaded display at reasonable interactive rates (i.e. several frames per second). Surface position and tangency can be manipulated using a mouse, Polhemus 3Space IsoTrak, or VPL DataGlove, as described.

A couple of caveats may become apparent in our description of the direct manipulations. These manipulations are local in nature, relying on the support of the basis functions to determine their area of effect. As a result, one of our geometric manipulations applied in a highly refined region will have little effect. They are currently only of use for local deformations. Since our goal is to rid the designers of dependencies upon the underlying representation, such direct manipulations must be applicable over a user-defined area. We are currently implementing a method to provide this *regional control*.

Another problem is the asymmetry that can result when the knot spacing is highly non-uniform. Once a mechanism is in place for applying direct manipulation over arbitrary regions, we can add additional knots to balance out the parametric spacing, then deal with the added knots in a well-behaved manner. As part of our regional control scheme, we are extending the work of Forsey and Bartels [9] to avoid insertion of entire knot lines that can lead to data explosion.

With direct manipulation and regional control, we will have gone a long way in reducing the basis-dependent attributes in the interaction with tensor product surfaces. We are also looking into extending our list of geometric constraints to provide intuitive control of surface curvature. We will continue to pursue interactive schemes for "virtual hands," particularly as devices more sophisticated than the DataGlove become available.

References

[1] Richard H. Bartels and John C. Beatty. A Technique for the Direct Manipulation of Spline Curves. In Graphics Interface '89, pages 33–39, London, Ontario, 1989. Morgan Kaufmann Publishers, Palo Alto, California.

[2] Eric A. Bier. Snap Dragging: Interactive Geometric Design in Two and Three Dimensions. Technical Report EDL-89-2, Palo Alto Research Center, Xerox Corporation, Palo Alto, California, September 1989.

[3] George Celniker and Dave Gossard. Deformable Curve and Surface Finite-Elements for Free-form Shape Design. Computer Graphics [SIGGRAPH '91 Conference Proceedings], 25(4):257–266, 1991.

[4] Michael Chen, S. Joy Mountford, and Abigail Sellen. A Study in Interactive 3-D Rotation Using 2-D Control Devices. Computer Graphics [SIGGRAPH '88 Conference Proceedings], 22(4):121–129, 1988.

[5] J. H. Clark. Designing Surfaces in 3D. *Communications of the ACM*, 19(8):454–460, 1976.

[6] Elizabeth S. Cobb. *Design of Sculptured Surfaces using the B-Spline Representation*. PhD thesis, Department of Computer Science, University of Utah, Salt Lake City, Utah, 1984.

[7] Sabine Coquillart. Extended Free-Form Deformation: A Sculpturing Tool for 3D Geometric Modeling. Computer Graphics [SIGGRAPH '90 Conference Proceedings], 24(4):187–196, 1990.

[8] Gerald Farin. *Curves and Surfaces for Computer Aided Geometric Design*. Academic Press, San Diego, California, second edition, 1990.

[9] David R. Forsey and Richard H. Bartels. Hierarchical B-Spline Refinement. Computer Graphics [SIGGRAPH '88 Conference Proceedings], 22(4):205–212, 1988.

[10] Barry Fowler and Richard Bartels. Constraint Based Curve Manipulation. *IEEE Computer Graphics and Applications*, 1992. Submitted for publication.

[11] Charles Loop and Tony DeRose. Generalized B-spline Surfaces of Arbitrary Topology. Computer Graphics [SIGGRAPH '90 Conference Proceedings], 24(4):347–356, 1990.

[12] Thomas W. Sederberg and Scott R. Parry. Free-form Deformation of Solid Geometric Models. Computer Graphics [SIGGRAPH '86 Conference Proceedings], 20(4):151–160, 1986.

[13] David Weimer and S. K. Ganapathy. A Synthetic Visual Environment with Hand Gesturing and Voice Input. SIGCHI Bulletin [Human Factors in Computing Systems – CHI '89 Conference Proceedings], pages 235–240, 1989.

[14] William Welch, Andrew Gleicher, and Andrew Witkin. Manipulating Surfaces Differentially. *Proceedings, Compugraphics '91*, September 1991. Also available from Carnegie Mellon University as Technical Report CMU-CS-91-175.

COMPUTER INTERACTIVE SCULPTURE

Supercomputing Research Center

CENTRAL PURPOSE

As a sculptor I want to experience and avail to others vital compelling forms. I desire access to quantitative measured forms as well as qualitative expression. Computers offer powerful tool possibilities. Other sculptors find this so, cf., [4, 9, 14]. It is not enough for me to make models of mathematical equations or CAD structures, although the capability to do that is sometimes important. I invest my sculpture with a wide range of knowledge. My sculpture process tends to involve direct carving or cutting away of material. It is more fashionable in sculpture today to do constructions or addition. I prefer the more interesting and difficult subtraction processes. While I make aesthetic artifacts, many of our functional artifacts are made by industrial cutting processes that are relevant to me.

As a research mathematician I have had the good fortune to discover mathematics as a design language for sculpture, cf., [3, 15]. My use of this design language folds naturally into our current computer technology. Mathematics is an invisible art form of profound social and scientific significance. Computer graphics makes mathematics visible, I take the next step.

In this paper I discuss two of my successful sculptural forms, *Umbilic Torus NC* and *Umbilic Torus NIST*. I have done a series of each using two different kinds of computer interaction. These and my related sculptures are in permanent collections, e.g., [10, 11, 12, 13] and have been exhibited widely, e.g., [6, 7, 8].

E-mail: helamanf@super.org
Typeset by $\mathcal{A}_{\mathcal{M}}\mathcal{S}$-TEX

MATHEMATICAL DESIGN

I begin by plunging directly into the design considerations for *Umbilic Torus NC* and *Umbilic Torus NIST*. This looks like raw mathematics but it is not in the usual sense because my motivations in writing it down are sculptural, cf., [3, 5]. The setting is the stratification of the space $\mathbf{R}^4$ of real coefficients of binary cubic forms by the action of the general linear group. Stratification means the orbits and the relationship among them. The correspondence between the points in $\mathbf{R}^4$ and the cubic forms is given by

$$(a, b, c, d) \in \mathbf{R}^4 \leftrightarrow f = ax^3 + bx^2y + cxy^2 + dy^3$$

The general real linear group $G = GL(2, \mathbf{R})$ consists of the real invertible 2×2 matrices, $\begin{pmatrix} \alpha & \beta \\ \gamma & \delta \end{pmatrix}$, where the condition of invertibility of this matrix is that the determinant $\alpha\delta - \beta\gamma$ be non-zero. These matrices will be regarded as acting on the two variable vector (x, y) as a column vector by left matrix multiplication The group action is defined by the mapping

$$\begin{pmatrix} \alpha & \beta \\ \gamma & \delta \end{pmatrix} : \begin{pmatrix} x \\ y \end{pmatrix} \rightarrow \begin{pmatrix} \alpha & \beta \\ \gamma & \delta \end{pmatrix} \begin{pmatrix} x \\ y \end{pmatrix},$$

or

$$\begin{pmatrix} x \\ y \end{pmatrix} \mapsto \begin{pmatrix} \alpha x + \beta y \\ \gamma x + \delta y \end{pmatrix}$$

This in turn gives an action on cubic forms by substituting these images in the cubic form and multiplying out. Thus the form $ax^3 + bx^2y + cxy^2 + dy^3$ becomes

$$(a\alpha^3 + \alpha^2 b\gamma + \alpha c\gamma^2 + d\gamma^3)x^3 +$$

$$(3a\alpha^2\beta + \alpha^2 b\delta + 2\alpha b\beta\gamma + 2\alpha c\delta\gamma + \beta c\gamma^2 + 3d\delta\gamma^2)x^2y +$$

$$(3a\alpha\beta^2 + 2\alpha b\beta\delta + \alpha c\delta^2 + b\beta^2\gamma + 2\beta c\delta\gamma + 3d\delta^2\gamma)xy^2 +$$

$$(a\beta^3 + b\beta^2\delta + \beta c\delta^2 + d\delta^3)y^3.$$

These four coefficients are linear in the four original coefficients a, b, c, d and define a 4×4 matrix

$$\begin{pmatrix} \alpha^3 & \alpha^2\gamma & \alpha\gamma^2 & \gamma^3 \\ 3\alpha^2\beta & \alpha^2\delta + 2\alpha\beta\gamma & 2\alpha\delta\gamma + \beta\gamma^2 & 3\delta\gamma^2 \\ 3\alpha\beta^2 & 2\alpha\beta\delta + \beta^2\gamma & \alpha\delta^2 + 2\beta\delta\gamma & 3\delta^2\gamma \\ \beta^3 & \beta^2\delta & \beta\delta^2 & \delta^3 \end{pmatrix}.$$

This matrix has the determinant $(\alpha\delta - \beta\gamma)^6$ which is the sixth power of the determinant of the original real invertible 2×2 matrix. This new 4×4 matrix is invertible if and only if the original matrix it is representing is invertible. This 4×4 matrix is an important example of a *group representation*.

The cubic $ax^3 + bx^2y + cxy^2 + dy^3$ can be completely factored over the complex numbers $\mathbf{C}$,

$$ax^3 + bx^2y + cxy^2 + dy^3 =$$

$$(r_1x + s_1y)(r_2x + s_2y)(r_3x + s_3y),$$

for $r_1, s_1, r_2, s_2, r_3, s_3 \in \mathbf{C}$. This gives three ratios or lines given by the pairs $r_j, s_j, j = 1, 2, 3$. We can think of them as lines because non-zero scaling of the form corresponds to non-zero scaling of the pairs. The ratios correspond to roots of the cubic and can be classified into five types: hyperbolic umbilics, two complex, one real root, e.g., $x^3 + y^3$; elliptic umbilics, three real distinct roots, e.g., $x^3 - 3xy^2$; parabolic umbilics, three real, two equal roots, e.g., x^2y; exceptionals, three real equal roots, e.g., x^3, and the origin. These root types correspond to orbits of the group of dimensions $4, 4, 3, 2, 0$ respectively.

The discriminant of the cubic is an invariant under the linear changes of variable we have been considering. The cubic discriminant is

$$\left(-\left(b^2c^2\right) + 4ac^3 + 4b^3d - 18abcd + 27a^2d^2\right).$$

The parabolic umbilics are those (a, b, c, d) such that

$$-\left(b^2c^2\right) + 4ac^3 + 4b^3d - 18abcd + 27a^2d^2 = 0.$$

The 'hyperbolic umbilics at infinity' and 'elliptic umbilics at infinity' are those (a, b, c, d) such that

$$-\left(b^2c^2\right) + 4ac^3 + 4b^3d - 18abcd + 27a^2d^2 < 0$$

$$-\left(b^2c^2\right) + 4ac^3 + 4b^3d - 18abcd + 27a^2d^2 > 0$$

respectively. The root types and orbits amount to the same things. The discriminant is homogeneous in the four variables so it suffices to look at orbits of forms represented by points on the 3-sphere,

$$\{[a, b, c, d] \mid a^2 + b^2 + c^2 + d^2 = 1\}.$$

This reduces the dimensions above to $3, 3, 2, 1$, ignoring the origin. The situation is now in a sculpture appropriate space.

In the complex number representation for the real cubic forms; the four real coefficients can be replaced by two complex numbers. Consider the real part of the complex cubic form

$$\Re\left(uz^3 + vz^2z^*\right),$$

where $z = x + y\mathbf{i}$, the complex conjugate $z^* = x - y\mathbf{i}$, and $u = u_1 + u_2\mathbf{i}$, $v = v_1 + v_2\mathbf{i}$. The linear transformation relating the a, b, c, d and the u, v coefficient sets

$$\begin{pmatrix} a \\ b \\ c \\ d \end{pmatrix} = \begin{pmatrix} 1 & 0 & 1 & 0 \\ 0 & -3 & 0 & -1 \\ -3 & 0 & 1 & 0 \\ 0 & 1 & 0 & -1 \end{pmatrix} \cdot \begin{pmatrix} u_1 \\ u_2 \\ v_1 \\ v_2 \end{pmatrix}$$

has determinant 16 and inverse

$$\frac{1}{4} \cdot \begin{pmatrix} 1 & 0 & -1 & 0 \\ 0 & -1 & 0 & 1 \\ 3 & 0 & 1 & 0 \\ 0 & -1 & 0 & -3 \end{pmatrix}.$$

There are two interesting planes of forms here, $u = 0$ or the v−plane or the $\Re(vz^2z^*)$ form and $v = 0$ or the u−plane or the $\Re(uz^3)$ form. They are interesting because the group $\mathbf{C}^\times$ contains the rotations $e^{\mathbf{i}\theta}$ which acts on each of these forms and corresponding planes in a simple way. At least it looks simple when written as complex multiplication instead of matrix multiplication. Here is the action of this circle group on the form as it acts by complex number multiplication

$$e^{\mathbf{i}\theta} : z \mapsto e^{\mathbf{i}\theta}z,$$

to give

$$e^{\mathbf{i}\theta} : \Re\left(uz^3 + vz^2z^*\right) \mapsto$$

$$\Re\left(ue^{3\mathbf{i}\theta}z^3 + ve^{\mathbf{i}\theta}z^2z^*\right).$$

Geometrically this means

$$(u, v) \mapsto (ue^{3\mathbf{i}\theta}, ve^{\mathbf{i}\theta}),$$

or that u gets rotated thrice whilst v is rotated once. We will use this observation below twice.

Consider the plane $u = 1$, the unit translate of the v−plane, or the real cubic forms $\Re\left(z^3 + vz^2z^*\right)$. The question is how does the discriminant variety intersect this plane or these forms. The discriminant variety consists of those forms having double roots at least. For which v's will there be double roots? Since $\Re\left(z^3 + vz^2z^*\right)$ is homogeneous in z and $z = 0$ is accounted for, we may suppose that the roots have absolute value one, $|z| = 1$, or that $z = e^{\mathbf{i}\theta}$. In this case

$$\Re\left(z^3 + vz^2z^*\right) =$$

$$\frac{1}{2}\left(e^{3i\theta} + e^{-3i\theta} + v\left(e^{i\theta} + e^{-i\theta}\right)\right).$$

For what v's does this form have a double root and hence be on the discriminant variety? This is the same form after multiplying by $e^{i\theta}$ to get

$$\frac{1}{2}\left(e^{4i\theta} + e^{-2i\theta} + v\left(e^{2i\theta} + 1\right)\right).$$

The derivative of this form is supposed to vanish since we want v's giving a double root, so, after solving for v, we have

$$v = -2e^{2i\theta} + e^{-4i\theta}.$$

A more recognizable version of this equation is had by rewriting the variable $\theta = \frac{1}{2}(\phi - \pi)$,

$$v = 2e^{i\phi} - e^{-2i\phi}, 0 \le \phi < 2\pi.$$

This is the locus of a point on a circle of radius 1 rolling inside a circle of radius 3, otherwise known as a hypocycloid of three cusps. This includes the case of all three roots of the cubic form being identical. In this case the second derivative of the form vanishes,

$$\frac{dv}{d\phi} = 2ie^{i\phi} - 2ie^{-2i\phi},$$

which when set equal to zero gives

$$e^{3i\phi} = 1 = e^{2i\pi k}$$

and

$$v = 3e^{\frac{2i\pi k}{3}}, k \in \mathbf{Z},$$

which latter is the set of the three cube roots of unity scaled by three.

These scaled cube roots of unity are cusps of the curve because a tangent line is defined there as everywhere else on the curve, but there is no tangent circle defined there but is everywhere else.

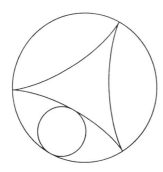

FIGURE 1. Hypocycloid of Three Cusps

Cycloids in general are defined in terms of a circle of radius B rolling without slippage inside or outside a circle of radius A. The equation in complex variable form is

$$z = (A + B)e^{iB\varphi} - Be^{i(A+B)\varphi},$$

where $B > 0$ gives an epicycloid (the smaller circle rolling outside the larger circle) and $B < 0$ gives a hypocycloid (the smaller circle rolling inside the larger circle). If $B = 0$ we just get the point $z = 0$. If $(A, B) = (3, -1)$ we get the hypocycloid of three cusps above. If $(A, B) = (1, 1)$ we get the cardioid which we shall see below.

We have chosen to look at those of the form $\Re\left(z^3 + vz^2z^*\right)$. This says that the form $(u, v) = (1, 0)$ or $(a, b, c, d) = (1, 0, -3, 0)$ is included which has negative discriminant -108 and the form has three distinct real roots and is therefore an elliptic umbilic. The hypocycloid we have discovered lies in the plane given by $u = 1$ or the $v-$plane. This plane gets moved by the unit circle group. Recall the u thrice while v once. Otherwise said, one third rotation of v while u rotates once. This means that the hypocycloid rotates one cusp over while $u = 1$ moves to $u = e^{2i\pi}$. The hypocycloid has three fold symmetry, so the resulting surface closes. We are looking at this torus with a hypocycloid cross-section from the point of view of the $(e^{2i\phi}, v)$ geometry. This torus does indeed present us with a picture of the parabolic umbilic surface, but keep in mind that we are looking at this singular set from a chosen perspective, one where the elliptic umbilic point $(u, v) = (1, 0)$ and all other elliptic umbilic points are inside the bounded part of the hypocycloid; the hyperbolic umbilic points are are all outside the hypocycloid and this is the unbounded part of the space.

Could we choose instead of $(u, v) = (1, 0)$ the case of $(u, v) = (0, 1)$? This gives us the forms in the plane $v = 1$, the unit translate of the $u-$plane, or the real cubic forms $\Re\left(uz^3 + z^2z^*\right)$. The question is how does the discriminant variety intersect this plane or these forms. The discriminant variety consists of those forms having double roots at least. For which u's will there be double roots? Since $\Re\left(uz^3 + z^2z^*\right)$ is homogeneous in z and $z = 0$ is accounted for, we may suppose that the roots have absolute value one, $|z| = 1$, or that $z = e^{i\theta}$. In this case

$$\Re\left(uz^3 + z^2z^*\right) =$$

$$\frac{1}{2}\left(u\left(e^{3i\theta} + e^{-3i\theta}\right) + e^{i\theta} + e^{-i\theta}\right).$$

For what u's does this form have a double root and hence be on the discriminant variety? This is the same form after multiplying by $e^{3i\theta}$ to get

$$\frac{1}{2}\left(u\left(e^{6i\theta} + 1\right) + e^{4i\theta} + e^{2i\theta}\right).$$

111

The derivative of this form is supposed to vanish since we want u's giving a double root, so, after solving for u, we have

$$-3u = -2e^{-2i\theta} + e^{-4i\theta}.$$

To recognize this equation as a cycloid rewrite the variables $\theta = \frac{-\varphi}{2}$ and $u = -\frac{w}{3}$ to get

$$w = 2e^{i\varphi} + e^{2i\phi}, 0 \le \varphi < 2\pi.$$

This is the locus of a point on a circle of radius 1 rolling outside a circle of radius 1, otherwise known as an epicycloid of one cusp, or a cardioid. This includes the case of all three roots of the cubic form being identical. In this case the second derivative of the form vanishes,

$$\frac{dw}{d\varphi} = 2ie^{i\varphi} + 2ie^{-2i\varphi},$$

which when set equal to zero gives

$$e^{i\varphi} = -1 = e^{(2k+1)i\pi}$$

and

$$v = -\frac{1}{3}e^{(2k+1)i\pi},$$

for k in the integers $\mathbf{Z}$ and v is the single point $\frac{1}{3}$.

This scaled fraction point is a cusp of the curve because a tangent line is defined everywhere on the curve, and there is a tangent circle defined everywhere but at that point.

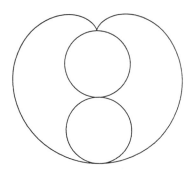

FIGURE 2. Epicycloid of One Cusp or a Cardioid

This time we have chosen to look at those of the form $\Re\left(uz^3 + z^2 z^*\right)$. This says that the form $(u,v) = (0,1)$ or $(a,b,c,d) = (1,0,1,0)$ is included which has positive discriminant 4 and the form has one real root and two distinct complex roots and is therefore a hyperbolic umbilic. The epicycloid we have discovered lies in the plane given by $v = 1$ or the u−plane. This plane also gets moved by the unit circle group. Recall the u thrice while v once. Otherwise said, one third rotation of v while u rotates once. This means that the epicycloid in the u−plane rotates once while $v = 1$ moves to

$v = e^{\frac{2i\pi}{3}}$. The epicycloid has bilateral symmetry, and this puts the epicycloid in the same position. Moving through the next two thirds puts the epicycloid back twice again to its original position. We are looking at this torus with a hypocycloid cross-section from the point of view of the $(u, e^{2i\varphi})$ geometry. This torus does indeed present us with a picture of the parabolic umbilic surface, but keep in mind that we are looking at this singular set from a chosen perspective, one where the hyperbolic umbilic point $(u,v) = (0,1)$ and all other hyperbolic umbilic points are inside the bounded part of the epicycloid; the elliptic umbilic points are all outside the epicycloid and they form the unbounded part of the space of forms.

I have summarized symbolically a collection of perhaps $10K$ years of some of the most important ideas in mathematics. Indeed, many of these ideas are foundation stones of contemporary computer graphics. I have reformulated them in a way to express them in three dimensional or physical materials. These are priceless ideas which I work into otherwise worthless stone or bronze.

NC: NUMERICAL CONTROL

The initials 'NC' represent 'numerically controlled' a phrase which originated in 1952 at the Servomechanisms Laboratory of MIT which was subcontracted by Parsons, Inc., who was commissioned by the U.S. Air Material Command to automate helicopter rotor blade manufacture. SL-MIT modified a Cincinnati Hydrotel milling machine to operate from binary punched tape. *Umbilic Torus NC* is more complex than the early rotor blades, but owes its existence to the continued development of this technology.

By 1988 when I was ready to do the *Umbilic Torus NC* at the Brigham Young University Robotics Laboratory, the largest machine available there was a Cartesian 3-axis Kearney & Trekker, VB-2. This machine could still read paper tape. Fortunately it was also interfaced with a PC. As it was we had to install an on board hard disc to accomodate all of the quill moves for the *Umbilic Torus NC*. The source of the data load arose from the fact that while the *Umbilic Torus NC* has spatial symmetry that symmetry is not particularly compatible with the Cartesian structure of the 3-axis machine.

The central problem in any NC application is tool path. The ball end mill approximates a sphere of positive radius and tool offsets had to be computed in advance whatever tool path was selected. Since the *Umbilic Torus NC* is a complex surface the normals to this surface at any point were computed symbolically and parametrically prior to computing the tool offsets.

For aesthetic and it turned out practical reasons, cf., [5], I selected the tool path for the *Umbilic Torus NC* to be a surface filling curve. The parametric single domain for the vector valued function defining the *Umbilic Tori* is essentially a square. It is not enough to define this domain square with inequalities. To machine the torus, points within the square domain have to be accessed in an ordered path. This ordered path is to be followed by a cutting tool. The surface filling curves offer effective ways of covering a single domain square and hence covering the image object.

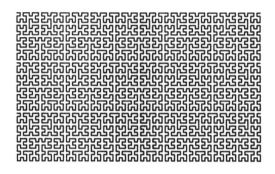

FIGURE 3. Hilbert Surface Filling Curve in the Domain of the *Umbilic Torus NC*

The Hilbert curve, which is a 2-adic version of Peano's suite of q-adic curves is defined (up to scale) recursively by the following set of ordered points. Begin with $H[0] = (0,0)$. Then for $n \geq 1$, define

$$H[n] = H[n-1] \cdot \begin{pmatrix} 0 & 1 \\ 1 & 0 \end{pmatrix}$$

$$\sqcup$$

$$(2^{n-1}, 0) + H[n-1]$$

$$\sqcup$$

$$(2^{n-1}, 2^{n-1}) + H[n-1]$$

$$\sqcup$$

$$(2^{n-1} - 1, 2^n - 1) - H[n-1] \cdot \begin{pmatrix} 0 & 1 \\ 1 & 0 \end{pmatrix}$$

where $\sqcup$ is an ordered union of the sets of points. The straight line segments which join the points in order become space curves on the *Umbilic Torus NC*. Further details can be found in [4, 5].

I encountered two difficulties with this NC technology: rigidity and scaling. The computer driven milling machine is essentially a mindless robot, the tool path and trajectory have to be specified in complete detail in advance. While it can do very well certain kinds of elegant, accurate, and reproducible work, it is very difficult to interrupt or reposition. After the programming is done you hope you like what you see. Once the general hardness, toughness, etc., of the material to be

FIGURE 4.   Hilbert Surface Filling Space Curve in the Image of the *Umbilic Torus NC*

cut is determined the material is not relevant and not a part of the process. As for scaling, how big can a robot be? Milling machines tend to be built around the space in which they do the cutting, they don't reach out anywhere. They are profoundly expensive to build and maintain. The capital cost of equipment like the VB-2 used for the *Umbilic Torus NC* was between $\frac{1}{8}M\$$ and $\frac{1}{4}M\$$. This gives a active cutting region of four or five cubic feet maximum at a capital cost of $25K\$$ per cubic foot.

The interactive aspect of NC milling of a three dimensional object is limited to the computer graphics previewing of the image, the tool path, the trajectory of the cutting apparatus.

VIP: VIRTUAL IMAGE PROJECTION

The concepts involved in the virtual image projection system were certainly motivated by the difficulties with rigidity and scaling described above. Addressing scaling, the active cutting region has increased to twenty seven cubic feet at a capital cost of $0.37K\$$ per cubic foot. While there are sacrifices in accuracy in the present system, they are not there in principle [1].

The virtual image projection system offers the possibility of human interaction in a positive way. Software for selection of tool trajectories is difficult to develop and is not available in generality. Yet the relative positioning involved in global tool trajectory selection is something humans are well equipped to do. Humans are less well equipped to do absolute quantitative positioning.

A virtual image projection system strengthens the latter and allows a wide range of interactive choices of when and where to approach the desired image. The software makes it very easy to reposition the virtual image after relocating the material. Also, the system is independent of any particular tool, so that a variety of tools can be used to address the material. This allows a sensitivity to the material which is important for direct carving in natural stone. The process can be interrupted, new images superimposed, and 'quoted' in rescaled form.

FIGURE 5. A bronze *Umbilic Torus NC* sitting on an enlarged Carrara marble quotation of a fragment of itself. Note the Hilbert curve articulation in the marble

The idea of the virtual image projector is simple yet powerful: Invert a 3D digitizer. The computer is used as a kind of oracle. Inquiries are made about the location of the desired image which can be thought of as present in the material. Specifically, give the computer the software capability of calculating the nearest distance from a point on the uncut material to the image. We will refer to the uncut material as 'the block' since the system has been used primarily for quantitatively carving stone.

On the ceiling of my studio is a fixed triangle with a string potentiometer at each vertex. Three steel cables under tension meet at a 'point' plectrum and can be pulled down to touch the block. The potentiometer outputs are digitized and the information interfaced with a Mac II. A foot mouse (rat) is used to click the points into the Mac II.

FIGURE 6. SP 1, the ceiling triangle with string potentiometers at the end points. The operator's finger can be seen in the plectrum forming a vertex of a tetrahedron under tension

Three general position registration points are selected on the block. These three points are labelled in some specific order. Three distinct labelled points in general position on a block suffice to determine the position and location of the block before and after a rigid motion. If the block is moved then the three points are touched with the plectrum and clicked into the Mac II.

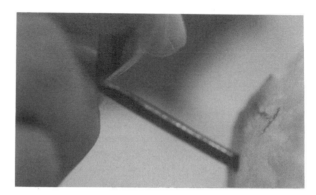

FIGURE 7. Note the operator's finger in the plectrum forming a vertex of a tetrahedron under tension and touching the registration point labelled **1**

The three general position registration points in order can be thought of as rows of a 3×3 invertible matrix. The position and orientation of the block is implicit in this matrix. For example, think of the general decomposition of the $n \times n$ invertible matrices

$$GL(n, \mathbf{R}) = \Delta(n) \times D(n) \times SO(n)$$

into lower triangular unipotent, diagonal, and orthogonal matrices, e.g., Gram-Schmidt orthogonalization. In the case of $n = 3$, $\dim \Delta(n) = 3$ and $\dim SO(n) = 3$ where the semi-direct product $\Delta(n) \rtimes SO(n)$ corresponds to the group of rigid motions. There is software for relocating the three registration points on the block as well as for realigning the virtual image with the new block position.

FIGURE 8. The block face with holes drilled to the millimeter depths indicated

The virtual image in this application is resident in the Mac II in the form of parametric equations. In indication of how these parametric equations were designed is in the mathematical design paragraph above. Finding the right parametric equations to do specific things is non-trivial. The parametric equation set could be replaced by a previously digitized data set, systems of splines, nerbs, etc. The software includes an algorithm which calculates from any given point in space the nearest distance from that point to the virtual image.

FIGURE 9. One side of the block has been excavated to the depths of the holes drilled in the stone to the nearest distance to the virtual image. The virtual image is becoming less virtual

Given a point on the block and the nearest distance, one can safely remove and entire sphere of radius that nearest distance and center that point on the block. The closer to the virtual image one is, the smaller the sphere. In principle it does not matter what direction one drills from the point; in fact one drills short to account for the diameter of the drill.

FIGURE 10. The block has now been turned over. The three labelled registration points are clicked off in order so that the virtual image is also 'turned over'

The other side of the block has been quantitatively carved after drilling to an acceptable accuracy. With this equipment, accuracy can be achieved to a millimeter or two. This piece has some undercut features which were extrapolated. Three small registration holes that were drilled into the block were left as reminders of the quantitative origins of the piece.

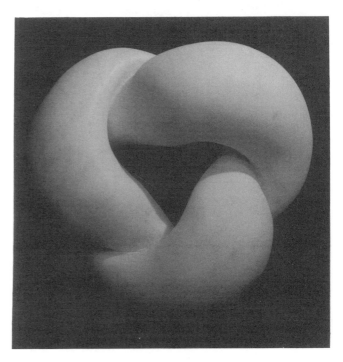

FIGURE 11. Frontal view of the *Umbilic Torus NIST*. Note that the curve of cusps goes once the long way and thrice the short way

FUTURE

The next generation of Virtual Image Projector, SP 2, scheduled to be installed in my sculpture studio for testing and evaluation, has six instead of three digitized cables. These are arranged in Stewart platform format, cf., [1]. The six cables terminate in pairs in the vertices of a ceiling triangle and in the vertices of a neutrally bouyant triangle with a rigidly affixed tool. The operator interactively flies the triangle. Tool tip position (x, y, z) coordinates and tool orientation (pitch, roll, yaw) are available from the digital readout mounted on the triangle. Software options include spatially parallel hole drilling to the depth of the virtual image. This system allows for an active cutting region (with undercuts possible) of four cubic yards at a capital cost of $0.25K\$$ per cubic foot.

A twenty foot version of this Stewart platform with a chain saw attachment has been built at NIST. Larger systems with spans of hundreds of feet are feasible, [1].

ACKNOWLEDGEMENTS

I wish to thank Professor Jordan Cox and his asso-

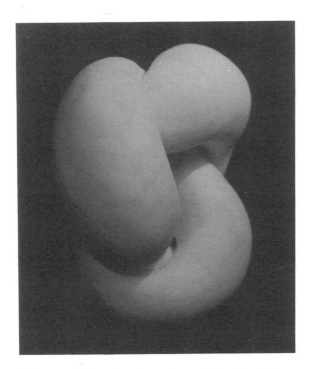

FIGURE 12. Quarter view of the *Umbilic Torus NIST*. Note the cardioid cross-section devolving about the curve of cusps and the natural veins of the Carrara marble

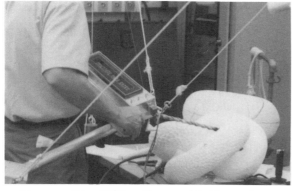

FIGURE 13. SP 2, a Stewart Platform structure coupling tool tip position and tool orientation with six digitized cable lengths

ciates at the Robotics Laboratory, Crabtree Building, Brigham Young University, Provo, Utah, and Division Chief James Albus and his associates at Robot Systems, Computer Maufacturing Engineering, National Insititute for Standards and Technology, Gaithersburg, Maryland for their creative colleagial relationships.

REFERENCES

1. James Albus, *A New Type of Robot Crane*, National Institute of Standards and Technology (NIST), preprint, 15 July 1991.
2. James Albus, Helaman Ferguson, Samuel Ferguson, et al.,, *String-Pot Measurement System*, National Institute of Standards and Technology (NIST), preprint, 1990, 26 pages and 15 drawings.
3. James W. Cannon, *Mathematics in Marble and Bronze: The Sculpture of Helaman Rolfe Pratt Ferguson*, Cover and Twenty-one Figures, The Mathematical Intelligencer **13** no. 1 (Winter 1991), 30-39.
4. Stewart Dickson, Chair, *The Third Dimension: It's not a Virtual One*, A Panel of Sculptors: Helaman Ferguson, Frank McGuire, Bruce Beasley, Rob Fisher, Stewart Dickson, Proceedings of ACM SIGGRAPH '91: Panels, Las Vegas, Nevada. 28 July - 2 August 1991.
5. Helaman Ferguson, *Two Theorems, Two Sculptures, Two Posters*, 75th Anniversary Issue of the Mathematical Association of America, Cover and Sixteen Figures, American Mathematical Monthly **97** no. 7 (August-September 1990), 589-610.
6. Helaman Ferguson, *Theorems in Stone and Bronze*, New York Academy of Sciences, 2 East 63rd Street, New York, New York 10021, 2 May through 16 July 1991.
7. Helaman Ferguson, *Umbilic Torus NC and Umbilic Torus NIST*, Infinite Illusions, exhibition at S. Dillon Ripley Center, The Smithsonian Institution, Washington, D. C., 10 September through 10 October 1990.
8. Helaman Ferguson, *Theorems in Stone and Bronze*, The Marsh Gallery of the University of Richmond, Richmond, Virginia 23173, 10 October through 10 November 1991.
9. Helaman Ferguson, *Quantitative Direct Carving with the Albus-NIST Virtual Image Projector*, Workshop at the University of Richmond, Sculpture Studio, Special Programs Building, October 10, 1-3 p.m..
10. Helaman Ferguson, *Umbilic Torus NC*, Permanent Collections: The University of California at San Francisco, Medical School Library, Parnassus, San Francisco, California; The Mathematical Association of America, 1529 Eighteenth Street N.W., Washington, D.C. 20007; Syracuse University, Department of Mathematics, Syracuse, New York; Chiron-Daiichi, Tokyo, Japan; Springer-Verlag, Heidelberg, Germany..
11. Helaman Ferguson, *Umbilic Torus NIST*, Permanent Collection: Institute for Defense Analyses, Alexandria, Virginia.
12. Helaman Ferguson, *Thurston Hyperbolic Knotted Wyes II*, Permanent Collection: Geometry Center, University of Minnesota, Minneapolis, Minnesota.
13. Helaman Ferguson, *Hyperbolic Figureight Knot Double Torus II*, Permanent Collection: Mount Holyoke College, South Hadley, Massachusetts.
14. Michael Haggerty, *3D Mathematics in Wood and Stone*, Displays on Display, Charles A. Csuri, Editor, IEEE Computer Graphics and Applications **11** no. 5 (September 1991), 7-10.
15. Ivars Peterson, *Equations in Stone*, Cover and Seven Figures, Science News **138** no. 10 (September 8, 1990), 147, 152-154.

Designing Solid Objects Using Interactive Sketch Interpretation

David Pugh
School of Computer Science
Carnegie Mellon University

ABSTRACT

Before the introduction of Computer Aided Design and solid modeling systems, designers had developed a set of techniques for designing solid objects by sketching their ideas on pencil and paper and refining them into workable designs. Unfortunately, these techniques are different from those for designing objects using a solid modeler. Not only does this waste a vast reserve of talent and experience (people typically start drawing from the moment they can hold a crayon), but it also has a more fundamental problem: designers can use their intuition more effectively when sketching than they can when using a solid modeler.

Viking is a solid modeling system whose user-interface is based on interactive sketch interpretation. Interactive sketch interpretation lets the designer create a line-drawing of a desired object while *Viking* generates a three-dimensional object description. This description is consistent with both the designer's line-drawing, and a set of geometric constraints either derived from the line-drawing or placed by the designer. *Viking*'s object descriptions are fully compatible with the object descriptions used by traditional solid modelers. As a result, interactive sketch interpretation can be used with traditional solid modeling techniques, combining the advantages of both sketching and solid modeling.

David Pugh
School of Computer Science
Carnegie Mellon University
Pittsburgh, PA 15213-3890
dep@cs.cmu.edu

1 INTRODUCTION

Sketching has long been an important element of the design process. For hundreds of years, people have designed by making quick, abstract drawings or "sketches." Sketching was used both to specify embryonic concepts and to refine these concepts into workable designs. Thirty or so years ago, the advent of Computer Aided Design (CAD) and solid modeling systems began to revolutionize some aspects of the design process. These programs let designers create a model of a three-dimensional object on the computer. This model can then be analyzed in ways that would be difficult or impossible without the computer. For example, CAD systems and associated programs can display realistic images, do stress analyses, and generate milling machine programs from the computer's model of the object.

Unfortunately, the CAD revolution did not extend to at least two critical aspects of the design process: exploring new ideas and refining these ideas into workable designs. With current CAD systems, the model typically changes in large, discontinuous steps. The designer is often forced to fully specify a change before he or she has a chance to see how it interacts with the rest of the model. This makes "feedback driven" design, in which the designer uses feedback from one change to guide the next change, difficult on a solid modeler: the magnitude of each change is too large to let the designer use his or her intuition effectively. As a result, designers will often use pencil and paper to "work out" a change before making the change on the computer.

The techniques used to design objects on pencil and paper are different from those used to design objects on a solid modeler [13]. Sketching, in this context, is a visual and intuitive process in which a drawing is refined over time by making small, incremental changes. At each point in the process, the designer uses feedback from one change – the appearance of the modified sketch – to guide the next change. The continual feedback lets the designer use his or her intuition effectively.

This paper presents a solid modeling system, *Viking*, that lets the user design three-dimensional objects using techniques normally used to create and refine two-dimensional

117

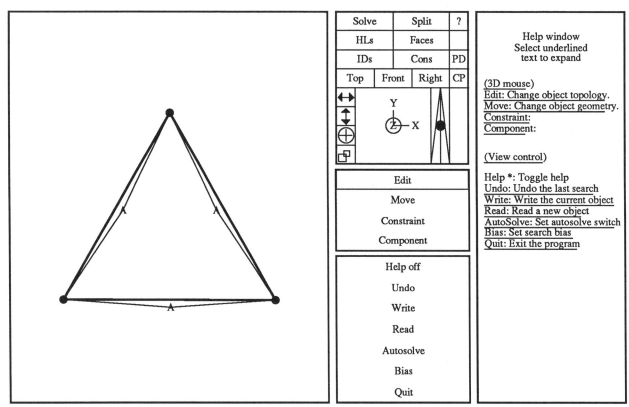

Figure 1: *Viking*'s display.

sketches. *Viking* uses interactive sketch interpretation to create a "what you draw is what you get" user-interface. Users can create a line-drawing of a desired object and use sketch interpretation to generate a three-dimensional object that is consistent with the line-drawing. Users can also place geometric constraints on the object. These constraints, together with a set of constraints derived from the line-drawing, are used to define a vertex geometry in subsequent interpretations. Geometric constraints let the user create precisely dimensioned objects. The resulting user-interface combines the power of traditional solid modeling systems with the continuous feedback of sketching.

2 THE *VIKING* SOLID MODELER

Viking extends the direct manipulation metaphor to three-dimensional object design by letting the user modify an object by changing its line-drawing. For most changes, deducing an appropriate change in the object description is trivial. For example, if the user erases a line, delete the corresponding edge. With other changes, such as making a line-segment visible, there is no obvious corresponding change in the object description. Sketch interpretation is used in these cases to generate a new object description that is consistent with the modified line-drawing.

Sketch interpretation divides the task of interpreting a line-drawing into two parts: finding a surface-topology and solving for a vertex geometry. The first part is done by generating surface-topologies that are consistent with the line-drawing until one that is acceptable to the user is found. The

second is done by using a geometric constraint solver to find a vertex geometry that satisfies a system of constraints either derived from the line-drawing and the proposed surface-topology, or placed by the user. The surface-topology and vertex geometry combine to form a three-dimensional object description that is consistent with both the line-drawing and the constraints.

2.1 *VIKING*'S USER-INTERFACE

Figure 1 shows *Viking*'s display after creating an equilateral triangle. The left window shows a line-drawing of underlying object description and the upper center window shows the view transform used to generate the line-drawing. Both windows let the user directly modify their contents. The user can, for example, move a vertex by dragging it to a new location with the mouse. The user can also dynamically change the view transform by dragging the mouse across the orientation triad, rotating the view about an axis perpendicular to the mouse's motion [9].

The line-drawing displays more than just an object's shape. Thick, thin and double lines respectively correspond to edges adjacent to zero, one and two faces in the object description. Circles correspond to vertices that can be moved by the constraint solver when solving for a vertex geometry. Triangles correspond to vertices whose positions are considered fixed constants by the constraint solver. Constraints are drawn in a variety of ways. Distance constraints, for example, are shown by thin, bent lines. In Figure 1, the "A" symbol at the bend indicates that all three sides of the triangle have the same length.

The four items shown in the center window of Figure 1 (*Edit, Move, Constraint* and *Component*) correspond to the four most commonly used modes in *Viking*. These modes determine how mouse actions in the line-drawing's window are interpreted. If the user enters either *Constraint* or *Component* modes, the center window is overwritten with a specialized menu.

Edit mode is used for changing the appearance of the line-drawing displayed in the image window. While in it, the user can draw new edges, erase old ones and change the visibility of line-segments. For the first two actions, both the line-drawing and the underlying object description change. For the last action, only the line-drawing changes: the underlying object description is not always modified: the Autosolve switch, located on in the bottom center window, determines whether *Viking* will automatically generate a new interpretation after the user changes the visibility of a line-segment, or wait until the user explicitly requests a new interpretation.

Move mode is used for placing tacks, and moving vertices and edges. Tacks are simple constraints that either lock a vertex into a fixed position or force an edge to pass through a point in space. If the Autosolve switch is on, *Viking* will use the constraint solver to maintain the constraints as the user drags a vertex or edge around with the mouse. Otherwise, the vertex or edge will follow the mouse without maintaining the constraints.

Constraint mode is used for placing or editing geometric constraints on the object. The constraint menu lets the user select a constraint template and then define constraints by picking vertices or edges to "fill in" the blanks. The user can also modify or delete previously defined constraints. Whenever the user adds a constraint, *Viking* will attempt to find a solution to the new system if the Autosolve switch is turned on.

Component mode is used for manipulating groups of vertices, edges and faces. Every component has a coordinate transform that defines the effective position of its vertices. The coordinate transform is generated from eleven variables that control a component's size (using both an axis-independent variable and three axis-dependent variables), position, and orientation (using quaternions [12]). The user can lock or free these variables independently and the constraint solver can manipulate the free variables when solving for a vertex geometry.

2.1.2 SKETCHING IN THREE-DIMENSIONS

Sketching is traditionally done in only two dimensions. With *Viking*, however, sketches are three-dimensional entities. This both aids and hinders the user. A three-dimensional "sketch" can help the user visualize the object it represents. But it also means the user must specify the location of each vertex in three-dimensions.

A simple mechanism for specifying a vertices' approximate location is needed. If the user can place every vertex near its correct position, then the user can rotate the object and the line-drawing will behave intuitively. This lets the user continue the design process until he or she knows enough to start using constraints to specify the vertices' position precisely. Also, since the vertices start close to a geometry that satisfies the constraints, the constraint solver will need less time to find a solution.

Geometric constraints are not, by themselves, a good mechanism for specifying approximate vertex positions. In part, this is because the constraint solver works best when all vertices are near a solution. Relying on the constraint solver to move a vertex a significant distance is, at best, time consuming and often results in unexpected and unwanted solutions (assuming any solution is found). A more fundamental problem with using constraints for rough positioning, however, is their precision. Often, users do not know the precise location of a vertex until late in the design process. Using constraints to position a vertex before the user knows its precise location is time consuming since the constraints will have to be changed later, when the precise dimensions are known. It can also be intimidating: people do not like answering questions until after they know the answers.

The user can position a vertex in three-dimensions by showing where it "should be" in two different views. Unfortunately, this technique forces the user to work in two different views, which is difficult. For example, it is not always obvious which vertex in one view corresponds to which vertex in the other.

When no other information is available, *Viking* uses a simple rule when drawing edges: both end-points have the same z-coordinate in the display's coordinate space. For many cases, such as drawing a short edge from an existing vertex, this is sufficient. In other cases, neither this method nor the alternatives given above suffice. Because of this, *Viking* provides two additional mechanisms to let the user easily specify the location of a vertex in three-dimensions: preferred directions and cutting planes.

Preferred directions are three-dimensional vectors. When the user draws an edge, *Viking* draws short lines parallel to each preferred direction at the new edge's origin. As the user moves the mouse, the edge's endpoint is projected onto the closest preferred direction.

Preferred directions can be defined in two ways. First, the user can define vectors in object space, such as the x, y and z axes, for preferred directions. Any new edge, no matter where it is drawn, will be able to use these preferred directions. Second, the user can put preferred directions on automatic. In this case, *Viking* automatically defines preferred directions depending on the context in which the user started to draw the new edge. If the user is drawing an edge from an existing vertex, then the preferred directions are defined to be parallel to each of the edges radiating from the vertex. If the user is drawing an edge from an existing edge, then one preferred direction is defined to be parallel to the edge and, for each adjacent face, a preferred direction is defined to lie in that face's plane and be perpendicular to the edge. If these rules generate one preferred direction, then two preferred directions are added that are perpendicular to the original preferred direction and each other. If two preferred directions were generated, then a third preferred direction perpendicular to the first two is added.

A cutting plane is a plane defined in object space. Cutting planes are a tool for both positioning a vertex in three-dimensions and helping the user visualize the object's three-dimensional structure. The user can position a vertex in three-dimensions by moving it parallel to the cutting plane or parallel to the cutting plane's normal.

The user can manipulate the cutting plane by moving it parallel to its normal, changing the orientation of its normal, and controlling the way in which it is displayed. The user can, among other things, make the cutting plane opaque or translucent, highlight the intersection of the cutting plane with the object, show the orthogonal projection of the object onto the cutting plane, and draw height poles between each vertex and the cutting plane.

3 IMPLEMENTATION

Viking's implementation of interactive sketch interpretation uses two distinct data-structures: one holds the current object description and the other holds the line-drawing displayed to the user. The user can modify the line-drawing and most changes automatically propagate to the current object description, maintaining consistency between the two data-structures. The user can also change the viewpoint, in which case the line-drawing is recreated from the new view transform and the current object description.

Sketch interpretation generates a new object description when the user makes a change that can not be propagated to the object description automatically. *Viking*'s sketch interpretation algorithm splits the task of generating a new object description into two parts: finding a surface-topology that is consistent with the line-drawing and solving for a vertex geometry that satisfies the object's implicit and explicit constraints. Together, the surface-topology and the vertex geometry completely describe a three-dimensional object. The new object description is consistent with both the line-drawing created by the user and any geometric constraints he or she may have specified.

Viking uses arc-labeling [10], an extension of Huffman-Clowes line-labeling [3, 8] to non-trihedral vertices, to generate a surface-topology from a line-drawing and an old object description. The surface-topology defines a set of faces that are consistent with the line-drawing. Since line-drawings can have many different interpretations, *Viking* uses heuristics to seek out the more desirable interpretations first. *Viking* generates surface-topologies in order of increasing cost, where the cost is based on several heuristics, including:

- how similar the surface-topology is to the current ob-

ject's surface-topology and

- if the user has given a preferred object type, how close the surface-topology is to the user's preferred type.

Surface-topologies are generated until the user either accepts one or aborts the search. In my experience, the desired surface-topology is normally the first surface-topology found.

Once an acceptable surface-topology has been found, a non-linear constraint solver finds a vertex geometry that satisfies a system of geometric constraints. These constraints fall into three categories:

- world: every face is a planar polygon.

- image: visible lines are in front of obscuring faces.

- explicit: constraints explicitly defined by the user.

The first two types of constraints are implicit constraints since they are automatically generated by *Viking*. World and explicit constraints are always part of the system of equations used by the constraint solver. Image constraints are only used when finding a vertex geometry after generating a new surface-topology for the object.

The constraint solver uses an algorithm developed by Bullard and Biegler [2]. This algorithm repeatedly solves a system of linear equations derived from the non-linear equations and their first derivatives until the global error is reduced below a threshold. The vertex positions from the current object are used as the initial solution for the new system of constraints. The solver tends to move the vertices only in small, well controlled steps and, as a result, solutions tend not to differ unnecessarily from the vertex geometry in the current object.

Once an acceptable surface-topology and vertex geometry have been found, *Viking* replaces the current object description with the new interpretation. A new line-drawing is then generated from the new current object description and the current view transform. The user can manipulate the new line-drawing just like the old one, letting the user continue the cycle of modification and interpretation.

4 EXAMPLES

4.1 CREATING A CHAIR

This section describes a session using *Viking* to create an "easy chair." This example is somewhat contrived (for example, chairs are not normally made from homogeneous blocks) but it does convey the flavor of *Viking*'s user-interface. It also demonstrates how modifying the line-drawing can be used as a substitute for constructive solid geometry. It took me less than two minutes to transform the cube in Figure 2a into the chair in Figure 2i.

Preferred directions (see Section 2.1.2) were on automatic throughout this example. As a result, whenever the user started to draw an edge, *Viking* defined a set of context

120

dependent vectors that could be used to position the edge's endpoint in three-dimensions. For example, preferred directions made it possible to draw the new edge in Figure 2b so that it was parallel to the edge between the upper and lower vertices at the right and back of the cube.

Figure 2a shows the initial object, a cube loaded from a library of standard objects. The first step in turning this cube into a chair is to add a raised back. Figure 2b shows the user drawing a new edge up from the upper-right corner of the cube. The user has finished drawing the edges for the chair's back in Figure 2c and is in the process of hiding the line-segments that would be obscured if the chair's back was solid and opaque.

In Figure 2d, the user deleted one unwanted vertex and is in the process of deleting the other (the user must pick a vertex twice to delete it: the first pick highlights the selected vertex, the second deletes is). These vertices are unwanted because deleting them and redrawing the missing edges ensures that the chair's back is a single, planar surface. If these vertices had not been deleted, *Viking* would have found an interpretation in which the chair's back and sides were each formed by two faces.

Deleting a vertex also deletes its adjacent edges and faces, although *Viking* preserves the hidden status of line-segments whose obscuring face is deleted. For example, in Figure 2d, the line at the bottom-back of the cube is drawn with a single, thin line (indicating that it is adjacent to only one face) since the top, back and right faces of the cube were deleted when the first vertex was deleted. Also, the entire line remains hidden, even though the face obscuring its right segment has been deleted.

Figure 2e shows the user redrawing some of the edges that were deleted when the user deleted the unwanted vertices, in preparation for using sketch interpretation to generate a new object description. Figure 2f shows, from a different viewpoint, the user starting to draw a lowered seat on the first interpretation found for Figure 2e. Since the user had set the search bias to prefer solid objects, *Viking* sought out an interpretation corresponding to a solid object. As a result, the interpretation contains faces that were not needed to generate an object description consistent with Figure 2e since they would have been hidden by the rest of the chair.

The user has finished drawing a lowered seat for the chair in Figure 2g and is in the process of removing some unwanted and unnecessary edges. In Figure 2h, the user is exposing the line-segments that would be visible if the chair's seat was lower than its arm rests. Figure 2i shows, from a different viewpoint, the first interpretation found for Figure 2h.

Even though the chair looks correct in Figure 2i, the geometry is not correct. For example, some edges that should be parallel to each other are skewed about 10°. These problems can be fixed in a minute or two by using geometric constraints. But, since the next example demonstrates the constraint solver, that part of the design process is skipped.

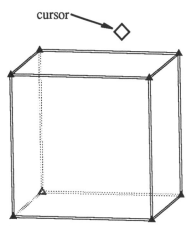

Figure 2a: Initial object: a unit cube.

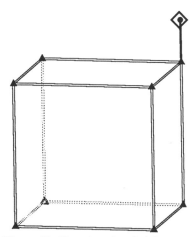

Figure 2b: Drawing the chair's back.

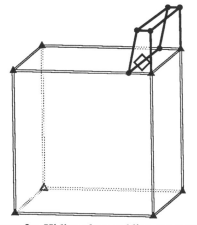

Figure 2c: Hiding obscured line-segments.

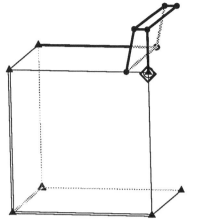

Figure 2d: Remove unwanted vertices and edges.

Figure 2g: Remove unwanted edges.

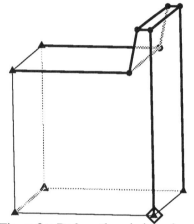

Figure 2e: Redraw the missing edges.

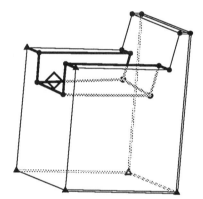

Figure 2h: Exposing visible line-segments.

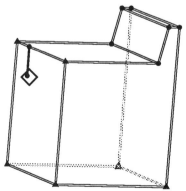

Figure 2f: Drawing the chair's seat.

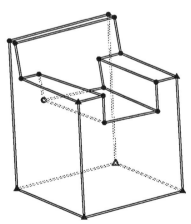

Figure 2i: The "completed" chair.

4.2 AN EXERCISE IN GEOMETRY

Suppose you have the following problem: if you place a solid equilateral tetrahedron face to face with a solid equilateral octahedron, how many faces does the resulting polyhedron have? The polyhedra are positioned and sized so that three of the tetrahedron's vertices coincide with three of the octahedron's vertices. Answering this question, by using *Viking* to create the object shown in Figure 3l, takes me less than three minutes.

Figure 3a shows the user starting to draw the two polyhedra. In Figure 3b, the user has changed the view transform by rotating it about the horizontal axis and is in the process of completing the octahedron's wire-frame. Figure 3c shows the user hiding the line-segments at the "back" of the polyhedra. Figure 3d shows the first interpretation found after hiding the rest of the line-segments that should be obscured.

The edges in Figure 3d were drawn without using either preferred directions or a cutting plane to position the vertices in three-dimensions. The user made no attempt to draw the edges so that they all had exactly the same length. Instead, geometric constraints will be used to turn these "rough sketches" into equilateral polyhedra.

Figure 3e shows the effect of adding and solving for equal length constraints on the tetrahedron's edges. Figure 3f shows the effect of placing a similar set of constraints on the octahedron. The bent lines and "A" symbols indicate that all of the tetrahedron's edges have the same length. The bent lines and "B" symbols do the same for the octahedron's edges. In both Figures 3e and 3f, the vertices have moved to accommodate the constraints. Figure 3g, in which display of the constraints has been turned off, shows the two polyhedra from a different direction.

In Figure 3h, the user has added, but not yet solved for, constraints forcing three of the tetrahedron's vertices to be coincident with three of the octahedron's vertices. The bent line and "0" symbol indicates that the distance between the vertices should be zero. Figure 3i shows the solution found by the constraint solver to the system described in Figure 3h. Figures 3h and 3i have, despite appearances, identical surface-topologies: the constraint solver moved the vertices without changing the underlying structure.

In Figure 3j, the view transform has been changed to give a view "straight-down" one of the edges where the tetrahedron and octahedron are in contact. This view suggests that the vertices to either side of this edge are co-planar, forming a single four-sided face. In Figure 3k, the user has merged the six coincident vertices into three vertices, deleted the unwanted edges, and generated a new, seven-sided, interpretation. Figure 3l shows Figure 3k with all constraints hidden. Since all faces must be planar, *Viking* would not be able to find a vertex geometry for Figure 3k unless the quadrilateral faces were planar polygons. The answer, therefore, to the question posed at the beginning of this section is that a tetrahedron and octahedron form a seven-sided polyhedra.

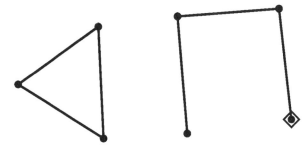

Figure 3a: Drawing the polyhedra.

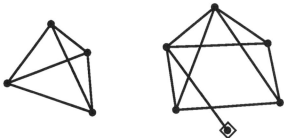

Figure 3b: Completing the wire-frames.

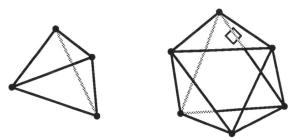

Figure 3c: Hiding obscured line-segments.

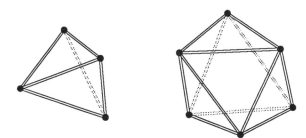

Figure 3d: Generating an interpretation.

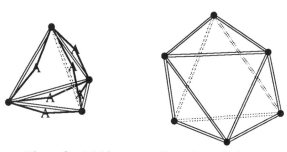

Figure 3e: Making an equilateral tetrahedron.

123

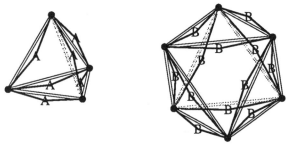

Figure 3f: Making an equilateral octahedron.

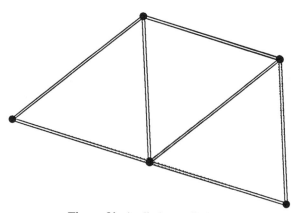

Figure 3j: An "edge-on" view.

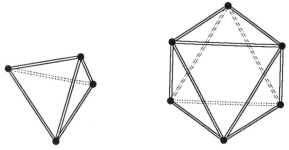

Figure 3g: Viewing from another direction.

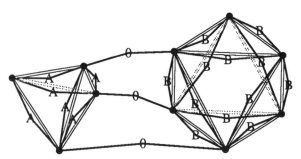

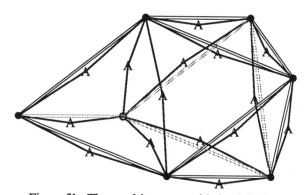

Figure 3k: The resulting seven-sided polyhedra.

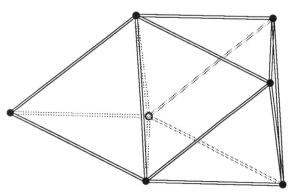

Figure 3h: Before solving the coincidence constraints.

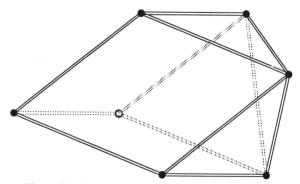

Figure 3i: After solving the coincidence constraints.

Figure 3l: Figure 3k with the constraints hidden.

5 FUTURE WORK

Viking's user-interface has some significant weaknesses. Some of these are problems should not be difficult to solve. Others do not seem to have easy solutions. These problems are presented in the order that they will be addressed in future research.

CAD modeling interface

Currently, *Viking* provides few of the capabilities found in conventional solid modeling systems. For example, *Viking* can neither calculate the mass of an object nor find the intersection of two objects. Combining conventional solid modeling capabilities and interactive sketch interpretation should not be difficult: *Viking*'s underlying object description is equivalent to the boundary representation description used by some solid modelers.

Explicit constraints specification

Viking's users must explicitly specify every geometric constraint. Other constraint based design systems, such as Snap-Dragging [1] [5], provide mechanisms for defining constraints implicitly. Incorporating similar mechanisms into *Viking* could alleviate one of the more tedious aspects of *Viking*'s user-interface.

Planar faces and straight edges

Viking can, currently, only interpret line-drawings of objects with planar faces. The sketch interpretation algorithm can be easily extended to objects with non-planar faces. Modifying the rest of *Viking* however, is more difficult: planar faces provides one of the better implicit constraints and designing a good user-interface for letting the user specify which faces are non-planar and controlling the shape of a non-planar face is not easy.

Quadhedral vertices

Viking can only analyze line-drawings in which every vertex is adjacent to four or fewer edges. This is because *Viking*'s sketch interpretation algorithm must match every intersection in the line-drawing to an entry in a fixed intersection library. This library contains all possible intersections of two, three and four lines. The program used to generate *Viking*'s intersection library, however, is already capable of generating entries for intersections of five or more lines. Adding this capability to *Viking* should not be difficult.

Simple polygonal faces

Faces in *Viking* must be simple, planar polygons: no internal holes or repeated edges or vertices. It should be possible to extend the algorithm to allow more complicated faces, although it may not be worth the extra processing time required. The current version of *Viking* lets the user simulate holes and the like by using artifact edges.

Explicit topology specification

Viking's sketch interpretation algorithm uses the presence of hidden lines-segments to automatically reject inconsistent interpretations. The downside of this is that the user must correctly indicate which line-segments are hidden. This can be a tedious and time-consuming process.

Viking lets the user generate a blind interpretation, in which the visibility cues are ignored and, therefore, the user does not have to indicate which line-segments are hidden. Blind interpretations are slower and less discriminating than conventional interpretation, since visibility cues can not be used to reject unwanted topologies. Despite this, it is often easier to generate a blind interpretation and manually reject unwanted topologies than it is to indicate which line-segments are hidden and generate a standard interpretation.

5.1 OPEN PROBLEMS

The following section describes problems that do not seem to have easy solutions.

General view

Viking's sketch interpretation algorithm can only interpret line-drawings that correspond to a general view of an object. A general view is one in which a small change in the view direction makes correspondingly small change in the line-drawing [11]. So, for example, a general view could not contain any faces that are "edge-on" to the viewer (such as Figure 3j).

This is a problem, since engineering drawings often do not correspond to general views. However, it is not clear how significant this problem is. Engineering drawings often used specialized viewpoints because, historically, specialized views were easier to draw or because they illustrated a particular point. Specialized views are not, for the most part, easier to interpret than general views and both types of views are easy to generate using the computer.

One possibility for generating interpretations of specialized views is to use graph based algorithms [4] [7]. These algorithms do not depend on the viewpoint, generating a surface-topology by finding a planar embedding of an object's vertex-edge graph. Unfortunately, these algorithms probably could not be modified to use *Viking*'s search heuristics.

Sketch interpretation performance

Viking's sketch interpretation algorithm is not as fast as one might wish, taking almost three minutes to generate an interpretation of a line-drawing containing 100 points. The time required to generate an interpretation seems to be roughly proportional to the square of the number of points in the line-drawing. Although

125

faster workstations and more efficient algorithms may alleviate this problem, it is not realistic to expect that *Viking*'s sketch interpretation algorithm could be used on large objects (which might three or four orders of magnitude more complex than the objects created in Sections 4.1 or 4.2). It should, however, be possible to automatically partition a large object and use sketch interpretation on only the relevant parts.

Constraint satisfaction performance

 Viking's constraint solver is used in two basic modes: when one or more constraints have been added and *Viking* must solve for a solution and when the user is moving a vertex by dragging it with the mouse and wishes to maintain the pre-existing constraints. The response time when dragging is far slower than desired, often taking several seconds to find a solution that satisfies all the constraints. It might be possible to use differential constraints [6] to improve response times when dragging.

6 CONCLUSIONS

Viking is a solid modeling system that uses interactive sketch interpretation to combine the simplicity of pencil and paper sketches with the power of a solid modeling system. *Viking* lets designers draw the object they wish to create and then modify it by changing the line-drawing to make it "look right." Each action is obvious from context, leaving the designer free to concentrate on the design itself and not how to convey it to the solid modeler.

This ease of use comes without sacrificing any of the capabilities intrinsic to solid modeling systems. As with other solid modeling systems, *Viking* lets the designer manipulate the underlying object description as if it were a solid object. This provides the designer with a powerful tool for visualizing an object's structure. For example, the designer can wiggle the object by dynamically changing the view transform or drag a translucent cutting plane through the object to see where vertices lie with respect to one another in three-dimensions. And, although *Viking*'s user-interface is based primarily on sketching, the designer can create precisely dimensioned models by using geometric constraints. This combination of sketching and solid modeling techniques creates an effective user-interface for developing ideas into practical designs.

REFERENCES

[1] Eric Bier. Snap-dragging in three dimensions. *Computer Graphics*, 24(2):193–204, March 1990. Proceedings 1990 Symposium on Interactive 3d Graphics.

[2] L.G. Bullard and L.T. Biegler. Lp strategies for constraint simulation. In *AIChE '89 Conference Proceedings*, November 1989.

[3] M. B. Clowes. On seeing things. *Artificial Intelligence*, 2:79–116, 1971.

[4] S. Mark Courter and John A. Brewer III. Automated conversion of curvilinear wire-frame models to surface boundary models; a topological approach. In *SIGGRAPH '86 Conference Proceedings*, pages 171–178, 1986.

[5] Michael Gleicher and Andrew Witkin. Creating and manipulating constrained models. Technical Report CMU-CS-91-125, Carnegie Mellon University, 1991.

[6] Michael Gleicher and Andrew Witkin. Differential manipulation. *Graphics Interface*, pages 61–67, June 1991.

[7] Patrick M. Hanrahan. Creating volume models from edge-vertex graphs. In *SIGGRAPH '82 Conference Proceedings*, pages 77–84, 1982.

[8] D. A. Huffman. Impossible objects as nonsense sentences. *Machine Intelligence*, 6:295–323, 1971.

[9] S. Joy Mountford Michael Chen and Abigail Sellen. A study in interactive 3-d rotation using 2-d control devices. In *SIGGRAPH '88 Conference Proceedings*, pages 121–129, 1988.

[10] David Pugh. Interactive sketch interpretation using arc-labeling and geometric constraint satisfaction. Technical Report CMU-CS-91-181, Carnegie Mellon University, 1991.

[11] P. V. Sanker. A vertex coding scheme for interpreting ambiguous trihedral solids. *Computer Graphics and Image Processing*, 6:61–89, 1977.

[12] Ken Shoemake. Animating rotation with quaternion curves. In *SIGGRAPH '85 Conference Proceedings*, pages 177–186, 1985.

[13] Rob Woodbury. Searching for designs: Paradigm and practice. *Building and Environment*, 26(1):61–73, 1991.

Interactive Graphics for Plastic Surgery:

A Task-Level Analysis and Implementation

Steven Pieper

Joseph Rosen

David Zeltzer

Thayer School of Engineering
Dartmouth College
Hanover, NH 05037

Medical Center
Dartmouth College
Hanover, NH 05037

Computer Graphics and Animation Group
MIT Media Laboratory
Cambridge, MA 02139

ABSTRACT

We have implemented a system for Computer-Aided Plastic Surgery. Planning plastic surgery procedures is complex because the surgeon needs to stretch and reshape the patient's skin to replace missing tissue while minimizing distortion of the surrounding tissue. Traditional planning techniques rely on the surgeon's experience to select among a myriad of possible procedure designs. While mathematical techniques for predicting the outcome of surgery have been proposed in the past, these are not in widespread use by surgeons because they require the surgeon to perform manual constructions and geometric calculations. Our system makes the analysis process easier by allowing the surgeon to draw the surgical plan directly on a 3D model of the patient. An automatic mesh generator is used to convert that drawing into a well-formulated problem for finite element analysis.

Key Words

Interactivity, 3D Graphics, Computer-Aided Surgery, Plastic Surgery, Surgical Simulation.

1. INTRODUCTION

This paper describes our experience designing a Computer-Aided Plastic Surgery (CAPS) system. The system provides surgeons with a computer graphics environment in which they can explore the biomechanical implications of surgical alternatives. The CAPS system uses a combination of interactive 3D computer graphics, automatic mesh generation algorithms, physically-based modeling using the Finite Element Method, and animated visualization of the surgical result. We have implemented the system and have had it evaluated by a number of practicing plastic surgeons with very positive results.

Computerized planning represents an important development for plastic surgeons because their current techniques do not allow iterative problem solving. Today, a surgeon must observe and perform many operations to build up the experience about the effect of changes in the surgical plan. Each of these operations is unique, and it is difficult to isolate the effects of different surgical options since the result is also influenced by many patient specific variables. The CAPS system allows exploration of the various surgical alternatives with the ability to modify the existing plan, or to create a new plan from scratch. This process may be repeated as many times as needed until the surgeon is satisfied with the plan.

In our view, it is crucial that the user interface to the system not burden the physician with the implementation details of the computational model Specifically, the physician should not be required to manipulate points and polygons, or nodal points and elements of the finite element model. Our work follows a task-level analysis[33] of the goals of plastic surgery: in this system the surgeon only deals directly with the problems associated with the task --- identifying the clinical problem, selecting the surgical procedure to apply, and specifying the execution of the procedure. All other aspects of the analysis are carried out automatically. The interface to the CAPS system is designed to simulate the process of drawing on the patient's skin with a marker, as is done when the surgery is transferred to the patient in the operating room.

The remainder of this paper describes the techniques used in the implementation of the CAPS system. This is motivated by a review of related work and a brief discussion of the goals of plastic surgery and the problems faced by the clinician. The following sections describe the simulation model, and the clinician's interface to the system. We then look in detail at the mesh generation algorithms that convert the surgical plan into a well-formed problem for finite element analysis.

2. BACKGROUND

Previous work has concentrated on either building mathematical models of the soft tissue mechanics in order to analyze specific test cases, or on imaging systems that present renderings of volumetric scans of the patient. Our work is an attempt to bring these two components together with a powerful user interface. This results in a system where the simulation procedures are attached to the graphical model --- a combination which allows the surgeon to operate on the graphical model in a manner directly analogous to operating on the real patient. This approach is crucial for the successful clinical application of mechanical analysis of soft tissue because without the assistance of a computer graphics tool the surgeon has neither the time nor the training to formulate a specific surgical case at the level of detail required for analysis.

Mechanical Analysis of Plastic Surgery

Previous research in biomechanical analysis of plastic surgery has not included methods for automatically converting a surgical plan into a form appropriate for the analysis programs. For example, in her work on analysis of plastic surgeries, Deng describes a system in which the user is required to type an input file which describes the incision geometries, regions of tissue to simulate, and constraint conditions on the tissue in terms of their world space coordinates[11]. Kawabata and his coworkers describe their techniques for analysis of surgical procedures but report no method for automatically generating a mesh for a particular plan[16]. Larrabee discusses the problem of modeling arbitrary incision geometries using graphical input devices, but the solution he proposes requires the user to define each of the dozens of analysis nodes and elements[18]. While Larrabee's approach is useful for small two-dimensional analyses (which is the way Larrabee used it), the approach becomes unmanageable for three-dimensional structures with a greater number of nodes. The user interface and mesh generation techniques described in this paper begin to address these three-dimensional problems.

Computer Graphics Models of Skin

Waters describes a system based on the for simulating the expressive action of facial muscles through a combination of pre-defined action units[30]. Waters and Terzopoulos subsequently extended this technique to include physically-based dynamics of the skin in response to the muscle action[31]. However, their system could not be used directly for plastic surgery simulation because it does not support cutting and suturing. In addition, their physical model is based on the mass-and-spring lattice approach, which we feel is more difficult to control and less accurate than the finite element method.

Volumetric Approaches

Previous computer graphics work has emphasized special purpose rendering algorithms for visualization of data obtained from volumetric scans of the patient[22;19;9], or geometric methods for extracting and repositioning pieces of the volume data[7;28]. Our approach differs since the CAPS system integrates a biomechanical simulation with a graphic presentation.

Interactive Computer Graphics for Surgical Simulation

The terms *surgical simulation*[24] and *Computer-Aided Surgery*[21;5] have both been used to refer to the combination of physically based modeling of the human body and interactive computer graphics applied to planning and analysis of surgical procedures. In an example of this approach, Delp *et al.* have created a system for simulating tendon transfer operations on the lower extremity[10]. This system includes a geometric model of the major bones of the hip and leg, a kinematic model of six joints, and a mechanical model of 43 muscle-tendon actuator units. A 3D graphics interface can be used to select and move tendon attachment points. Thompson *et al.* have developed a similar system for hand surgery[27]. Our work on the CAPS system is most similar in spirit to, and was inspired by the work of these groups.

3. GOALS OF PLASTIC SURGERY

The goal of plastic surgery is to create a proper contour by making the best distribution of available materials. Operations take place on relatively limited surface areas and, in local procedures, skin cover is not brought from distant areas.* Rather, skin should be borrowed and redistributed in the area where the operation is being carried out. In this way, surgeons should be able to perform typical plastic operations that will restore proper form to distorted surfaces. Different maneuvers are used in various combinations as either simple or complex figures. The location, form, and dimensions of the incisions necessary for plastic redistribution of tissues determine the plan of the operation.

A. A. Limberg, M.D.[20]

Applications of plastic surgery include repairing lesions caused by disease, replacing skin lost to burns or amputations, rebuilding features misshapen by injury or birth defects, and removing excess tissue to reduce the visual effects of aging[13]. This is accomplished through the precise application of surgical techniques including excision (removal) of tissue, direct closure of a wound site, and a variety of flap transposition and rearrangement surger-

---

* In contrast to skin grafting operations.

ies. Each of these results in a redistribution of the available tissue and requires the application of plastic surgery principles to produce the optimum contour.

An example plastic surgery (simulated on the CAPS system) is shown in figures 6 and 7. This procedure combines excision of a tumor with two flap transpositions. The flap transpositions have the effect of using tissue from the area surrounding the excision to relieve the stress caused by covering the wound. The resultant effects on the surrounding tissue contour can be seen. This includes distortions, redistribution, and standing cones (dog ears) at the point of rotation of the flaps. The CAPS system can be used to compare various flap transposition and excision options, and provides an environment that allows the surgeon to iteratively approach the planning problem.

4. THE PATIENT MODEL

The model of the patient used in the CAPS system is a combination of patient specific geometric data and a generic mechanical model of the soft tissue.

Sources of Patient Geometric Data

The patient specific geometry we have used to date is derived from either a Cyberware surface scan of the patient[8] or from a CT scan. The Cencit scanner system is also a promising technology for use in this application[29]. The mesh generation algorithms make use of a cylindrically-mapped range image of the type produced by the Cyberware and Cencit scanners. In order to create a solid model of the skin, our current system assumes a constant soft tissue thickness when working with this type of data. Full volumetric scans (CT or MR scans) of the patient provide enough information to create a solid model with the appropriate variation in soft tissue thickness. We have experimented with some techniques for building models directly from volumetric scans[25], however, we feel that the surface scanners will be more appropriate for use in plastic surgery because of the time, expense, and radiation hazards associated with volumetric scanners. In the future we will be working on techniques for creating a generic map of facial soft tissue thickness in order to generate more accurate solid models from surface scan data.

Model of Soft Tissue Biomechanics

The finite element method is a well established technique for biomechanical analyses[12] and provides a basis for detailed modeling of skin nonlinearities[11]. Finite element methods can also be used to model the shape changes and force generating properties of other parts of the body, such as the muscles[6]. Although we use a relatively simple linear solution technique in the CAPS system, the user interface and mesh generation techniques described below can be used directly with a nonlinear finite element back end. The finite element module of the CAPS system uses the displacement-based formulation to solve the elasticity equilibrium equations. The implementation closely follows the procedure described in Bathe[1]. Readers are referred to Bathe's excellent text for further details on the implementation of finite element codes.

Visualization of the Finite Element Model

The two components of the patient model, the scan of the patient and the finite element mesh, exist different resolutions. A typical Cyberware patient scan contains 512x256 range and color samples, while the finite element meshes we can easily simulate contain only 50 elements, with each element covering approximately a square inch of skin. In order to display the full resolution of the original scan data both before and after the finite element solution (corresponding to pre- and post-operative conditions), we use the following texture and displacement mapping technique. First, we subdivide the outer face of each element into micropolygons (the outer face being the one which lies on the skin surface). The position of each micropolygon vertex is transformed back into cylin-

128

drical coordinate space, and the θ and z coordinates are used to sample the Cyberware range and color data (a bilinear interpolation is used to sample between pixels). The color value is stored as the vertex color of the micropolygon vertex. The sampled range point is transformed back into cartesian space and used as the position of the micropolygon vertex. The user can select the number of micropolygons created for each element and thus can visualize the full resolution of the Cyberware data. We maintain a data structure for each micropolygon vertex in which we store the vector from the point on the surface of the element to the corresponding position on the range data.

This vector is then used to display the full resolution post-operative model. The output of the finite element solution is a set of displacements for each nodal point in the finite element mesh. These nodal displacements are interpolated through the element to define a displacement vector at each point in the element. Thus, for each micropolygon vertex, there is a displacement vector. By adding the finite element displacement vector to the range data displacement vector, we can generate post-operative images using the full resolution of the original scan. Images generated using this method are shown in figure 7.

5. SPECIFYING THE PLAN
The heart of the interactive system is the user interface which allows the surgeon to input the parameters of the surgical procedure. For this task, we selected an interface based on a combination of 2D and 3D computer graphics techniques using the X Window System with the Motif toolkit, and on a set of 3D interaction tools built on top of the Starbase graphics library from Hewlett Packard. The CAPS system is built on top of the bolio simulation system[32]. The clinician is presented with an X Window System screen containing a menu bar and buttons, and a 3D graphics window showing a rendered image of the geometric model of the patient. The user controls the 3D view of the patient model and modifies other rendering parameters using the mouse. The user interface also allows the surgeon to switch between the pre- and post-operative patient geometry, or to animate the transition between them.

Mouse actions are used to select points on the rendered image of the patient. These points are used to define the incision lines on the skin surface and the tissue to be excised. The system converts this into a data structure for subsequent use by the mesh generator.

Operating on the Surface
Planning the operation on the skin surface requires a technique for mapping selections on the screen window back onto the surface of the object, i.e., a mouse click on the window should pick a point on the patient model which appears directly beneath the mouse location. For use in their 3D object painting system, Hanrahan and Haeberli describe a technique for hardware-assisted calculation of this location that makes use of an object ID buffer[15].

Since our graphics hardware did not support this feature, we implemented this operation with ray tracing as follows. A ray is cast from the view point to the selected point on the view plane and is intersected with a polyhedral reconstruction of the scan data.

The polyhedron is created by making vertices at the scan data sample points (transformed from source data space to world coordinates) and connecting each set of four adjacent vertices with a polygon. This operation requires checking the ray against each of the polygons in the polyhedral reconstruction. To reduce the number of polygons, a filtered version of the source data is used. The operation could be made more efficient with octree sorting of the polygons or other ray tracing optimizations. It turned out that we did not need to explore this since the point is picked on a 2D image, and feedback can be given instantly when the button is pressed; the system can then be calculating the 3D intersection in the background while the user is selecting the next point.

After a set of points on the surface is created, it is useful to be able to pick a point by clicking the mouse on that point. Again, we chose a ray tracing approach to select the nearest point to the ray from the view point through the picked point on the view plane.

Defining a Hole: Incision
An incision through the skin is topologically a hole, but geometrically it is infinitesimally thin until it is deformed by the mechanical simulation. Rather than requiring the user to draw a hole by entering the points on both sides of the incision, the incision is entered by picking a sequence of points corresponding to the cutting path of the scalpel. This list of points is then converted into a loop of points describing the hole. Figure 2 illustrates this mapping. The points are entered by selecting locations on the skin surface using the screen space to skin surface transformation described in the previous section. The incision line can be modified by picking one of the points and moving it.

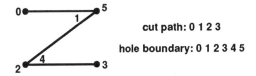

cut path: 0 1 2 3

hole boundary: 0 1 2 3 4 5

Figure 2. This figure shows the relationship between the cutting path entered by the surgeon and the boundary of the incision hole. The surgeon selects the points 0, 1, 2, and 3 to define a simple Z-plasty incision. The system adds points 4 and 5 coincident with points 2 and 1. The boundary of the hole is then stored as the ordered list 0, 1, 2, 3, 4, 5. Note that no tissue was removed in the incision shown. Tissue could be removed by interactively picking and moving the points 1, 2, 4, or 5 in order to enclose the tissue to remove within the hole boundary.

Modifying the Hole: Excision
An excision of tissue is defined by picking one of the points in the hole border and offsetting it from its corresponding point on the other side of the hole, with the result that the hole is no longer infinitesimally thin. Moving one border point creates a quadrilateral, while moving more than one creates an arbitrary polygonal shape. A simple point picking algorithm cannot be used for this picking operation because the two points on either side of the hole are coincident. A modified algorithm could be devised to distinguish between coincident points by determining on which side of

Figure 1. This figure shows the node numbering and pattern for an elliptical excision, both before and after wound closure. The surgeon originally enters the points 0, 1, 2, and 3. The system then adds points 4 and 5, initially coincident with 2 and 3. The surgeon then moves points 4 and 5 to enclose the excision region.

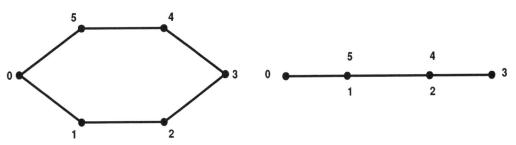

129

the incision line the user picks. In our current prototype a menu selection is used to indicate the point to be moved.

Closing the Hole: Suturing

Suturing refers to the sewing together of edges of the incision. In the finite element simulation, this is accomplished by suture constraint equations for the individual nodes in the continuum mesh. Even for a simple wound closure, dozens of pairs of nodes must constrained together in order to suture the entire wound. Selecting each pair of nodes by hand would be unnecessarily tedious. Instead, the continuum mesh generator automatically creates a list of nodes to be sutured from a description of which edges of the hole border are to be brought together. Figure 1 shows the pre- and post-operative topology desired for a simple excision. For this configuration, the edge sutures are specified as ((0,1), (0,5)), ((1,2), (5,4)), and ((2,3), (4,3)). When the same point is included in both of the edges to be sutured, the mesh generator recognizes this as a corner being closed and does not define any sutures for the nodes corresponding to that point. The suture edges for the Z-plasty shown in figure 2 are ((5, 0), (5, 4)), ((2, 1), (2, 3)), and ((0, 1), (3, 4)). In the CAPS system, the suture edges are specified by selecting a menu item corresponding to the type of surgical procedure being performed (e.g. elliptical excision or Z-plasty). This technique works because the suture relationships depend only on the pre-defined topology of the procedure and not the interactively specified geometry. The menu item approach has the advantage that the suture conditions do not need to be re-entered for each simulation of the same surgical procedure.

The drawback of this menu-based approach is that in order to simulate a new procedure, the suture relationships described above must be worked out by hand and added to the user interface configuration file. While this is not a very difficult task, a more flexible solution would be to allow the user to define the suture relationships by selecting pairs of wound edges. The system could differentiate between coincident edges by determining which side of the incision line the user picked. Picking edges in the proper sequence would then define the suture relationships for the surgical procedure. These suture relationships could then be added to the menu for use in future analyses.

6. MESH GENERATION

The surgical plan is entered in the CAPS system using a graphical interface which corresponds to the way the surgeon draws on the patient's skin in the operating room. An important part of this interface is the mesh generator, which creates a well-formed finite element mesh directly from the surgical plan and the original scan of the patient geometry.

The mesh generation algorithm consists of two major steps: surface meshing and continuum meshing. The surface meshing portion of the algorithm grows a mesh out from the incision hole border along the skin surface. Surface meshing is performed in a normalized cylindrical space ignoring the r (radial) coordinate. After the surface mesh is generated, the mesh is snapped back to the skin surface by looking up the r coordinate in the Cyberware range data.

The continuum meshing portion of the algorithm refers to the process of creating a continuum finite element mesh representing the skin thickness. This is accomplished by growing the surface mesh radially in from the skin surface to the bone surface along the r axis. Triangles are extruded into wedge elements and quadrilaterals are extruded into cuboid elements. Edges shared by polygons in the surface mesh are extruded into shared faces in the continuum mesh. Each vertex in the surface mesh defines a set of nodes in the continuum mesh which lie along the line from that vertex to the central axis of the cylindrical space of the patient scan data. Note that this extrusion process assumes that the incision cuts into the skin along the r axis.

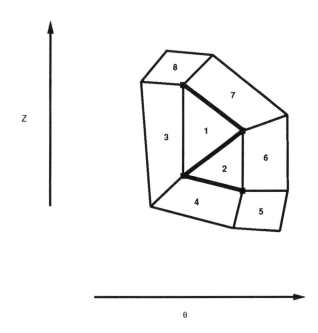

Figure 3. A surface mesh generated from a Z-plasty incision. The original incision lines are indicated in bold. The first stage of the surface meshing algorithm traverses the border of the incision hole and identifies the two concave regions which become surface mesh polygons 1 and 2. The second stage of the algorithm adds polygons 3, 4, 5, 6, 7, and 8. Polygons 5 and 8 result from vertices that were "expanded" because they meet at too sharp an angle.

Figure 4 shows a cross section of the nodes and elements created by the continuum mesh algorithm. Heavy lines are edges from the surface mesh, and filled circles are nodes from the surface mesh.

A suture condition specified between two edges on the incision boundary is converted into suture constraints between each pair of nodes generated from those edges. Nodes on the bottom layer of the continuum mesh which do not have suture constraints are marked as fixed in all three degrees of freedom. All other nodes in the continuum mesh are unconstrained.

Surface Meshing Algorithm

The surface meshing approach used in the CAPS system is based on the automatic mesh generation work of Chae and Bathe[3;4]. Their algorithm, which addresses the problem of automatic meshing of CAD parts such as a plate with holes drilled in it, works by creating layers of elements along the borders of the object and working inward until the rows meet. We have modified this approach to work outward from the incision boundary hole and have made the algorithm create quadrilateral elements wherever possible.

Our algorithm consists of two stages: 1) Traverse the border of incision looking for angles larger than a set threshold t_1, convert them to triangles in the surface mesh and update the border. This process continues until no more angles need to be filled. 2) Go around the border adding a layer of quadrilaterals of thickness l_1: a quadrilateral is added for each edge in the border, and an extra quadrilateral is added at edges which join at an angle less than a specified threshold t_2.

Stage 1 is implemented as follows. For each vertex v_i in the border list, examine the angle between the edges (v_i, v_{i+1}) and (v_{i+1}, v_{i+2}).* If this angle is greater than t_1, add triangle (v_{i+2}, v_{i+1}, v_i) to the surface mesh and delete vertex v_{i+1} from the border list. Continue this process until no more triangles are added in a complete traversal of the border list. After stage 1, the region defined by the border list will be nearly convex (no concavities will be greater than t_1).

Stage 2 has two substages: creating the new border list and joining the new and old border lists with quadrilaterals. The first substage proceeds as follows. Create an empty list to store the new border. For each vertex v_i in the current border list, let n_1 be the outward normal from edge (v_{i-1}, v_i) and n_2 be the outward normal from edge (v_i, v_{i+1}). Examine the angle between the edges (v_{i-1}, v_i) and (v_i, v_{i+1}). If the angle is greater than t_2 then add a vertex to the new border with vertex position of $v_i + l_1 (n_1 + n_2)$. If the angle is less than t_2 then mark v_i as expanded, and add three vertices to the new border with vertex positions of $v_i + l_1 n_1$, $v_i + l_1 (n_1 + n_2)$, and $v_i + l_1 n_2$.

The second substage of stage 2 is to connect new and old border lists with quadrilaterals as follows. Let j index the new border list and i index current border list; initialize i and j to zero. For each vertex v_i, if v_i is marked as expanded, add quadrilateral $(v_i, v_j, v_{j+1}, v_{j+2})$, increment j by two. Add quadrilateral $(v_i, v_j, v_{j+1}, v_{i+1})$. Increment i and j by one. Make the new border the current border. The entire stage 2 process is repeated once for each layer to be added to the surface mesh. Figure 3 shows the surface mesh generated for a Z-plasty incision.

Continuum Meshing Algorithm

Generation of the continuum mesh from the surface mesh is accomplished by extruding the surface mesh inward along the r axis to form solid elements and then making a mapping from vertices and polygons in the surface mesh to nodes and elements in the continuum mesh. First we look at the numbering of nodes in the standard isoparametric element, then we look at the numbering of the vertices and edges in the surface mesh, and then at the correspondence between these numbering schemes. The continuum meshing algorithm converts the surface mesh into an arbitrary number of layers of elements, each layer being of an arbitrary thickness.

Figure 5 shows the standard finite element used in the CAPS system. The algorithm must generate elements with the proper node ordering. Nodes 0-3 called the top_nodes, are the corners of face 0; nodes 4-7, called the bottom_nodes, are the corners of face 1; nodes 8-11, called the top_mid_nodes are the nodes in the middles of the edges on the top face; nodes 12-15, called the bottom_mid_nodes are the nodes in the middle of the edges on the bottom face; nodes 16-19, called the center_nodes are the nodes in the center of the edges joining face 0 to face 1.

In the surface mesh we have a set of vertex points connected by a set of polygons. Each polygon has a list of the vertices which defines its shape. An edge of the polygon is defined by each pair of vertices in the list and by the last and first vertices in the list. A data structure is maintained for each layer of elements which keeps track of the numbering of nodes in the layer. As each node is created, its position is calculated and its index in the list of nodes for the structure is recorded in the layer data structure.

For the top layer of elements, the top_nodes are positioned at the points of the surface mesh vertices, The positions of the top_mid_nodes of the top face are calculated by taking the midpoints of each polygon edge and offsetting those points to lie on the skin surface. The positions of the bottom_nodes are calculated by offsetting the positions of the top_nodes in r by the thickness of the layer. The positions of the bottom_mid_nodes are calculated by offsetting the positions of the top_mid_nodes by the thickness of the layer. The positions of the center_nodes are calculated by offsetting the positions of the top_nodes by one half the layer thickness. For continuum meshes with more than one layer of elements

---

* Accesses to vertices in the node list wrap around if the $i+n$ is greater than the length of the list. Similarly, negative indices wrap back to the end of the list.

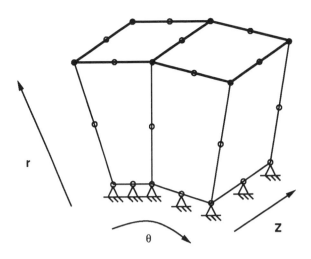

● **Surface mesh vertex**

○ **Continuum mesh node**

Constrained node

Figure 4. Two elements from a continuum mesh. this shows the relationship between the surface mesh polygons (corresponding to the top faces shown in bold) and the continuum elements. The continuum mesh algorithm generates elements extruded along the r (into the skin) following the topology defined by the surface mesh. The bottom layer of nodes are constrained to remain fixed to represent the bony support. The figure shows a single layer of 20 node elements.

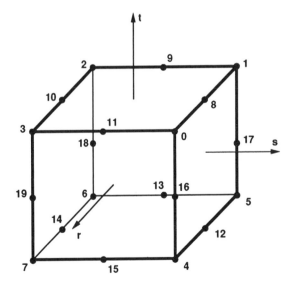

Figure 5. Node numbering for the standard 20 node isoparametric element used in the CAPS system.

in the r direction, subsequent layers of elements are generated in an analogous manner with the exception that rather than creating new nodes for the top_nodes and the top_mid_nodes, the indices of the previous layer's bottom_nodes and bottom_mid_nodes are copied instead.

Once all the nodes have been created, the elements must be created. One element per layer is created for each polygon in the surface mesh. These elements must contain a correctly ordered list of the node indices. This list of indices for the top_nodes is obtained by looping through the vertices of the polygon and looking up the node indices from the data structure of the layer corresponding to the top the element. The indices for the bottom_nodes and the center_nodes are obtained in the same manner, but using the appropriate node indices from the layer data structure. The list of indices for the top_mid_nodes and the bottom_mid_nodes are found by looping over the edge list for each polygon and finding that edge's index in the list of edges for the surface mesh; that index is then used to find the appropriate node index by looking up the node in the appropriate layer data structure.

Triangles in the surface mesh are handled as a special case by creating wedge shaped elements. This can be accomplished by collapsing one of the side faces of the isoparametric element. In this case, only 15 nodes are created for the element, and a shared node index is used for nodes 2, 10, and 3, for nodes 18 and 19, and for nodes 6, 14, and 7.

7. RESULTS

To date the system has been used in two ways. We have been able to use the system to simulate a number of plastic surgeries of the face and have obtained good visual match between the simulation results and post-operative photos of actual patients. In addition, we have shown the system to over a dozen practicing plastic surgeons and have obtained very positive feedback. Surgeons have noted, for example, that this system is completely different than any current form of surgery planning because it contains an actual model of the elasticity of the skin. This critical feature is missing from most current planning techniques such as drawings or paper models. The other planning techniques which do have some model of skin elasticity (namely cadavers or animal models) do not allow easy iterative design of the procedure.

8. Future Work

Physical modeling of human soft tissue presents many challenges which can only be addressed by making simplifying assumptions about the behavior of the tissue. The complexity of the tissue includes the fact that it is alive, that it has a complex structure of component materials, and that its mechanical behavior is nonlinear[17;23]. The design of the CAPS system, we have attempted to model those features of the tissue which have direct bearing on the outcome of plastic surgery, but in doing so it ignores the following effects: the physiological processes of healing, growth, and aging are not included in the model; the multiple layers of material which make up the skin are idealized as a single elastic continuum;

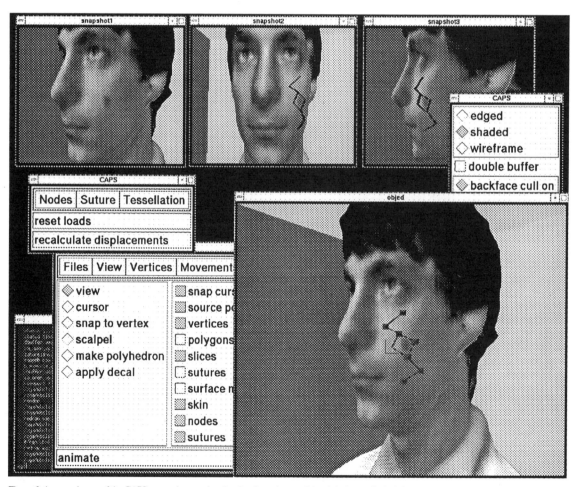

Figure 6. A screen image of the CAPS system in operation showing the patient model and the interactively defined surgical plan.

and the system uses only a linear model of the mechanical behavior of the tissue and does not include a model of the pre-stress in the tissue (i.e., the skin does not open up when cut). Under these assumptions, the model gives an estimate of the instantaneous state of the tissue after the procedure has been performed.

These assumptions could be relaxed to build a more complete model of tissue behavior. The complex structure of the tissue could be addressed by creating a more detailed finite element mesh with multiple layers of differing material properties. The nonlinear mechanical response of the tissue could be better approximated using a nonlinear finite element solution technique. Both of these improvements will make the solution process more computationally complex, but will become more feasible as computers become faster. We plan to perform a series of clinical trials to identify the parameters which have the most influence in the surgical result and to obtain accurate estimates of the elastic and viscous moduli of the soft tissue.

The incorporation of physiological processes presents a more fundamental problem, since the processes themselves are not well understood. In this realm, the physical modeling approach offers a possible method for determining the action of these processes. For example, if the physical model is calibrated such that it gives a nearly exact prediction of the immediate post-operative state of the tissue, then subsequent changes in the patient's skin due to healing could be determined by changing the material property assumptions of the model until it again matches the skin. It is possible that this analysis would lead to a method of predicting the effect of healing which could then be included in the planning system.

The field of plastic surgery simulation is still very new and there are many promising directions for future work. For example, more work is needed to improve modeling of the soft tissue to more accurately model its nonlinear mechanical response and its long term physiological changes. In the future, we would also like to see improved user interface techniques to give the surgeon more control over the direction and depth of the incisions. The current incision technique is adequate for planning surface incisions, but cannot be used for internal surgery.

9. CONCLUSIONS

Simulation of plastic surgery presents many challenging problems which can be addressed by interactive 3D graphics techniques. Each patient presents the surgeon with a unique set of problems for which there are many possible courses of action. The surgeon's goal is to optimize the rearrangement of tissue, to correct the tissue deficiency, and to minimize distortion of the surrounding tissue.

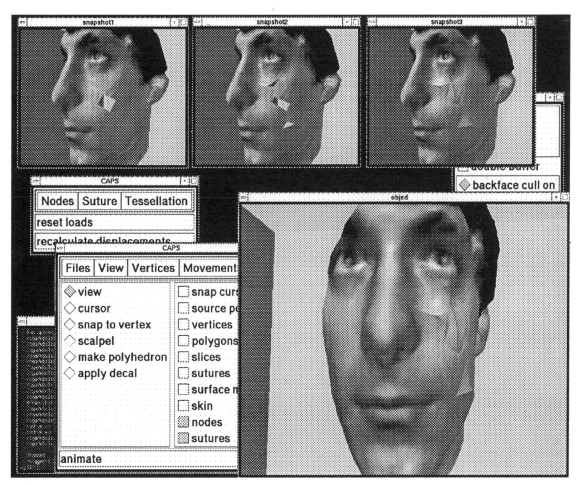

Figure 7. A screen image of the CAPS system in operation showing the simulated results of the operation.

The surgical plan must take into account the complex geometry and mechanical behavior of the soft tissue.

In this paper we have shown how a task level analysis of the plastic surgery planning problem has guided our development and implementation of a computer-aided plastic surgery system. The user interface techniques and mesh generation algorithms we have presented directly address the requirements of the task without burdening the surgeon with the implementation details of the finite element model. Our approach has been well received by clinicians, who report that they would be comfortable using this system to plan operations. However, before we take that step, we will be putting the software through a series of clinical trials to validate the simulation results through retrospective analysis of case histories.

10. ACKNOWLEDGMENTS

This work was supported in part by NHK (Japan Broadcasting Co.) and by equipment grants from Apple and Hewlett Packard. The authors would like to thank David Sturman for being a willing virtual patient.

11. BIBLIOGRAPHY

1. Klaus-Jurgen Bathe, Finite Element Procedures in Engineering Analysis, Prentice-Hall, Englewood Cliffs, New Jersey, 1982.

2. Mike Cedars M.D., Plastic Surgeon, Berkeley, California, Personal Communication.

3. Soo-Won Chae, On the Automatic Generation of Near-Optimal Meshes for Three-Dimensional Linear-Elastic Finite Element Analysis, Ph.D. Thesis, MIT (1988).

4. Soo-Won Chae and Klaus-Jurgen Bathe, On Automatic Mesh Construction and Mesh Refinement in Finite Element Analysis, Computers & Structures, Maxwell Pergamon Macmillan plc. (1989) 32:3/4 pp. 911-936.

5. Grace Hwa-Pei Chang, Computer-Aided Surgery -- An Interactive System for Intertrochanteric Osteotomy, SM Thesis, MIT (1987).

6. David Chen, Pump It Up: Simulating Muscle Shape From Skeleton Kinematics A Dynamic Model of Muscle for Computer Animation, Ph.D. Thesis, MIT (1991).

7. Court Cutting, M.D., Fred L. Bookstein, Ph.D., Barry Grayson, D.D.S., Linda Fellingham, Ph.D., and Joseph G. McCarthy, M.D., Three-Dimensional Computer-Assisted Design of Craniofacial Surgical Procedures: Optimization and Interaction with Cephalometric and CT-Based Models, Plastic and Reconstructive Surgery, 77:6, pp. 877-885, (June, 1986).

8. Cyberware Laboratory, Inc. Monterey, California.

9. Robert A. Drebin, Loren Carpenter, Pat Hanrahan, Volume Rendering, Computer Graphics, 22:4, pp. 65-74 (August, 1988).

10. S. Delp, P. Loan, M. Hoy, F. Zajac, S. Fisher, and J. Rosen, An Interactive Graphics-Based Model of the Lower Extremity to Study Orthopaedic Surgical Procedures, IEEE Transactions on Biomedical Engineering, Special issue on interaction with and visualization of biomedical data, 37:8, (August, 1990).

11. Xiao Qi Deng, A Finite Element Analysis of Surgery of the Human Facial Tissues, Ph.D. Thesis, Columbia University (1988).

12. Richard H. Gallagher (ed.), Finite Elements in Biomechanics, Wiley Interscience (1982).

13. William C. Grabb M.D. and James W. Smith M.D., Plastic Surgery, Little, Brown and Company, Boston (1986).

14. Mark Gorney, M.D., Plastic Surgeon, Personal Communication.

15. Pat Hanrahan, Paul Haeberli, Direct WYSIWYG Painting and Texturing on 3D Shapes, Computer Graphics 24:4, pp. 215-223 (1990).

16. Hidehiko Kawabata, M.D., Hideo Kawai, M.D., Kazuhiro Masada, M.D., Keiro Ono, M.D., Computer-Aided Analysis of Z-Plasties, Plastic and Reconstructive Surgery 83:2, pp. 319-325 (February 1989).

17. R. M. Kenedi, T. Gibson, J. H. Evans, J. C. Barbenel, Tissue Mechanics, Phys. Med. Biol. 20:5, pp. 699-717 (1975).

18. Wayne F. Larrabee Jr., M.D., A Finite Element Model of Skin Deformation, Laryngoscope, pp. 399-419 (July, 1987).

19. Mark Levoy, A Hybrid Ray Tracer for Rendering Polygon and Volume Data, IEEE Computer Graphics and Applications 10:2, pp. 33-40 (March, 1990).

20. A. A. Limberg, M.D., The Planning of Local Plastic Operations on the Body Surface: Theory and Practice, Government Publishing House for Medical Literature, Leningrad, U.S.S.R. (1963), english translation S. Anthony Wolfe, M.D., D. C. Heath and Company (1984).

21. R. W. Mann, Computer-Aided Surgery, RESNA 8th Annual Conference, Memphis, Tennessee (1985).

22. Derek R. Ney, Elliot K. Fishman, Donna Magid, and Robert A. Drebin, Volumetric Rendering of Computed Tomographic Data: Principles and Techniques, IEEE Computer Graphics and Applications 10:2, pp. 24-32 (March 1990).

23. Richard M. Peters, Biomechanics and Surgery, in Biomechanics: Its Foundations and Objectives, Prentice-Hall, Englewood Cliffs, New Jersey (1972).

24. Steve Pieper, David Chen, Scott Delp, Michael McKenna, David Zeltzer, and Joseph Rosen, Surgical Simulation: From Computer-Aided Design to Computer-Aided Surgery, Proceedings of IMAGINA '92, Monte Carlo (January 1992).

25. Steven Pieper, CAPS: Computer-Aided Plastic Surgery, Ph.D. Thesis, MIT (1991).

26. Steven Pieper, More Than Skin Deep: Physical Modeling of Facial Tissue, SM Thesis, MIT (1989).

27. David E. Thompson, William L. Buford, Jr., Loyd M. Myers, David J. Giurintano, and John A. Brewer, A Hand Biomechanics Workstation, Computer Graphics 22:4, pp. 335-343 (August 1988).

28. Michael W. Vannier, M.D., Jeffrey L. Marsh, M.D., James O. Warren, M.D., Three Dimensional Computer Graphics for Craniofacial Surgical Planning and Evaluation, Computer Graphics 17:3, pp. 263-273 (July 1983).

29. Michael W. Vannier, Tom Pilgram, Gulab Bhatia, Barry Brunsden, and Paul Commean, Facial Surface Scanner, Computer Graphics and Applications 11:6, pp. 72-79 (November 1991).

30. Keith Waters, A Muscle Model for Animating Three-Dimensional Facial Expression, Computer Graphics 21:4, pp. 17-24 (1987).

31. Keith Waters and Demetri Terzopoulos, A Physical Model of Facial Tissue and Muscle Articulation, Proceedings of the First Conference on Visualization in Biomedical Computing, Atlanta, Georgia, pp. 77-82 (May 22-25, 1990).

32. David Zeltzer, Steve Pieper, and David Sturman, An Integrated Graphical Simulation Platform, Proceedings of Graphics Interface '89, London, Ontario, pp. 266-274 (June 19-23, 1989).

33. David Zeltzer, Task-level Graphical Simulation: Abstraction, Representation, and Control, in Making Them Move: Mechanics, Control, and Animation of Articulated Figures, Norman Badler, Brian Barsky & David Zeltzer (eds.), Morgan Kaufmann Publishers, Inc., San Mateo, California, pp. 3-33 (1991).

3DM: A Three Dimensional Modeler Using a Head-Mounted Display

Jeff Butterworth, Andrew Davidson,
Stephen Hench and T. Marc Olano

Department of Computer Science, Sitterson Hall
University of North Carolina
Chapel Hill, NC 27599-3175

Abstract

3dm is a three dimensional (3D) surface modeling program that draws techniques of model manipulation from both CAD and drawing programs and applies them to modeling in an intuitive way. 3dm uses a head-mounted display (HMD) to simplify the problem of 3D model manipulation and understanding. A HMD places the user in the modeling space, making three dimensional relationships more understandable. As a result, 3dm is easy to learn how to use and encourages experimentation with model shapes.

1   Introduction

The use of interactive 3D environments has increased the demand for complex 3D models.[9] The 3D environments that provide a sense of telepresence or "virtual reality" require a large number of models in order to give the user the illusion of being in a specific place. This demand for more models has highlighted the fact that most modeling systems are difficult to use for all but a small number of experts.[9] Through identification and removal of some of the fundamental obstacles to modeling we hope to make it accessible to more users.

Typical techniques used to select and display objects are a major hindrance to 3D modeling.[3] To place an object in 3D requires six parameters: the position (three) and the orientation (three). Most modeling systems (modelers) must settle for a 2D mouse augmented by a keyboard for this purpose. This mismatch results in difficult placement and picking of objects in modeling space. The display of models usually takes the form of a projection onto a 2D monitor. This has the effect of making spatial relationships unclear. Technological improvements to 3D model display and manipulation hardware can remove these barriers to model creation and understanding.

Current virtual reality technology provides one solution to more intuitive modeling. A HMD system gives the ability to understand complex spatial relationships of models by placing the user in the model's world. Within this type of system, a hand-held pointing device supplies users with the ability to specify 3D relationships through direct

3D manipulation. As a result, the user can build the virtual world from *within* the virtual world.

Our source of inspiration for designing a user interface for a HMD-based modeler is the current software used for 2D modeling. At one time, creating 2D models required cumbersome CAD programs. This software took a long time to learn and often did not provide real-time interaction. Now, however, 2D drawings can be manipulated by even the most casual users of personal computers. This revolution is in part the result of intuitive drawing programs like MacDraw. One of the keys to MacDraw's success is its inherent simplicity. Most work done with it requires no reading or use of the keyboard. Rather, it provides a palette of tools which is always available next to the model. To change modes, the user simply selects the tool from the palette using the mouse. The process of 3D modeling can become more accessible if some of the lessons learned from this evaluation of 2D modeling can be applied to 3D modeling systems.

This paper presents a HMD-based system called **3dm** which simplifies the task of 3D modeling by implementing the concepts introduced above. Basic techniques for working within 3dm's virtual world are described to show how users access the various features. The implementation of 3dm is described through a presentation of its most useful commands. Finally, the results of actually using 3dm are presented with an emphasis on new techniques that can be applied within other virtual worlds.

2   Prior Work

A large body of work has been done on 3D modeling. Although 3D *input* devices have been used to enhance modelers, very little modeling has been done with a HMD. Some examples of modeling with six degree-of-freedom input devices are [1] and [8], but both of those used traditional 2D displays. Previous uses of HMD systems have concentrated more on exploration of virtual worlds rather than creating or modifying them. Some examples of this work with HMD's can be found in [5].

Modeling using a HMD system has been explored by Clark.[4] Users of Clark's system created parametric surfaces by manipulating control points on a wire-frame grid. This system highlighted the utility of using a HMD for improved understanding and interaction with models. Like Clark's system, 3dm relies on a HMD to help simplify modeling, but 3dm's intuitive user interface design also makes it easy to learn and use.

135

3   Implementation

3dm was developed using a VPL eyephone as the display device and Polhemus trackers to track the head and hand. A 6D 2-button mouse, developed at UNC-CH, was the input device. The images were rendered using the Pixel-Planes 4 and Pixel-Planes 5 high-performance graphics engines developed at UNC-CH.[6][7] Currently, all models created with 3dm are made up of hierarchical groups of triangles.

3.1   User Interface

In addition to the model, the virtual world of 3dm contains the components of the user interface. The most important of these are the toolbox and the cursor. The cursor follows the position of the hand-held mouse, giving the user a sense of hand position in the modeling space. The toolbox is the means by which most actions are performed.

Some of the user interface components are simply helpful markers that can be turned off, unlike the toolbox and the cursor, which are always visible. The user stands on a "magic carpet" which marks the boundaries of where the tracking system operates. Remaining within tracker range is important because the virtual world will begin to tilt as the user moves farther out of range. Below the magic carpet lies a checkered ground plane, above which the model is usually created. Additional reference objects, such as coordinate axes, can be turned on by the user.

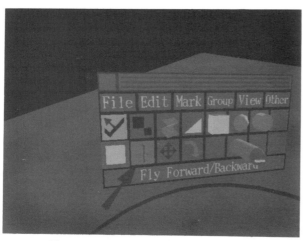

Figure 1: The toolbox as seen by the user.

The toolbox initially appears suspended in space near the user's waist, but it can be moved to a more convenient location. The toolbox remains attached to the user as he or she moves around the modeling space, or it can be disconnected and left anywhere above the magic carpet. The toolbox is organized into cells containing 3D icons. Each icon represents either a tool, a command, or a toggle. Many of these icons can optionally appear in pulldown menus at the top of the toolbox in order to reduce clutter.

Icons perform actions when they are selected with the cursor. Tools change the current mode of operation as reflected in the shape of the cursor. For instance, when the user reaches into the toolbox and selects the flying tool, the cursor takes the form of an airplane. Selecting a command performs a single task without changing the current mode of

operation. Toggles change some global aspect of 3dm. An example is the snap-to grid toggle, which restricts cursor movement to a 3D grid when it is on.

Exploring the model provides understanding of its 3D shape, so 3dm supports multiple methods of navigating in the modeling space. The HMD system used for 3dm allows the user to walk through the model space a few paces in any direction. Walking simply does not provide the range of movement needed for most models, so 3dm supports "flying," a commonly used method of traveling through virtual worlds.[2] Flying consists of translating the user through model space in the direction that the cursor is pointing. Flying moves the magic carpet, which carries the user and the toolbox along. A method of navigation that is the complement of flying is "grabbing" the world. Grabbing the world allows the user to attach the modeling space to the cursor and then drag and rotate it. Grabbing can be used to bring a feature of the world to the user rather than forcing the user to walk or fly to the feature.

Models often require manipulation at vastly different scales. To facilitate this type of work, the user can be scaled using a process called *growing* and *shrinking*. This scaling does not affect the model: it changes the user's relative size with respect to the model. The user could shrink down to bird size in order to add eyelashes to a model of an elephant and then grow to the size of a house to alter the same model's legs. Since the user can become disoriented by all of these methods of movement, there is a command that immediately returns the user to the initial viewpoint in the middle of the modeling space.

The user receives continuous feedback in a variety of ways. The HMD system provides all visual input to the user, so the display must be updated between 15 and 30 times per second. Even during file loading and other slow operations, the screen is updated and the head is tracked. Rubber banding is implemented in many situations: when defining a new triangle, scaling or moving an object, and extruding. Predictive highlighting shows the user what *would* be selected if a mouse button were pressed. This highlighting is used in the toolbox, and even more importantly, when marking vertices. Whenever the cursor is near a model, the nearest vertex is highlighted, giving the user an indication of which vertex would be operated on before actually attempting the operation.

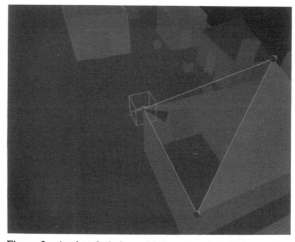

Figure 2: A triangle being added to a model. Demonstrates rubber banding and snapping to nearby vertices.

3.2 Tools and Commands

Although many tools are available in the 3dm toolbox, it is more useful to understand the general classes of tools supplied to the user than to enumerate all of the specific tools. Most of these tools were chosen because of their proven utility in pre-existing modelers.

3.2.1 Surface Creation

Surface creation is the central purpose of most 3D modeling, so 3dm provides more than one method for creating surfaces. A triangle creation tool exists for generating both single triangles and triangle strips. The corners of these triangles are specified by pointing and clicking the mouse, so the triangles are created in their desired locations rather than appearing in a "building" area and then being moved into the model space. Pre-existing vertices may be used during triangle creation to allow triangles to share corners or entire edges, making seamless connections easy.

The extrusion tool supplies a more powerful and more specialized method of triangle creation. This tool allows the user to either draw a poly-line or select one from edges already in the model and stretch it out into an extruded surface. The extrusion is performed by dragging the leading edge of the surface with the mouse. Because the mouse can be twisted and translated arbitrarily during the extrusion, it becomes easy to create complex surfaces with this tool. In addition, the leading edge of this new surface can be scaled and then extruded again as many times as necessary. This form of extrusion can rapidly create such objects as walls, legs, tree trunks, and leaves.

The last surface creation tools facilitate creation of standard surface shapes. Currently box, sphere, and cylinder tools exist. They each allow the user to interactively stretch out an arbitrarily proportioned wireframe representation of a standard shape. When the wireframe representation has the desired proportions, it is turned into a triangulated surface.

3.2.2 Editing

Since surfaces are rarely in exactly the desired shape upon creation, it is important that surface editing be an easy operation. The most commonly used editing tool is the mark/move tool. This tool provides a method of grasping and moving arbitrary portions of the model. Not only can entire objects be grabbed and moved with the mouse, but selected groups of vertices can be moved in order to distort part of an object. Scaling can also be performed on either entire objects or groups of vertices. During both movement and scaling, the user sees the model changing in real time. This interaction decreases the number of edits needed to make a desired change. The marking aspects of this tool are used to mark arbitrary portions of the model for operations with other tools.

Familiar editing operations from drawing programs are a group of 3dm commands that facilitate rapid experimental changes. An arbitrary number of triangles or entire objects can be cut, copied, pasted and deleted. These commands provide easy reuse of existing objects.

An undo/redo stack is provided for reversing any number of operations from any tool or command. As operations are performed, the changes they cause to the model are stored in the undo/redo stack. The undo command can then be used to pop changes off of this stack to undo as many operations as necessary. These undo operations can themselves be undone with the redo command. The undo/redo commands encourage experimental changes to the model because no operation can cause permanent damage.

3.2.3 Hierarchy

The hierarchical features of 3dm provide methods for organizing complex models. "Grouping" can be used to associate triangles and possibly other groups to more easily manipulate them as a whole. These groups can be *instanced*. An instance is similar to a copy of a group that can be arbitrarily translated, rotated, and scaled. However, the difference between an instance and a copy is that the instances of a group are all linked to the same basic shape. If this shape is changed, then the change is reflected in all instances at once. An example where instancing would be useful is in a model of a large building. Suppose that hundreds of chairs were in this building. If one model of a chair were instanced many times to make these chairs, then a change to a single chair would be reflected in hundreds of places throughout the building.

Groups can be organized into a hierarchy represented by a directed acyclic graph. This type of hierarchy is particularly well-suited to modeling articulated figures. The ability to instance groups and impose a hierarchy on them helps to organize models.

4 Results

Actual modeling sessions have shown that 3dm is efficient for rapidly prototyping models. Organic shapes, like rocks and trees, have proven to be particularly good subjects for 3dm. These shapes are easily created in 3dm because it provides a good sense for spatial relationships. Users of 3dm have commented that they feel a sense of control, because they can reach out and grab any part of the model with ease. The ability to make these quick modifications encourages the user to experiment with shapes until they are satisfactory. However, 3dm has shown weakness in the area of constraints and models that traditional CAD and drawing programs create well. For instance, 3dm has no way of keeping two polygons parallel, causing some models to appear irregular.

The extrusion tool is an example of a traditional modeling tool that has become even more powerful because of its use in a HMD framework. In most modeling systems, extrusion is performed by moving one or two spatial parameters at a time. 3dm users often alter many parameters at once during an extrusion by twisting *and* translating the new surface. Extrusion in 3dm often consists of many short extrusions. In between these short operations the leading edge of the extruded surface is often scaled and twisted. The result is that complex surfaces can be rapidly created with an easy to use tool.

Some initial solutions to 3dm's lack of constraints have been to add toggles in the toolbox for a snap-to grid and a snap-to plane. The snap-to grid constrains the position of the cursor to the nodes of a regular 3D grid. The resolution of the snap-to grid is dynamically modified to be appropriate to the user's current "grown" or "shrunk" size. The snap-to plane gives the ability to constrain cursor movement to 2 dimensions. The snap-to constraints help in making regular objects, such as mechanical parts.

5   Conclusion

3dm draws techniques of model manipulation from both CAD and drawing programs and applies them to modeling in an intuitive way. A HMD modeling system uses these tools to simplify the problem of 3D model manipulation and understanding.

3dm is a step toward making 3D modeling accessible to unsophisticated users. It supports users' natural forms of interaction with objects to give them better understanding of the shapes of their models. Even a novice user can understand how to manipulate a model by reaching out and grasping it. Users are encouraged to experiment with model shape because 3dm facilitates making rapid changes. The effects of a change to a model can be clearly understood because the user can explore the model using a variety of intuitive navigation techniques.

Advanced users are also empowered by 3dm. Many of the tools borrowed from existing modeling systems become more powerful when used with a HMD. One source of increased utility is the fact that complex operations can involve simultaneous modification of many spatial parameters. Examples of tools that take advantage of this are object placement and extrusion, which both allow combinations of rotation and translation in a single step. By concentrating more functionality into each operation, fewer operations are needed to perform a task and models can be created faster.

6   Acknowledgements

We would like to thank Rich Holloway and Erik Erikson for VLIB and all of their software and hardware support. We would also like to thank Henry Fuchs, Fred Brooks, and the whole Pixel Planes team for supplying us with the graphical environment needed to implement 3dm.

References

[1] Badler, Norman I., Kamran H. Manoochehri, David Baraff. Multi-Dimensional Input Techniques and Articulated Figure Positioning by Multiple Constraints. Proceedings of the Workshop on Interactive 3D Graphics, October 1986. Sponsored by ACM SIGGRAPH.

[2] Blanchard, Chuck, Scott Burgess, Young Harvill, Jaron Lanier, Ann Lasko, Mark Oberman, Michael Teitel. Reality Built For Two: A Virtual Reality Tool. *Computer Graphics,* 22(2):35-36, March 1990. Symposium on Interactive 3D Graphics.

[3] Brooks, Frederick P. Jr. Grasping Reality Through Illusion: Interactive Graphics Serving Science. *Keynote address at the Fifth Conference on Computers and Human Interaction.* Published in CHI '88 Proceedings, May 1988, 1-11.

[4] Clark, James H. Designing Surfaces in 3-D. *Communications of the ACM*, 19(8):454-460, August 1976.

[5] Fisher, S. S., M. McGreevy, J. Humphries, W. Robinett. Virtual Environment Display System. Proceedings of the Workshop on Interactive 3D Graphics, October 1986. Sponsored by ACM SIGGRAPH.

[6] Fuchs, Henry, Jack Goldfeather, Jeff P. Hultquist, Susan Spach, John D. Austin, Frederick P. Brooks, Jr., John G. Eyles, John Poulton. Fast Spheres, Shadows, Textures, Transparencies, and Image Enhancements in Pixel-Planes. *Computer Graphics*, 19(3):111-120, February 1985. SIGGRAPH '85 Conference Proceedings.

[7] Fuchs, Henry, John Poulton, John Eyles, Trey Greer, Jack Goldfeather, David Ellsworth, Steve Molnar, Greg Turk, Brice Tebbs, Laura Israel. Pixel-Planes 5: A Heterogeneous Multiprocessor Graphics System Using Processor-Enhanced Memories. *Computer Graphics*, 23(3): 79-88, July 1989. SIGGRAPH '89 Conference Proceedings.

[8] Sachs, Emanuel, Andrew Roberts, David Stoops. 3-Draw: A Tool for Designing 3D Shapes. *IEEE Computer Graphics & Applications*, November 1991, 18-26.

[9] Sproull, Robert F. Parts of the Frontier are Hard to Move. *Computer Graphics*, 22(2):9, March 1990. Symposium on Interactive 3D Graphics.

Volume Seedlings

Michael F. Cohen, James Painter, Mihir Mehta, Kwan-Liu Ma
Department of Computer Science
University of Utah
Salt Lake City, Utah 84112

Abstract

Recent advances in software and hardware technology have made direct ray-traced volume rendering of 3-d scalar data a feasible and effective method for imaging of the data's contents. The time costs of these rendering techniques still do not permit full interaction with the data, and all of the parameters effecting the resulting images. This paper presents a set of real-time interaction techniques which have been developed to permit exploration of a volume data set. Within the limitation of a static viewpoint, the user is able to interactively alter the position and shape of an area of interest, and modify local viewing parameters. A run length encoded cache of volume rendering samples provides the means to rerender the volume at interactive rates. The user locates and plants "seeds" in areas of interest through the use of data slicing and isosurface techniques. Image processing techniques applied to volumes (i.e. volume processing), can then automatically form regions of interest which in turn modify the rendering parameters. This "region growing" of "seedlings" incrementally alters the image in real-time providing further visual cues concerning the contents of the data. These tools allow interactive exploration of internal structures in the data which may be obscured by other imaging algorithms. Magnetic Resonance Angiography (MRA) provides a driving application for this technology. Results from preliminary studies of MRA data are included.

1 Introduction

Three dimensional scalar fields (or volumes) of data arise in a number of applications from computer simulation of physical phenomena to data gathered for medical diagnostic use via CAT scans and Magnetic Resonance. Rendering images directly from the volume has been demonstrated to be an effective method for visualizing such data [7, 9, 11, 12, 14, 19, 27, 29]. Volume rendering avoids many artifacts which may arise when intermediate graphics primitives are required [7, 13].

Volume images are constructed either in image order by sampling the volume along a ray from an eye point through the data or by projection of the data directly onto the pixel array. Differences in algorithms also deal with the order in which the samples are processed, either front to back as in ray tracing [12], or back to front analogous to a painter's algorithm. Ray tracing algorithms process a pixel at a time, while in projection techniques, a singe sample or data point may effect an area of pixels around the sample in some way via "splatting" [28], or projecting of a representative area onto the screen [22, 29].

As in earlier image synthesis techniques, acceleration methods focus on exploiting coherence in the image and in the data, and/or by progressively refining the image to provide rough results early in the rendering process [11, 15]. However, high quality images still require many seconds or minutes. Thus interactive exploration of volume data sets via these techniques is still not feasible. Changes in viewing parameters, mappings of data values to opacity or color, or enhancing regions of interest require complete new renderings.

The research presented here exploits the coherence across *all possible images from a given viewpoint* to provide interactive rendering rates for high quality images. The starting point of this algorithm is the volume ray casting technique as presented by Levoy [12, 15]. Earlier work in raytracing [21] has shown that a view dependent cache can be exploited to good effect when surface properties and light source intensities need to be adjusted while view position and geometry remain unchanged. In this paper we apply a similar idea to ray casting based volume rendering. The method described here caches rendering information at each sample point along each ray. The cache allows new images based on changes in rendering parameters to be generated *as the changes are made*, providing an interactive loop for volume exploration.

Local areas of interest within the volume can be indicated by the user planting a "seed" in the volume. Local rendering parameters can then be modified based on location relative to the seed. The basics of interactive use of local rendering modification through the use of "volume seeds" has been discussed in an earlier paper [17], and will be summarized in the next section. Problems in the earlier system included excessive storage requirements, and difficulty in placing and forming regions of interest.

The paper continues with a discussion of the use of coherence in the sample caching process followed by a description of new interactive positioning tools utilizing an integration of slicing and isosurface techniques. We then describe the use of image processing techniques generalized to volumes (volume processing) to automatically generate matte volumes modifying local rendering parameters. In this way, the seed sprouts into a "seedling" to enhance the rendering in connected regions of particular interest. Rendering parameters such as opacity are then based on minimum distance from the seedling. Image processing methods have been applied to volumes to *segment* the volume into discrete regions [18, 25, 26]. However, it should be noted that, in the application described here, the seedling itself is never rendered directly, but rather the volume of data continues to be rendered with directly, but rather the volume of data continues to be rendered with volumetric techniques with modified parameters based on position relative to the grown region.

Much of the motivation for the development summarized above has come from a medical application. In particular, imaging of data arising from Magnetic Resonance Angiography (MRA), in which the focus of attention is on exploring the vascular structure within the brain or other regions of the body. MRA techniques are used to diagnose malformations and aneurisms within the brain's blood supply, and to plan surgical and catheterization procedures. The intricate nature of the vascular structure as well as the somewhat noisy data capture require the ability to focus attention on specific vessels as potential anomalies are discovered. Results of the use of the above algorithms on this application will be presented and discussed.

2   Volume Seeds

Ray traced volume rendering involves sampling the data volume at evenly spaced points along a ray, computing a local illumination and opacity value and composing the result with earlier samples along the ray. Individual sample contributions are computed from trilinearly interpolated values from surrounding voxels, where each voxel contains a data value and an estimated gradient determined through finite differencing from its neighbors. The interpolated value and gradient provide arguments to mapping functions to determine color and opacity at the sample point. These color and opacity values may be a derived from a simple mapping from value to RGB (or opacity) or be determined from more complex statistical procedures intended to classify the likelihood of a particular material (e.g., bone, muscle) being present at a particular location [7].

The final illumination contribution at each sample point is computed from the color, opacity, local normal (estimated from the gradient of the data), and direction vectors to the eye and lights. These parameters to a Phong lighting model produce the final illumination at each sample point. Finally each sample illumination value is composited with earlier samples along the ray based on the accumulated opacity along the ray. Sampling can stop when the accumulated opacity approaches unity.

2.1   Image Coherence from a Static Viewpoint

By examining the volume rendering process described above, the required calculations can be broken into the two categories, those which are independent and dependent on mappings from *position and value* to *color and opacity*. Map-independent computations include:

- gradient calculation at voxels,

- determination of rays, and sample points along each ray,

- trilinear interpolation of data values and gradients to the sample points,

- the determination of local shading parameters, e.g. angles between view vector, light vector(s), and normal,

- and evaluation of a monochrome local lighting model, (i.e. independent of color and opacity).

Map-dependent calculations include only:

- mapping of data and position values to opacity and color,

- final evaluation of the local illumination,

- and compositing sample value illumination for final pixel color.

The above lists illustrate the fact that most of the computation is map-independent. However, the remaining map-dependent calculations leave a wide discretion for modification of the final image. This includes changes in:

- the mapping from value to color,

- the mapping from value (and/or the length of the gradient) to opacity,

- and position based variation in color and/or opacity.

By providing interactive tools to modify the local mapping to color and opacity, a user can create new renderings in interactive times (less than one to five seconds at 480x480 resolution on an SGI 240GXT). The locality of the mappings is controlled by the interactive specification of *matte volumes* [7]. By planting a *seed* at a point in the volume, opacity values can be modified as a function of the distance from the seed location. This allows the user to focus attention on particular regions of interest. By adding a binary decision indicating if the sample is in front or behind an imaginary plane through the seed, virtual cut-aways can also be produced in the same way. A final acceleration to the rendering process can be made by recognizing that only a local region of screen space will be effected by a new seed location when the matte volume is limited in size. Details of the matte volume functions and cut-away techniques can be found in Ma et al [17].

2.2   Sample Data Caching

The ability to quickly modify the image based on new matte volumes and the related mappings depends on caching the map-independent information at each sample point. This includes the partially computed illumination value and trilinearly interpolated data value for lookup into the interactively modified mappings. Unlike standard volume rendering, the storage of samples along a ray cannot stop when opacity reaches unity since opacity values can be changes interactively. The current implementation stores a two byte illumination value, and one byte data value per sample. Although the three bytes per sample is compact, this may require substantial memory, on the order of 150 Mb for a 500x500 image with 200 samples per ray. This problem can be largely ameliorated for most data sets by run-length encoding the sample values along each ray. In particular, if some range of values, e.g. zeros indicating empty space, can be a priori ruled as transparent, then both the storage and subsequent rerenderings can often be reduced by one to two orders of magnitude. The run length encoding is accomplished by stealing a bit from the 16 bit illumination value.

3 Seed Positioning

The need for the user to locate and position seeds to indicate areas of interest requires the ability to easily move and position a cursor in the three dimensions of the volume. Visual feedback for this process should provide clues both about the cursor's position and some indication of the volume's content to allow a seed to be placed near a region with a suspected anomaly. A multi-modal approach has been taken to serve these needs. Operations which can be performed smoothly in real time include manipulation of a rough 3D isosurface model and display of data on a slice through the volume.

Isosurface and slice display provide the basis for the user interface which has been developed. A low resolution isosurface is computed from a downsized data set by a polygonization algorithm [3, 16]. This provides enough detail to give the user a correspondence between the data set and what can be seen in the volume rendered image. A slice through the data volume orthogonal to the view direction indicates the depth position. A "screen door" transparency rendering of the slice permits continued view of the portion of the isosurface behind the slice. Finally, the coloration of the isosurface is based on distance from the slice plane, white away from the plane, and red where the plane slices the isosurface. Color plate 1 shows the full screen presented to the user in the Volume Seedlings system. The slicer/isosurface interface is in the upper left. Seeds can be deposited on the slicing plane which will then effect the subsequent rendering of the volume in the upper right.

Thus, the user can, in real-time, manipulate both the rotation of the isosurface and position of the slice plane. By pointing to some point on the resulting image, a seed is placed at the depth of the slice plane and in the location of the cursor. The volume rendering can then be modified based on the new seed location.

4 Volume Seedlings

A single seed highlights a spherical region around the seed point. In many applications, however, the shape of the region of interest within the volume is not strictly spherical, but rather is *data dependent*. The idea of Volume Seedlings is to use the seed point as a base from which to sprout a seedling along paths of "maximum interest", thus highlighting the region of interest.

Identifying regions of interest within the volume is closely related to the computer vision problem of identifying regions of interest within an image. Hence the seedling growth algorithm is similar to region growing algorithms described in the computer vision literature [1] and 2d seed fill algorithms described in the computer graphics literature [8, 24]. One important difference is a primary interest in the intermediate states of the growth process. Computer vision region growing algorithms are primarily concerned with a final segmentation of the image. A similar problem of extracting closed regions in a volume of data has been addressed by Miller et al [18],

The seedling growth algorithm used in the work presented here is voxel based. A *priority queue* [20] of voxels is maintained determining voxels within the volume which need to be explored. Initially, the priority queue contains only the user specified seed. At each growth step, the highest priority voxel is extracted from the priority queue and its 26 neighboring voxels are examined. The priority assigned to each voxel within the queue is based on the "degree of interest" of that voxel. We have currently experimented with linear combinations of three priority functions:

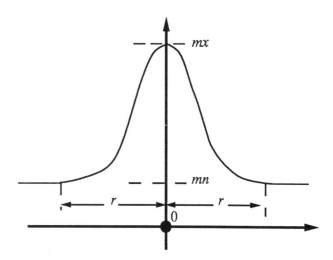

Figure 1: A graphical illustration of the opacity matte as a function of the distance from the seedling.

- classification based

  The priority of a voxel is based on its material classification. A voxel is given a higher priority the greater its percentage of some user specified desired material. This priority function encourages growth within regions of this material.

- gradient based

  The priority of a voxel is based on the magnitude of the gradient at the voxel. High gradient values indicated a surface boundary between materials so this priority function encourages growth along the surfaces boundaries.

- position based

  The priority of a voxel is based on the distance from the original seed point, thus encouraging growth of the seedling near the position indicated by the user.

Many other priority functions are possible.

In addition to the continuous priority function, a discrete test is used to eliminate many voxels. Thus, the neighbors are inserted in the queue only if:

- they haven't been visited before

- they pass an "eligibility" test

The eligibility test is not required but can significantly reduce the size of the priority queue by eliminating obviously uninteresting voxels. Currently, our eligibility test is a simple threshold on the priority, thus voxels are included in the queue only if their priority indicates at least a modicum of interest.

The seedling growth process yields a set of voxels, in priority order, defining a region of interest within the volume. The region of interest is highlighted through the use of an opacity matte as before for a single seed. The opacity matte volume is based on a function of the distance to the *closest* voxel of the seedling as illustrated in Figure 1.

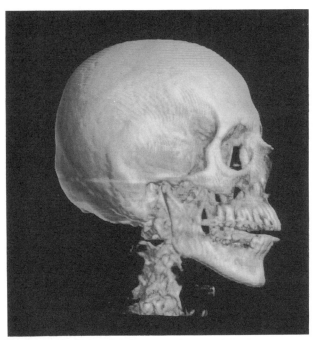

Figure 2: Traditional volume rendering of the UNC Chapel Hill CT head data.

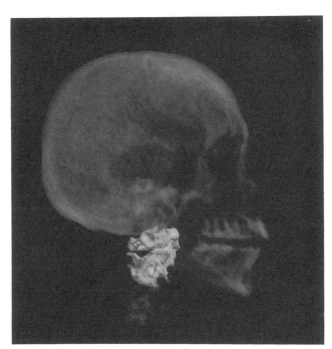

Figure 3: A seed point is used to highlight a spherical area in the data set.

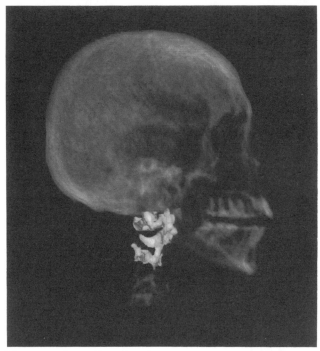

Figure 4: A gradient based seedling is used to highlight a structure in the data set.

The seedling opacity matte is computed according to the following formula:

$$\alpha(p) = mn + (mx - mn) \cdot \beta(mindist(p,s), r)$$

$$\beta(d,r) = \begin{cases} cos^2(\frac{\pi}{2} \cdot \frac{dist}{r}) & \text{if } dist < r, \\ 0 & \text{otherwise.} \end{cases}$$

where $mindist(p,s)$ is the minimum distance between any voxel of the seedling s and the sample point p in three-space. The mn, mx and r parameters are specified by the user.

In essence, r is used to control how wide an area the user wants to see. Surfaces outside this area should be semi-transparent or fully transparent, determined by mn. Mx is used to indicate how much enhancement is to be made to the area near the seed. Note that the opacity matte is never stored explicitly but is instead computed on the fly from the distance to the seedling.

By adding one additional byte to the sample cache to hold the distance to the nearest point in the seedling, images can be computed incrementally. As each new voxel of interest is extracted from the priority queue, only rays representing pixels which pass near the new voxel need to be processed. The minimum distance from a sample point to any point on the seedling is maintained by updating the distance only when the new point on the seedling is closer than any previously processed points (as in a Z-buffer algorithm).

Interactive changes can be made to the matte function mn, mx, and r parameters, as well as the color and opacity maps based on data value, without invalidating the cache. The rerenderings are thus very rapid due to the sample distance caching and the fact that only a small portion of the image space is affected by each new voxel added to the region of interest. The current implementation on an SGI 240GTX extracts new seedling points and rerenders the volume image approximately 10 times per second. This dynamic nature of the seedling growth also provides visual cues to the user.

Figures 2, 3, 4 illustrate the use of seeds and seedlings on the CT head set from the UNC Chapel Hill Volume Data Sets. Figure 2 is a normal volume rendering of the data set without the use of a seed. Figure 3 uses a seed point to highlight a spherical region in the neck area. Figure 4 shows a seedling grown from the same seed point using a gradient based seedling growth priority function. Figure 4 uses a smaller opacity matte radius than Figure 3 to focus on the seedling itself rather than a broader area around the seadling. Notice that Figure 4 does a much better job of isolating the region of interest.

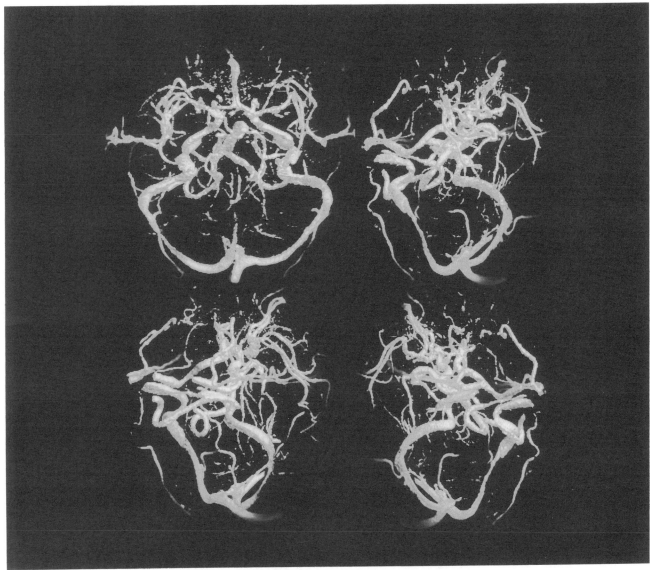

Figure 5: Four views of the MRA vascular data set.

5 Magnetic Resonance Angiography

Magnetic Resonance Angiography (MRA) is used to extract the vascular structure from within soft tissues like the brain. Visualizing the vascular structure can help in diagnosing malformations such as anuerisms and blockages, and/or help prepare surgical procedures such as catheterization through the vessels, or other invasive procedures designed to not disturb the vascular structure. The non-invasive nature of MRA over traditional angiography makes this diagnostic approach safer and thus more widely applicable. Unfortunately, MRA data capture cannot extract single vessels as can be done by selective dye release from a catheter in traditional angiography.

The vascular structure in MRA is captured by taking advantage of the fact that blood flows within the veins and arteries. The signal which is received is related to the time in which individual molecules are within the bounds of a thin slice through the body. Difficulties arise due to noisy data capture, or dropouts due to vessels which lie in the plane of excitation.

The most common visualization method used is a simple Maximum Intensity Projection (MIP) in which, as the name implies, a simple projection of the data onto a pixel grid is performed in which the pixel values are given the maximum value along a corresponding ray through the volume. A series of such images from different angles are viewed in succession to provide depth cues. However, single frames lose all or most of the depth information, and the sequence does not provide the full range of geometric information visible from more sophisticated algorithms.

The goals of the Volume Seedlings approach is to provide the three dimensional visual cues captured by volume rendering, while providing interactive tools to explore the data set and extract individual vessels for closer examination. Other work has been done in this area to extract single vessels through connectivity information. Cline et al selected a single voxel value and extracted all voxels of the same value connected to a seed point, and projected these voxels directly onto a screen [4, 5]. Other imaging techniques for MRA have been described as well [2, 6, 10, 23], however, not in the context of interactive systems with the

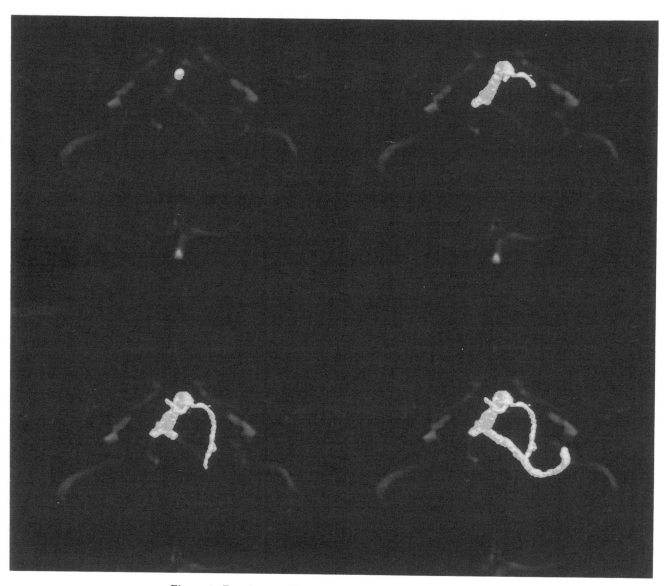

Figure 6: Four intermediate steps in the growth of a seedling.

use of volume rendering as the final imaging method.

Figure 5 shows four views of the vascular structure within the brain of a patient suffering from an anuerism. One single large seed in the center of the volume is used to capture most of the vessels while eliminating the vessels at the outer edges which complicate and obscure the interior. (These images are rendered at full 1K x 1K resolution as opposed to the 480x480 resolution in interactive mode.) After selection of a seed in the area of the anuerism a seedling is grown to extract the region of interest (Figure 6). The four images show the progress of the seedlings growth at four stages.

6   Conclusion

The ability to interactively isolate regions of interest within a volume rendering context has been discussed. By growing Volume Seedlings within the data set according to "interest" functions, features which may otherwise be hidden by the image complexity or by opaque regions can be examined. A description of an interactive volume exploration system has been described. Finally, the use of these techniques in the context of Magnetic Resonance Angiography to highlight individual vessels has been demonstrated.

The application of image processing and computer vision techniques to the problems involved in scientific visualization is an exciting area for exploration. It is expected that other more sophisticated region growing algorithms will be applicable in a wide variety of applications.

Acknowledgments

Partial support for this research was provided by a grant by International Business Machines for scientific visualization. Assistance in acquiring MRA data and other advice was given by Allen Sanderson. Dr. Wayne Davis and Dr. H. Ric Harnsberger of the department of Neuroradiology at the University of Utah supplied the MRA data and consulted on the development of the Volume Seeds system. Marc Levoy provided insight needed to interpret the UNC CT head data. Elena Driskill implemented an early version of the data slicer used in the interactive system. Video production assistance was provided by Robert McDermott and James Rose.

References

[1] BALLARD, D. H., AND BROWN, C. M. *Computer Vision*. Prentice-Hall, Inc., 1982.

[2] BARILLOT, C., GIBAUD, B., SCARABIN, J., AND COATRIEUX, J. 3D Reconstruction of Cerebral Blood Vessles. *IEEE Computer Graphics and Applications 5*, 12 (Dec 1985), 13–19.

[3] BLOOMENTHAL, J. Polygonization of Implicit Surfaces. *Computer Aided Geometric Design 5* (1988), 341–355.

[4] CLINE, H., DUMOULIN, C., HART, JR., H., LORENSEN, W., AND LUDKE, S. 3D Reconstruction of the Brain from Magnetic Resonance Images using a Connectivity Algorithm. *Magnetic Resonance Imaging 5*, 5 (1987), 345–352.

[5] CLINE, H., LORENSEN, W., HERFKENS, R. J., JOHNSON, G. A., AND GLOVER, G. H. Vascular Morphology by Three-Dimensional Magnetic Resonance Imaging. *Magnetic Resonance Imaging 7*, 1 (1989), 45–54.

[6] CLINE, H. E., DUMOULIN, C. L., LORENSEN, W. E., SOUZA, S. P., AND ADAMS, W. J. Connectivity Algorithms for MR Angiography. *Book of Abstracts, Society of Magnetic Resonance in Medicine 1* (Aug. 1990), 59.

[7] DREBIN, R. A., CARPENTER, L., AND HANRAHAN, P. Volume Rendering. *Computer Graphics (Proceedings of SIGGRAPH 1988) 22*, 4 (August 1988), 65–74.

[8] FISHKIN, K. P., AND BARSKY, B. A. A Family of New Algorithms for Soft Filling. *Computer Graphics (Proceedings of SIGGRAPH 1984) 18*, 3 (July 1984), 235–244.

[9] KAJIYA, J., AND HERZEN, B. Ray Tracing Volume Densities. *Computer Graphics (Proceedings of SIGGRAPH 1984) 18*, 3 (July 1984), 165–174.

[10] KRASKE, W. F., AND COLLETTI, P. M. VOXAR 3-D Curvilinear Feature Description for Graphic Presentation and Analysis of MR Angiography(MRA) Aquisitions. *Book of Abstracts, Society of Magnetic Resonance in Medicine 1* (Aug. 1990), 59.

[11] LAUR, D., AND HANRAHAN, P. Hierarchical Splatting: A Progressive Refinement Algorithm for Volume Rendering. *Computer Graphics (SIGGRAPH '91 Proceedings) 25*, 4 (July 1991), 285–288.

[12] LEVOY, M. Display of Surfaces from Volume Data. *IEEE Computer Graphics and Applications* (May 1988), 29–37.

[13] LEVOY, M. A Taxonomy of Volume Visualization Algorithms, August 1990. SIGGRAPH 1990 Course Notes 11, Voulme Visualization Algorithms and Architectures.

[14] LEVOY, M. Efficient Ray Tracing of Volume Data. *ACM Transactions on Graphics 9*, 3 (July 1990), 245–261.

[15] LEVOY, M. Volume Rendering by Adaptive Refinement. *Visual Computer 6*, 1 (February 1990), 2–7.

[16] LORENSEN, W. E., AND CLINE, H. E. Marching Cubes: A High Resolution 3D Surface Construction Algorithm. *Computer Graphics (Proceedings of SIGGRAPH 1987)*, 4 (July 1987), 163–169.

[17] MA, K.-L., COHEN, M., AND PAINTER, J. Volume Seeds: A Volume Exploration Technique. *The Journal of Visualization and Computer Animation* (1991 (To Appear)).

[18] MILLER, J. V., BREEN, D. E., LORENSEN, W. E., O'BARA, R. M., AND WOZNY, M. J. Geometrically Deformed Models: A Method for Extracting Closed Geometric Models from Volume Data. *Computer Graphics (SIGGRAPH '91 Proceedings) 25*, 4 (July 1991), 217–226.

[19] SABELLA, P. A Rendering Algorithm for Visualizing 3D Scalar Fields. *Computer Graphics (Proceedings of SIGGRAPH 1988) 22*, 4 (August 1988), 51–58.

[20] SEDGEWICK, R. *Algorithms*. Addison-Wesley, 1988.

[21] SÉQUIN, C. H., AND SMYRL, E. K. Parameterixed Ray Tracing. *Computer Graphics (Proceedings of SIGGRAPH 1989) 23*, 3 (August 1989), 307–314.

[22] SHIRLEY, P., AND TUCHMAN, A. A Polygonal Approximation to Direct Scalar Volume Rendering. *Computer Graphics (San Diego Workshop on Volume Rendering Proceedings) 24*, 5 (Nov. 1990), 63–70.

[23] SIEBERT, J. E., AND ROSENBAUM, T. L. Projection Algorithm Imparting a Consistent Spatial Perspective for 3D MR Angiography. *Book of Abstracts, Society of Magnetic Resonance in Medicine 1* (Aug. 1990), 59.

[24] SMITH, A. R. Tint Fill. *Computer Graphics (Proceedings of SIGGRAPH 1979) 13*, 2 (August 1979), 276–283.

[25] TRIVEDI, S. S., HERMAN, G. T., AND UDUPA, J. K. Segmentation Into Three Classes Using Gradients. *IEEE Transactions on Medical Imaging 5*, 2 (June 1986), 116–119.

[26] UDUPA, J. K. Interactive Segmentation and Boundary Surface Formation for 3-D Digital Images. *Computer Graphics and Image Processing 18* (1982), 213–235.

[27] UPSON, C., AND KEELER, M. V-buffer: Visible Volume Rendering. *Computer Graphics (Proceedings of SIGGRAPH 1988) 22*, 4 (August 1988), 59–64.

[28] WESTOVER, L. Footprint Evaluation for Volume Rendering. *Computer Graphics (SIGGRAPH '90 Proceedings) 24*, 4 (July 1990), 367–376.

[29] WILHELMS, J., AND GELDER, A. V. A Coherent Projection Approach for Direct Volume Rendering. *Computer Graphics (SIGGRAPH '91 Proceedings) 25*, 4 (July 1991), 275–284.

NPSNET: Constructing A 3D Virtual World

Michael J. Zyda*, David R. Pratt, James G. Monahan, Kalin P. Wilson
Naval Postgraduate School
Department of Computer Science
Monterey, California 93943-5100
zyda@trouble.cs.nps.navy.mil
*contact author

Abstract

The development of 3D visual simulation systems on inexpensive, commercially available graphics workstations is occurring today and will be commonplace in the near future. Such systems are being constructed to move through and interact with 3D virtual worlds. There are a variety of goals for these systems, including training, planning, gaming and other purposes where the introduction of the physical player may be too hazardous, too expensive or too frivolous to be tolerated. We present one such system, NPSNET, a workstation-based, 3D visual simulator for virtual world exploration and experimentation.

Virtual World Systems

The attention to virtual world systems is particularly appealing to the researchers of the Graphics and Video Laboratory of the Department of Computer Science at the Naval Postgraduate School as our focus for years has been on the production of prototype 3D visual simulation systems on commercially available graphics workstations [9,18-25]. 3D visual simulation systems have many of the characteristics of virtual world systems in that their purpose has long been for visualizing and interacting with distant, expensive or hazardous environments. If we turn off some of our physical modeling, we can even simulate non-existent 3D environments, so we feel quite comfortable under the virtual worlds umbrella.

We do not study the construction of our 3D visual simulators on specially-designed graphics hardware. We instead assume that such hardware is available from commercial workstation manufacturers. We build 3D visual simulators on inexpensive graphics workstations instead of specially-designed hardware because of our observation that the performance numbers from the manufacturers are so suggestive.

NPSNET: Overview

The Graphics and Video Laboratory has been developing low-cost, three-dimensional visual simulation systems for the last six years on Silicon Graphics, Inc. IRIS workstations. The visual simulators developed include the FOG-M missile simulator, the VEH vehicle simulator, the airborne remotely operated device (AROD), the Moving Platform Simulator series (MPS-1, MPS-2 and MPS-

3), the High Resolution Digital Terrain Model (HRDTM) system, the Forward Observer Simulator Trainer (FOST), the NPS Autonomous Underwater Vehicle simulator (NPSAUV), and the Command and Control Workstation of the Future system (CCWF).

Our current visual simulation efforts are on the NPSNET system, a workstation-based, 3D visual simulator that utilizes SIMNET databases and networking formats. The DARPA-sponsored SIMNET project had the goal of developing a low-cost tank simulator that provided a "70% solution" to the tank-war-gaming problem [17].

Unfortunately, the SIMNET system delivered has its graphics hardware and software suffering from a rigid specification based on 1983 graphics technology and was not designed to take advantage of ever faster and more capable graphics hardware and processor power. Low-cost for the project meant $250K per station. Instead, the contractor designed its own graphics platform, its own processing system, and wrote software that worked only on that platform. In NPSNET, we want to be somewhat more flexible BUT still interact with the DARPA investment.

The NPSNET system is an attempt to explore the SIMNET domain using a readily available graphics workstation, the Silicon Graphics, Inc. IRIS workstation in all its incarnations (Personal IRIS, GT, GTX, VGX...), instead of the contractor produced hardware. Our starting point is that we assume databases and network packet formats in a form similar to those utilized by the actual SIMNET system but allow the flexibility for continuing evolutions in efficiency.

NPSNET is a real-time, 3D visual simulation system capable of displaying vehicle movement over the ground or in the air. Displays show on-ground cultural features such as roads, buildings, soil types and elevations. The user can select any one of 500 active vehicles via mouse selection and control it with a six degree of freedom spaceball or button/dialbox. In between updating events, all vehicles are dead reckoned to determine their current positions. Speed in three dimensions and the location of the vehicle can accurately be predicted as long as the speed or direction of the vehicle does not change. Vehicles can be controlled by a prewritten script, or can be driven interactively from other workstations, as the system is networked via Ethernet. Additionally, autonomous players can be introduced into the system via a programmable network "harness" process (NPSNET-HARNESS).

As obvious from the above overview, NPSNET is in many ways a departure from the goals of SIMNET. We can "push the envelope" of real-time, workstation-based virtual reality while providing *a workstation-based SIMNET node.* We present our plan for the overall NPSNET effort in the following sections to provide an understanding of what is required to construct such a system.

SIMNET Database Display Work

The first effort in any virtual world development is obtaining the data that represents the world to be modeled. For 3D visual simulations, this usually begins with a large 2D grid of elevation data that is turned into a 3D terrain carpet.

Once the terrain carpet has been extracted and displayed, attention then turns to on-ground cultural features and 3D vehicle *icons*. On-ground cultural features include roads, forest canopies, trees, building, corrals and other stationary objects. Many cultural features are provided in 2D and have to be projected onto the terrain. Significant work must be done to accomplish this. There is the pre-processing work to turn 2D linear features like roads into 3D, correctly projected onto the terrain carpet. Projecting planar 3D road segments onto the terrain carpet is also not easy. The problem is that it requires projecting the road polygons onto the same place as the terrain carpet. Under z-buffering, the standard hidden surface elimination method for graphics workstations, coplanar, coincident polygons cause what is known as z-buffer *tearing* [1]. We see scan lines alternately colored with the underlying terrain color and the road color. We solve this by drawing the underlying terrain polygon first into the RGB planes with z-buffering on but modifications to the z-buffer off. We then draw the road overlay. Modifications to the RGB planes are then turned off and the underlying terrain polygon is again drawn, this time with modifications to the z-buffer on. This procedure must be done for all coplanar features in the system. It requires that underlying layers be drawn multiple times and in an ordered fashion. The visual simulator must handle this in a general fashion. It is just part of the complexity of building such systems.

3D vehicle *icons* are the next consideration in constructing our virtual world system. We call them 3D icons in that the goal is not realism but rather low resolution indicators of players on the terrain. Low resolution means whatever level of detail the user of the final system is willing to live with.

Hierarchical Data Structures for Real-Time Display Generation

If the modeled world is simple, just blasting all the polygons through the graphics pipeline ought to get satisfactory display results. Since NPSNET uses data from the SIMNET Database Interchange Specification (SDIS) for an actual 50km x 50km terrain area of Fort Hunter-Liggett, California and has a resolution of one data point for every 125 meters [6], this will not do.

Hierarchical data structures are the heart of any complex real-time, 3D visual simulator. Such data structures, in conjunction with viewing information, provide for the rapid culling of polygons comprising the terrain carpet, the cultural features, the 3D icons and any other displayable objects. The purpose of this operation is to minimize or reduce the flow of polygons through the graphics pipeline of the workstation's hardware. A classic reference to understand this problem in more detail is [2]. The culling operation is performed through the traversal of a data structure that spatially partitions the displayable data. The appropriate hierarchical data structure to use is problem domain dependent. As we have adopted NPSNET to additional tasks, we have had to modify and change our data structure.

Expanding the Terrain Area

In order to increase performance, the initial NPSNET dataset has been divided into 2500 text files based on the one kilometer standard of the military "grid square" with each file containing data for one square kilometer. These were preprocessed into binary format and three additional lower resolutions generated (250, 500 and 1000 meter), together with fill polygons for each level. The final

form of the dataset is 2500 binary files, each containing a multiple-resolution (4 level) description of the terrain for one square km, stored as a heap-sorted quadtree [7,12].

The final format for the binary terrain data files is designed for fast access using the C function *fread()*. All polygon descriptions are stored in memory-image format, therefore, no data conversion has to be done during paging. The 2500 files resulting from preprocessing contain:

❑ Count of polygons in each node of full four level quadtree (85 total).

❑ Total polygon descriptions in the file.

❑ Multi-resolution description of terrain in this square kilometer stored in quadtree heap-sort order, lower resolutions first (Figure 1).

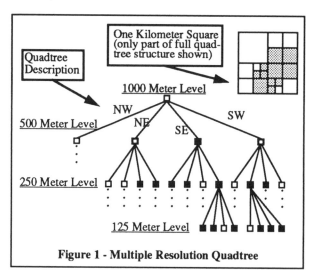

Figure 1 - Multiple Resolution Quadtree

As the final dataset is too large to store in main memory at one time, and we do not wish to limit the simulation to some smaller area, paging terrain data through a dynamic algorithm is required.

A 16km x 16km active area was chosen based on considerations for memory size of available workstations, frame rates, required field of view and desired range of views. This amount of terrain data is in main memory at any given time and available for rendering. Sixteen kilometers allows a seven kilometer field of view in all directions for immediate rendering with one kilometer acting as a buffer to ensure terrain is fully paged in before attempting to render it (Figure 2).

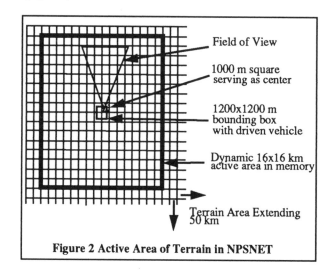

Figure 2 Active Area of Terrain in NPSNET

On multi-processor workstations, the simulator does not wait for additional terrain to be paged in. Instead, the additional CPUs are used to page in the terrain in parallel.

Terrain Paging Algorithm

When the simulator is initialized, the driven vehicle is centered on a 16 x 16 active area. The indices of the center one kilometer square containing the driven vehicle become the notional center. Data is loaded into the appropriate elements of a 50 x 50 array, and a bounding box is established around the driven vehicle (centered on the index of the center square). When the driven vehicle reaches the bounding box in any direction, memory space is freed in the direction opposite of travel, terrain is paged in the direction of travel, and the bounding box moves.The size of the bounding box can be adjusted as required by vehicle speed/turn rate characteristics. Terrain paging is independent of the hierarchical data structure implemented.

Terrain Rendering

Terrain rendering involves several steps in NPSNET:
❑ Determine which 1000m x 1000m squares are actually in the field of view.
❑ Determine resolution within each 1000m x 1000m square (there may be at most two resolutions), including which fill polygons are needed.
❑ Render the terrain.

Two algorithms are involved. One checks to see if a polygon is within the field of view by calling a procedure that checks for the intersection of a point (each point of the polygon) and a polygon (the triangle composing the field of view) [3]. The other determines the resolution, essentially which nodes of the quadtree to render, by checking the intersection of nodes with concentric circles corresponding to ranges of the resolutions [13]. The circle-rectangle and point-polygon intersection algorithms are applied repetitively to render only terrain within the field of view and at the appropriate resolution levels. Figure 3 depicts multi-resolution within the field of view. NPSNET is graphics bound. Therefore, the computational expense of the above algorithms is better than rendering terrain not actually in the field of view.

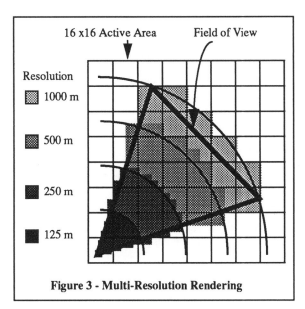

Figure 3 - Multi-Resolution Rendering

Implementation of the above has resulted in a doubling of the performance of the simulation over high resolution rendering alone. However, performance when large numbers of objects (trees, vehicles) are present in the viewing area does not change.

NPSOFF: Overview

The development of interesting virtual world systems requires the modeling of many different graphical objects. How these objects are represented in the system plays a major part in determining the capabilities and efficiency of the system. We use a simple, flexible object description language to model graphical and some non-graphical aspects of our objects called NPSOFF.

NPSOFF is a language system that consists of "tokens" that represent graphical concepts. These tokens are combined in an ASCII file to represent an object. The object can then be referenced by an application in an abstract manner. The application does not need to know the details of how the object is composed. The level of abstraction that NPSOFF provides offers numerous advantages that are discussed below. NPSOFF objects can have varying levels of complexity to represent a wide range of graphical objects and environments. NPSOFF also serves as a standard for application development. This makes general purpose tools plausible and extremely useful.

Functional Description

The NPSOFF language can be broken down into tokens. In early versions of the language, the tokens corresponded almost one for one to GL functions. Later versions have added more abstraction and flexibility. The language tokens simplify the interface to the GL library by labeling components and help encapsulate some of its complexity.

NPSOFF extends the GL interface by allowing many system settings to be named. Naming system definitions allows us to build libraries of commonly used settings like materials and textures.

NPSOFF tokens generally belong to one of three categories: definition, display or characteristics/composition. The definition tokens define graphics system settings. Definition tokens define lights (normal and spot), lighting models (normal and two-sided), materials, textures, and colors. Definition tokens are named and stored in tables for later access.

Display or execution tokens make up the bulk of NPSOFF. Display tokens represent a change in graphics system state or graphics primitives. They are stored in a sequential display list in the order that they appear in an NPSOFF file. Example tokens that change the system state are: *setmaterial, setlight, settexture*, etc. Each of these tokens has a name argument that corresponds with an earlier definition. In the case of *setlight*, the named light is associated with one of seven possible light numbers [14]. These state tokens make it easy to manipulate the graphics pipeline. Complex lighting and shading effects can be done with NPSOFF in a simple and straightforward way.

The graphics primitives used in NPSOFF are: polygons, surface (polygon with vertex normals), triangular mesh and lines. Additional display tokens perform manipulations of the system matrix stack. NPSOFF objects and components of objects can be transformed within the object definition file. The tokens *loadmatrix, multmatrix, pushmatrix, popmatrix, rotate, scale* and *translate* define stack manipulations.

The third category of NPSOFF tokens allow the user to define object characteristics and composition. This allows a high level of abstraction and supports complex graphics techniques. Two of the main abstractions are composite objects and polygon decaling. NP-

SOFF objects can be named and contain nested object definitions. The nested definitions can contain any display tokens. This structure allows multiple related objects to be treated as a single object for graphics display. It also minimizes the duplication of primitive definitions. Objects are defined with the *defobject* token and displayed with the *callobject* token. This structure is flexible and useful for building complex objects from simpler sub-objects.

Using an NPSOFF object is also simple. Essentially the user needs to use only three function calls to access and display an object. There are many more programmatic entrypoints to NPSOFF but many of them deal with in-memory manipulation that is not needed for standard use. They are used primarily by tools that build or manipulate NPSOFF objects.

Physical Modeling Support

In the past, simulations developed in the Graphics and Video Laboratory have each handled physically-based modelling (PBM) independently and internally. The latest extension of the NPSOFF system is an object-oriented PBM system [8]. These enhancements give NPSOFF objects physical characteristics and provide mechanisms to control an object's motion given a list of internal and external forces on the object. Objects are handled in an enclosed reference called the "environment". All objects that participate in the NPSOFF PBM system are members of the environment.

The NPSOFF PBM system models object rigid-body dynamics using a Newtonian framework. An object can be given many physical properties using the *defphysics* token. These properties include the object's initial location and location constraints in the environment, initial orientation and orientation constraints, initial linear and angular velocities and constraints on each, the object's mass and center of mass, the object's ability to absorb forces (elasticity), the dimensions of a bounding volume and a local viewpoint for the object. Each object can also use its own system of measurement. The *defunits* token allows the user to specify the units of measurement for dimensions, force magnitude and mass. This capability was incorporated to accommodate the use of object models from various sources. The PBM system uses reasonable constant or calculated defaults for all physical characteristics so none of the properties is required to be present when object physical characteristics are defined.

Forces are defined and added to an object's force list with the *defforce* token. Two types of forces are supported: deforming and non-deforming. Deforming forces are used for object explosions and bending. Non-deforming forces are used to alter an objects linear and angular velocities. Forces can be specified as awake or asleep. This allows the selective application of previously defined forces. The characteristics of a force defined with *defforce* are: type (deforming/non-deforming), origin relative to object center and origin constraints, force direction vector, magnitude and magnitude constraints and force state (asleep/awake).

The run-time interface of the NPSOFF PBM system is simple and flexible. Once the PBM environment has been initialized, the user can add or delete objects from the environment, add and modify global forces, modify object physical characteristics, add and modify object force characteristics and modify object and force states. The environment is processed once each display cycle. The processing involves resolving forces, calculating object states and displaying the objects. The NPSOFF PBM system provides us with a simple environment to model object dynamics and interaction. This is one of our first steps to add more physical reality to our applications.

Advantages

NPSOFF provides many advantages to the researchers in the NPS Graphics and Video Laboratory:

❑ NPSOFF allows an application independent description of graphical objects. Objects can be designed and maintained by general purpose tools. Collections of objects can be built and shared with other researchers.

❑ NPSOFF adds a level of abstraction that greatly simplifies application development. Also, by having a large collection of common objects, developers can concentrate on how objects should be used rather than designing and rendering the objects.

❑ NPSOFF provides a simple, object oriented, run-time interface to an object. Functions such as read_object(), display_object() and delete_object() all operate on individual objects in memory. Many functions are provided so flexible manipulations are possible.

❑ The stand-alone, reusable nature of NPSOFF objects encourages the use of common libraries of definition tokens such as materials and textures.

Support Tools

The wide use of NPSOFF in our laboratory has led to a variety of tools to aid in the design and maintenance of NPSOFF objects. These tools include: The OFF calculator, NPSME - a material editor, NPSTE - a texture editor, NPSICON - a model builder and NPSMOVER - a physically based design editor.

The OFF calculator allows in memory manipulation of NPSOFF objects using a simple command line interface. Using the OFF calculator, objects can be transformed (transformation applied to all primitives), primitives can be added to an object, graphical objects (spheres, boxes, etc.) can be added to an object and objects can be concatenated.

NPSME is a material editor that helps manage libraries of materials [26]. It reads and writes material definitions. Material definitions can be selected from the library for viewing and editing. The material editor helps us to maintain a large collection of material definitions used by NPSOFF objects in our applications. The ability to interactively design and modify material definitions is very important to rapid application development.

NPSTE is a texture editor that helps manage libraries of NPSOFF texture definitions [26]. NPSTE can use images in many formats as textures. Portions of an image can be copied and used as a texture image. Textures can be viewed on any NPSOFF object using either the texture coordinates specified in the object or automatically generated coordinates using the GL function *texgen()* [14]. Textures can be edited using a simple pixel editor. Finally, a texture definition can be saved in a library of textures and the library saved as an NPSOFF file. The texture editor lets developers interactively create, select and view textures independent of a developing application.

NPSICON is an interactive object design tool [10]. NPSICON lets a developer design or modify NPSOFF objects using a set of predefined building blocks. NPSICON is designed to be used primarily to build vehicular models. Objects can be edited and transformed in many ways and then saved to an NPSOFF file. NPSICON allows rapid prototyping of vehicular objects for use in applications. It also allows developers to modify existing models quickly and easily.

NPSMOVER provides an environment for users to design and test physical dynamics of NPSOFF objects [8]. NPSMOVER reads any NPSOFF file and assigns default physical characteristics if not present. The user can then adjust all physical characteristics of the object. Forces can be defined and added to an object's force list using interactive controls. Once the object's initial conditions, constraints and characteristics are set and the forces acting on the object are specified, the dynamics can be "turned on". The user can observe the effects of the forces and make necessary adjustments. Once the user is satisfied, the object can be saved to an NPSOFF file with all the needed tokens. The NPSMOVER tool provides a simple, interactive environment to view and adjust an object's basic dynamic behavior.

NPSOFF Future Directions

Current and future projects at NPS are working to extend and improve NPSOFF including support for defining inter-object relationships and constraints. This would allow the composite object structure to be extended to where each subobject has physical properties and affects the behavior of the whole object. Also the notion of linked objects will be explored in the context of NPSOFF. This will allow the realistic modeling of such things as vehicle controls (e.g. aircraft stick movement changes control surface which changes forces on whole aircraft).

Another area that future research will address is animation support within NPSOFF. Support for continuously animated portions of an object (vehicle antennae) or constraint management of subobjects (doors, arms, etc.) would be very useful to our researchers. Such a system would benefit from the standardization that NPSOFF provides and offer much more capabilities to developers.

The NPSOFF system is object-oriented in its design and use but is implemented in a non-object oriented language. Modifying or extending the current system is time consuming and error prone. We are currently redesigning NPSOFF to be truly object-oriented and implementing it in C++. The main benefits of moving to an object-oriented implementation will be increased extensibility through inheritance and polymorphism and better maintainability.

Collision Detection

In earlier versions, NPSNET did not detect nor respond to vehicle collisions. Without collision detection and response, the realism was poor. Even with texturing, environmental effects and realistic looking vehicles, the virtual world falls apart the first time one vehicle drives through another. A possible solution to this problem would be to prevent interpenetrations by bouncing objects off of each other after any contact, but this is rarely accurate. Another possible solution is to destroy the objects involved in collisions. A third option is to combine these two solutions along with varying stages of damage to involved objects depending upon the physical characteristics of the involved objects. The current version of NPSNET detects and responds to collisions between objects in real-time. Detection is sufficiently fast to allow the time needed to respond properly. Response time is dependent upon the level of physically-based modeling.

Collisions with Fixed Objects

The algorithm for collisions with fixed objects constantly checks moving vehicles to determine if a collision has occurred. The position of the moving vehicle is updated constantly. Consequently, as soon as a vehicle is moved and its position is updated, it is checked for a collision. In order to maintain a real-time speed, the scope of the collision detection is severely limited. A collision with fixed objects is checked only if the moving vehicle is below a threshold elevation. All fixed objects are in some way attached to the terrain and thus below that threshold elevation. If an object is below that elevation, NPSNET runs through a linked list of fixed objects which are attached to the current gridsquare.

Collisions with Moving Objects

A collision with other moving objects is more complicated since any other moving vehicle or object has the potential for colliding with the vehicle we are checking. The potential exists for checking up to 500 vehicles and any of their expendable weapons. Consequently, the scope of the collision detection range has been limited in several ways.

As soon as each vehicle is moved, its position is checked against the position of the neighboring vehicles. If the X or Z position of any other vehicle is within 100 meters of the checked vehicle then those two vehicles are sent to the second level check. At the second level check, the distance between the two vehicles is calculated. If this distance is less than the combined radii of the two vehicles, then a collision has occurred and the third level collision check is done. A rudimentary form of ray tracing determines the actual point of collision.

If worst case numbers are used to determine the implicit range limitations of all vehicles, it can be shown why this culling is fairly accurate. Reasonable speed limitations of the various types of vehicles are used to calculate worst cases for each (Table 1). Consequently, the movement across more than two gridsquares within one tenth of a second, one frame, is unlikely.

Table 1: VEHICLE MOVEMENT LIMITATIONS

	KPH	m/sec	Frames/sec	m/Frame
Land	60	16.6	10	1.66
Sea	50	13.8	10	1.38
Air	1000	277.7	10	27.7

Collision detection is accomplished by determining if one object's bounding sphere has interpenetrated another. The radius used in the spherical check is the maximum distance from the center of the object to the furthest outer vertex. In the collision response portion of the system, the actual object's penetration point is determined. A slightly smaller value than the actual radius of the object is used for the radius. This produces a more realistic collision possibility since it increases the likelihood of an actual collision of the checked objects and not just their spheres. Once the collision has been detected, the extent of damage and collision response are determined.

Collision Response

Collision response is handled by a function which takes into account speed and angle of impact, mass of the objects involved, explosive potential, resistance to destruction, moldability of the objects, rigidity and fabricated spring forces which determine the bouncing-off effect and likelihood of survivability. Each of these factors is weighted in order to provide as realistic an effect as possible while maintaining the environment in real-time.

Moving Objects

In the case where two moving objects impact, all of the physically-based modeling characteristics of each object must be considered. The collision point must be known to create realistic responses in the involved objects. The collision point determines the point for any type of bending, crumpling and molding. Moreover, if the point of collision is part of a wall that is interconnected to several other walls then there will have to be corresponding responses in those interconnected walls. The only way to find the collision point is through ray tracing.

The first ray is shot from the center of a moving object towards the center of an adjacent object to determine a possible point of collision. This collision may simply be between the bounding spheres of the two objects and not the actual objects themselves. The intersection between the first ray and the second object's bounding sphere is used to specify the direction of a second ray originating from the adjacent object's center.

The second ray determines if one of the object's actual polygons was penetrated. This second ray is the ray used in Haines' algorithm. This algorithm from Glassner [4] was adapted for use in the collision point determination. It involves running through the list of polygons that comprise the adjacent object and determining if the second ray intersects the plane containing the polygon. If no intersection is found once all of the polygons have been checked, then only the spheres were penetrated and not the objects themselves.

Reactions

The proper response is performed by comparing the characteristics of two objects involved in the collision. For fixed objects, the responses include several degrees of damage, based upon the speed and mass of the colliding object. Up to three levels of damage plus the original undamaged fixed object are available for display after a collision. For mobile objects, the response depends upon the angle of impact as well as the speed and mass of the two involved objects. The mobile object reacts by either bouncing away or being destroyed and exploding. In the special case of contact by munitions, the only response is an explosion.The limited number of options available for the response to the collision keep the response fast to maintain the real-time criteria. The collision point and direction of travel are passed to another module that handles physically-based modeling of object movement. This function's implementation can be seen in [8].

SIMNET Networking Integration

SIMNET networking integration is part of our NPSNET efforts on software structures for world modeling in that networking provides the locations and actions of other players in our visual simulators. We use Ethernet and TCP/IP multicast packets of our own design for the current NPSNET system. We are in the process of integrating the networking system with the SIMNET standard packets as the full description and documentation is now available. This connection to SIMNET will provide players, weapons firing and other state information with which we can test our world modeling efforts. At a later stage, we hope to examine some of the available work on higher speed networks, such as FDDI, as it becomes commercially available and relevant.

NPSNET-HARNESS Structure

The NPSNET-HARNESS process was developed to allow the rapid integration of different components into the NPSNET simulation system and in partial response to Ethernet's speed and addressing limitations [15]. The high level structure of the network harness is shown in Figure 4. The harness is divided into two main sections, the Network Daemon and the User Program Interface, which communicate via shared memory. The principle purpose of the Network Daemon is to provide low level data and network management support for user written NPSNET "player" programs. Player programs developed by users are stand alone applications that provide specific world interaction functionality.

The User Program Interface consists of a set of routines that allow the programmer to interact with the network at a higher level of abstraction. These functions include setting up the shared memory

space with the network daemon, creation of a network read key, message formatting, and the actual reading and writing of network messages.

Message Types

One of the interesting things about the Ethernet network is that it is more efficient to have a few long messages rather then many short messages[16]. This influenced the creation of five message types and formats.

The message types, NEWSTATMESS and DELSTATMESS, are used when a a station enters the network and when it no longer is an active player in the networked environment. These are used solely as administrative messages and do not affect the appearance of any vehicle.

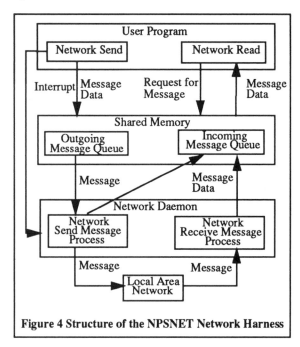

Figure 4 Structure of the NPSNET Network Harness

One of the features of NPSNET is the capability of allowing the user to change vehicles during the execution of the simulation. The SWITCHMESS notifies all the other nodes on the network that the user has changed vehicles. This does not affect the appearance of any of the vehicles.

The UPDATEMESS is the largest message used in NPSNET and it is also the most common, accounting for almost all the network traffic. Before we discuss this message, the concept of the state of the vehicle must be covered. As mentioned previously, the vehicle's position is updated only after a speed or direction change. The tilt and roll of the vehicle can be derived from the location on the terrain and need not be sent across the network. Additionally, the orientation of the turret, the gun elevation, vehicle destruction, and weapons firing all change the state of the vehicle. Whenever any of these state parameters change, a message must be sent to update the other network nodes.

Since it is more efficient to have a few long messages rather then many short ones, we combined all of the vehicle state parameters into a single message. This has the additional benefit of updating all of the vehicle parameters at the same time to ensure accurate placement and orientation of the vehicle.

NPSNET-HARNESS Future Directions

Currently there are two major efforts underway concerning NPSNET-HARNESS. The first of these is the porting of the system to Sun SPARC workstations. We envision providing the user a standard network interface for both the IRIS and Sun workstations. This will allow the development of Autonomous Agents (AA) and Semi-Automated Forces (SAF) that can interact with the vehicles that are driven on the IRIS workstations. Our 100+ departmental Sun workstations would then serve as a distributed multiprocessor.

The second major effort is the utilization of the SIMNET Protocols [11]. As shown in Figure 5, we plan on constructing an interface between the User Program and the Network Daemon to convert the format of the protocols between the internal and external protocol. This will later be extended to the DIS Protocols [5] as well. The use of a translator will isolate the programmer from changes in the protocols. Naturally, we will increase the number of messages available to the user when we use the new protocols, but the old message formats will remain.

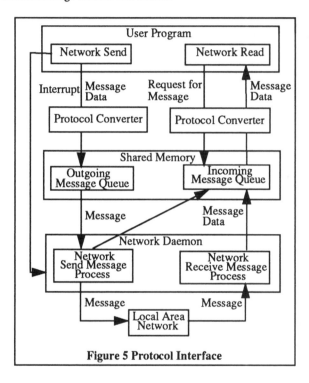

Figure 5 Protocol Interface

Semi-Automated Forces

The current DARPA SIMNET system has a semi-automated forces (SAF) component in it. The SAF system provides autonomous players to SIMNET when sufficient numbers of actual, interactive players are not available or affordable. The Graphics and Video Laboratory has considerable experience in generating such players as our visual simulation efforts have a close coupling to our department's artificial intelligence and robotics efforts [20,21]. We are continuing those efforts and expanding that work to take advantage of the available parallel processing capabilities of our workstations.

NPSNET-MES: Overview

Earlier versions of NPSNET used randomly guided vehicles to populate the battlefield. These vehicles had very little intelligence and were only capable of firing back at an attacker or running away.

It is not enough to have random vehicles moving about the battlefield without a mission; we must populate the battlefield with combat formations that act semi-autonomously as well. The NPSNET Mobility Expert System (NPSNET-MES) provides realistic semi-automated forces (SAF) to introduce sufficient numbers of unmanned players into the system to make the simulation more challenging and exciting. NPSNET-MES consists of two components: a path generation module and a vehicle controller module. The path generation module determines the SAF route and mission based upon the SAF controller input. The vehicle controller module uses the programmable harness, NPSNET-HARNESS, to multicast data packets via Ethernet to control the SAF vehicles during the simulation. NPSNET-MES integrates SAF into an already existing network simulator such that no changes are necessary to NPSNET.

Problem Description

One of the major objectives of our work is to determine the best approach to integrate semi-automated forces into an already existing simulation. The following are the minimum capabilities of the semi-automated forces: The SAF controller specifies a path that includes start and goal points with possible way points along the route. The SAF must negotiate all known obstacles without hitting them in a relatively optimal path. The SAF vehicles within a SAF formation must follow the lead SAF vehicle such that they maintain relative positions and do not collide with each other. The SAF controller specifies the number of combat formations as well as the number of vehicles, speed and type of each combat formation. When a SAF vehicle is killed, it no longer moves. NPSNET-MES integrates the SAF into the existing NPSNET without any change to the system. Once the SAF controller determines the SAF prerequisite information, NPSNET-MES makes that information available to NPSNET for use during the simulation. These basic considerations drive the requirements for the NPSNET-MES prototype system.

Integration with NPSNET

To get the desired results, NPSNET-MES is designed to act in a stand alone mode. This means that NPSNET-MES integrates the SAF into NPSNET by using the existing set of programmable network harness routines, NPSNET-HARNESS. The main problem separates into two distinct subsets: designing semi-automated forces that can navigate and travel a specified path and transmitting the information generated by the first part.

Path Generation Module

This module is a 2D map/interface that the SAF controller uses to perform SAF vehicle placement and route selection. The SAF controller is able to control the SAF parameters, such as number of SAF formations, number of vehicles in each SAF formation, and type of SAF vehicles and input a desired path with intermediate rendezvous points as well as a speed for each path segment.

NPSNET-MES stores this information in a file available to the vehicle controller module. The path selection criteria for this module is not an optimal path, rather it is a relatively simple path that is found quickly. This module generates a path based on *a priori* obstacle information using a circle world.

Computational versus *a priori* Path Planning

The path generation module's path generation algorithm uses a modified breadth-first search of a bounding box rather than the more traditional artificial intelligence approach of *a priori* generated paths because it is more efficient and less complex. The computational approach searches the bounding box, shooting a line between the start and goal to determine if the goal is visible from the start. If the path has an obstacle, then the path finder is called recursively until a path is found around obstacles enroute to the goal. The NPSNET-MES path generation module algorithm bounds the search area using the start and goal points to limit the search within a box.

An *a priori* path generation produces paths for the entire database requiring a longer amount of time and more memory to store those paths for quick access than a computational generation. The recursive path planner grows in a linear fashion versus a non-linear growth for the more traditional *a priori* method (Figure 6).

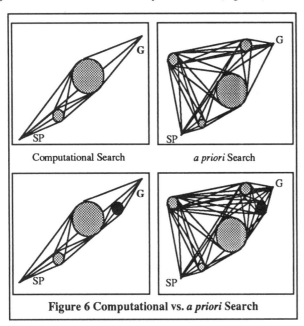

Figure 6 Computational vs. *a priori* Search

Path Generation Module

The path generation module is the interface for NPSNET-MES with NPSNET. This program places the generated paths in a sorted linked list by ascending order of time. A path point time is a running total time for the vehicle from the start up to that point. Using the system clock to maintain relative time, the paths are taken off a priority list. The NPSNET-HARNESS sends updated messages reflecting the new vehicle position, direction, and speed to NPSNET. NPSNET receives the path data and the SAF vehicles respond to the vehicle controller commands ensuring that the SAF vehicles stay on track with the generated paths.

NPSNET-MES Results

NPSNET-MES provides a relatively efficient solution to finding a good path for the SAF vehicles. The path found by the path generation module does not attempt to find the best solution only a good solution, since the human that it emulates usually only finds a good solution when conducting path planning. The vehicle control module provides the necessary interface between NPSNET-MES and NPSNET so that the SAF forces travel as they would in real life.The system provides a realistic friend or foe force on the simulation battlefield. NPSNET-MES effectively integrates SAF into NPSNET. This system is a prototype for research, therefore it has many potential capabilities that can be added at a later time.

Path Generation Module Limitations

❏ No dynamic path planning for the SAFs to react to other players during the simulation.
❏ Produces only one combat formation type for the entire mission.
❏ Terrain slope considerations are not incorporated in the path planning algorithm.

The most serious limitation with the system is the inability of the SAF to react to other players in the simulation. The SAF missions are pre-set before the simulation begins and cannot be altered once it commences. This was a design decision made at the outset of the project. The deficiency can be corrected by incorporating a local path generation capability within the vehicle controller module. When a SAF comes within range of an active player, the vehicle controller module path generation function would generate a local path around the moving obstacle and then the SAF reenters the previous path at the closest point.The path generation module places all follow-on vehicles in a column of wedges. This is a good movement formation, but there are many occasions where other formations would be appropriate. This additional flexibility is possible by giving the SAF controller some options during his path planning preparation. Terrain slope considerations are not incorporated into the path generation module because the design calls for a fast and efficient path planner. Terrain analysis requires more computation per path segment since the path generator evaluates each path segment terrain slope for terrain selection.

Path Generation Module Limitations

❏ Limited SAF vehicle reaction to active simulation players.
❏ Projected and actual path plots deviate due to clock speed and network transmission times.

A design decision was made early in the design phase rejecting multiple reaction capabilities. The SAF vehicles die when attacked because NPSNET-MES no longer sends update positions and reduces the speed to zero. By increasing the number of items that the vehicle controller module checks from the network, the reaction capability is upgradeable.

The final limitation is not a serious one since deviations are small and the shifting movement is not conspicuous. To fix the problem, the system must be able to operate at the millisecond rate or faster since the path points are in an ascending order queue. Some path points may have the same time stamp causing a delay for at least one of the SAF vehicles. NPSNET-HARNESS is not able to operate faster than its current rate due to hardware system limitations. The limitations create a bottleneck because there is only a single wire and single port on the Ethernet. There will always be some error due to transmission time delay, but this effect is negligible as long as the machines are in relative proximity.

Aural Cues for 3D Visual Simulation

A realistic virtual world must include aural cues about the objects in the world. These cues should provide feedback about the user's environment and actions taking place. A recent addition to NPSNET is the support of sound feedback to the user.

The addition of sound to a complex virtual world is itself complex. Often, parallel event generated sounds are routed to sound devices which are serial in nature. This imposes a severe limitation that must be worked around.

One solution we are investigating involves a process that can intelligently manage requests for sound issued from NPSNET.

This process would have several responsibilities:

❑ Receive sound requests, resolve multiple similar sounds into a single sound that can represent them and throw away requests of significant age.
❑ Coordinate requests for continuous sounds (e.g. background noise, other vehicular noise, etc.).
❑ Manage the use of multiple sound production devices (e.g. samplers, keyboards, MIDI devices, etc.).
❑ Facilitate the use of 3D sound.

This sound manager process would allow NPSNET to deal with sounds in a fairly abstract manner. Only knowledge of classes of sounds would need to be shared between NPSNET and the sound manager. This will allow us to modify the sound manager easily without affecting NPSNET.

Currently, sound support in NPSNET is limited. We use a Macintosh IIci running in-house software to play digitized sound files. The Macintosh is connected to an IRIS workstation running NPSNET by a serial link between RS-232 ports. When NPSNET wants to produce a sound, it issues a request for a specific sound to be played by the Mac via the serial port. The Macintosh queues the request, locates and plays the sound in the system resource. There are several limitations to this solution:

❑ NPSNET must know specific sound names that exist on the Macintosh and request them by name.
❑ Currently all sound files on the Macintosh must reside in the system folder. This limits the number of sounds that are available.
❑ Only discrete sounds are currently used. There is no notion of continuous sounds.
❑ A single device with one channel is used to reproduce the sound. This can lead to a backlog of requested sounds.
❑ The queue of sound requests on the Macintosh can become overloaded due to the above backlog. This can result in lost sounds, delayed sounds or queue overflow.

Ongoing work with sound and NPSNET is approaching the model outlined above. We are beginning to investigate high quality sound samplers and MIDI devices attached to the Macintosh to collect, create and reproduce various sounds. Sophisticated sound editing, sequencing and control software on the Mac give us many options for creatively employing aural feedback in NPSNET. Support for 3D sound is also under research.

Since many sounds are object-based, NPSOFF objects will support the description and management of sound that pertain to themselves. The sound control with NPSOFF will provide a standard use of sounds and facilitate the collection of sound definitions just as we collect materials and textures.

We believe that sound is an integral part of any serious virtual world simulation. We are actively pursuing efficient, extensible and effective solutions to integrating sound into NPSNET.

NPSNET: Current Performance

The current NPSNET system runs on a variety of platforms. Our highest performance system in the laboratory is the Silicon Graphics, Inc. IRIS 240 VGX with 64MB CPU memory. The VGX system is listed by the manufacturer as being capable of some 1 million triangles per second, z-buffered and Gouraud-shaded. On that system with terrain texturing on, NPSNET shows 6 frames/second with many objects in the display and 9 frames/second with few visible objects. The system has a switch to turn off texturing of the terrain and the frame rate roughly doubles respectively.

The performance of NPSNET is not affected by the addition of the collision detection and response modules as it is. The response time for detection of fixed objects is adequate regardless of the speed of the moving objects. However, for collisions between two high speed objects, collision detection is sometimes slow.

Fully Interactive and Detailed Virtual Worlds

While the NPSNET virtual world is not yet complete (and may never be), it is still a consequential and somewhat useful system. The NPSNET project itself is a good study of the complexity of constructing 3D virtual worlds with available commercial technology and why fully interactive and detailed virtual worlds are not yet even on the horizon despite media promises. We are optimistic and hope that by "pushing the envelope" of real-time, workstation-based virtual reality, we are finding a way to reach the goal of a fully interactive and detailed virtual world.

Acknowledgments

We wish to acknowledge the sponsors of our efforts, in particular George Lukes of the USA Engineer Topographic Laboratories, Michael Tedeschi of the USA Test and Experimentation Command, John Maynard and Duane Gomez of the Naval Ocean Systems Center, San Diego, LTC Dennis Rochette, USA of the Headquarters Department of Army AI Center, Washington, D.C. and Carl Driskell of PM-TRADE.

References

1. Akely, Kurt, "The Hidden Charms of the Z-Buffer," *IRIS Universe*, Vol. 11, March 1990, pp. 33-34.

2. Clark, James, "Hierarchical Geometric Models for Visible Surface Algorithms," *CACM*, Vol. 19, No. 10, October 1976, pp. 547-554.

3. Fichten, Mark and Jennings, David, *Meaningful Real-Time Graphics Workstation Performance Measurements*, M.S. Thesis, Naval Postgraduate School, Monterey, California, December 1988.

4. Glassner, Andrew, editor, *An Introduction to Ray Tracing*, Academic Press, San Diego, CA, 1990, pp. 35-78

5. Institute for Simulation and Training, "Protocol Data Units for Entity Information and Entity Interaction in a Distributed Interactive Simulation", Military Standard (DRAFT), IST-PD-90-2, Orlando, FL, September 1991.

6. Lang, Eric and Wever, Peters, *SDIS Version 3.0 User's Guide: Interchange Specification, Class Definitions, Application Programmer's Interface*, BBN Systems and Technologies, Bellevue, WA, August 1990.

7. Mackey, Randall, *NPSNET: Hierarchical Data Structures for Real-Time Three-Dimensional Visual Simulation*, M.S. Thesis, Naval Postgraduate School, Monterey, California, September 1991.

8. Monahan, James, *NPSNET: Physically-Based Modeling Enhancements to an Object File Format*, M.S. Thesis, Naval Postgraduate School, Monterey, CA, September 1991.

9. Nizolak, Joseph Jr., Drummond, William T. Jr., and Zyda, Michael J. "FOST: Innovative Training for Tomorrow's Battlefield," Field Artillery, HQDA PB 6-90-1, February 1990, pp. 46-51.

10. Polcrack, Jane, *Using Solid Modeling Techniques to Construct Three-Dimensional Icons for a Visual Simulator*, M.S. Thesis, Naval Postgraduate School, Monterey, CA, September 1991.

11. Pope, Arthur, "The SIMNET Network and Protocols", BBN Report No. 7102, BBN Systems and Technologies, Cambridge, MA, July 1989.

12. Samet, Hanan, "Applications of Spatial Data Structures", Addison Wesley, 1990, p. 426.

13. Shaffer, Clifford, "Fast Circle-Rectangle Intersection", *Graphics Gems*, Ed. Andrew Glassner, Academic Press, Boston, 1990, pp. 51-53.

14. Silicon Graphics Computer Systems Inc., Graphics Library Reference Manual, C edition, IRIS-4D series, 1990

15. Silicon Graphics, Inc. "Network Communications," Document Version 1.0, Document Number 007-0810-010, Mountain View, CA, 1990.

16. Tanenbaum, Andrew, "Computer Networks", Second Edition, Prentice Hall, Englewood Cliffs, NJ, 1989, pp. 146-148.

17. Thorpe, Jack "The New Technology of Large Scale Simulator Networking: Implications for Mastering the Art of Warfighting," *Proceedings of the Ninth Interservice Industry Training Systems Conference*, November 1987.

18. Zyda, Michael "3D Visual Simulation for Graphics Performance Characterization," NCGA '90 Conference Proceedings, Vol. I, 22 March 1990, pp. 705-714.

19. Zyda, Michael, Fichten, Mark, and Jennings, David H. "Meaningful Graphics Workstation Performance Measurements," Computers & Graphics, Vol. 14, No. 3, 1990, Great Britain: Pergamon Press, pp.519-526.

20. Zyda. Michael, McGhee, Robert, Kwak, S., Nordman, D.B., Rogers, R.C., and Marco, D. "3D Visualization of Mission Planning and Control for the NPS Autonomous Underwater Vehicle," IEEE Journal of Oceanic Engineering, Vol. 15, No. 3, July 1990, pp. 217-221.

21. Zyda, Michael, McGhee, Robert, McConkle, Corinne M., Nelson, Andrew H. and Ross, Ron S. "A Real-Time, Three-Dimensional Moving Platform Visualization Tool," Computers & Graphics, Vol. 14, No. 2, 1990, Great Britain: Pergamon Press, pp.321-333.

22. Zyda, Michael, McGhee, Robert, Ross, Ron, Smith, Doug and Streyle, Dale "Flight Simulators for Under $100,000," IEEE Computer Graphics & Applications, Vol. 8, No. 1, January 1988, pp. 19-27

23. Zyda, Michael and Pratt, David "3D Visual Simulation as Workstation Exhaustion," Proceedings of Ausgraph 90, Melbourne, Australia, 10 - 14 September 1990, pp. 313-328.

24. Zyda, Michael and Pratt, David "Zydaville," on ACM SIGGRAPH Video Review, Vol. 60, August 1990, entitled "HDTV & The Quest for Virtual Reality". The video segment shows our NPSNET system and a brief interview of Professor Zyda.

25. Zyda, Michael and Pratt, David "NPSNET: A 3D Visual Simulator for Virtual World Exploration and Experimentation, "1991 SID International Symposium Digest of Technical Papers, Volume XXII, 8 May 1991, pp. 361-364.

26. Zyda, Michael, Wilson, Kalin, Pratt, David, and Monahan, James, *NPSOFF: An Object Description Language for Supporting Virtual World Construction,* Naval Postgraduate School, Monterey, CA, October 1991, in preparation.

Networked Virtual Environments

Brian Blau,   Charles E. Hughes,
J. Michael Moshell and Curtis Lisle

Institute for Simulation and Training
and
Department of Computer Science
University of Central Florida
Orlando, Florida 32816

ABSTRACT

The Virtual Environment Realtime Network (VERN) is an object oriented testbed for the interconnection of environments over a network of graphical workstations. VERN is based on extensions to the networking technology of the DARPA sponsored SIMNET combined combat training system and the Distributed Interactive Simulation protocol being developed as a DOD standard. It allows for multiple participants to interact in an environment, sharing ideas and solving problems, regardless of their physical locations. Furthermore, dramatic reconstructions of historical events for education or entertainment will be possible. Indeed, much of the impact of VERN is likely to result from the ability of participants to learn from each other even if they and their machines are separated by long distances.

INTRODUCTION

Virtual Reality/Virtual Environments (VE) describes a multi-sensory real-time simulation that immerses the participant in a multi-dimensional (usually 3D) graphical space, allows freedom of movement within the space, and supports interactions including the modification of most features of the space itself [10,13]. Additionally, a VE system may include modeling tools for world construction, rendering tools for viewing, storage mechanisms for saving memorable experiences, I/O devices for controlling aspects of the space and communication ports for shared environments.

Recently, research in the VE field has now turned its attention to networking issues for shared experiences. Two phases must be considered : rendering (distribution of graphical data) and computation (distribution of the physical model). The Visual Systems Laboratory (VSL) at IST is currently working on both of these problems.

Our efforts have produced two software systems : ANIM and VERN. ANIM is an interactive graphical simulation system with support for devices like SpaceBalls and gloves (VSL Input Paw). Modeling tools, such as Alias (high end rendering tool, Alias Research), MultiGen (tool for CIG databases, Software Systems) and S1000 (SIMNET's CAD system, BBN) are used to build environments which are inputs for the system. ANIM has been extended using VERN protocols and can now operate on several computers, distributing the computations of the objects as well as distributing the space itself. This paper will focus on VERN and how systems like ANIM can use VERN to distribute virtual objects, computational load and user interactions across multiple simulation platforms.

Simulation Network (SIMNET) [7,12] is a project sponsored by the Defense Advanced Research Projects Agency (DARPA) and was designed and built by BBN Laboratories Inc. and Perceptronics Inc. It allows for collective team training in combined arms scenarios. All of the simulators are networked via EtherNet and the communication model is based on the "dead reckoning" paradigm [8]. VE applications are a far more demanding simulation than SIMNET, because in a truly useful virtual world, every object is dynamic. In traditional simulators, only a small collection of moving objects can be maintained.

As a follow-on to the homogeneous SIMNET system, the US Army has explored the possibility of expanding these concepts to address the networking of large numbers of dissimilar training devices. The next important step in this research is the development of a standard communications protocol for Distributed Interactive Simulations (DIS) [8].

Interactive simulations in the SIMNET and DIS worlds perform computations and communicate by a dead reckoning model. Each object in the simulation has a host machine which will process its dynamics. All other machines have representations of the object which maintain an approximation to the current state of the object. The approximation of a simulation object's state is computed by a dead reckoning algorithm.   This computation is usually an extrapolation of the object's position based on velocity. When the host object realizes that the dead reckoning model has deviated significantly from the dynamic model (probably because of user input), an update message is sent to all other representations of the object on every other machine.

DESCRIPTION OF VERN v1.2

VERN v1.2 was developed to meet the needs of the simulation community as a vehicle for development of networked environments as well as to break new ground in the development of interactive VE systems.   This implementation is an extensible object oriented class hierarchy where the communications, dead reckoning and process control are abstracted to the highest levels. Most importantly, VERN extends the notion of dead reckoning into a distributed physical model.

VERN evolved from a non-realtime Smalltalk-80 prototype [2,3,4]. Version 1.2 is implemented in C++ and

157

currently runs on Silicon Graphics and Sun Sparc UNIX systems.

The communications protocol forms the software basis for an environment that will support experiments with a network of visual simulators operating in a single simulation. This environment will contain dynamic and static objects. For example, terrain over which objects move may be dynamic while buildings in a city may be static. Objects in the simulation communicate with each other without having to know the host machine on which the receiving object resides. Each object assumes that all objects are in its own local memory. Under the VERN protocol, messages bound for remote objects are intercepted and routed accordingly.

Players and Ghosts

Each real world object participating in the simulation is represented by a software object called a Player. The Player resides on the object's home machine. If human or external input is required by the Player, the data is read and processed on the Player's home machine. The main responsibility of the Player is to accurately maintain state information, read and process inputs, provide feedback usually in the form of real-time graphics, and inform the network of any significant state changes that deviate from the dead reckoning model.

In order to facilitate communication between Players residing on separate machines, each Player has an associated Ghost located on every machine involved in the simulation. Thus in an N Player simulation on M networked machines, each machine is guaranteed to have exactly N objects representing all players. Such a configuration allows Players to communicate locally with any other Player (represented by its Ghost). It is the responsibility of the Ghost either to respond directly to the message, or to forward it to the actual Player.

Ghosts are approximations of their associated Players. That is, the state of a Ghost is not always as precise (algorithmically) as the Players, but this approximation is adequate for visualization and dynamics. All Ghosts that are associated with a single Player are synchronized at any given instant in simulation time through the use of the system clock, message passing and dead reckoning. When the Player realizes that its Ghosts are going to be inaccurate, the Player then communicates the correct state information to all Ghosts.

Message Types

There are two types of messages to which Players and Ghosts respond: queries and commands. Queries are messages which can be processed entirely by the Ghost. Commands are messages that must be passed on to the Player. Thus, a message that requests state information would be considered a query while a change of behavior message would be a command.

Class Hierarchy

VERN v1.2 was designed using the object oriented paradigm. The classes that comprise the highest levels of the hierarchy contain the code for handling all of the communications and process control protocols. This hierarchy is considered a white box framework [6] because the user (programmer) of the system must follow the structures that the abstract classes establish. Figure 1 shows the abstract class hierarchy of VERN v1.2.

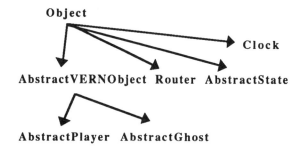

Figure 1. Class Hierarchy for VERN v1.2

There are additional classes not shown here which represent communication support structures such as mailboxes, addresses, and sockets. The following describes each of the abstract classes.

class AbstractVERNObject :
This class contains the virtual methods which handle actions to be performed in each simulation loop. For example, initializations, maintenance of the local mailbox (repository for messages), and access to the state information.

class AbstractPlayer :
This class defines the basic components of the simulation Player. Virtual methods in the class are used to support such activities as processing of incoming messages, internal state configuration and message creation.

class AbstractGhost :
This class defines the "view" of a Player as seen by other local and remote Players. A simulation Player located on a workstation can communicate with another Player only through its AbstractGhost. An instance of this class contains limited state information which is useful to other Players. When the state of the Player changes significantly from the dead reckoned state, a message is sent to all AbstractGhosts to reflect the new value.

class AbstractState:
This class defines the state variables used in the AbstractPlayer. Each implementation will inherit from this class and use it as a guide. The class AbstractVERNObject has an instance of AbstractState as one of its instance variables.

IMPLEMENTATION DETAILS

To write a Player/Ghost program, the programmer must create concrete subclasses of the abstract classes listed above. For example, consider the definition of a moving ball. The classes that must be created are MovingBallPlayer (subclass of AbstractPlayer), MovingBallGhost (subclass of AbstractGhost), and MovingBallState (subclass of AbstractState). These new classes must then be compiled, linked and executed. Further examples of Players may be found in [2].

The first classes that must be created is a subclass of Abstract Player and AbstractGhost. There are two methods that must be reimplemented in the new Player. These are processMsg and computeNextState. The Player must also have a constructor method to create instances.

Method : constructor

The purpose of constructor methods in C++ is to provide a default way to instantiate new instances of a class. In our case, a string containing the name of the Player is the required parameter. The main function of the constructor is to initialize the state instance variable.

Method : processMsg

Since C++ does not internally support machine to machine communications, a low level messaging system is necessary. Support for sending raw packets of data between UNIX processes has been supplied. The responsibility of creating and interpreting the raw data is left to the Player.

The purpose of processMsg is to interpret and respond to incoming messages. It is important to note that messages may arrive from many different Players. Each raw message contains the source, destination, data and type.

Method : computeNextState (for Player)

This method serves two purposes. The first is to perform any internal processing which might be required by the Player. For example, calculate new position and velocity based on current simulation time. The second purpose of this method is to update the state information of the Player.

Method : computeNextState (for Ghost)

The objective of this method is to compute the Ghost's approximate state model. The Ghost determines the next state of the player, without any additional information coming from the player. This is how dead reckoning is implemented within VERN. Each Ghost performs this message once each simulation loop.

In order to facilitate complete freedom in defining state information of a Player's object, an AbstractState was created. This abstract class provides default definitions of methods that must be reimplemented. It defines no instance variables. This means that the concrete Player class must define and maintain all of its own instance variables. The main methods in this class are comparison operators such as == and !=, mathematical operators such as + and -, and the assignment operator =. There are no other restrictions placed on the addition of subclassses.

EXECUTING THE SIMULATION

Previous versions of the VERN used a synchronized clock as the simulation coordinator. Using this synchronization system enabled the state of the Player to know (via a local dead reckoning) the Ghost's exact state at every tick of the clock. Although this is important, it can be accomplished using the computers' real-time clocks. This allows each computer to execute as fast as possible and it also reduces the communications overhead of clock maintenance.

The function of the Router is to maintain the connections to the outside world, maintain a list of active local and global Players, and route messages according to their source and destination. All of the routers know the locations of the other routers and the addresses of all

objects. This global information allows the router to make decisions about the direction of the message. The Router's main loop asks each of the local objects to run one simulation cycle. During this cycle, objects execute the inherited methods above.

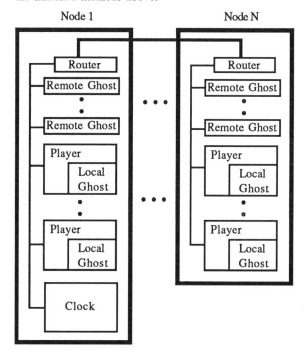

Figure 2. Process Architecture of VERN v1.2

Additionally, the Router can report the current simulation configuration and detect simulation errors. When a Player leaves the simulation, the Router immediately realizes which Player is missing and then reports this to all Routers in the system. Figure 2 shows the overall system architecture of VERN v1.2.

There are additional system functions worth mentioning. An automatic update is has been added. This forces the Player to update its Ghost at a specified interval (usually 3-5 seconds) even if no update is needed. This function is useful when the communication system drops packets. Using this function provides for reliable Player/Ghost synchronization.

An additional system parameter is called "dynamic update." Dead reckoning algorithms have a base threshold on which an update is based. The dynamic update is another threshold which provides the user with some control. The dynamic update threshold specifies the amount of error in the dead reckoning algorithm. For example, if the user is interacting with the environment at a detailed level, then the dynamic update will be set to a small value, resulting in accurate synchronization between Player and Ghost.

One last feature is called "update tracking." When a Ghost receives an update message from the Player, usually the position has changed significantly. If the update tracking is set to "jump", then the object will disappear from its current location and reappear at its updated location, causing a visual disturbance. If the update tracking is set to smooth, then the object will track evenly to its new position. This tracking will occur over a number of frames and the amount of smoothing can be set as a system parameter.

ISSUES FOR DISCUSSION

There are many issues that arise in research projects of this nature. It is useful to note that VERN v1.2 is only one part of a larger project to develop VEs, and its main purpose is to show proof of concept. Below are a few interesting topics that emerged from this implementation.

Communications

The base communications between different machines is accomplished with a "broadcast" UNIX socket. Broadcast sockets distribute their packets to anyone listening. Socket communications using the broadcast mechanism are not guaranteed: messages sent may not reach their final destination. Additionally, broadcast is convenient for local communications but may not be useful in long haul systems. By experiment, the performance advantages of broadcast messages outweigh the risk of occasional lost messages. Point-to-Point sockets are the main means for long haul communication. VERN has been tested over private communication lines as well as on the nation-wide Internet.

It should be noted that the lowest level communications were written in-house. There was a study of language based communications systems, such as those that support TimeWarp and Actor [5,1]. It was determined that these systems are useful, but our need to learn and experience workstation based communications outweighed their use. Implementing VERN using an Actor or TimeWarp paradigm is possible and is part of our future research.

Object Oriented Design Using C++

This is probably one of the most interesting parts of the VERN. One of the main arguments against the use of C++ as the base language for the VERN is that is does not fully support polymorphism. Dynamic binding of method calls is restricted in some cases because of the strict type checking. Since the design of this project incorporates abstract classes, a language with flexible support of dynamic binding and type checking would be more suitable. Smalltalk would be a suitable alternative and may solve some of these problems, but it is not yet available on a wide variety of workstations.

Performance

The performance of VERN has been measuerd and a detailed description of experiments can be found in [3]. Currently, running on a network of 2 Sun Sparcs and 4 Silicon Graphics workstations, VERN v1.2 can achieve 300-350 frames/second. The test environment consisted of 5 balls bouncing in a closed box. We have conducted extensive experiments on non-trivial environments and the results are encouraging. We expect frame rates of 5-10 per second with an environment consisting of 1000 objects (~10k polygons).

Future Directions of VERN

The major goals of the next version are to improve efficiency, investigate other distributed simulation systems, experiment with extended environments and continue work on long haul communications.

The design of this project represents only one limited view of VE system development. Frameworks, like VERN, need to be combined with other object oriented systems to form complete VE systems. This project and others, like ANIM, are likely to pave the way to robust systems. These new VE's will contain physical modeling, real-time control of objects, decentralized clocks and spatial division of computations in an object oriented framework. The next level of research for this project will look at these issues to determine commonality and reusability which will extend the functionality of the entire system.

ACKNOWLEDGEMENTS

Many thanks are due to Jinxiong Chen and Xin Li for their excellent ideas and late nights. Also, thanks goes to Ernie Smart for his continuing support. This research project is supported by the Army's Project Manager for Training Devices, Department of Defense, contract no. N61339-90-C-0041.

REFERENCES

[1] Agha, G., *Actors: A Model of Concurrent Computation in Distributed Systems*, MIT Press 1986.

[2] Blau, B. "How To Implement Networked Simulation Players Using VERN v1.05." VSL Document 91.4. Institute for Simulation and Training, University of Central Florida, Orlando, FL. April, 1991.

[3] Blau, B., "Performance Measurements of VERN v1.2," VSL Document 91.37, Institute for Simulation and Training, University of Central Florida, Orlando, FL. Jan, 1992.

[4] Hughes, C. E., Blau, B., et. al, "Dynamic Terrain Project: The Virtual Reality Testbed Smalltalk Prototype." VSL Document 90.14, Institute for Simulation and Training, University of Central Florida, Orlando, FL, Nov, 1990.

[5] Jeffferson, D., et. al., "Distrubuted Simulation and the Time Warp Operating System," 11th ACM Symposium on Operating Systems Principles, Austin, TX, In, Operating Systems Review, vol. 25, no. 5, p77-93, 1987.

[6] Johnson, R. E and Foote, B., "Designing Reusable Classes." *Journal of Object Oriented Programming*, 22-35, June/July, 1988

[7] Johnston, R. S., "The SIMNET Visual System." *Proceedings of the 9th ITEC Conference*, Washington D.C. Nov, 1987.

[8] McDonald, L. B. and Bouwens, C. 1991. "Rationale Document for Protocol Data Units for Entity Information and Entity Interaction in a Distributed Interactive Simulation." Institute for Simulation and Training Publication IST-PD-90-1-Revised, University of Central Florida, Orlando, FL. (Jan)

[9] Moshell, J. M., et. al, "Networked Virtual Environments for Simulation and Training," *1991 International Simulation Technology Conference*, Orlando, FL, Oct, 1991.

[10] Pentland, A. P., "Computational Complexity Versus Simulated Environments," Special Issue on 1990 Symposium on Interactive 3D Graphics, In *Computer Graphics*, vol. 24, no. 2, March 1990.

[11] Pope, A., "The SIMNET Network and Protocols." BBN Report No. 7102. BBN Systems and Technologies Advanced Simulation Division, Cambridge, Mass. July, 1989.

[12] Pope, A., "The SIMNET Network and Protocols." BBN Report No. 7102. BBN Systems and Technologies Advanced Simulation Division, Cambridge, Mass. July, 1989.

[13] Rheingold, H., *Virtual Reality*, SummitBooks, 1991, ISBN 0-671-69363-8.

A Framework for Dynamic Visual Applications

Mark A. Tarlton and P. Nong Tarlton

Microelectronics and Computer Technology Corporation

Abstract

The Mirage system is an object-oriented framework for constructing interactive visual applications. It takes a model-based approach to application development by providing a representation system for graphics, interaction, and time-based dynamics. This paper will provide a brief overview of the architecture, examples of its use, and a comparison to alternative approaches.

1.0 Introduction

The goal of this work is to create a foundation for animated, interactive 3D graphics that will reduce the time and expertise required to produce visual applications. Our hypothesis is that a model-based approach to application development provides significant advantages over more conventional procedural programming techniques.

To test this hypothesis, we have developed a foundation for interactive 3D graphics that supports this paradigm. It combines elements of object-oriented programming and frame-base knowledge representation to provide the functionality of window systems, graphics systems and animation systems.

2.0 Modeling Methodology

The modeling process begins by describing elements of an application domain in terms of the primitive elements of the representation system. These new classes of objects are domain-specific primitives that map their domain attributes onto graphical attributes. They are then used to create models in the desired domain. As the domain attributes change through the evaluation or simulation of the model, the effects propagate down to the low-level graphical attributes. The resulting structure is then interpreted to produce the desired visual presentation.

In Mirage, modeling is accomplished through the use of a representation system. The purpose of the representation system is to provide a framework for describing the elements and behavior of a

Authors' address: 3500 West Balcones Center Drive, Austin, TX 78759.

mtarlton@mcc.com, (512) 338-3620, nong@mcc.com (512) 338-3344

system in a modular, declarative style. The developer creates a model by manipulating elements and attributes of the representation system. The representation framework then provides the necessary infrastructure to handle rendering, flow of control and event management. The intent is to hide details, such as how rendering is to be done, and focus instead on what the result is to be.

The representation system employed resembles a simple frame-based knowledge representation system[6]. The primary elements are:

- classes and instances of objects,
- object attributes and values,
- operations on objects, and
- relations between objects.

Models are created by making instances of objects, setting the attribute values of the objects and composing the objects via various relationships, such as a "component" relation.

The graphics representation system of Mirage is where an application specifies what is to appear on the screen, while the renderers interrogate the model and perform the hardware-specific operations required to present an interpretation of the model on the screen. (see Figure 1). The final result of interpretation depends

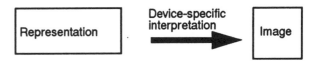

Figure. 1. Representation and interpretation

upon the specific type of interpreter being used and upon the resources available to the interpreter. For example, different graphics interpreters may behave differently depending upon the specific architecture of the graphics subsystem they are using or the degree of realism desired. Similarly, a different type of interpreter may produce an interpretation showing a part/whole structure diagram rather that the literal appearance of the model elements.

The advantages of the modeling approach to graphics are:

- it reduces complexity via declarative, constructive style of usage,
- it supports a variety of rendering styles and platforms,
- it is usable either by programming or through knowledge-based or interactive tools.

3.0 The Mirage System

A representation system for 2D and 3D graphical presentations has been defined and a prototype (Mirage) has been implemented in C++ under Unix for both the Silicon Graphics Inc. Graphics Library (SGI-GL) and for X Windows/PEX. This prototype has been used successfully to construct interactive applications including scientific visualizations for the Superconducting Super Collider Laboratory and a virtual reality, retail shopping system for the NCR Corporation. The system consists of the following elements:

- a graphics substrate that supports interactive 3D graphics in a heterogeneous networked environment,
- a temporal representation that allows the dynamic aspects of a system to be specified, and
- an event-manager for describing the cause-effect behavior of the system due to user and system interactions.

3.1 Graphics

The representational framework for static graphics combines hierarchical graphics, object-oriented programming, and frame-based knowledge representation techniques. This framework has been described in more detail in [9,10]. The class lattice of Figure 2.

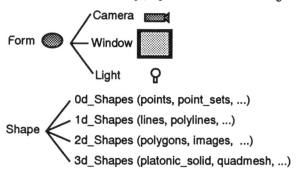

Figure 2. Classes

presents the graphical classes. The class Form represents objects with spatial attributes such as location, scale, orientation and shape. Each Form defines a local coordinate system in space. Forms may be combined hierarchically. Forms by themselves have no direct appearance but instead have a shape attribute which may be filled by one or more instances of a Shape sub-class. Figure 3. shows how instances of these classes can be used to create a visual presentation. From the top down, an instance of class Window is viewing the "world" through an instance of class Camera. The "world" is an aggregation of Forms where the part-whole structure is defined by the Component relation. The result of interpreting this structure is shown in the upper right corner of Figure 3. as an image on a workstation display.

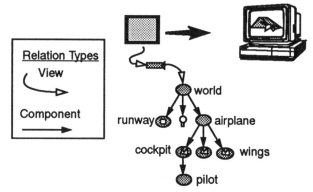

Figure 3. Airplane and runway scene

In this framework, Windows, Cameras and Lights all inherit from the Form class, so that they may be placed in a scene like any other graphical object. As a result, synthetic cameras which may be attached to other objects as shown in figure 4 are directly supported.

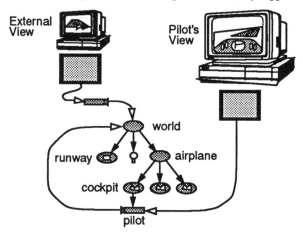

Figure 4. Synthetic camera example

In this example, the display on the left shows an external view of the scene, while the display on the right shows the pilot's view from the cockpit. In a similar fashion, A Window may be placed in a scene and then treated as a Form with the difference being that its appearance is determined by the Cameras and scenes it is viewing.

The preliminary results have shown that having Camera and Window be sub-classes of Form makes interface composition both simpler and more flexible than with the more traditional approaches. This follows from the fact that all objects have a common subset of attributes and behaviors, and there are very few constraints on how they can be combined. The result is a simple, consistent model of how graphical scenes are described.

Furthermore, by making the representation declarative and by enforcing the separation between representation and interpretation, a high degree of display-architecture independence and support of multiple display presentations are possible. The resulting architecture appears well suited to supporting dynamic, interactive graphics in a networked environment.

3.2 Animation

Time-dependent behavior is represented using a framework similar to that used in the graphics sub-system. The dynamic behavior of objects is defined by constructing a graph-based representation of temporal objects. The nodes in the graph, Activity (see Figure 5.), represents objects with a temporal extent, that is, one that exists over some interval of time. An Activity also defines a tempo-

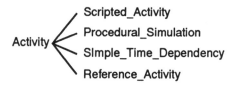

Figure 5. Temporal classes

ral coordinate system. The actual behavior of an Activity is specified by specializing the Activity class and expressing the time-dependent behavior procedurally for the new sub-class. For example, Figure 6a. shows time being mapped onto the rotation at-

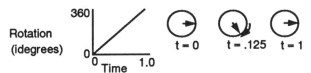

Figure 6a. Rotating-wheel activity.

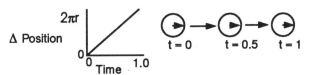

Figure 6b. Moving-wheel activity

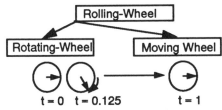

Figure 6c. Rolling-wheel activity structure

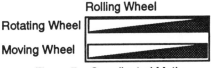

Figure 7a. Coordinated Motion

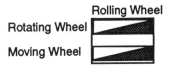

Figure 7b. Fast, Coordinated Motion

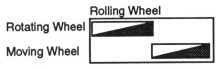

Figure 7c. Disconnected Motion

tribute of a wheel so that as time goes from 0 to 1, the wheel rotates 360 degrees. This behavior is represented by the Activity "rotating-wheel". Similarly, Figure 6b. shows time being mapped onto translation of the wheel, to produce the effect of the wheel moving a distance equal to its circumference over 1 unit of time ("moving-wheel" activity).

Next, a hierarchical temporal coordinate system is introduced in which each node in the graph corresponds to a temporal activity of some duration and which acts as a time-frame for all sub-activities. Complex activities are then created by composing simpler sub-activities under a parent activity. The result is that Activities may be composed hierarchically in the same way that graphical objects are. Figure 6c. shows the result of combining the rotating-wheel Activity with the moving-wheel Activity to define a new, more complex "rolling-wheel" Activity.

An Activity defines a one-dimensional coordinate system for time. Activities can be "scaled" and "translated" in time in much the same way that the graphical elements (Forms) are manipulated in space. Scaling an Activity affects the rate and duration of the Activity, while translating an Activity defines when the activity will occur relative to its parent's time-frame.

Figure 7. shows three variations of the "Rolling-Wheel" Activity. In the Figure 7a., the wheel rolls one complete turn in one unit of time. In Figure 7b., the Rolling-Wheel Activity has been scaled by 0.5 relative to its parent activity (not shown) and as a result, occupies one half the time as before and therefore rolls twice as fast. In the third case, Figure 7c., each of sub-activities (Rotating-Wheel, and Moving-Wheel) have been scaled by 0.5 and the Moving-Wheel activity has been translated 0.5 time units. The behavior here is that during the first 0.5 time units of the Rolling-Wheel Activity, the wheel rotates one complete turn, and then during the second 0.5 time units, the wheel moves a distance equal to its circumference.

The behavior of an Activity can be described using a simple state-machine (see Figure 8.). The transitions between states is determined by the change in local-time between samples and invoke methods on the Activity. For some types of activities, the methods triggered by state transitions may be no-ops.

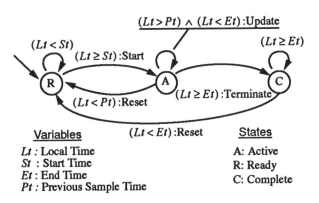

Variables

Lt : Local Time
St : Start Time
Et : End Time
Pt : Previous Sample Time

States

A: Active
R: Ready
C: Complete

Figure 8. Activity state transition model

The behavior of an Activity is procedurally specified through the following methods:

- Start - Begin execution of activity, create and initialize any resources required for the activity.
- Update - Advance activity to new local time.
- Terminate - Finish activity and release any resources no longer needed.
- Reset - Reset activity to initial state.

This framework allows time to flow forwards and backwards, be reset to an earlier time or jump to a later time, and allows a variety on non-linear time-warps [7] to be applied to Activity sub-graphs providing effects such as slow-in-slow-out dynamics.

As indicated in Figure 5., the class Activity may be specialized in various ways to create different types of time-based behaviors. Instances of the various classes may be combined within a single Activity structure allowing some dynamics to be produced via execution of scripts while other dynamic behaviors to be controlled by procedural simulations.

Gibbs[4] proposes a similar framework for audio and video media which suggests that this framework may be appropriate for combining animation, interactive simulation, and other media types.

3.3 Events

The third part of the system is the Event Manager. Events may be generated by the user through interactive devices or within the system itself. A rule-based framework is used to describe how events are to be interpreted and what actions are to be performed in response to the various events.

In the Event Manager, the four primary classes are Events, Proposers, Actions, and Contexts. Events are the mechanism that communicate the description of significant states that the system achieves. Events occur within Contexts which provide a scoping of events. Proposers are triggered by specific patterns of events and either schedule Actions, or inject new Events into the system. Actions manipulate either the underlying application, the graphical presentation or the temporal model of the system.

The purpose of an Action is either to produce an interpretation of the triggering Event, or to cause some function to be performed in response to the Event. An interpretation of an event or pattern of events may result in new events being created that contain the interpretation. This event framework is sufficient to handle user interaction, and discrete-event style simulation.

4.0 Related Work

There are many papers in the literature describing object-oriented graphics systems[1,2,3,5,8]. Typically these systems are either two-dimensional interactive systems, or three dimensional off-line animation or rendering systems. A recent system that shares many of the same objectives as this work is the Brown Animation and Graphics System, BAGS [11]. Both BAGS and Mirage attempt to replace the traditional modeling / animation / rendering pipeline with a framework suited to interactive applications. In doing so, both systems build upon object-oriented programming foundations to produce systems that are flexible and extensible. The systems differ however, in several important respects.

First, BAGS defines its own delegation-based language for graphics, while Mirage builds upon existing, class-instance languages such as C++ or CLOS. While the delegation approach used by BAGS provides a great deal of flexibility during execution, in practice much of the functionality can be provided using more conventional languages. Use of a standard language makes integration of the graphical elements with the application easier, since the interface elements and application can be built from the same object-oriented programming language.

Next, the BAGS designers have chosen to tie the time-dependent elements of the system closely to the graphical elements. The result is to change graphical attributes such as location or orientation from simple values to time-dependent functions. In BAGS, time is a special global variable. Hierarchical time is not explicitly supported, and effects such as localized time warps are more difficult to achieve.

Finally, Mirage provides a separate framework for managing events and actions. Events may result from either user actions (e.g., mouse clicks), or from within the system (e.g., collision detection, or application event). The event manager provides a framework for interpreting patterns of events and scheduling actions which result from the events. It also provides a mechanism though which interleaved events in multi-participant systems can be organized, and controlled to provide correct execution without undue serialization of execution.

5.0 Conclusions

In summary, the approach presented here addresses the issues of dynamic graphics by defining a declarative representation system for graphics, animation and interaction. Mirage also introduces the concept of windows as three-dimensional graphical objects and a hierarchical framework for animation. By using object-oriented programming and declarative representational techniques, superior modularity and ease of use are achieved as compared to current systems. The feasibility of this approach is demonstrated through a working prototype and example applications.

References

[1] ACM SIGGRAPH '87 course notes, "Object-Oriented Geometric Modeling and Rendering" (July 27-31, 1987).

[2] Barth, Paul S. "An Object-Oriented Approach to Graphical Interfaces," ACM Transactions on Graphics, Vol. 5, no. 2 (April 1986) pp. 142-172.

[3] Borning, Alan. "ThingLab -- A Constraint-Oriented Simulation Laboratory." Xerox Palo Alto Research Center Technical Report SSL-79-3 (July, 1979) 100 pages.

[4] Gibbs, Simon. "Composite Multimedia and Active Objects." Proceedings of OOPSLA'91 (Phoenix, Arizona, Oct. 6-11, 1991) . In SIGPLAN Notices Vol. 26, no 11 (Nov. 1991) pp. 97-112.

[5] Grant, Eric, Amburn, Phil, and Whitted, Turner. "Exploiting Classes in Modeling and Display Software", IEEE Computer Graphics and Applications. Vol. 6, no. 11 (Nov. 1986) pp. 13-20.

[6] Minsky, Marvin A. "A Framework for Representing Knowledge" The Psychology of Computer Vision. ed. Patrick Winston. McGraw-Hill, New York. (1975)

[7] Reynolds, Craig W. "Description and Control of Time and Dynamics in Computer Animation," SIGGRAPH '85 Tutorial : Advanced Computer Animation. (July 23,1985) pp. 31-56A.

[8] Smith, Randall B. "The Alternate Reality Kit: An Animated Environment for Creating Interactive Simulations," Proceedings of 1986 IEEE Computer Society Workshop on Visual Languages, CS-IEEE, (Los Alamitos, CA.) pp. 99-106.

[9] Tarlton, Mark A., Tarlton, P. Nong , and Poltrock., Steven E. "GrafBag: An Object- Oriented Graphics Package." MCC Technical Report Number HI-418-86-P. (Dec. 1986).

[10] Tarlton, Mark A., and Tarlton, P. Nong. "Pogo: A Declarative Representation System for Graphics" Object-Oriented Concepts, Databases and Applications. ed. W. Kim and F. Lochovsky. ACM Press, Addison-Wesley. (1989)

[11] Zeleznik, Robert C., Conner, D. Brookshire, Wioka, Matthias M., Aliaga, Daniel G., Huang, Nathan T., Hubbard, Philip M., Knep, Brian, Kauman, Henry, Huges, John F. , and van Dam, Andries. "An Object-Oriented Framework for the Integration of Interactive Animation Techniques." Proceedings of SIGGRAPH'91 (Las Vegas, Nevada, July 29-Aug. 2, 1991). In Computer Graphics Vol. 25, no. 4 (July 1991) pp. 105-112.

Linear Constraints for Deformable B-Spline Surfaces

George Celniker[a] and Will Welch[b]

[a]celniker@slcs.slb.com,
Schlumberger Laboratory for Computer Science, P.O. Box 200015, Austin, Texas 78720

[b]william.welch@cs.cmu.edu,
School of Computer Science, Carnegie Mellon University, 5000 Forbes ave, Pittsburg, PA 15213

ABSTRACT

We describe a method for preserving a set of geometric constraints while interactively sculpting a free-form B-spline surface. The surface seeks a fair shape by minimizing an appropriate global energy function. The user controls the surface through the creation and manipulation of geometric constraints such as interpolated points and curves.

We represent the free-form surface as a B-spline surface, and formulate a quadratic deformation energy in terms of this basis. Constraints are represented as gradients of quadratic functionals which have a global minimum value when the constraint is satisfied. These constraints are linear in the surface degrees of freedom, and are maintained during surface minimization by transforming the constrained surface equations into an unconstrained system with fewer degrees of freedom.

Point, curve, and normal constraints are formulated with reference to a tensor-product B-spline surface. By extension, formulations are applicable to any linearly blended surface.

1 INTRODUCTION

We are interested in developing an easy to use modeling method for building shapes with free-form surfaces. In conventional free-form modeling schemes the user must manage both a large number of control parameters as well as difficult to perceive relationships between them to achieve application specific effects.

The strategy we propose to address this problem is to find a modeling technique that separates the surface representation from the surface modeling operators. In this approach one modeling operator might modify many degrees of freedom simultaneously to create one highly leveraged modeling effect. We believe that interactive free-form surface design based on energy minimizing surfaces and geometric constraints can be exploited to achieve this separation.

Energy minimizing surfaces mimic the behavior of everyday physical objects providing the user with a familiar metaphor for modifying shape with forces in an intuitive manner. Surfaces can be pushed, pulled, and inflated to get desired shapes. The form of the energy functional determines the properties of the shape being sculpted. We use a functional that causes the surface to minimize its area while distributing curvature over large areas to form very smooth and graceful shapes.

We divide modeling operators into two classes: sculpting tools and geometric constraints. Sculpting tools are implemented as sets of forces such as pressure, springs and gravity to produce qualitative effects like enlarge, attract, and flatten. Interacting sculpting loads are naturally handled by adding the effective force vectors at each point on the surface into a net force. Such surface modeling approaches have been discussed in [3,4,21].

In contrast, geometric constraints are specified as analytic conditions which the surface must satisfy explicitly. Such constraints, including point and curve skinning, and tangency and normal conditions, allow precise control over a portion the surface, and are therefor a means of knitting free-form shapes to analytic shapes.

This paper deals with enforcing geometric constraints while sculpting on deformable surfaces. Much of the recent work in constraint based systems for geometric modeling have concentrated in preserving relationships between simple parameterized objects such as lines and circles. These efforts have been applied to kinematics [8], dynamics based animation [20], and constraint based geometric modeling [8,17]. Previous work for enforcing constraints on parametric surfaces and curves have been based on penalty methods without deformable surfaces [1,20], transformation based constraints limited to the explicit degrees of freedom in the surface representation with deformable surfaces [4], and Lagrangian constraints [19].

In this paper, we restrict ourselves to a linearly blended surface (a tensor-product B-spline surface), and consider the class of geometric constraints which are linear functions of the explicit degrees of freedom of the shape representation. Such constraints can be imposed on the surface by a linear transformation of the constrained surface equations which reduces them to a smaller, unconstrained system in which the constraints are implicitly satisfied. It is then possible to perform other operations (such as surface minimization in the presence of applied sculpting forces) on the remaining surface degrees of freedom without violating the constraints.

We show how this technique may be used to constrain any parametric point on the surface to remain at a fixed location in 3-space, constrain parametric curves in the surface to maintain fixed profiles in 3-space (fixed-parameter curve-skinning), and constrain the 3-space surface normals along a parametric curve. The method is directly applicable to any surface representation which is a linear blend of its control parameters. In this paper B-spline basis functions are used.

2 DEFORMABLE B-SPLINES

A deformable surface is designed to mimic real physical behavior. Like a physical surface, a deformable surface's deformation behavior is modeled by minimizing a global energy functional which describes how much energy is stored in the surface for any deformation shape. The deformation energy used in this work is of the form.

$$E_{deformation} = \int_\sigma (\alpha \ \text{stretch} + \beta \ \text{bending}) \, d\sigma \qquad 1$$

where α and β are weights on stretching and bending.

This produces a surface which tends to minimize its area to avoid folding and to distribute curvature over large regions to make very graceful shapes. The quadratic functional used in this work is made from the linearized stretching and bending terms

$$E_{surface} = \int_\sigma \left[\begin{pmatrix} (\alpha_{11}w_u{}^2 + 2\alpha_{12}w_uw_v + \alpha_{22}w_v{}^2) \\ + (\beta_{11}w_{uu}{}^2 + 2\beta_{12}w_{uv}{}^2 + \beta_{22}w_{vv}{}^2) \end{pmatrix} - 2\,f\,w \right] dudv \qquad 2$$

where w is the surface shape, a contiguous set of points in 3-space represented with parametric variables u and v as

$w = w(u,v) = [x(u,v),y(u,v),z(u,v)]$ with
w_u as shorthand for $\partial w/\partial u$ and
w_{vv} as shorthand for $\partial^2 w/\partial v^2$ and
$f = f(w,t)$ denoting the applied sculpting forces which are changed over time t by the user.

The above problem is discretized by approximating the minimal surface shape w by w^h a weighted sum of continuous shape functions. In this paper, we use the tensor-product B-spline basis as discussed by [Piegl] for the shape functions yielding

$$w(u,v) \approx w^h(u,v) = \sum_{i=0}^n \sum_{j=0}^m P_{i,j} N_{i,p}(u) N_{j,p}(v) \qquad 3$$

where $P_{i,j}$ are the familiar [nxm] grid of B-spline control points and $N_{i,p}$ are the univariate B-spline basis functions of order p defined recursively as

$$N_{i,0}(u) = \begin{cases} 1 \text{ if } u_i \le u < u_{i+1} \\ 0 \text{ otherwise} \end{cases} \qquad 4$$

$$N_{i,p}(u) = \frac{u - u_i}{u_{i+p} - u_i} N_{i,p-1}(u) + \frac{u_{i+p+1} - u}{u_{i+p+1} - u_{i+1}} N_{i+1,p-1}(u) \qquad 5$$

where u_i are the knots forming a vector $U = \{u_0, u_1, \ldots u_r\}$. By convention, knots at the ends of the B-spline are repeated p+1 times so that a B-spline curve with r knots will have n control points where $r = n + p + 1$. The range of u is limited to $u_p \le u \le u_{r-p}$. In this work B-splines are of 3rd order setting $p = 3$ and $N_{i,p}$ is abbreviated as N_i.

The B-spline approximation for shape w^h is substituted back into the original minimum principle yielding a discrete matrix minimum problem

$$\min \ (x^T \, K_\sigma \, x - f_\sigma^T \, x) \qquad 6$$

where the unknowns are ordered into a vector as $x^T = [P_{0,0} \ P_{0,1} \cdots P_{m,n}]$. K_σ and F_σ define the stiffness matrix and forcing vector. These terms are given by

$$K_\sigma = \int_\sigma \Phi_b^T \, \bar\beta \, \Phi_b + \Phi_s^T \, \bar\alpha \, \Phi_s \, dudv \quad \text{and} \quad f_\sigma = \int_\sigma \Phi^T \, f \, dudv \qquad 7$$

where $\Phi_b = \begin{bmatrix} \Phi_{uu} \\ \Phi_{vv} \\ 2\Phi_{uv} \end{bmatrix}$ $\Phi_s = \begin{bmatrix} \Phi_u \\ \Phi_v \end{bmatrix}$

and $\bar\alpha = \begin{bmatrix} \alpha_{11} & \alpha_{12} \\ \alpha_{12} & \alpha_{22} \end{bmatrix}$ $\bar\beta = \begin{bmatrix} \beta_{11} & & \\ & \beta_{22} & \\ & & \beta_{12} \end{bmatrix}$

and $\Phi = [N_0(u)N_0(v) \ N_0(u)N_1(v) \cdots N_m(u)N_n(v)]$ an ordered set of basis functions.

The minimum of equation 6 is found by solving

$$K_\sigma x = f_\sigma(w,t) \qquad 8$$

Simple mass and damping effects are added to the surface as

$$M\ddot{x} + B\dot{x} + K_\sigma x = f_\sigma(w,t)$$

where $M = \rho I$, $B = \mu I$, I = Identity matrix, and ρ is a mass density and μ is a stabilizing damping term.

166

These equations are integrated through time by using finite differences for the temporal derivatives which results in a matrix equation relating the shape at time $t+\Delta t$ to the shape and sculpting loads at time t and $t-\Delta t$

$$K x_{t+\Delta t} = F(f_t, x_t, x_{t-\Delta t})$$

Solving for x generates the control point locations used to generate the surface in equation 3. The matrices K_σ and K are symmetric and positive definite due to the form of the selected energy functional. The local support property of the B-spline basis functions make K_σ sparse.

3 CONSTRAINTS BY NULL-SPACE PROJECTION

An attractive way to enforce constraints on a system of equations is to transform it into an unconstrained system of equations with fewer degrees of freedom. We do this for systems of linear equations by projecting the system of equations onto the subspace of solutions which satisfies the constraints. General linear constraints are written as

$$A x = b \qquad\qquad 9$$

where the vector x represents the degrees of freedom, each row of the $m \times n$ matrix A ($m < n$) represents a linear constraint on x, and the vector b represents the values of these constraints. Given a particular solution x_0, the space of satisfying vectors for the system can be expressed as

$$x = Z y + x_0 \qquad\qquad 10$$

where the columns of the $n \times z$ matrix Z span the null-space of A, and the vector y represents a reduced set of z unconstrained degrees of freedom. Substituting equation 10 into 9 shows that Z has the property that $A Z y = 0$ for all y. The number of columns in Z is n minus the number of independent rows in A because each independent constraint in A removes one degree of freedom from the system.

Given Z and x_0, the minimization problem of equation 8 can be projected onto this reduced space as

$$Z^T K Z\ y = Z^T F - Z^T x_0 \qquad\qquad 11$$

Equation 10 regenerates a properly constrained solution x to the original minimization problem for each unconstrained solution y of the projected minimization problem.

There are any number of stable ways of calculating Z (see Gill et al.). In general, selecting a subset of A's columns on which to base Z is a delicate procedure, especially in the presence of nearly-dependent constraint rows (Golub and Van Loan, Matrix Computations, p 571).

A very simple procedure for computing Z is to apply Gaussian elimination with full pivoting to the system

$A x = 0$, reducing the first $n-z$ rows of A to the identity. This produces the specially factored matrix A'

$$A' = \begin{bmatrix} I & R \\ 0 & 0 \end{bmatrix} \text{ in the relation } A'x = \begin{bmatrix} I & R \\ 0 & 0 \end{bmatrix} \begin{bmatrix} x_d \\ y \end{bmatrix} = 0 \qquad 12$$

that explicitly separates the x degrees of freedom into dependent and independent sets. The identity submatrix is associated with the $n-z$ dependent degrees of freedom x_d which are "removed" from equation 11 by constraints and the R submatrix is associated with the remaining independent degrees of freedom in y. Each dependent constraint in A produces a zero row at the bottom of the A' matrix. The null-space basis Z is found by observing that $A'x = 0$ is true whenever $x_d = -Ry$ so that

$$0 = A'x = A'\begin{bmatrix} x_d \\ y \end{bmatrix} = A'\begin{bmatrix} -R \\ I \end{bmatrix} y = A'Zy = 0 \text{ and } Z = \begin{bmatrix} -R \\ I \end{bmatrix} \qquad 13$$

where I is the $z \times z$ identity matrix. Note that full pivoting is absolutely essential during this procedure if a well-conditioned basis is to result (orthogonal factorizations such as the SVD or QR are in general better conditioned, though more computationally expensive).

It is important to note that this technique successfully generates Z in the face of redundant constraints in A. Redundant constraints can be either compatible as in the case of multiple hinges supporting a single door or conflicting. In our system we identify conflicting constraints when solving for x_0. We treat all dependent constraints as compatible when solving for Z since Z is not affected by the particular values of the constraints. In this system a new x_0 is computed each time the user changes a constraint value, while a new Z is only computed each time a constraint is added or deleted.

4 GEOMETRIC CONSTRAINTS

We distinguish between two kinds of geometric constraints, frozen and tracked. A frozen constraint is added to the system at a particular time by freezing some geometric property of the surface while allowing the rest of the surface to vary. A tracked constraint varies the value of the constraint over time also causing the surface to deform. Our current strategy for exploiting constraints is to first freeze in constraints and then to track them. A frozen constraint has the advantage that at least the current surface configuration is guaranteed to satisfy the constraint.

4.a Point Constraints

The simplest constraint to visualize is a freezing point constraint. A particular surface point, identified by a parametric location (u^0, v^0), is fixed to its current position for all future times $t+\Delta t$. The constraint equation is generated from the B-spline surface equation and the current values of the control points $P_{ij}(t)$ as

$$w(u^0, v^0) = \sum_{i=0}^{n} \sum_{j=0}^{m} P_{i,j}(t) \, N_{i,p}(u^0) \, N_{j,p}(v^0) \qquad 14$$

Each constrained point generates one additional constraint equation that is added to the constraint matrix $\mathbf{A}$.

4.b Curve Constraints

The curve constraint is considerably more complicated than the point constraint. The constraint allows any curve lying within the surface to be frozen at time t such that the rest of the surface can be sculpted in future times without violating the frozen shape. The constraint equations for the curve are generated by considering a positive definite error functional over the length of the curve as

$$\varepsilon = \int_{curve} 1/2 \left(c(s) - c^0(s)\right)^2 ds \qquad 15$$

where $c(s)$ = 3d shape of the curve in the surface given by

$$c(s) = w(t(s)) = \sum_{i=0}^{n} \sum_{j=0}^{m} P_{i,j} \, N_{i,p}(u(s)) \, N_{j,p}(v(s)) \qquad 16$$

$$= \sum_{i=0,j=0}^{n,m} P_{ij} \, N_{ij}(t(s))$$

where $t(s) = [u(s) \; v(s)]$, a curve lying in the surface and $c^0(s)$ = the target 3d curve shape at time t = 0.

The value of the error functional for the curve constraint is both zero and a minimum when the curve $c(s)$ is exactly equal to the curve $c^0(s)$. We can formulate this as a linear constraint by requiring that the error functional always be at a minimum -- that its gradient with respect to the degrees of freedom be 0. The constraint that each term of the gradient be 0 yields one linear constraint equation for each degree of freedom in the system.

Finding the minimum error value ε will automatically satisfy frozen constraints. However, this will not be generally true for tracking constraints where $c^0(s)$ is allowed to change over time. In such situations the system will find the solution which best satisfies all the constraints e.g. finds the most minimum value available for ε given the shape representation but will not guarantee satisfying the constraints exactly e.g. the value of ε might not equal zero. In this work we limit ourselves to frozen constraints.

The linear curve constraint equations are

$$\frac{\partial \varepsilon}{\partial P_{ij}} = \int_{curve} \left(c(s) - c^0(s)\right) \left(\frac{\partial c(s)}{\partial P_{ij}} - \frac{\partial c^0(s)}{\partial P_{ij}}\right) ds = 0 \qquad 17$$

For the B-spline basis functions

$$\frac{\partial c(s)}{\partial P_{ij}} = N_{ij}(t(s)) \quad \text{and} \quad \frac{\partial c^0(s)}{\partial P_{ij}} = 0 \text{ for a freezing constraint.}$$

Once integrated, the above equations yield a linear set of equations in P_{ij}, $\mathbf{Cx} = \mathbf{v}$. A row in $\mathbf{C}$ is given by

$$C_{kl} = \int_{curve} \left(\sum_{i=0,j=0}^{n} P_{ij} N_{ij}(t(s))\right) N_{kl}(t(s)) \; ds \qquad 18$$

and the associated term in V is given by

$$v_{kl} = \int_{curve} \left(\sum_{i=0}^{n} P_{ij}^0 N_{ij}(t(s))\right) N_{ij}(t(s)) \; ds \qquad 19$$

The curve constraint generates one constraint equation for each control point in the surface. Typically, most of these constraints are redundant or zero equations leaving the surface several degrees of freedom in which to continue moving. In our system we generate all nonzero constraints and depend on the construction of the $\mathbf{Z}$ matrix to eliminate the redundant constraints.

4.c Surface Normal Constraints

We formulate a constraint on the surface normal along a curve as a pair of constraints. The surface normal at a point in the surface is in the direction of the cross product of any two independent surface tangent vectors at that point. In particular, surface tangents in the direction of a curve and normal to a curve generate the surface normal as

$$\mathbf{n} = |\mathbf{w}_t \times \mathbf{w}_n| \qquad 20$$

where $\mathbf{n}$ = surface normal at a point on the surface and
$\mathbf{w}_t$ = surface tangent in the direction of the curve and
$\mathbf{w}_n$ = surface tangent in the direction normal to the curve in parameter space.

The surface tangents $\mathbf{w}_t$ and $\mathbf{w}_n$ are related to the parametric derivatives $\mathbf{w}_u$ and $\mathbf{w}_v$ along the length of the curve $c(t(s))$ by the linear rotation

$$\begin{bmatrix} \mathbf{w}_t \\ \mathbf{w}_n \end{bmatrix} = \begin{bmatrix} u_s & v_s \\ -v_s & u_s \end{bmatrix} \begin{bmatrix} \mathbf{w}_u \\ \mathbf{w}_v \end{bmatrix} \qquad 21$$

where u_s and v_s are the components of the normalized curve tangent in parametric space given as $t_s = [u_s, v_s]$.

The functions $\mathbf{w}_u$ and $\mathbf{w}_v$ along the length of the curve are

$$c_u(s) = w_u(t(s)) = \sum_{i=0}^{n} \sum_{j=0}^{m} P_{i,j} \frac{d\,N_{i,p}(u(s))}{du} N_{j,p}(v(s)) \qquad 22$$

and

$$c_v(s) = w_v(t(s)) = \sum_{i=0}^{n} \sum_{j=0}^{m} P_{i,j}\, N_{i,p}(u(s)) \frac{d\,N_{j,p}(v(s))}{dv}$$

The error functionals for the constraints are written as

$$\varepsilon_t = \int_{curve} \left(c_t(s) - c_t^0(s)\right)^2 ds \ \ \text{and} \ \ \varepsilon_n = \int_{curve} \left(c_n(s) - c_n^0(s)\right)^2 ds \qquad 23$$

$$\text{where} \begin{bmatrix} c_t \\ c_n \end{bmatrix} = \begin{bmatrix} u_s & v_s \\ -v_s & u_s \end{bmatrix} \begin{bmatrix} c_u \\ c_v \end{bmatrix}$$

Like the curve constraint, finding the minimum of the error functionals ε_t and ε_n with respect to the degrees of freedom P_{ij} yield the sets of constraint equations to be enforced. The combination of constraining the curve's tangent shape c_t and the curve's normal shape c_n acts to constrain the surface normal along the length of the curve. Note that the constraint on curve shape c can replace the constraint on c_t since constraining the curve's shape automatically constrains the higher order surface derivatives along the length of the curve.

5 RESULTS

The techniques discussed in this paper were implemented in an interactive sculpting design package that runs on a Silicon Graphics workstation. An example of the system's modeling capability is shown in Figure 1. The surface in figure 1 is a 3rd order tensor-product B-spline with an 8x8 array of control points. The surface is constrained to interpolate the closed curve shown as a heavy dark line. The constraint eliminates 24 of the original 64 system degrees of freedom. Pressure sculpting loads are applied to the surface inside the closed constraint. The sequence of images in Figure 1 are produced by varying the magnitude of the pressure force interactively with a slider bar. The curve constraint is enforced exactly at all times while the surface is sculpted.

6 CONCLUSIONS AND FUTURE WORK

An interactive modeling system designed to sculpt free-form surfaces in the presence of point and curve constraints based on the techniques described in this paper is implemented on a Silicon Graphics Workstation. The system supports interactive sculpting under any combination of frozen constraints. Based on this experience we make the following conclusions.

We have formulated a strategy for enforcing linear constraints on linearly blended surfaces in interactive time. Using the B-spline basis functions as a shape representation we have shown how this strategy can be used to enforce a rich range of geometric constraints. We have shown how to constrain a point in the surface, and the shape of a curve

lying in the surface, as well as its higher order derivatives. Exploiting the first order surface derivative constraint we were able to build a surface normal constraint.

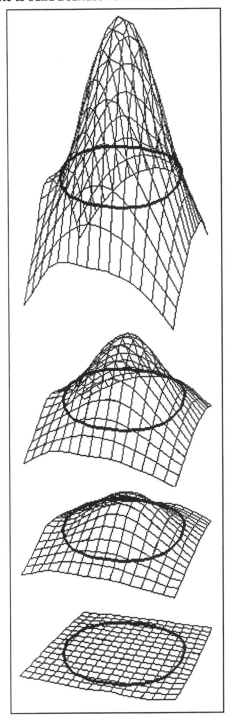

Figure 1. A closed curve constraint applied to a surface

An important limitation to the technique presented is that the shape of the geometric constraint in the surface's uv-plane must remain fixed over time. Otherwise, the nonlinearity of the surface basis functions produce nonlinear constraint equations. Although techniques are available for solving nonlinear constraint problems they tend to be inappropriate for interactive systems since they depend on iterative refactorizations of the basis. What is needed in future work is a good solution for selecting suitable parameterizations for constraints. Such a solution would enable a very exciting system for modeling with generalized curve skinning.

Another limitation of the system described here involves the discretization error of the surface approximation. The curve constraint and energy minimization techniques used here find the minimum solution for a given surface representation, but such a solution may or may not be an acceptable approximation to the true solution. Discretization error for curve constraints results in the surface pulling away from the constraint curve when its ability to exactly represent the solution curve is exceeded. Discretization error for the minimum surface solution shows up as "bad leverage" between closely placed point constraints within a single surface patch (pulling slightly on a point near a constrained point can cause large deflections in the total surface shape). A practical implementation of these constraint techniques should include an automatic surface refinement mechanism sensitive to such errors.

REFERENCES

1. Baumgarte, J., "Stabilization of Constraints and Integrals of Motion in Dynamical Systems", Computer Methods in Applied Mechanics and Engineering, 1972

2. Bloor, M.I.G. and Wilson, M.J., "Blend Design as a Boundary-Value Problem", Theory and Practice of Geometric Modeling, Wolfgang Staber and Hans-Peter Seidel (Eds.), 1989

3. Celniker G., Gossard D., "Deformable Curve and Surface Finite-Elements for Free-Form Shape Design", Proceedings Siggraph '91, Las Vegas Nevada, 28 July - 2 August 1991

4. Celniker G., ShapeWright: Finite Element Based Free-Form Shape Design, M.I.T. Ph.D., Dept. of Mechanical Engineering, September, 1990

5. Gill, Phillip and Murray, Walter and Wright, Margaret, Practical Optimization, Academic Press, 1981.

6. Golub, Gene and Van Loan, Charles, Matrix Computations, 2nd ed., p 571. Johns Hopkins University Press, 1989.

7. Kass, Michael and Witkin, Andrew, and Terzopoulos, Demetri, "Snakes: Active Contour Models", International Journal of Computer Vision, 1988

8. Kramer, Glen A., Solving Geometric Constraint Systems: A case study in kinematic, MIT Press, 1991, Cambridge Mass.

9. Lancos Cornelius, The variational Principles of Mechanics", 4th Edition, Dover,. 1970

10. Light, R.A. and Gossard, D.C., "Modification of Geometric Models through Variational Geometry", Computer Aided Design, 1982, vol. 14, no. 4

11. Nielson, G.M., "Some piecewise polynomial alternatives to splines in tension", in Barnhill, RE and Riesenfeld, RF (eds) Computer Aided Geometric Design, Academic Press, 1974

12. Nowacki, H. and Reese, D., "Design and fairing of ship surfaces", in Barnhill R.E. and Boehm, W. (eds), Surfaces in CAGD, North-Holland, Amsterdam, pp 121-134, 1983

13. Piegl, Les, "On NURBS: A Survey", IEEE Computer Graphics and Applications, Jan 1991

14. Platt, John, "Constraint Methods for Neural Networks and Computer Graphics", PhD thesis, California Institute of Technology, 1989

15. Pramila, A., "Ship Hull Surface design using finite elements", Int. Shipbuild. Prog. Vol. 25 No. 284, pp. 97-107, 1978

16. Schweikert, D.G., "An interpolation curve using a spline in tension", Journal of Math and Phys. No 45, pp. 312-317, 1966

17. Serano, D. and Gossard, D.C., "Constraint Management: A prerequisite to Conceptual Design", in Knowledge Based Expert Systems in Engineering: Planning and Design, Sriram, D. and Adey, R.A., editors, Computational Mechanics Publications, UK, 1987

18. Strang, Gilbert, Introduction to Applied Mathematics, Wellesley-Cambridge Press, Massachusetts, 1986

19. Welch, W., and Gleicher, M. and Witkin, A., "Manipulating surfaces differentially", proceedings Compugraphics 91 (Springer Verlog) also Carnegie Mellon Technical report CMU-CS-91-75

20. Witkin, Andrew, and Fleischer, Kurt, and Barr, Alan, "Energy Constraints on Parameterized Models", Proceedings Siggraph '87, Anaheim, July 27-31 1987

21. Terzopoulos, Demetri and Platt, John and Barr, Alan and Fleischer, Kurt, "Elastic Deformable Models", ACM, Computer Graphics, vol. 21, no. 4, July, 1987

22. Zienkiewicz, The Finite Element Method, third edition, McGraw-Hill Book Co., U.K., 1967

Integrating Constraints and Direct Manipulation

Michael Gleicher*
School of Computer Science
Carnegie Mellon University

ABSTRACT

In this paper, we present techniques for integrating constraint and direct manipulation approaches to geometric modeling. Direct manipulation positioning techniques are augmented to provide the option of making the relationships they establish persistent. *Differential constraint* techniques are used to maintain these relationships during subsequent editing. Issues in displaying and editing constraints are also addressed. By integrating constraints with direct manipulation, it is possible to build systems that provide the power of explicit representation of geometric relationships and the properties which make direct manipulation so attractive.

INTRODUCTION

Geometric relationships between parts are an important element in geometric models. From the earliest days of interactive systems[13], the benefits of using constraints to explicitly represent these relationships have been known. Although many have discussed the value of constraints, constraint-based approaches have not been successful in practical systems. Their success has been hindered by a large number of difficult issues.

In contrast to the failure of constraints, direct manipulation systems have been successful for geometric modeling tasks. Users control the geometry of objects by interactively grabbing and pulling them, with continuous update providing feedback. Such systems employ snapping techniques, such as grids, to aid in establishing relationships, but these relationships are immediately forgotten. They are neither explicitly represented nor automatically preserved. It is the user's job to maintain them during subsequent editing.

In this paper we combine the two approaches: snapping techniques establish relationships and constraint techniques maintain them during subsequent dragging. Our integrated approach distinguishes the problem of establishing relationships from that of maintaining them during subsequent edit-

*School of Computer Science, Carnegie Mellon University, Pittsburgh, PA 15213-3890. gleicher@cs.cmu.edu

ing. This separation allows us to skirt several difficult issues in constraint-based systems. Integration with direct manipulation addresses issues in solving, specifying, debugging, displaying and editing constraints.

The *Briar* drawing program demonstrates our approach. When direct manipulation snapping establishes a new relationship, *augmented snapping* provides the user with the option of transforming it into a persistent constraint. *Differential constraint* techniques can maintain these during dragging. Direct manipulation techniques also address editing constraints.

ESTABLISHING RELATIONSHIPS IN DRAWINGS

Previous constraint-based systems have operated in what we call a "specify-then-solve" approach to constraint usage. In such systems, the user describes the model by declaring relationships which must hold true and the system configures the model to meet these requirements. This approach allows a user to specify the important aspects of a design and have the system resolve the details. Because the system explicitly represents the relationships, it can insure that these constraints continue to hold during subsequent editing.

There are problems in using the specify-then-solve approach. One is "solving" the constraints – finding a new configuration of the geometric model which meets the set of requirements. This is difficult because, in general, systems of non-linear algebraic equations must be solved from arbitrary starting points. While this problem is intractable[11], systems can usually operate by limiting the class of constraints which can be handled (as done by [6, 14]) or using temperamental numerical techniques (as done by [9, 12]). If no configuration is found that satisfies the constraints, it can be difficult to determine whether none exists or if the solver was just unable to find one. If no solution exists, the conflicts must be diagnosed and debugged. If the solver does find a new configuration, it must help the user understand how and why it jumped to the new state.

These three challenges, solving constraint-satisfaction problems from arbitrary starting points, presenting state jumps to users, and coping with conflicts, must be addressed to build a specify-then-solve system. However, these issues only arise when the constraint mechanism is used to reconfigure the model to establish new relationships. To skirt these difficult issues, we separate the task of maintaining existing relationships from that of initially satisfying them.

Our systems use direct manipulation to establish relation-

171

ships and use constraint techniques for maintaining them during subsequent editing. Constraints are only generated for relationships which exist in the drawing. They start out satisfied so there is never a need to jump from an arbitrary state to a consistent one. There are no constraint-satisfaction problems to solve or state jumps to explain. There is no concern about conflicting or unsatisfiable constraints, since there exists at least one configuration which meets the constraints.

MAINTAINING RELATIONSHIPS

When initial solutions are provided, the task of constraint techniques changes; instead of establishing the relationships, constraint-based techniques are used to maintain them. Rather than jumping from an inconsistent state to one where the constraints are met, constraint techniques permit users to drag models and have the constraints enforced as the drawing follows with continuous motion. We call this facility to drag constrained models *Differential Constraints*.

Unlike solving non-linear algebraic equations, good techniques exist for maintaining constraints during dragging. We use techniques which treat the motion of the model as a differential equation and provide methods for maintaining sets of non-linear constraints by solving systems of sparse linear equations[4]. Alternatively, solving can be accomplished using a standard constraint-solving approach: the model is repeatedly perturbed slightly, then re-solved.

Fast computers and good algorithms allow update rates which give the appearance of continuous motion. This rapid feedback is essential. Although the trajectory the model follows is not part of the resulting drawing, this animation makes it possible for users to employ their perceptual skills to connect states of the drawing with many things changing between them[2].

Differential constraints provide a natural way to incorporate constraints into a conventional drawing system. Objects are dragged the same way, except that relationships can be maintained among them. This allows the drawing process to be incremental: each new relationship added to a drawing does not disturb previously established ones.

The ability to directly manipulate constrained models helps address many of the issues in constraint-based systems. It provides an easy way for the user to explore underconstrained spaces, permitting them to experiment with models to understand how they work, or why they do not. The existence of a direct manipulation facility means that all parts of the model do not need to be specified by constraints. If it is difficult to devise a way to describe an aspect of a drawing with constraints, direct manipulation can be used instead.

Constraints can aid in the direct manipulation process by providing the user with "extra hands" to hold things in place. Providing the user with "lightweight constraints" which are easy to place temporarily to aid in manipulation is a useful feature in modeling systems.

SPECIFYING CONSTRAINED MODELS

Rather than using constraints, our approach, like most direct manipulation systems, uses *gravity* to help users establish relationships in models. The drawing cursor follows the motion of the pointing device, but snaps to locations which will establish relationships in the model when it is close to them. This idea of gravity has existed for a long time, having been demonstrated as early as Sketchpad[13]. The most common variant of gravity is the uniform grid. A more interesting technique is Snap-Dragging[1] which extends gravity by expanding the set of snapping targets to include intersections and construction lines.

Gravity is successful at helping a user establish relationships in models, but previous systems promptly forget these relationships once the positioning operation is complete. To employ constraint maintenance, these newly established relationships must be made into persistent constraints. The user could be required to explicitly identify the constraints, but this creates excess work: each relationship is specified twice, once to establish it and once to identify it as a constraint. Previous systems have attempted to infer constraints after drawing operations by looking at the resulting drawing[10], or at a trace of user actions[7]. Because this information typically does not specify the relationships unambiguously, these systems relied on heuristics or asked the user to resolve the ambiguity[8]. Our approach augments positioning methods so they, in addition to location, unambiguously specify the relationships which are being established.

Our *augmented snapping* technique lets direct manipulation positioning specify constraints as well as location. It enhances the snapping operation so that it generates constraints. The basic idea is that cursor placement operations contain information about why an object was positioned where it was, and can, therefore, also provide a constraint specification. Suppose the user, while dragging an object, moves the pointer near another object so that the cursor and the point being dragged snap to the second object. Snapping has helped the user establish a relationship between the dragged point and the target object. We provide the user with the option of making this relationship persistent so it can be preserved during subsequent editing.

When a snapping operation occurs, the system acknowledges it by showing the newly established relationship to the user. The user has the opportunity to accept the new relationship, transforming it into a persistent constraint. To make the constraint creation process more transparent, the default can be to accept new constraints. [1]

Augmented snapping permits direct manipulation techniques to be integrated with constraints. Since snapping is used for all drawing operations, such as creating and moving objects, all of these operations can specify constraints. Constraint generation is opportunistic, as the user draws, constraints are

---

[1] Although we provide an "accident-prone" mode where acceptance is not the default, we find that it is seldom used.

created when relationships are established. Aside from the occasional rejection (or acceptance, if that is not the default) of a constraint, the interface should not require any additional effort from the user. Such an interface feels just as fast and clean as the non-augmented version.

As a constraint specification technique, augmented snapping offers other advantages. It does not require the user to learn new commands for each type of constraint since a uniform interface creates all constraints. Because it provides both constraints and an initial configuration that satisfies them, augmented snapping cannot create conflicting constraints.

Careful attention to the user interface is crucial to making augmented snapping work. Feedback must show the snapping operations to the user so it is clear what relationship is being established. When a new relationship is established, it must be displayed prominently enough that it is clear what constraint will be created, but not be obtrusive to hinder the drawing process.

Augmented snapping only generates constraints for relationships which are unambiguously specified by the user's actions. A snapping operation unambiguously specifies a relationship, but if multiple objects coincide, it can be ambiguous which to snap to. Feedback, which clearly shows which object is snapped to, and a cycling mechanism to choose between potential snapping targets resolves this problem. Pruning the set of objects that are snapped to (for example, avoiding snaps which would create a redundant constraint) avoids excess cycling.

Augmented snapping does not guess about the user's intentions. It relies on the construction process to obtain constraints. The user may construct a model in a manner which does not convey the desired constraints. To curtail this, it is important to design modeling operations which make it easy to convey what is intended, rather than just what is convenient to express. For example, making two objects be the same size should be no more work than making them both be the same fixed size.

VISUAL REPRESENTATIONS FOR CONSTRAINTS

Constrained drawings have more state that must be displayed to the user than non-constrained ones do. A system must convey to the user not only the geometry of the model, but also the constraints. The user must be able to edit this structural information as well as the geometry. Although textual languages for describing constraints, such as in [9, 14] are easy to edit, they are distinct from the drawing and can be difficult to connect to their corresponding places in the model. Visual representations[5, 12] superimpose symbols for constraints directly on the model. Unfortunately, devising clear visual representations is challenging and editing such representations is often difficult.

When differential constraints are used, the continuous motion and ability for users to experiment with models can convey much of the information about the constraints. We also use a visual representation for constraints.

The problem of editing constraints transcends visual representations. Before being able to delete or modify a constraint, the user must figure out which constraints to alter. We have developed methods for editing constraints which avoid this problem by having the users edit constraints by referring to the desired effects, not to the constraints themselves. Instead of pointing at constraints, users directly manipulate objects to show how they are to move. For example, constraint maintenance can be disabled so objects move freely. Constraints which are broken are clearly noted to the user. When maintenance is restarted, violated constraints are removed. A variant is a "rip" command which allows the user to pull part of an object free from its constraints.

Designing the semantics of the constraints properly can also reduce problems in the visual language. For example, when a group of points is connected together, an equivalence class is used rather than a large number of binary connection relations. This is also significant since it removes the need to remember which point is connected to which other point if some are to be disconnected.

DRAWING WITH CONSTRAINTS

To explore the integration of constraints and direct manipulation, we have built a drawing program called *Briar*[2][3]. A direct manipulation drawing technique called Snap-Dragging[1] is augmented to specify constraints. Differential constraint techniques are used to maintain these relationships as the user modifies the drawing. Augmented Snap-Dragging also serves as the basis for a visual representation for the constraints.

Snap-Dragging enhances the usefulness of gravity. The cursor snaps not only to the edges of objects, but also to interesting points in the scene such as intersections and vertices of objects. Relations other than contact are created in Snap-Dragging through *alignment objects:* objects that are not part of the drawing *per se,* but exist only to be snapped to. The original Snap-Dragging work includes several types of alignment objects, each corresponding to types of relationships which are useful in drawings. The usefulness of alignment objects is further enhanced by making them easy to place.

Snap-Dragging provides two operations for positioning points in two dimensions: snapping the cursor to a point, such as a vertex, and snapping the cursor to an object's edge or curve. These operations correspond directly to *Briar's* two basic constraints, "points-coincident" and "point-on-object" respectively. The two snapping operations combined with alignment objects allow a user to establish a wide variety of relationships. Similarly, the two basic constraints are combined with alignment objects to enforce a similarly large set of relationships. For example, a distance constraint can be expressed using a fixed size circle.

---

[2]It is called Briar because, like the plant it is named for, things stick together inside it.

Augmented Snap-Dragging also provides the basis for *Briar's* visual representation of constraints. Constraints are displayed just as they are specified: using the two basic elements along with alignment objects. Although *Briar* can handle a wide variety of relationships, users need not learn a large number of constraint creation commands or display symbols. *Briar* provides several methods for altering constraints by direct manipulation of objects, including disabling constraint maintenance and commands to "rip" parts of objects free of their constraints.

Briar's display employs many mechanisms to convey its state to the user. Objects light up when snapped to and the cursor changes shape to indicate the type of snapping operation. Newly established relationships are shown in distinctive colors which signify whether or not they will become constraints.

THREE DIMENSIONAL SYSTEMS

Extending a system like *Briar* to three dimensional modeling poses a new set of challenges. For modeling tasks, the set of possible spatial relationships between objects is much richer, and more complex, than in 2D. However, this richness and complexity is also a strong motivation for the development of constrained interaction techniques for 3D. Direct manipulation techniques to establish spatial relationships are not as developed as their two dimensional counterparts. A more pragmatic concern is that our reliance on feedback already causes *Briar* to use almost all available perceptual cues, such as texture, hue, brightness, size, and motion, leaving little for the increased visual demands of 3D.

Techniques such as augmented Snap-Dragging, differential constraints, and visual alteration of constraints make it possible to build systems which integrate constraints and direct manipulation. Such systems can combine the power of representing geometric relationships with the fluency and intuitive interfaces which have made direct manipulation so successful.

Acknowledgments
This research was funded in part by Apple Computer, a fellowship from the Schlumberger Foundation, and an equipment grant from Silicon Graphics. I would like to thank Andy Witkin for his assistance with this work. I would also like to thank everyone who has commented on this paper, especially Will Welch, David Pugh, and Bruce Horn, for helping make it more readable.

REFERENCES

[1] Eric Bier and Maureen Stone. Snap-dragging. *Computer Graphics*, 20(4):233–240, 1986.

[2] Jock Machinlay George Robertson and Stuart Card. Cone trees: Animated 3d visualizations of hierarchical information. In *Proceedings CHI '91*, pages 189–194, May 1991.

[3] Michael Gleicher. Briar - a constraint-based drawing program. In *CHI '92 Formal Video Program*, 1992. SIGGRAPH video review, in press.

[4] Michael Gleicher and Andrew Witkin. Differential manipulation. *Graphics Interface*, pages 61–67, June 1991.

[5] Mark Gross. Relational modeling: A basis for computer-assisted design. In Maclcolm McCullough, Williadm J. Mitchell, and Patrick Purcell, editors, *The Electronic Design Studio (Proc. CAAD Futrues '89)*, pages 123–146. MIT Press, 1989.

[6] Jiarong Li. Using constraints in interactive text and graphics editing. In P. A. Duce and P. Jancene, editors, *Eurographics*, 1988.

[7] D. L. Maulsby, K. A. Kittlinz, and I. H. Witten. Metamouse: Specifying graphical procedures by example. *Computer Graphics*, 23(3):127–136, July 1989.

[8] Brad A. Myers and William Buxton. Creating highly-interactive and graphical user interfaces by demonstration. *Computer Graphics*, 20(4):249–258, 1986.

[9] Greg Nelson. Juno, a constraint based graphics system. *Computer Graphics*, 19(3):235–243, 1985.

[10] Theo Pavlidis and Christopher Van Wyk. An automatic beautifier for drawings and illustrations. *Computer Graphics*, 19(3):225–234, 1985.

[11] William Press, Brian Flannery, Saul Teukolsky, and William Vetterling. *Numerical Recipes in C*, chapter 9.6, page 286. Cambridge University Press, Cambridge, England, 1986.

[12] Steven Sistare. Interaction techniques in constraint-based geometric modeling. In *Proceedings Graphics Interface '91*, pages 85–92, June 1991.

[13] Ivan Sutherland. *Sketchpad: A Man Machine Graphical Communication System*. PhD thesis, Massachusetts Institute of Technology, January 1963.

[14] Christopher J. Van Wyk. A high level language for specifying pictures. *ACM Transactions on Graphics*, 1(2):163–182, April 1982.

Interactive Modeling Enhanced with Constraints and Physics— With Applications in Molecular Modeling

Mark C. Surles
Department of Computer Science
University of North Carolina at Chapel Hill
Chapel Hill, NC 27599-3175

Abstract

Interactive modeling systems that continually maintain a physically-realistic representation of an object combine advantages of interactive graphics and batch simulations. In this paper I address two advantages of incorporating physics into *Sculpt,* an interactive protein modeling system. First, time-consuming model correction is avoided by maintaining a physically-valid model throughout a modeling session. Second, additional cues about model properties can arise when a chemist interactively guides a simulation rather than views a cine loop from a pre-computed simulation. I argue these benefits with examples from sessions with *Sculpt.* A chemist can interactively move atoms while *Sculpt* automatically maintains proper bond topology and atom separations. *Sculpt* models bonded and non-bonded atom interactions for medium-size proteins (800 atoms) at 0.6 updates per second on a Silicon Graphics 240 using a constrained energy minimization method.

CR Categories and Subject Descriptors: I.3.5 [**Computer Graphics**]: Computational Geometry and Object Modeling; I.3.6 [**Computer Graphics**]: Methodology and Techniques; I.J.2 [**Computer Applications**]: Physical Sciences.

Additional Keywords and Phrases: Physically-based modeling, interactive modeling, constraint systems, scientific visualization.

1. Introduction

Within the last ten years a trend in computer graphics has been to increase scene realism by using physically-based models. Animators use physically-based modeling to create realistic detailed behavior. Most animations generated with physically-based modeling, to date, required minutes to hours of computation for each frame. This large computation time has kept physically-based modeling out of interactive graphics systems except with small, simple models. However, increased

computer speeds now permit adding physically-based models to interactive systems. I have picked a large modeling problem with simple properties to study issues that arise in modeling physical properties in an interactive graphics system.

Protein modeling systems represent molecules containing one hundred to several thousand atoms. The systems can be classified as interactive or batch (though some interactive systems have batch processing). Most interactive systems maintain bonded properties such as fixed bond lengths and angles by restricting operations to rotation of segments about particular bonds. The performance of interactive systems is only limited by the display capability of the graphics system since the modeling operations are only rotations. Batch simulations model variance in bond lengths and angles *and* interactions among non-bonded atoms over relatively near and far distances. Accurately modeling all these properties requires batch computation, even for small proteins.

Today an interactive, physically-based modeling system, called *Sculpt,* models non-bonded atom interactions for medium-size proteins (800 atoms) on a Silicon Graphics 240 at 0.6 updates per second. *Sculpt* lets a chemist interactively move atoms while automatically keeping correct bonded properties and non-bonded atom separations using a constrained energy minimizer. Compared to many other physically-based modeling systems in computer graphics, *Sculpt* models simpler properties (e.g. angles versus volumes) and minimizes static strain energies rather than functions of object dynamics. However, system performance now allows investigation into issues that arise when physically-based modeling is applied to complex real applications.

Chemists that collaborate on the project believe interactive, physically-based modeling will relieve many manual modeling tasks, allowing more work in less time, and provide additional cues about protein behavior. In this paper I present two improvements the system provides that result from modeling physical properties interactively. First, the system removes the often laborious task of fixing a physically-invalid model after a modeling session. Though interactive systems such as Sybyl [15] maintain fixed bond lengths and angles, they make the chemist keep non-bonded atoms at appropriate separations. Second, the system provides a new medium for exploring protein properties by allowing interactive, guided simulation. This should combine benefits of interactive graphics and batch simulations.

2. Related work

Physically-based modeling frequently aids computer animations by automating detailed motion planning and complex object interactions. Miller generates realistic snake motions by modeling muscle contractions with springs and friction against surfaces [9]. Witkin models the energy and momentum of a Luxo lamp jumping hurdles and ski jumps [18]. Terzopoulos models energy in elastically deformable objects such as cloth to create animations of flags [14]. These examples simulate the motion of objects by first stating application-specific conditions about the objects and scene and then solving Newton's equations of motion.

Similar applications use *constraints* to restrict the allowable states of objects and express dependencies among objects. Barzel uses constraints in animation to specify paths for objects [4]. Witkin uses geometric constraints to assemble models [16], and he describes a system that lets a user interactively connect and manipulate objects such as a mechanical assembly or tinker-toy [17]. Constraints maintain constant volume in incompressible solids [12] and restrict penetration when a ball strikes a trampoline [11].

3. Driving problem – protein modeling

A protein, to a first approximation, contains fixed bond lengths, fixed bond angles, and some planar segments. Figure 1-A shows three sequential segments in a protein with vectors representing bonds between atoms and gray areas denoting planar regions. The only degrees of freedom in the figure are rotations about the N-C and C-C bonds that enter and leave each planar segment. A linear sequence of the segments comprise the protein *backbone*. Attached to the atom between each segment (C) are *sidechains* (not shown) with additional fixed length and angle properties. Superimposed onto this geometric model are non-bonded attractions and repulsions. Attractions hold nearby atoms together, while repulsions maintain a minimal separation between all atom pairs.

Chemists often use brass models (Kendrew models) to study geometric properties and relationships in a protein. Brass models contain segments shown in Figure 1-A connected with rotational joints about the N-C and C-C bonds. Manipulating such a model with one's hands aids understanding of relationships. However, the models have two drawbacks. First, the model's size becomes difficult to hold and manipulate when dealing with large molecules (e.g. an 800-atom brass model of the protein in Color Plate 1 is 80 centimeters wide when 2 cm of brass represents 1 Ångstrom, a typical bond). Second, brass models do not represent attractive and repulsive interactions among non-bonded atoms.

Chemists use computers to model large proteins and non-bonded atom interactions. Interactive modeling systems resemble brass models by allowing only rotations about particular bonds. The limiting factor in interactive systems is display rate of the graphics machine. Batch simulations model non-bonded atom interactions and more accurately model bond lengths and angles (these do vary, though by only a few percent).

Protein modeling provides a good driving problem for research in interactive physically-based modeling. First, the benefits of interactive graphics and batch simulations are each well established. Second, real users want such a system and will provide valuable assistance in its development. Third, the size of useful models requires improved algorithms for interactive modeling on current machines. Fourth, many aspects of protein modeling are similar to other problems. For example, the inherent three-dimensional structure requires addressing mechanical modeling issues similar to those encountered in articulated-figure motion and computer-aided design. Fifth, understanding the interplay of properties in proteins during the modeling requires good visualization paradigms.

4. *Sculpt's* interface and performance

Sculpt continually maintains realistic protein properties as a chemist moves an atom. *Sculpt* lets a chemist move an atom by first attaching a spring between the atom and the cursor and then dragging the cursor in a desired direction. Throughout the dragging process, *Sculpt* polls the cursor position and adds the strain energy of that spring to the energy in the protein. *Sculpt* then finds a local minimum of the total energy that also maintains rigid bond lengths, angles, and planar segments. *Sculpt* also lets a chemist insert a spring that continually pulls an atom towards a given three-dimensional position.

The color plates show photographs of *Sculpt* sessions. Depth-cued vectors represent bonds between atoms; cyan denotes the central backbone, and tan denotes sidechains connected to the backbone. Gold coils show springs attached by a chemist to pull atoms toward positions denoted by the gold thumbtacks. Color Plate 1 shows a model containing 760 atoms of a medium-sized protein called Felix [8]. The model contains 2205 constraints (bond length, angle, and others) and approximately 8005 energy functions (attraction, repulsion, and others). The backbone in Color Plate 1 winds through four helices (purple cylinders highlight the two on the left). Color Plate 2 shows a model composed of the two helices highlighted in Color Plate 1. The model contains 355 atoms, 1027 constraints, and approximately 3450 energy functions. The text in Color Plate 2 names several of the sidechains.

Sculpt maintains approximately 0.7 updates per second with the model in Color Plate 1 and 1.5 updates per second with the model in Color Plate 2, on a Silicon Graphics 240-GTX [2]. An update includes the following steps: evaluate protein properties (bond lengths, angles, attractions, and repulsions) and their derivatives, minimize the energy and satisfy the constraints, update atom positions, and display the results. Though this performance is twenty times too slow for smooth interaction, our chemist collaborators believe the performance already provides enough interactivity on medium-size proteins that new, useful research can be accomplished that could not previously be undertaken. The system is described in greater detail in [13].

5. Maintaining a consistent model

Users of interactive modeling systems (not only molecular) often unintentionally move objects into a configuration that violates required properties of the application—producing an invalid model database. For example: moving an endpoint so that an originally constrained line is no longer horizontal; moving a wall without adjusting those adjoining it; leaving cables dangling in a car engine after moving the alternator; moving atoms closer than electron shells allow.

Changing a computer object so that it mimics the properties of its physical counterpart can be arbitrarily complex. Most modeling applications leave this task to the user. For example, moving a wall in an architectural model requires that a user rejoin all the adjacent walls and then ensure those changes did not invalidate the model. Some molecular modeling systems let a user invoke a batch energy minimizer to move atoms into a valid arrangement. However, such automated post-processing methods can change the model differently than the user intends.

An interactive modeling system that maintains a physically-valid model throughout user modifications eliminates the model re-idealization task. This section presents two protein-modeling examples to illustrate complexities that can arise in manual and automated methods for repairing the invalid models.

5.1. A simple edit requiring complex repairs

A common operation in molecular modeling requires flipping a planar segment (peptide) in the backbone, surrounded closely by neighboring atoms, by 180 degrees. Figure 1 shows two stages of the flip operation. Figure 1-A shows the center segment and its neighbors before a flip. Lines represent bonds between atoms and hashed areas represent rigid planar segments. Each atom contains an electron shell that (to a first approximation) cannot intersect other electron shells. Figure 1 represents the shells with circles (notice the circles do not intersect in Figure 1-A). Most systems only allow rotations about the C–C and C–N bonds so that bond lengths, angles and planar groups do not change. This makes the flip difficult by itself since one rotation affects all the atoms further along the chain. Figure 1-B shows the center segment flipped 180 degrees after an appropriate sequence of rotations. The model now requires repairs because the circles overlap.

Manual correction. A chemist can manually adjust the atom positions to remove the intersections in Figure 1-B. Moving an atom requires that a chemist choose appropriate combinations of rotations so that other segments do not move. Moving one atom usually causes interference with another, which then requires additional repairs. Correctly fitting the flipped segment often causes small changes that propagate through the entire protein. In practice this problem is much harder because a chemist fits spheres rather than circles and approximates non-bonded atom interactions by getting the spheres to touch. Professor Jane Richardson, a collaborator from Duke University's Biochemistry Department, usually adjusts models manually after operations such as this flip. This example takes on the order of fifteen minutes.

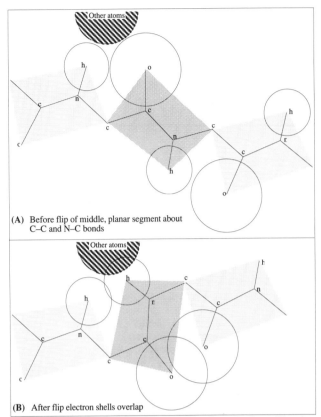

(A) Before flip of middle, planar segment about C–C and N–C bonds

(B) After flip electron shells overlap

Figure 1: Modeling errors introduced by flipping a rigid planar segment.

Batch minimization. A chemist can also use a batch minimization package to remove the intersections. Such packages find a local minimum of the ensemble energy associated with the overlapping shells. These work well if the atom shells only slightly overlap. Overlaps greater than, say, twenty percent contain very large strain energy that cause minimization packages to make large changes to the model. Batch routines often resolve such interactions by moving atoms the chemist did not intend to change. Professor Richardson interleaves some manual intervention with energy minimization to avoid these undesirable changes.

Interactive minimization. Performing this operation in *Sculpt* requires approximately thirty seconds (depending on the size of the protein). A chemist tugs the atoms from one orientation to another while *Sculpt* continuously adjusts segments along the chain to accommodate the change. Throughout the operation, *Sculpt* maintains a valid protein model. *Sculpt* does nothing here that batch minimization systems cannot perform. The difference is the small minimization time in *Sculpt* allows the system to continuously minimize the energy rather than do it once after the user interaction.

5.2. A complex task requiring exorbitant re-idealization

This example requires changing the orientation of two helices between Color Plate 2 and 3 by unwinding the lower helix, counter-clockwise by ninety degrees, and winding the upper helix, clockwise by ninety degrees, similar to unrolling a scroll. The helical structure must remain after the operation. The task first requires large structural changes to the model (to twist the helices) and then local adjustments to remove hundreds of contacts among the sidechains (tan vectors). Color Plates 2 and 3 show the model before and after the operation. Text is attached to nearby sidechains to emphasize the change between the pictures; yellow indicates nearby sidechains before, and white indicates nearby sidechains after the operation.

Interactive minimization. Professor Richardson performed this task with *Sculpt* in approximately thirty minutes. She spent most of the time turning the helices by applying radial tugs to the atoms to get a uniform twist. (A future version of the systems will include rigid segments to reduce the time for this operation.) The system maintained proper bond lengths and angles throughout the session. She used the final ten minutes of the session arranging sidechains to change the contacts among their atoms.

Manual solution. Solving this task manually, without energy minimization, is not feasible. One can turn the helices in two ways. The first way requires choosing the appropriate rotation angles between segments. This is an extremely complex, inverse-kinematics problem involving hundreds of joints. The second way involves breaking the connection (backbone) between the two helices, rotating each helix, and rejoining the connection. Rejoining the connection with proper geometry is very difficult, though easier than the inverse-kinematics problem. Once the two helices are turned, a chemist must resolve hundreds of contacts between sidechain atoms. Professor Richardson attempted to solve this task manually but quit after several frustrating days and was never fully satisfied with the results.

Batch minimization. A chemist could specify target positions for some atoms (if such end positions are known) and invoke an energy minimization package. The minimizer chooses a path to move the atoms along towards their targets. Certain paths can tear the model apart in order to reach the target (e.g. through the middle of a structure). Instead of solving the problem with one minimization, a chemist may choose subgoals along a path to the target and run minimizations for each subgoal. This approach works better than the manual solution, but the turnaround time between subgoal minimization limits the number of steps picked along the path. Continuously running a minimization as a chemist moves atoms to targets is the same as choosing an infinite sequence of subgoals and running batch minimizations on each.

6. Interactive, guided simulation

Interactive modeling of physical properties is essentially a form of interactive, guided simulation. Placing a user in the computation-loop of a simulation that once required hours or days we hope will provide greater insights to properties and relationships in a model. This section discusses benefits of interactive simulations compared to batch simulation and interactive graphics without simulations and discusses complications of scientific visualization in interactive simulations.

6.1. Simulation

Simulations can illustrate molecular properties not easily incorporated into brass models such as attractions and repulsions between non-bonded atoms. Though a chemist understands individual attractions and repulsions between two atoms, comprehension of hundreds of simultaneous interactions becomes very difficult. Simulations are typically used to examine specific atom interactions in a molecule. A simulation requires that a chemist choose model parameters, run the simulation, and view the results in a cine loop. If the results do not show the specific interaction, the steps are repeated with new parameters. Simulations have uncovered important molecular properties, but long turnaround times have kept this from being a common exploration tool for most researchers.

Sculpt lets a chemist explore non-bonded interaction while interactively moving atoms. Professor Richardson believes interactively exploring protein models with non-bonded interactions will improve perception of subtle relationships within proteins. In several sessions Professor Richardson has seen unexpected reactions that, upon closer examination, resulted from non-bonded interactions competing against other properties such as bond rotations.

Interactive modeling of physical properties augments benefits from batch simulations with features from interactive graphics. Today chemists use interactive graphics to study a static structure or series of structures from pre-computed simulations. Interactively controlling the view and display parameters provides more cues about a molecule's structure and nature than does viewing multiple, static images. Guiding an interactive simulation while immediately viewing the results lets the user remain continually engaged in the modeling process. I believe this provides greater situational awareness of complex relationships within a model than viewing cine loops of simulations. Guiding an interactive simulation lets a user stumble upon unexpected reactions in the model that may go unnoticed in batch simulations (the Ahah! phenomenon). Also more users will experiment with the models as turnaround time is shortened.

One advantage batch simulations, viewed with cine loops, have over interactive simulation is the ability to replay the simulation. Since a cine loop is a sequence of frames, a user can easily move backwards in the sequence to study a particular property. Unless a system saves all user actions during an interactive simulation, a user cannot readily return to a previous state. Like an on-going laboratory experiment, an event cannot be repeated without re-running the experiment from the beginning with the same steps.

6.2. Visualization of non-bonded forces

Near-neighbor interactions among non-bonded atoms play an important role in protein conformations by holding those atoms together at fixed distances. A protein modeling system should convey these interactions to help a chemist tightly pack the protein's interior. These interactions, unfortunately, are not as simple to display as a bond (vector connecting atoms). Figure 2 plots the potential energy of the van der Waal interaction between two atoms as a function of their separation (1 Ångstrom = 10^{-10} meters). The plot shows a maximum attractive (negative) energy, E_m, at a separation of R_m. The energy decreases nonlinearly as the separation increases from E_m. The energy becomes repulsive, increasing at a different nonlinear rate, as the separation decreases from E_m. Each atom in a protein, on average, interacts with ten atoms within a six-Ångstrom radius (the model in Color Plate 1 contains 7,577 van der Waal interactions). A useful visualization of a non-bonded interaction should convey the type (attractive or repulsive), magnitude, and ideal separation, R_m.

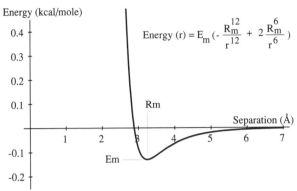

Energy (r) = $E_m (- \dfrac{R_m^{12}}{r^{12}} + 2 \dfrac{R_m^{6}}{r^{6}})$

Figure 2: Van der Waal potential energy between two atoms.

Sculpt displays van der Waal interactions that have an energy magnitude greater than a user-defined threshold. A partial spherical shell is placed around both of the interacting atoms and aligned along a vector between them (see Color Plate 4). Currently a shell with a solid angle of 0.4π steradians (ten percent coverage) represents the weakest interaction. Solid angle increases with the magnitude of the interaction. Weak interactions are represented by dot spheres, and strong interactions are represented by wireframe spheres. A dot-sphere indicates that an interaction exists without distracting the user and consuming as much screen space as the wireframe sphere. Blue denotes attraction, and red denotes repulsion.

Color Plate 4 illustrates this visualization on a small model. The photograph shows a spring attached to a planar ring (highlighted with a purple tube) that pulls one atom into another. Notice the wireframe shells around the two atoms labeled with text. The shells bend rather than intersect so that the vector in the two shells do not interfere visually. Intersecting wireframe shells are difficult to associate with their respective atoms.

7. Adding physical modeling to interactive graphics systems

The physically-based modeling module in *Sculpt* is inserted into the control flow of an interactive graphics systems with minor modifications. The white boxes in Figure 3 list the sequence of actions in the interactive graphics system: the system receives a user action (e.g. mouse movement), interprets it (move an atom by one Ångstrom in a given direction), applies the change to the model database (change the coordinates of atom), and displays the next frame. The shaded box shows the additional step that modifies the user action according to properties of the application (e.g. also adjust distances to neighboring atoms).

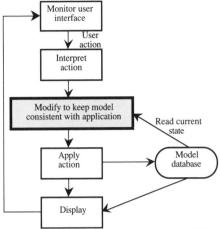

Figure 3: Steps in an interactive modeling system for processing a user action.

The control-flow presented in the white boxes is similar to the event loop of many graphics systems [7]. The remainder of this section discusses some implementation issues addressed in *Sculpt* that may be useful to others wishing to incorporate physically-based modeling into interactive graphics systems.

7.1. Constrained minimization

Sculpt implements the shaded box in Figure 3 with a constrained minimizer in the following manner. *Sculpt* converts a user action into a potential energy function (e.g. a spring to pull atoms). *Sculpt* then finds a local minimum of the total system energy (from protein and user) that also satisfies the set of bond length and angle constraints. Mathematically, the minimizer solves the following problem:

Given:
$\mathbf{x}$	model state (e.g. vector of atom positions)
Energy($\mathbf{x}$)	sum of potential energies in model
Constraint($\mathbf{x}$)	vector of constraint functions

Solve:
minimize	Energy($\mathbf{x}$)
such that	**Constraint**($\mathbf{x}$) = **0**.

The minimizer finds the solution using a method of Lagrange multipliers as discussed in [6], [17] and [13]. The minimizer determines changes in atom positions. The changes are sent to the next module in Figure 3 (Apply action) which then updates the model database.

Other constrained-minimization approaches fit within the framework of Figure 3. Witkin minimizes a potential energy function [16] associated with the physical state of elastic models. Amburn minimizes costs associated with design goals [3]. Phillips uses kinematic constraints to reduce allowable joint movements in an articulated figure while minimizing costs associated the positioning goals [10].

179

7.2. Positioning

Direct versus indirect positioning. Directly moving an object to a new location can violate constraints. For example, moving one end of a fixed-length line segment extends its length if the other end cannot move. Indirect positioning by attaching a spring to an object and tugging the other end avoids this problem. If no opposing force prevents movement in the direction of the tug, the result is the same as direct manipulation. However, if the object cannot move in the direction of the tug, the indirection increases the potential energy in the system (because the spring stretches) but does not invalidate the model.

Tugging objects also lets a user move atoms from one local minimum to another. Figure 4 shows an example where user intervention overcomes a local energy minimum. Arrows show the direction and strength of the attractions among atom T and the fixed-position atoms F_1 and F_2. Figure 4-A shows the initial state with atom T attracked more by F_1 than F_2. The tug in Figure 4-B (indicated with the dashed arrow) pulls the atom towards F_2. Figure 4-C shows the final result.

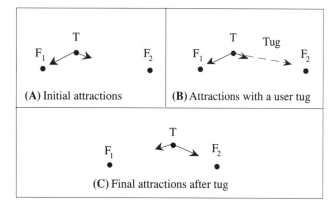

(A) Initial attractions   **(B)** Attractions with a user tug

(C) Final attractions after tug

Figure 4: A user spring pulls atom T between energy minima.

Which physics? Dynamics or statics. Physically-based modeling, as it has most often been used in computer graphics, aims to determine physically-realistic motions and trajectories of objects with specific physical properties (e.g. blowing flags [14] and jumping Luxo [18]). The approach solves Newton's second law, $\mathbf{F} = m\mathbf{a}$, which gives the *acceleration* of objects, and combines this with an initial position and velocity to determine motions.

In this work, stable conformations, not the trajectories of reaching them, are the concern. *Sculpt* achieves this by modeling potential energy rather than forces in a model. This gives *strains* between objects that the system minimizes. The objects never contain velocity information. Minimizing the potential energy (strain) moves the objects but does not induce momentum. This technique provides greater control over object positions and takes less computation.

7.3. Approximating stiff model components with constraints

Sculpt makes an approximation that dramatically improves performance without appreciably decreasing accuracy. Properties whose deformation requires very large strain energies relative to others in a model are replaced by rigid constraints. For example, a bond length is constrained to its ideal value since the potential energy increase for extending a bond is *five* orders-of-magnitude larger than that associated with a comparable increase in distance between two non-bonded atoms.

Minimizing functions with similar potential energies, subject to constraints, requires significantly less computation, in this application, than minimizing all the energies without constraints. Minimizing potential energy functions requires time-steps small enough to model the stiffest properties accurately. The time-step must decrease as the potential energy separation among the functions increases. Minimizing all the potential energy functions requires time-steps orders-of-magnitude smaller and, therefore, requires orders-of-magnitude more steps per screen update!

Is this approximation valid? Approximating bond-length, potential energy functions with rigid constraints reduces the accuracy of the physical model. However, the large potential energy signifies that bond-length variability is orders-of-magnitude smaller than the variability of other properties. Since the bond lengths hardly change, constraining them for increased performance is justified. *Sculpt* lets a chemist trade performance for accuracy when desired, by modeling lengths with potential energy functions.

An important principle influences this approximation—only compute what is significant. *Sculpt* follows this by only accurately modeling properties that can vary significantly and constraining the others. This approach can prove useful in other applications with wide variability in energy magnitudes.

8. Other applications

Removing model re-idealization and enhancing understanding of model properties will most likely arise in other interactive applications that incorporate physically-based modeling. The particular benefits and implementations are specific to the applications. However, similarity between the control-flow in *Sculpt* and other applications suggests that a generic, physically-based modeling module may eventually be developed. For now, the system development effort may be overkill for simple modeling applications and only justified for complex modeling applications. I conclude with two example applications that can benefit from adding physically-based modeling.

8.1. Architectural layout

Simple changes in a modeling system for architectural models (e.g. blueprints) often require numerous operations. For example, narrowing a corridor requires moving the corridor walls *and* lengthening the walls that connect to it. A large portion of the effort in the Building Walkthrough project [1] at the University of North Carolina at Chapel Hill is spent fixing and maintaining databases of models (these databases contain approximately 4,000 to 30,000 polygons). An automated radiosity calculation followed by viewing uncovers modeling errors, including walls not connected to ceilings and doors outside the plane of their walls. Most of the errors arise from previous database edits that left parts of the model inconsistent.

Applying constrained minimization to this application reduces these burdens. In the corridor example, constraints can require that moving the corridor wall also moves the connecting walls. Additional cost functions can increase as certain goals are not met such as rooms containing a certain area or being a given distance from an exit.

8.2. Drafting

Most interactive drafting and drawing systems ignore application-specific properties to reduce computation and broaden product applicability. They base operations (e.g. move, stretch) on individual, geometric primitives (polygons, lines, control points, etc.). Information regarding an object's construction is usually discarded. For example, MacDraw II lets a user construct a line constrained to the horizontal, but discards the horizontal requirement after construction [5]. The package does not restrict the line to the horizontal if a user later moves one of its endpoints. Keeping information about an object's structure and properties allows a system to maintain a consistent model throughout model editing.

9. Future work

The immediate goal for future work is to place *Sculpt* in a chemistry lab and gather results about its usefulness for solving daily protein-modeling problems. This should offer direction for future enhancements to the modeling and visualization components of the system.

The visualization issues offer large scope for future research. The near-neighbor visualization discussed in this paper is adequate, though not great. I will continue to examine the near-neighbor interactions. A much harder property to visualize is long-distance, electrostatic interaction. These interactions can extend between atoms on opposite sides of a molecule. Visualizing these interactions will be hard.

Finally, I plan to apply the techniques described in this paper to other applications. The input to the *Sculpt* system is a list of points with a set of length and angle functions defined on the points. Under one thousand lines of modeling code (out of ten thousand) is specific to molecules. With this framework I hope to examine interactive manipulation of skeletal figures without significant system development.

Acknowledgements

I thank Professors David and Jane Richardson of Duke University for continued guidance and encouragement. Professor Frederick Brooks provided many useful critiques about the research and the manuscript. Jane Richardson conceived and Jim Begley implemented the shells used in the visualization of non-bonded interactions. This work is supported by NIH National Center for Research Resources grant RR-02170.

References

1. Airey, J. M., Rohlf, J. H. and Brooks, F. P., Jr. Towards Image Realism with Interactive Update Rates in Complex Virtual Building Environments. *Symposium on Interactive 3D Graphics. 24*, 2 (1990), 41-50.

2. Akeley, K. and Jermoluk, T. High-Performance Polygon Rendering. *Computer Graphics. 22*, 4 (1988), 239-246.

3. Amburn, P., Grant, E. and Whitted, T. Managing Geometric Complexity with Enhanced Procedural Models. *Computer Graphics. 20*, 4 (1986), 189-195.

4. Barzel, R. and Barr, A. A Modeling System Based On Dynamic Constraints. *Computer Graphics. 22*, 4 (1988), 179-188.

5. *MacDraw II.* Claris Corporation, 1988.

6. Fletcher, R. *Practical Methods of Optimization.* John Wiley and Sons, 1987.

7. Foley, J. D., van Dam, A., Feiner, S. K. and Hughes, J. F. *Computer Graphics—Principles and Practice.* Addison-Wesley, New York, 1990.

8. Hecht, M. H., Richardson, J. S., Richardson, D. C. and Ogden, R. C. De Novo Design, Expression, and Characterization of Felix: A Four-Helix Bundle Protein of Native-Like Sequence. *Science. 249*, 4964 (1990), 884-891.

9. Miller, G. The Motion Dynamics of Snakes and Worms. *Computer Graphics. 22*, 4 (1988), 169-178.

10. Phillips, C., Zhao, J. and Badler, N. Interactive Real-time Articulated Figure Manipulation Using Multiple Kinematic Constraints. *Symposium on Interactive 3D Graphics. 24*, 2 (1990), 245-250.

11. Platt, J. *Constraint Methods for Neural Networks and Computer Graphics.* Ph.D. Dissertation, California Institute of Technology, 1989.

12. Platt, J. and Barr, A. Constraint Methods for Flexible Models. *Computer Graphics. 22*, 4 (1988), 279-288.

13. Surles, M. *Techniques For Interactive Protein Manipulation.* Ph. D. Dissertation Manuscript, University of North Carolina at Chapel Hill, 1992.

14. Terzopoulos, D., Platt, J., Barr, A. and Fleisher, K. Elastically Deformable Models. *Computer Graphics. 21*, 4 (1987), 205-214.

15. *Sybyl.* Tripos Associates, 1988.

16. Witkin, A., Fleischer, K. and Barr, A. Energy constraints on parameterized models. *Computer Graphics. 21*, 4 (1987), 225-232.

17. Witkin, A., Gleicher, M. and Welch, W. Interactive Dynamics. *Symposium on Interactive 3D Graphics. 24*, 2 (1990), 11-21.

18. Witkin, A. and Kass, M. Spacetime Constraints. *Computer Graphics. 22*, 4 (1988), 159-168.

Three-Dimensional Widgets

D. Brookshire Conner, Scott S. Snibbe, Kenneth P. Herndon,
Daniel C. Robbins, Robert C. Zeleznik,
Andries van Dam

Computer Science Department
Brown University
Providence, RI

ABSTRACT

The 3D components of today's user interfaces are still underdeveloped. Direct interaction with 3D objects has been limited thus far to gestural picking, manipulation with linear transformations, and simple camera motion. Further, there are no toolkits for building 3D user interfaces. We present a system which allows experimentation with 3D *widgets*, encapsulated 3D geometry and behavior. Our widgets are first-class objects in the same 3D environment used to develop the application. This integration of widgets and application objects provides a higher bandwidth between interface and application than exists in more traditional UI toolkit-based interfaces. We hope to allow user-interface designers to build highly interactive 3D environments more easily than is possible with today's tools.

Keywords

User Interface Design, Widgets, 3D Interaction, Virtual Reality

1 Introduction

Modern user-interface software is built using *widgets*, objects with geometry and behavior used to control the application and its objects. However, most of today's user interfaces for 3D applications take little advantage of the third dimension's added power, predominantly using 2D widgets. Commercial modeling and visualization systems typically present one or more 3D views surrounded by a large, hierarchical menu system, often with supporting dialog boxes and sliders. The menu system is sometimes replaced or augmented by another 2D interface widget such as a network or hierarchy editor. Direct interaction with the 3D world is limited primarily to interactive viewing, selection, translation, and rotation. 3D widgets used in these interactions include a 3D cursor, gestural translation, a virtual sphere, and direct manipulation of 3D spline points on paths or patches. While today's 3D applications clearly allow users to be productive with the current interface technology, we believe that they could be improved significantly by making greater use of 3D in the interface itself.

In virtual-reality systems, 3D interaction is especially crucial. However, the significant difficulties of 3D input and display have led research in virtual worlds to concentrate far more on the development of new devices and device-handling techniques than on higher-level techniques for 3D interaction [19]. Such interaction

goes no further than a straightforward interpretation of device data, such as using a Polhemus for a head tracker or a DataGlove for simple gestural recognition of commands such as select, translate and rotate. Some virtual-reality systems make use of menus floating in 3-space with 3D icons instead of 2D pixmap icons [3]. Besides the additional options for its position, however, such a menu provides no more expressive power than its 2D equivalent.

There are many reasons for the underutilization of 3D. First, almost all interaction techniques must be created from scratch, since essentially no toolkits of 3D interaction techniques exist. Second, such toolkits are difficult to develop until metaphors for 3D interfaces grow beyond their current infancy. Finally, we believe such a toolkit is intrinsically more difficult to create than its 2D counterpart because of the inherent complexity of 3D interaction.

Widget toolkits are well known for 2D applications (e.g., the Macintosh Programmer's Toolbox, OSF/Motif, XView) [17]. However, 3D graphics libraries such as PHIGS+ and SGI's GL provide very little support for interaction beyond simple device handling. The industry standard PHIGS+ provides only six widgets (pick, locator, stroke, choice, valuator, and string). Further, the application programmer cannot change their look or feel, and all except 3D pick correlation are low-level, providing little functionality beyond that provided by a physical device. Thus, application developers are left to implement basic interactive techniques such as virtual sphere rotation themselves.

Most paradigms and metaphors for 3D interfaces are less developed than those for 2D interfaces. Some 3D metaphors are the natural analogs of those familiar in 2D, such as 3D menus and rooms [14] [4]. However, research in 3D interfaces must develop new metaphors and interaction techniques to take advantage of the greater possibilities of 3D. The cone tree and perspective wall, designed at Xerox PARC [22] [13], demonstrate the potential of 3D representation and interactive animation.

User interfaces are inherently difficult to program [17]. 3D interfaces complicate interface design and implementation, since the interface must take into account such issues as a richer collection of primitives, attributes, and rendering styles, multiple coordinate systems, viewing projections, visibility determination, and lighting and shading. Further, 3D environments allow many more degrees of freedom than those easily specified with common interface hardware like mice. The interface can easily obscure itself, and 3D interaction tasks can require great agility and manual dexterity. Indeed, physical human factors are a central part of 3D interface design, whereas 2D interface designers can assume that hardware designers have handled the ergonomics of device interaction.

This paper reports some first steps towards the goal of creating a richly interactive 3D application development environment. After a more detailed discussion of the problems inherent in designing and implementing 3D widgets, we present a framework under development for their implementation, design, and use. By working with an object-oriented notion of a widget, we hope to provide a toolkit of modifiable and reusable 3D interaction techniques.

2   Extending Widgets

There are several points to consider when designing an environment for developing 3D widgets. Most fundamentally, what *is* a widget? How do existing notions of widgets derived from 2D environments extend to 3D environments? Secondly, how should a 3D application communicate with its 3D interface? Finally, what kinds of primitives are needed to build 3D widgets? 2D environments, like the X Window System, provide raster drawing primitives and event-based callback mechanisms. What sorts of primitives should a corresponding 3D environment provide?

2.1   Defining "widget"

We define a widget as an encapsulation of geometry and behavior used to control or display information about application objects. Although this definition is somewhat vague and general, it has the advantage of covering all the areas of the interface literature we have explored, from general constructs such as Garnet's Interaction Objects [16] and the Interactive Objects of Xerox's 3D Rooms [21] to very specific kinds of widgets such as those found in the X Toolkit or the Macintosh Toolkit.

The extent to which a 2D widget should be classified as consisting of behavior or of geometry varies widely. Some useful widgets are primarily geometric, such as the dividing lines and frames that serve to organize and partition an interface. Others, such as a gestural rotation widget in an object-oriented drawing program, have no inherent geometry. 3D widgets encompass a similar range of geometry and behavior. This makes our definition of the term "widget" useful for understanding interface problems that are not dimension-specific.

2.2   Comparing common 2D widgets and 3D widgets

Despite their often complex appearance, most 2D widgets have very simple behavior. They commonly have few degrees of freedom (usually only one) and support only a small range of values within a degree of freedom. Thus, while toggle buttons have bitmap icons to represent different states, they represent only a single bit of information, and similarly, sliders represent a single number within a range, usually only a small integer range.

3D space inherently has more degrees of freedom than 2D space: a rigid flying body has six degrees of freedom in 3D versus three in 2D. 3D graphics libraries are, in general, more capable of handling general transformations than their 2D counterparts. As noted, common 2D widgets rarely take advantage of all the degrees of freedom available to them. The use of multiple degrees of freedom to enhance interaction is thus largely unexplored potential, even in 2D [23], and 3D, with its greater degrees of freedom, has correspondingly greater potential. This potential must of course be handled with restraint: while we would like to be able to use several degrees of freedom simultaneously, using too many may make the widget too difficult to use. Rather, interface designers should be able to specify any subset.

The user interacts with most widgets, whether 2D or 3D, through manipulation involving motion and simple gestures that are interpreted directly, to produce, for example, a sliding button or a popup window. However, the user can gain more expressive power through interaction techniques that interpret and process movements and make possible more sophisticated interaction. For example, a calligraphic drawing program can attach a pen to a cursor by means of a simulated spring [9], a simple motion-control technique that makes possible a whole new range of drawings not easily created with a rigid pen-cursor linkage.

Both 2D and 3D widgets can benefit from more sophisticated reaction to user input. Interaction can potentially achieve substantial gains by using such techniques as dynamic constraints, inverse kinematics, and physical simulation as components of direct manipulation interfaces. These techniques currently appear only in systems designed explicitly to present or use them, such as demos or prototypes, but in the future, these techniques should be as accessible as any other component in the widget designer's repertoire [8].

2.3   Integrating the application and the user interface

User interfaces were originally designed by application programmers using the same tools they used to build applications. This produced interfaces that were tightly integrated with the application. Recently, however, interface design is more often done by specialists using UI development tools [17]. While this separation produces more consistent interfaces and more modular programs, it can also produce interfaces that are not as helpful as they could be if they were more specialized to the application — the interface designer is not only aided but also limited by the toolkit and its metaphors. In particular, as has been noted by those critiquing WIMP interfaces [8], today's toolkits are not oriented towards highly interactive applications.

Such highly interactive applications require a high bandwidth between the application and the user interface, particularly for semantic feedback [8]. Prior UI research indicates that this may be best accomplished if the application and the interface are part of the same development environment, with the same tools being used to build both [18]. An integrated environment has additional software engineering benefits. First, only a single paradigm must be learned, rather than one for the interface and another for the application. Also, separate paradigms can be hard to integrate at several levels: the conceptual level, the code implementation level, and the compile-debug level. Advocating integration is *not* a call to abolish modularity in application and interface design. Rather, it is a suggestion that the principles of modularity can be pushed too far. The reasons for separating the application from the user interface are valid, but the benefits of a single development environment may outweigh the benefits of using two, especially for 3D applications.

Consider the benefits of higher bandwidth between the application and the interface. A menu selection is a relatively small amount of input that specifies only an operation, operand, or attribute, leaving other parameters to be specified elsewhere (perhaps in another menu or a dialog box). Gestural interfaces, on the other hand, allow the user to specify operation, operand, and parameters in a single action [23], providing a faster interface and commands that do not depend on previous or further actions.

In addition to providing better input, a tighter integration between application and interface lets the application provide semantic feedback *while* the user is interacting. Structured program editors have provided this kind of functionality for many years through syntax checkers that check for or prevent syntactic errors as the user types. Similarly, some 2D graphical circuit design tools prevent the user from making physically impossible or illogical connections.

Existing UI toolkits do allow callbacks to alter a widget based on application feedback, but the mechanisms to do so are often clumsy and hard to use. Our interfaces are constructed in an environment called UGA [25] in which widgets can actively depend on the state of other widgets, in the same way that any other objects (e.g., the application's objects) in our system can depend on each other. Our widgets are not external to the application model. They are first class objects, indistinguishable from application objects. This provides the UI designer with all of our system's power for specifying behavior and geometry, and gives as high a bandwidth between application and interface as between application objects themselves, creating the possibility of interfaces that are tightly coupled with the application, both for input and for output.

We have advocated both 3D widgets and widgets that are tightly integrated with an application. The latter idea is the more powerful of the two, since it can apply to all areas of interface design. In the remainder of the paper, we consider tools applicable to integrated widgets and then examine some case studies of integrated 3D widgets.

3 Tools for Designing and Implementing Integrated Widgets

3D interfaces are presently too underdeveloped for us to specify a comprehensive library of tools for building useful interfaces. We have therefore devised an environment that provides a great degree of flexibility to design new 3D widgets. It is often pointed out that flexibility in a user-interface design environment is a double-edged sword, allowing novel and useful interfaces as well as novel and useless interfaces. Because of the undeveloped state of current 3D interfaces, however, we prefer to allow the possibility of some poorly conceived designs rather than rule out unexplored possibilities.

3.1 Dependencies and controllers

UGA supports the geometric components of widgets through its rich modeling environment. The system supports the behavioral aspects of widgets through one-way constraints called *dependencies* [25]. An object can be explicitly related to another object by using a dependency. Since widgets are first-class objects in UGA, they can use this dependency mechanism as easily as application objects can. For example, a cube can become a simple slider by constraining it to move only along its x axis, and a torus's inner radius can then depend on the x position of the cube.

To provide multi-way constraints and cyclical constraint networks [18], we use *controllers* [25], objects whose primary purpose is to control other objects. Thus, our dynamic constraint solver is encapsulated as a controller. Additionally, we encapsulate physical devices as controllers that filter and pass values to objects. Finally, we can use controllers to encapsulate simulation methods, such as inverse kinematics or collision detection. By employing controllers, widgets can make use of general constraints, hardware devices, and simulation techniques.

3.2 A dialog model for sequencing

Some researchers choose to separate UI design into two broad categories: data-oriented UI design, usually supported through constraints, and dialog-oriented UI design [11]. We find both models useful. In addition to the data-oriented mechanisms of dependencies and controllers, we provide a dialog model that uses augmented transition networks (ATNs). We use ATNs because the sequencing of an interface is explicitly declared and is more easily visualized in a hierarchical ATN than in context-free grammars or event systems [7].

A simple transition network is a finite-state automaton (FSA). A complex interface can be described as an FSA but the complexity produces a combinatorial explosion of FSA states. Augmented transition networks handle some of the limitations of simple FSAs (allowing such behaviors as definite loops without specifying intermediate states) by adding variables and conditional transition along arcs based on the values in the variables. Recursive transition networks are used to provide hierarchy for ATNs, by allowing control in one ATN be suspended until a recursively invoked ATN reaches its final state.

Normally, an ATN, even a recursive one, has only one current state. Therefore, some events that can happen at any time, such as an "abort" or "help" request, are especially cumbersome to specify, requiring an additional arc from every state in the ATN. By contrast, event systems have greater expressiveness than ATNs [7], since they can easily handle an "abort" or "help" event by simply adding a new event handler to process this event. This would seem to make event systems a better choice. However, notions of current state, history,

or context are more difficult to express in event systems. Consider a "help" event that should provide context-sensitive information. An event model must provide a different event for each context. On the other hand, an ATN can handle a uniform "help" event, with arcs corresponding to context-dependent actions looping back to each state or leading to one or more help states. We would like a dialog model that combines the best features of both ATNs and event handlers.

Thus, we modify the ATN model to allow possibly disconnected components of the state graph and more than one active state [12]. We can now represent a set of event handlers as a group of disconnected states in an ATN, one state per event handler, each with a single arc back to itself. The arc's input tokens represent the corresponding event handler's events, and the arc's action represents the handler routine. However, we can add explicit sequencing to this ATN. For example, in our model, it is easy to specify the sequence of events found in snap-dragging, described in Section 4.3, but relatively cumbersome to specify in an event model, because of the need to represent history.

Our dialog model also allows a clean separation of subparts of the interface (i.e., individual widgets or groups of widgets). The dialog specification of each subpart can be represented as a subgraph of the ATN that describes the specification of the entire interface. These subparts can run in parallel, corresponding to a situation in which several widgets are logically operating at the same time. This parallelism is very useful: we can, for example, use the mouse to control both a 3D cursor and a higher-level widget, such as the rack described in Section 4.5.

The components of this dialog model, such as the individual states in the ATN, are first-class objects in our system. Since the dialog model is embedded in the same environment as the application itself, dependencies can be used to establish the connections between the ATN and the application that allow each to modify the other.

3.3 Applying object construction techniques

The UGA system supports a rich set of modeling primitives and operations, including constructive solid geometry (CSG), volumetric sculpting, spline patch objects and deformations. Both geometric and non-geometric modeling techniques, such as hierarchical grouping, can be applied to widget creation. Geometric techniques are used to specify a widget's geometry. Correspondingly, since ATN states are first-class objects, they can be organized using non-geometric object grouping techniques. Thus, both a widget's geometry and behavior are specified in the same unified framework, the framework of the application objects it controls.

The underlying construction technique we use is *delegation*, where one object (the child) is created from a pre-existing object (the parent) [24] [10]. If the parent object is changed, the child changes as well. Since both the parent and its children are objects in the system, and any object can be a controller modifying other objects, one of the children can modify the parent object, and therefore modify itself and all of its siblings. Delegation provides the ability to change large portions of the interface at once. Furthermore, since delegation relationships are maintained at run time, we can modify the interface without recompiling. This allows rapid prototyping of interface designs.

4 Examples of 3D Widgets in Our System

Our user interface group has developed several simple 3D widgets in our framework. Some of these, such as the virtual sphere and the cone tree, duplicate other researchers' widgets; others are experiments with new paradigms for a 3D user interface. We present these widgets below, explaining the design process we used in creating them, and stress the progress made possible by rapid prototyping.

4.1 A virtual sphere

A virtual sphere rotation widget can be handled by a simple two-state ATN (Figure 1). The ATN processes mouse motion, passing the mouse positions to a function that maps the 2D mouse coordinates into another object's space, in this case producing a point on the surface of a sphere. The deltas between a series of these projections produce rotations. We can easily change the kind of object that mouse coordinates are mapped to, so as to produce a "virtual cube" or "virtual donut." This sort of modification of the interface can be done at run time.

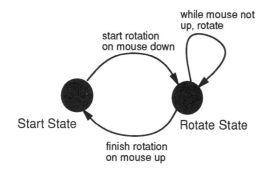

Figure 1: A two-state ATN for virtual sphere rotation

4.2 Handles

Object handles [6] are a 3D widget that contains more visual geometry than the virtual sphere widget. We can build handles with an arbitrarily complex appearance. Once they are built, we are free to establish dependencies on them or use them as a controller. Color Plate I shows various handles being used to translate, rotate and scale an object.

The same kind of constrained motion can be produced by holding down various modifier keys or different combinations of buttons [20]. However, a user presented with such an interface has no easy way to determine what the possible actions are. Handles allow constrained motion through intuitive direct manipulation: when a particular handle is selected, motion is constrained along or around the axis it describes. For example, clicking on an object-space translation handle located along an object's x axis limits translation to the x axis.

The visual feedback of a widget can range from the direct movement of the selected object to more complex widgets, such as handles that include numerical output and other quantitative indicators. Because our system provides rich support for geometry, the same set of primitives used for the application can be used to assemble widgets and their visual feedback. The behavior of handles can be produced without the corresponding geometry. An example is the creation of "hot spots" on an object that may or may not have a visual indication. The behavior of a virtual sphere can in turn be augmented with geometry — for instance, a semi-transparent sphere can be placed around the object during rotation to convey the behavior of the widget to the user more effectively. The flexibility of the system allows the widget designer and user to explore a wide range of options.

4.3 Snapping

With a more intricate ATN (Figure 2) we can perform simple snap-dragging [2]. A mouse's coordinates are used to generate a ray from the camera through the projection of the mouse's position onto the viewplane. If this ray intersects an object, the ATN lets the user choose a point on an object to snap to a point on another object. Since this is done with ray intersection, the point to snap

includes a complete Frenet frame [15] defined by the surface normal and tangents. When the user releases the mouse button and clicks again, the ATN begins checking to see if the ray specified by the mouse intersects another object. If so, this new object becomes the object to snap to. Again, the user can choose exactly which point to use, including the entire Frenet frame. When the user has chosen both points, the widget produces a transformation to align the two frames, and applies it to the first object.

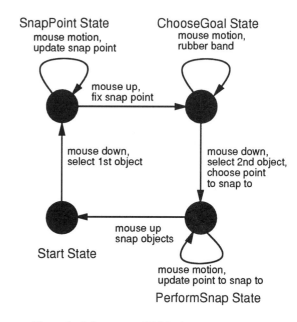

Figure 2: A four-state ATN for interactive snapping

By changing the states in the ATN, the user can experiment with different ways of specifying snap-dragging. Several different ATNs for different snapping techniques can be concurrently developed and experimented with, even at run time. For example, a user could develop a more complex ATN to allow the specification of the distance between the surfaces as well as the relative orientation of the Frenet frames.

4.4 A color picker

Color spaces are inherently multidimensional. To illustrate these spaces we can build a color picker in three dimensions and show how changes in the values affect the output color. Color plate II shows two interactive views of RGB color space and one interactive view of HSV color space. One view of RGB space is built with three sliders, each of which was specified using dependencies. Another view is built using a cubical marker that can translate within the bounds of a unit cube. Here, each axis of the cube's position represents a component of the color value. Thus, all three components can be specified simultaneously using 3D gestural translation. The third view is of HSV space. As in the RGB cube, the position of the spherical marker in the center represents the three components of the HSV color. The constraints on the sphere permit it to move around in the cone that represents valid HSV color values.

All of the spaces are different visualizations of the same data, kept consistent through the use of dependencies. Thus, a user can choose a color in one view and see how that color is represented in the other two. As the user interactively chooses a color, the other two color representations update accordingly. Users familiar with the RGB space can learn about the nature of HSV space by watching the motion of the HSV indicator as they move the RGB indicator.

4.5 The rack

Recall that the ATN states are first-class objects and that our system provides hierarchical grouping of objects. An ATN can pass control to another ATN through dependencies and controller mechanisms. Thus, pre-existing ATN's can be grouped together to form a more complex, hierarchical ATN (see Figure 3) that controls the sequencing of the lower-level ATNs. In other words, we can build more complex widgets out of pre-existing widgets.

To construct a more complex widget, we start with the simple rotation and translation handle widgets discussed in Section 4.2. By rearranging them and changing their connections, we combine them to form a "rack" for specifying high-level deformations such as twists, tapers and bends [1], shown in Color Plate IV.

Different handles specify the parameters to three deformations. The distance between the two upright handles specifies the range over which the deformation applies. The angle of the red handle on the end indicates the amount of bend, and the angle of the pink handle indicates the amount of twist, while the height of the blue handle indicates the amount of taper. By reconfiguring the rack, changing the number of handles and their respective behaviors, the user can control how the deformation is specified. Specialized racks that only bend, taper, or twist can be easily built. A new rack can be designed to apply wave deformations, or to allow both geometric transformations and nonlinear deformations at the same time.

Textual specification of a bend deformation requires four floating-point values and two vectors. The rack specifies all of these visually. The major axis of the rack specifies one vector, and the red handle specifies another vector, determining the angle and direction in which the object should bend. The floating-point values are all specified by how much particular handles are moved.

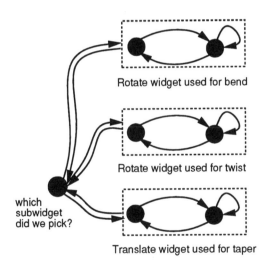

Rotate widget used for bend

Rotate widget used for twist

which
subwidget
did we pick?

Translate widget used for taper

Figure 3: Several ATNs can be combined to form a more complex widget. This widget specifies high-level deformations.

The rack is a widget that provides a more meaningful interface to complex deformations than a conventional widget such as a panel of independent sliders. Such a panel provides no semantic correlation: the user must extrapolate a single deformation from multiple independent slider positions. Thus, the rack serves to abstract out the essential characteristics of a deformation. When handles are used to translate an object in its own object space, the handles themselves give the user feedback on the orientation of that space, which might not be apparent from the object itself. Similarly, an object being deformed with the rack may be so geometrically complex that it has no clear axis around which to twist, bend or taper. The rack provides this axis, along with immediate and understandable feedback about the magnitude and effects of the deformations.

4.6 The cone tree

More complicated metaphors for 3D interfaces can be constructed and experimented with in our system. A large number of rotation widgets can be assembled into a Xerox PARC-style cone tree. Here, we use the cone tree to display the hierarchy of a 3D model (Color Plate III). The cone tree is itself an object in the system and can be freely manipulated as a whole.

The nature of this widget inherently requires motion control to animate the rotation of the subtrees. When we modify the cone tree, we can affect the underlying geometric hierarchy it represents. Moving subtrees of the cone tree to other nodes in the tree affects the hierarchy of the model that the cone tree represents. If we use other tools to modify the hierarchy, the cone tree's structure is also updated.

Since the cone tree is itself a widget, we can combine it with other widgets to make more intricate information browsers, much as simple rotation and translation widgets were composed above to make a deformation editor. We plan to explore using cone trees to represent portions of a hypermedia graph that are primarily hierarchical but have some cross-links, e.g., a multimedia technical paper with its various sections, subsections, references, and see-also's.

5 Conclusions

5.1 Accomplishments

We have presented a concept of 3D widgets as first-class objects encapsulating behavior and geometry that can be treated as any other objects in a 3D world. Their behaviors may be defined using complex control methods and user input techniques. We have provided a first implementation of these widgets within the UGA system. Widgets can be rapidly prototyped, modified, and combined into more complicated systems of widgets. Close integration with the application allows rich forms of interaction and feedback in our 3D applications.

5.2 Future work

Constructing 3D widgets is reasonably fast with our system. However, widget designers at present must be experts in the use of UGA. We hope to make specifying 3D widgets even more natural and intuitive than it is now, so that a far less technically expert designer can implement 3D widgets. Part of the complexity stems from limitations of dependencies. We might address these limitations with a more generic constraint model at the basic system level, making it easier to specify some of the complex relationships of 3D widgets. In addition, our system does not run as fast as we would like, even on today's high-end platforms. A large portion of time is spent evaluating dependencies. Unfortunately, the addition of a more generic constraint model is not likely to help performance. Thus, dependencies merit a close look, at both the conceptual and the implementation level.

We would like to continue developing individual widgets and exploring the potential of various techniques from the world of 3D graphics in interface design. We want to investigate the use of more sophisticated motion control, modeling and rendering techniques for 3D widgets. We can foresee widgets that will use dynamic constraints, physical simulation, volumetric techniques, particle systems, and even radiosity. Our application framework already includes many of these techniques, so it is simply a matter of their imaginative application in our system to make use of such techniques in 3D interfaces.

In addition, we are in the process of constructing full 3D applications and interfaces with the system presented. We believe the unusual nature of our widgets will provide some interesting avenues of exploration. Since the widgets are as much a part of the application as the application itself, it is straightforward to manipulate widgets with widgets. In other words, a user interface can be built by starting with simple widgets and using them to bootstrap more complex ones.

Finally, we hope to develop a high-level UIDS (user interface design system) [5] for our system. As previously noted, our system currently has no tools for making high-level specifications of an interface. Most commercial UIMSs, having been built on top of a widget toolkit, focus on appearance and geometry of widgets. Some research-level UIDSs handle behavior and sequencing. A UIDS suitable for our system would clearly have to be able to handle full application behavior and would perhaps be an Application Design System, a full-fledged programming environment for 3D interactive applications.

5.3 Acknowledgments

This work was supported in part by NSF, DARPA, IBM, Sun Microsystems, NCR, Hewlett Packard and Digital Equipment Corporation. Software contributions by Bitstream Inc., Pixar and Visual Edge Software Ltd. are gratefully acknowledged. We also thank Frank Graf for his help in implementing and extending the rack widget and Nate Huang for technical support.

References

[1] Alan H. Barr. Global and local deformations of solid primitives. In *Proceedings of the ACM SIGGRAPH, Computer Graphics*, volume 18(3), pages 21–30, July 1984.

[2] Eric A. Bier. Snap-dragging in three dimensions. In *Proceedings of the ACM SIGGRAPH, Computer Graphics*, volume 24(4), pages 193–204, March 1990.

[3] Jeff Butterworth, Andrew Davidson, Stephen Hench, and T. Marc Olano. 3DM: A three dimensional modeler using a head-mounted display. In *Proceedings of the 1992 Symposium on Interactive 3D Graphics*, 1992.

[4] Stuart K. Card, George G. Robertson, and Jock D. Mackinlay. The information visualizer, an information workspace. In *Human Factors in Computing Systems, Proceedings of the ACM SIGCHI*, pages 181–188. Addison Wesley, 1991.

[5] James Foley, Won Chui Kim, Srdjan Kovačević, and Kevin Murray. Designing interfaces at a high level of abstraction. *IEEE Software*, pages 25–32, January 1989.

[6] Tinsley Galyean, Melissa Gold, William Hsu, Henry Kaufman, and Mark Stern. Manipulation of virtual three-dimensional objects using two-dimensional input devices. Class project, Brown University, December 1989.

[7] Mark Green. A survey of three dialogue models. *ACM Transactions on Graphics*, 5(3):244–375, 1986.

[8] Mark Green and Robert Jacob. SIGGRAPH '90 workshop report: Software architectures and metaphors for non-WIMP user interfaces. *Computer Graphics*, 25(3):229–235, July 1991.

[9] Paul Haeberli. dynadraw. posted to comp.graphics, 1990. GL program.

[10] Brent Halperin and Van Nguyen. A model for object-based inheritance. In Peter Wegner and Bruce Shriver, editors, *Research Directions in Object-Oriented Programming*. The MIT Press, 1987.

[11] Scott H. Hudson. Graphical specification of flexible user interface displays. In *Proceedings of the ACM Symposium on User Interface Software and Technology*, pages 105–114, 1989.

[12] Robert J. K. Jacob. A specification language for direct-manipulation user interfaces. *ACM Transactions on Graphics*, 5(4):283–317, October 1986.

[13] Jock D. Mackinlay, George G. Robertson, and Stuart K. Card. The perspective wall: Detail and context smoothly integrated. In *Human Factors in Computing Systems, Proceedings of the ACM SIGCHI*. ACM SIGCHI, 1991.

[14] Microelectronics and Computer Technology Corporation. An introduction to the visual metaphors team's software releases. Video tape, 1986. TR# HI-344-86.

[15] Richard S. Millman and George D. Parker. *Elements of Differential Geometry*. Prentice-Hall, 1977.

[16] Brad A. Myers. Encapsulating interactive behaviors. In *Proceedings of CHI '89* (Austin, TX, April 30–May 4, 1989), pages 319–324. ACM, New York, May 1989.

[17] Brad A. Myers. User-interface tools: Introduction and survey. *IEEE Software*, pages 15–23, January 1989.

[18] Brad A. Myers, Dario A. Guise, Roger B. Dannenberg, Brad Vander Zanden, David S. Kosbie, Edward Pervin, Andrew Mickish, and Philippe Marchal. Garnet: Comprehensive support for graphical, highly interactive user interfaces. *IEEE Computer*, pages 71–85, November 1990.

[19] Randy Pausch. personal communication, 1991.

[20] Cary B. Phillips, Jianmin Zhao, and Norman I. Badler. Interactive real-time articulated figure manipulation using multiple kinematic constraints. In *Special Issue on the 1990 Symposium on Interactive 3D Graphics, Computer Graphics*, pages 245–250. ACM SIGGRAPH, ACM Press, March 1990.

[21] George G. Robertson, Stuart K. Card, and Jock D. Mackinlay. The cognitive coprocessor architecture for interactive user interfaces. In *Proceedings of the ACM Symposium on User Interface Software and Technology*, pages 10–18, 1989.

[22] George G. Robertson, Jock D. Mackinlay, and Stuart K. Card. Cone trees: Animated 3D visualizations of hierarchical information. In *Human Factors in Computing Systems, Proceedings of the ACM SIGCHI*. ACM SIGCHI, 1991.

[23] Dean Rubine. Specifying gestures by example. In *Proceedings of the ACM SIGGRAPH, Computer Graphics*, pages 329–337. ACM SIGGRAPH, Addison-Wesley, July 1991.

[24] Peter Wegner. The object-oriented classification paradigm. In Peter Wegner and Bruce Shriver, editors, *Research Directions in Object-Oriented Programming*. The MIT Press, 1987.

[25] Robert C. Zeleznik, D. Brookshire Conner, Matthias M. Wloka, Daniel G. Aliaga, Nathan T. Huang, Philip M. Hubbard, Brian Knep, Henry Kaufman, John F. Hughes, and Andries van Dam. An object-oriented framework for the integration of interactive animation techniques. In *Proceedings of the ACM SIGGRAPH, Computer Graphics*, pages 105–112. ACM SIGGRAPH, Addison-Wesley, July 1991.

Implementation of Flying, Scaling, and Grabbing in Virtual Worlds

Warren Robinett
Richard Holloway

Department of Computer Science
University of North Carolina
Chapel Hill, NC 27599-3175

ABSTRACT

In a virtual world viewed with a head-mounted display, the user may wish to perform certain actions under the control of a manual input device. The most important of these actions are flying through the world, scaling the world, and grabbing objects. This paper shows how these actions can be precisely specified with frame-to-frame invariants, and how the code to implement the actions can be derived from the invariants by algebraic manipulation.

INTRODUCTION

Wearing a Head-Mounted Display (HMD) gives a human user the sensation of being inside a three-dimensional, computer-simulated world. Because the HMD replaces the sights and sounds of the real world with a computer-generated virtual world, this synthesized world is called virtual reality.

The virtual world surrounding the user is defined by a graphics database called a *model*, which gives the colors and coordinates for each of the polygons making up the virtual world. The polygons making up the virtual world are normally grouped into entities called *objects*, each of which has its own location and orientation. The human being wearing the HMD is called the *user*, and also has a location and orientation within the virtual world.

To turn the data in the model into the illusion of a surrounding virtual world, the HMD system requires certain hardware components. The *tracker* measures the position and orientation of the user's head and hand. The *graphics engine* generates the images seen by the user, which are then displayed on the HMD. The *manual input device* allows the user to use gestures of the hand to cause things to happen in the virtual world.

BASIC ACTIONS

An *action* changes the state of the virtual world or the user's viewpoint within it under control of a gesture of the hand, as measured by the manual input device. The hand gesture initiates and terminates the action, and the changing position

and orientation of the hand during the gesture is also used to control what happens as the action progresses.

The manual input device may be a hand-held manipulandum with pushbuttons on it, or it may be an instrumented glove. In either case, the position and orientation of the input device must be measured by the tracker to enable manual control of actions. The input device must also allow the user to signal to the system to start and stop actions, and to select among alternative actions.

Certain fundamental manually-controlled actions may be implemented for any virtual world. These actions involve changing the location, orientation or scale of either an object or a user, as shown in Table 1.

	User	Object
Translate	fly through the world	grab (and move) object
Rotate	tilt the world	grab (and turn) object
Scale	expand or shrink the world	scale object

Table 1. Basic actions

Flying is defined here as an operation of translating in the direction pointed by the hand-held input device, with steering done by changing the hand orientation. This is different from the type of flying available in a flight simulator, where the user can not only translate but can also cause the virtual world to rotate around him by banking. However, translation-only flying is appropriate for a HMD because the user has the ability to turn and look in any direction, and to point the input device in any direction. We believe that keeping the orientation of the virtual world locked to that of the real world helps the user to navigate while flying through the virtual world.

Tilting the world is the ability to re-orient the virtual world relative to the user's orientation; that is, to turn the surrounding virtual world sideways. This is implemented by rotating the user with respect to the virtual world, which is subjectively perceived by the user as the entire virtual world rotating around him.

Scaling the world is the capability to shrink or expand the world relative to the user, as occurs to Alice in Wonderland when she drinks from the little bottle or eats the little cake. By setting up the action code properly, the user can shrink and expand the world while manually steering the center of expansion. This enables a powerful method of travel in very large virtual worlds: the user shrinks the world down until the destination is within arm's reach and then expands the world, continuously steering the center of expansion so as to arrive at the correctly-scaled destination.

Grabbing an object is picking up and moving a simulated object that appears in the virtual world. By analogy with real-world grabbing of objects, this includes the ability to rotate the held object before releasing it.

Scaling an object is just shrinking or expanding an individual object alone.

This paper seeks to answer the following question: How can the basic actions of flying, grabbing, scaling and tilting in a HMD system be specified and implemented?

PRIOR WORK

The first HMD was built in 1968 by Ivan Sutherland [8], but since it had no manual input device other than a keyboard, it did not allow actions controlled by manual gestures. At the University of Utah, a tracked manual input device called a "wand" was added to the system [9]. The tip of the wand was tracked in position but not orientation. The wand was used to deform the surfaces of virtual objects composed of curved patches [2].

In 1985 at NASA Ames Research Center, McGreevy and Humphries built a HMD which was later improved by Fisher, Robinett and others [3]. Under contract to NASA, VPL Research provided an instrumented glove, later named the "DataGlove," which served as a manual input device. The position of the hand and head were tracked with a Polhemus 3Space magnetic tracker. In 1986 using the glove input device, Robinett implemented on this system the actions of flying through the world, scaling the world, rotating the world, and grabbing objects.

Some of these actions, particularly flying and grabbing objects, have since been implemented on HMD systems at several sites. VPL Research began in 1989 selling commercially a HMD system that used a glove to control the actions of flying and grabbing [1]. At the University of North Carolina [7][5], the actions of flying, scaling and grabbing were controlled with a hand-held manual input device with pushbuttons on it which was made from a billiard ball.

COORDINATE SYSTEMS DIAGRAM FOR A HMD

Various coordinate systems co-exist within a HMD system. All of these coordinate systems exist simultaneously, and although over time they may be moving with respect to one another, at any given moment each pair of them has a relative position and orientation. The instantaneous relationship between two coordinate systems can be described with a transform that converts the coordinates of a point described in one coordinate system to the coordinates that represent that same point in the second coordinate system.

Although transforms exist between any pair of coordinate systems in the HMD system, certain pairs of coordinate systems have relative positions that are either constant, measured by the tracker, or are known for some other reason. These are the *independent transforms*, which are shown in relation to one another in Figure 1. In this diagram, each node stands for a coordinate system, and each edge linking two nodes stands for a transform between those two coordinate systems.

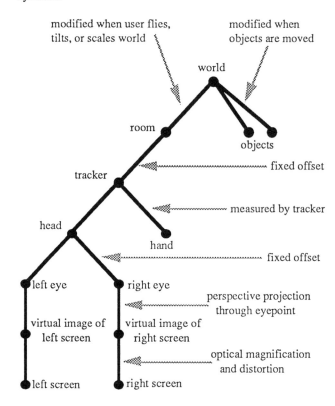

Figure 1. Coordinate systems diagram for a single-user HMD system

NOMENCLATURE FOR TRANSFORMS

We abbreviate the coordinate systems with the first letters of their names. The World-Object transform may be written as T_{WO}. Transform T_{WO} converts a point P_O in coordinate system O to a point P_W in coordinate system W.

$$P_W = T_{WO} \cdot P_O$$

This notation is similar to that used in [4]. Notice that the subscripts cancel nicely, as in [6]. Likewise, the composition of the transform T_{WO} going from O to W with the transform T_{RW} going from W to R gives a transform T_{RO} from O to R, with the cancellation rule working here, too:

$$T_{RW} \cdot T_{WO} = T_{RO}$$

The inverse of transform T_{WO} is written T_{OW}.

SPECIFYING ACTIONS WITH INVARIANTS

An action in a virtual world is performed by activating the input device, such as by pushing a button, and then moving the input device to control the action as it progresses. As an example, grabbing a simulated object requires, for each frame while the grab action is in progress, that a new position for the object be computed based on the changing position of the user's hand.

It is possible to precisely define grabbing and other actions with an *invariant*, which is an equation that describes the

190

desired relationship among certain transforms involved in the action. The invariant is typically stated as a relation between certain transforms in the current display frame and certain transforms in the previous frame. In the case of grabbing, the invariant to be maintained is that the Object-Hand transform be equal to its value in the previous frame while the grab action is in progress; in other words, that the object remain fixed with respect to the hand while it is being grabbed.

Starting from the invariant and a diagram of the coordinate systems involved, a mathematical derivation can be performed which produces a formula for updating the proper transform to cause the desired action to occur. For grabbing, this would be updating the Object-World transform to change the object's position and orientation in the virtual world.

Rigorously deriving the update formula from a simple invariant is much easier and more reliable than attempting to write down the update formula using the coordinate systems diagram and informal reasoning. Also, the matching of adjacent subscripts in the notation helps to check that the transforms are in correct order.

GRABBING AN OBJECT

To derive the update formula for grabbing, we first look at the relevant part of the coordinate system diagram, shown in Figure 2.

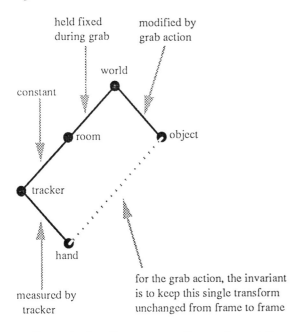

Figure 2. Coordinate systems diagram for grabbing an object

A way of describing the action of grabbing is that the Object-Hand transform T_{OH} remain unchanged from frame to frame, which is expressed by the invariant

$$T_{OH}' = T_{OH}$$

where the apostrophe in T_{OH}' indicates a transform in the current frame which is being updated, and no apostrophe means the value of the transform from the previous frame.

To move an individual object, the Object-World transform T_{OW} must be updated each frame in a way that preserves the invariant. To derive the update formula for grabbing, we start with the invariant and decompose the transforms on both sides based on the relationships among the coordinate systems as shown in the coordinate system diagram.

$$T_{OW}' \cdot T_{WR}' \cdot T_{RT}' \cdot T_{TH}' = T_{OW} \cdot T_{WR} \cdot T_{RT} \cdot T_{TH}$$

We then use algebraic manipulations to isolate the desired transform on the left side of the equation, remembering that these transforms are not commutative.

$$T_{OW}' \cdot T_{WR}' \cdot T_{RT}' = T_{OW} \cdot T_{WR} \cdot T_{RT} \cdot T_{TH} \cdot T_{HT}'$$
$$T_{OW}' \cdot T_{WR}' = T_{OW} \cdot T_{WR} \cdot T_{RT} \cdot T_{TH} \cdot T_{HT}' \cdot T_{TR}'$$
$$T_{OW}' = T_{OW} \cdot T_{WR} \cdot T_{RT} \cdot T_{TH} \cdot T_{HT}' \cdot T_{TR}' \cdot T_{RW}'$$

This is the update formula for grabbing, which updates the Object-World transform based on its previous value, the current and previous values of the Hand-Tracker transform (which changes as the hand moves), and the values of the intervening transforms between Tracker and World. The effect of executing this assignment each frame is to keep the object in a fixed position and orientation relative to the hand, even though the hand is moving around within the virtual world.

Another action which can be implemented in a similar manner is "grabbing the fabric of space." In this case, the user can grab and tilt the entire virtual world, rather than just a single object, by holding the World-Hand transform invariant while the hand rotates.

FLYING

The action of flying is translating the user through the virtual world in the direction pointed by the manual input device. The user steers by rotating the manual input device as the flight proceeds. A metaphor for this type of flying is that the user holds a rocket pistol in his hand, which drags him through the virtual world when he squeezes the trigger.

The manual input device is considered to point in a particular direction that is relative to its local coordinate system. This may be thought of as a 3D vector in Hand coordinates, where the vector's length specifies the flying speed and the vector's direction defines the direction the input device points. This vector defines a translation transform, $T_{HtranslateH}$, which moves a point in Hand coordinates to a new position in Hand coordinates. To implement flying, we first need to convert this transformation to operate on points in Room coordinates.

$$T_{RtranslateR}' = T_{RH}' \cdot T_{HtranslateH}' \cdot T_{HR}'$$

To make the user's position change within the virtual world, the World-Room transform must be modified each frame, so the invariant for flying is

$$T_{WR}' = T_{WR} \cdot T_{RtranslateR}'$$

which may be expanded to give the update formula for flying.

$$T_{WR}' = T_{WR} \cdot T_{RT}' \cdot T_{TH}' \cdot T_{HtranslateH} \cdot T_{HT}' \cdot T_{TR}'$$

SCALING THE WORLD

It is possible to shrink or expand the surrounding virtual world. This is comprehensible and effective because the user has direct perception of the size of and distance to virtual objects through stereopsis and head-motion parallax, and can therefore easily perceive the concerted motions of the objects in the virtual world expanding around a center of expansion, or shrinking towards a center of contraction.

The type of scaling used is uniform scaling, in which all three dimensions are always scaled by the same factor. There is always a center of scaling when uniform scaling occurs, and for the manually controlled action of scaling the world, it makes sense to locate the center of scaling at the user's hand. When expanding the world, the center of scaling is the point that virtual objects move away from as expansion occurs, and so to end up at a specific desired location within a formerly-tiny virtual world, the center of scaling must be repeatedly re-centered on the desired location as it emerges during expansion.

Implementing this action requires a derivation similar to that used for flying. An incremental scaling transformation in Hand coordinates, $T_{HscaleH}$, will use the Hand origin as the center of scaling. Below we give the invariant for scaling the world, and the update formula derived from it.

$$T_{WR}' = T_{WR} \cdot T_{RscaleR}'$$
$$T_{WR}' = T_{WR} \cdot T_{RT}' \cdot T_{TH}' \cdot T_{HscaleH} \cdot T_{HT}' \cdot T_{TR}'$$

GENERAL FORM

Upon examining the invariants for flying and scaling, we see a strong similarity between them: both invariants are of the form:

$$T_{WR}' = T_{WR} \cdot T_{R<transform>R}'$$

In fact, these two invariants for updating T_{WR} are examples of a more general technique for updating a transform between two coordinate systems based on a transform that occurs in a third coordinate system. The general form for updating the transform T_{AB} in terms of an action in coordinate system K is:

$$T_{AB}' = T_{AB} \cdot T_{BK}' \cdot T_{K<transform>K} \cdot T_{KB}'$$

where there may be an arbitrary number of coordinate systems between B and K, and T_{BK} is the product of the transforms that go between the two coordinate systems.

Using this general form, scaling an object about the hand is analogous to scaling the world about the hand:

$$T_{OW}' = T_{OW} \cdot T_{WH}' \cdot T_{HscaleH} \cdot T_{HW}'$$

CONCLUSIONS

The foregoing examples of grabbing, flying and scaling show how actions can be implemented that operate under continuous manual control by the user. For each action, the relationship between the motion of the hand and the transforms to be modified was precisely specified with an invariant. These invariants not only provided a concise and precise specification of each action, but also provided a starting point for a formal derivation that produced update equations which could be used directly to implement the actions.

Using invariants and derivations to produce the code to implement grabbing, scaling and flying is greatly superior to the method which is often used, namely, to just write down a sequence of transforms that looks right based on the coordinate system diagram. It is easy to get some of the transforms in the wrong order. The notation used in this paper provides a check against misordering the transforms by requiring adjacent subscripts to match. The HMD software at UNC was implemented using this notation and the formulas derived in this paper, and serves as proof that they work.

ACKNOWLEDGEMENTS

We would like to thank many people for their contributions to this work, starting with the HMD and Pixel-Planes teams at UNC, led by Fred Brooks and Henry Fuchs. We thank Fred Brooks for useful discussions about coordinate systems diagrams and nomenclature. This work builds on earlier work at NASA, and we would like to acknowledge the contributions of Scott Fisher, Jim Humphries, Doug Kerr and Mike McGreevy. We thank Ken Shoemake for help with quaternions and Julius Smith for rules-of-thumb about writing technical papers. This research was supported by the following grants: DARPA #DAEA 18-90-C-0044, NSF Cooperative Agreement #ASC-8920219, and DARPA: "Science and Technology Center for Computer Graphics and Scientific Visualization", ONR #N00014-86-K-0680, and NIH #5-R24-RR-02170.

REFERENCES

[1] Blanchard, C., S. Burgess, Y. Harvill, J. Lanier, A. Lasko, M. Oberman, M. Teitel. Reality Built for Two: A Virtual Reality Tool. *Proc. 1990 Workshop on Interactive 3D Graphics.* 35-36.

[2] Clark, J. 1976. Designing surfaces in 3-D. *Communications of the ACM.* 19:8:454-460.

[3] Fisher, S., M. McGreevy, J. Humphries, and W. Robinett. 1986. Virtual Environment Display System. *Proc. 1986 Workshop on Interactive 3D Graphics.* 77-87.

[4] Foley, J., A. van Dam, S. Feiner, J. Hughes. 1990. *Computer Graphics: Principles and Practice* (2nd ed.). Addison-Wesley Publishing Co., Reading MA. 222-226.

[5] Holloway, R., H. Fuchs, W. Robinett. 1991. Virtual-Worlds Research at the University of North Carolina at Chapel Hill. *Proc. Computer Graphics '91.* London, England.

[6] Pique, M. 1980. Nested Dynamic Rotations for Computer Graphics. M.S. Thesis, University of North Carolina, Chapel Hill, NC.

[7] Robinett, W. 1990. Artificial Reality at UNC Chapel Hill. [videotape] *SIGGRAPH Video Review.*

[8] Sutherland, I. 1968. A head-mounted three-dimensional display. *1968 Fall Joint Computer Conference, AFIPS Conference Proceedings.* 33:757-764.

[9] Vickers, D. 1974. Sorceror's Apprentice: head mounted display and wand. Ph.D. dissertation, Dept. of Computer Science, Univ. of Utah, Salt Lake City.

A Comparison of Head-tracked and Non-head-tracked Steering Modes in the Targeting of Radiotherapy Treatment Beams

James C. Chung
Department of Computer Science
University of North Carolina at Chapel Hill*

ABSTRACT

A controlled experiment was conducted to compare head-tracked and non-head-tracked steering modes in the performance of an abstract beam-targeting task. Collected data revealed a wide variety of mode preferences among the subjects. Subject performance, as measured by final score, task completion time and subject confidence, differed very little between the head-tracked steering modes taken as a group and the collective non-head-tracked modes. Some significant differences were observed between individual steering modes, both within and between the head-tracked and non-head-tracked groups.

INTRODUCTION

Current research at the University of North Carolina at Chapel Hill is investigating the possible benefits to be gained by applying head-mounted display (HMD) technology to radiotherapy treatment planning (RTP). Use of a head-mounted display for targeting of treatment beams suggests several possible steering modes for exploring the virtual world of the patient's anatomy. To determine which steering mode is best suited to our application, a user study was conducted to investigate the relative merits of the different steering modes.

Seven steering modes were used in an abstract beam-targeting task. Four modes used head-tracking information, while the other three modes did not. It was anticipated that head-tracking would provide an advantage in beam targeting through more natural steering and navigation that makes use of proprioceptive and vestibular information, which are absent in non-head-tracked methods.

Related work in movement through a virtual world is described in [1, 2, 3], but these studies do not deal with HMD's and head-tracking.

BEAM TARGETING

The key to successful beam targeting in radiation therapy treatment planning is to orient and shape the beams so that the entire tumor is covered by each beam while as little of the healthy surrounding tissue as possible is hit by the beams. Given the complex spatial arrangement of a patient's anatomy (tumors may be draped around healthy organs or have tendrils snaking out into the healthy tissue), this is usually not an easy task.

To evaluate the different steering modes, subjects were presented with an abstract anatomy model, consisting of a multi-colored spherical target (tumor analog) embedded in a collection of uniquely

colored monochromatic spherical dodges (organ analogs). (See Color Plate 1.) The subjects used each of the seven steering modes to manipulate the direction in which a conical virtual beam passed through the model. The beam was defined such that its source (cone vertex) was always a fixed distance from the target, its central ray (cone axis) passed throught the center of the target, and its divergence was just large enough to encompass the target. The subject was instructed to find the beam direction that afforded the smallest volume of intersection between the conical beam and the dodges, a task analogous to a radiotherapist trying to avoid radiosensitive organs with a treatment beam.

STEERING MODES

The term "steering mode" refers to the method used to change one's position or orientation in the virtual world. This is distinguished from navigation, which refers to understanding one's current position and orientation relative to other objects in the virtual world.

Head-Tracked

These modes are linked to movement of the subject's head and enable the subject to make use of vestibular (inner ear balance) and proprioceptive (muscles, tendons, joints) senses for navigation.

Walkaround (WLK). In Walkaround mode, the subject physically walks about in the virtual world containing the target/dodges model. The direction of the beam is defined by the vector from the subject's eyes to the center of the target. To better examine the model and target the beam from above and below, the subject is given the ability to vertically translate the model using a 6-D mouse. No other manipulation of the model is possible.

Walkaround/Rotation (WKR). This is the same as Walkaround mode, with the exception that the subject is able to also rotate the model about any axis in 3-space through its center by grabbing with the 6-D mouse. (See 6-D Mouse section below.)

Orbital (ORB). In Orbital mode the subject is constrained to always be looking at the center of the model from the beam source. Beam direction coincides with gaze direction. Unlike the Walkaround modes, Orbital mode uses only head orientation and ignores head position. As the subject's head turns, the model is observed to translate about the subject's head at a constant distance. (Hence the name Orbital.) Because the model undergoes no rotation, it can be viewed from any direction with a turn of the subject's head.

Immersion (IMM). In Immersion mode the subject views the model looking outward from the center of the target. Like Orbital mode, Immersion mode makes use of head orientation only and ignores

*CB#3175, Sitterson Hall, Chapel Hill, NC, 27599-3175.
chung@cs.unc.edu   (919) 962-1889

head position. When the subject's head turns, the subject's view sweeps across portions of the model from its fixed, central vantage point. The beam direction is defined by the subject's gaze direction, and the task of finding the best beam orientation becomes one of looking for the portion of the model with the biggest opening. Since the beam passes completely through the model, the subject is given the ability to reverse his gaze direction by holding down a button on the 6-D mouse, and can thereby examine the complete prospective beam path through the model.

Non-Head-Tracked

Although these modes do not make use of head-tracking information, the subjects still viewed the model through the HMD so that image quality was equalized over the seven modes. These three modes all place the subject's eye at the beam source, looking in the direction of the beam toward the target, and support exploration of prospective beam orientations by rotating the model in three-space.

Joystick (JOY). In Joystick mode the model is rotated with a velocity-control joystick. In addition to the left-right/forward-backward movement of the joystick, the cap of the joystick turns clockwise and counterclockwise to provide all three degrees of rotational freedom.

Spaceball (SPC). In this mode the model is rotated with a Spaceball*, an isometric, force-sensitive device that provides six degrees of translational and rotational freedom. This mode, however, uses only the three rotational degrees of freedom as a velocity control for rotation of the model in three-space.

6-D Mouse (SDM). In 6-D Mouse mode the orientation of the model is controlled with a custom-built, six degree-of-freedom mouse (tracker sensor embedded in a pool ball with two buttons). When either mouse button is held down, the rotational component of the mouse movement is directly linked to model rotation, and the subject sees the model rotate in the same manner as his hand.

BEAM'S-EYE VIEW

An important feature of a steering mode that may affect a subject's performance is whether or not it provides a "beam's-eye view." Beam's-eye view is the view seen by an eye coincident with the beam vertex and whose gaze vector coincides with the beam's central axis. With a beam's-eye view it is very easy to determine which dodges intersect the beam, for since the beam is defined to diverge just enough to exactly enclose the target, the silhouettes of those dodges will overlap with the silhouette of the target. In those modes that do not provide a beam's-eye view, it is more difficult for the subject to judge which dodges are hit by the beam.

Walkaround and Walkaround/Rotate modes do not provide beam's-eye views, because the subject's head cannot be physically constrained to align with the beam source. Immersion mode also does not provide a beam's-eye view, since the subject's eyepoint is constrained to stay at the target's center. The other four modes do provide beam's-eye views.

EXPERIMENTAL METHOD

The experiment was a one-factor within-subject investigation, with steering mode as the independent variable. Dependent variables measured were final score (volume of intersection between beam and dodges), task completion time, confidence in the final beam configuration, and rank orderings of the seven modes by ease of use and by preference.

Fourteen subjects were recruited from graduate students and staff members of the Departments of Computer Science, Radiation On-

---

*Spaceball™ is a registered trademark of Spatial Systems, Inc.
†3Space™ is a registered trademark of Polhemus Navigation Sciences.
‡EyePhone™ is a registered trademark of VPL Research, Inc.

cology, and Radiology at UNC. Each subject underwent 7 sessions, each of which used a different steering mode. The order of the steering modes used by each subject was varied according to a 7x7 latin square. Each session consisted of 3 practice trials followed by 3 test trials. Each trial used a unique target/dodge model.

In each trial the subject explored prospective beam orientations until the best one was found, at which time the subject stopped the trial. There was no time limit, nor any emphasis on task completion time—the subject was instructed to take as long as necessary to find the best beam path. A virtual marker (arrow pointing through the model) was provided to the subject to use as a reference. At any time the subject could issue a "mark" command, which aligned the marker with the current beam direction, and the marker would remain fixed in the model until a subsequent command was issued. The score and task completion time for the trial were recorded, as well as the subject's rating on a scale of 1 (no confidence)-10 (total confidence) of how confident he or she was that the best beam orientation had been found.

After all seven sessions were completed, the subject ranked the seven steering modes according to two criteria, ease-of-use of the steering mode and preference for performing the beam targeting task.

Equipment used included a Polhemus 3Space† tracker on an EyePhone‡ Model 2 head-mounted display, displaying images generated by UNC's Pixel-Planes 4 graphics processor.

RESULTS

Figure 1 presents histograms showing for each steering mode, the number of times it was ranked 1st, 2nd, ... 7th by ease-of-use and by preference. The plot for Walkaround Mode shows that most subjects found it to be one of the more difficult steering modes to use. The other three head-tracking modes have somewhat flat histograms, suggesting no general consensus on how easy they were to use. Of the non-head-tracking modes, the Joystick mode is widely considered an easy-to-use steering mode. Spaceball mode and 6-D Mouse mode both tended to be on the difficult side.

The preference rankings show that Joystick mode was widely pre-

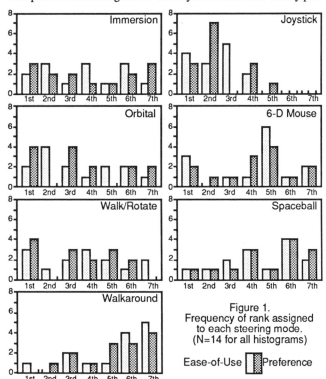

Figure 1.
Frequency of rank assigned
to each steering mode.
(N=14 for all histograms)

Ease-of-Use   Preference

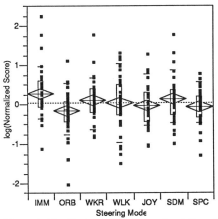

Figure 2. Distribution of log(Normalized Score) by Steering Mode

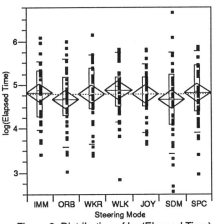

Figure 3. Distribution of log(Elapsed Time) by Steering Mode

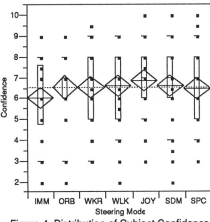

Figure 4. Distribution of Subject Confidence by Steering Mode

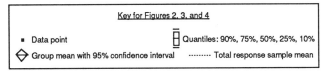

Key for Figures 2, 3, and 4

■ Data point   ▯ Quantiles: 90%, 75%, 50%, 25%, 10%

◇ Group mean with 95% confidence interval   .... Total response sample mean

ferred by the subjects, whereas Walkaround Mode was widely disliked. For Spaceball and 6-D Mouse modes subjects' opinions were on the less-preferred sides. On the other hand, Walk/Rotate and Orbital modes were on the more-preferred side of the scale. Immersion mode shows an interesting bimodal distribution, suggesting that subjects either loved it or hated it.

In order to factor out inter-model variability, each trial's score was normalized by the median score across subjects for the particular model used in that trial. Figure 2 shows the distribution of the logarithms of the normalized scores grouped by steering mode. As the best possible score is 0 (no intersection between beam and dodges), the more negative values represent better performance. Student's t-test reveals significant differences for the following inter-mode comparisons: IMM-ORB (α=0.0007), IMM-SPC (α=0.0069), SDM-ORB (α=0.0126), WKR-ORB (α=0.0187), IMM-JOY (α=0.0197). Head-tracked modes (IMM, ORB, WKR, WLK) taken as a group do not differ significantly from non-head-tracked modes (JOY, SDM, SPC).

Figure 3 shows the distribution of the logarithms of the task completion times grouped by steering mode. No significant differences are found in this data, neither between individual steering modes nor between head-tracked and non-head-tracked modes.

Figure 4 presents the distribution of subject's confidence rating grouped by steering mode. The only significant effect found in this data is the JOY-IMM comparison (α=0.0375).

Table 1 describes correlations between the dependent variables. Not surprisingly, ease-of-use and preference rank are highly correlated. Significant correlations are also found between subject confidence and ease-of-use, preference, and elapsed time. All three correlations are negative, indicating that a subjects' confidence decreased when

using difficult steering modes or modes they did not like, or when trials took a long time. Interestingly, score is not significantly correlated with any of the other variables.

DISCUSSION
Trial Replay

In addition to the statistical summaries presented above, a subjective review of each trial was conducted by playing back log files in which were recorded status information for the subject's head, the model and the beam at half-second intervals. By observing the trial replay with the HMD, it was possible to study how the subject moved and how the model was manipulated. The trial replay also traced the location of the beam source through the trial, quickly revealing which beam directions were considered, and perhaps more important, which directions were not considered.

In spite of being instructed to find the best possible beam direction, subjects usually terminated the trial before considering all possibilities. Presumably they were able to attain a good enough spatial understanding of the model without having to inspect it from all angles. Trials in which the model had been completely covered usually were usually of extremely long duration, with subject movement suggesting confusion and disorientation. In only a few cases did subjects follow a systematic search strategy, and these systematic searches would usually be abandoned after one candidate beam direction had been found. For the most part, subjects followed what might be called a "greedy" steering strategy, moving about the model in a manner based upon their current view of the model, and not upon some predefined plan. As a result, in most trials the traces of the beam source showed large "holes" that were never considered. From just watching the trial replay it is difficult to determine whether such holes were areas that were deliberately skipped or accidentally missed. Some of these areas corresponded to beam directions that were obviously bad, which might imply that those possibilities were deliberately skipped. Other holes contained prospective beam directions that were good enough to deserve consideration, implying that these areas were accidentally missed by the subject. In most cases the beam directions that required the subject to look straight up or straight down were not covered, as the HMD would exert very large torques on the subject's neck in these positions.

Most subjects relied very heavily on the marker to provide a reference point in the model. The marker served as a landmark that facilitated quick movement between two diametrically opposed

Correl. Coeff. (Signif. Prob.)	Ease-of-Use Rank	Preference Rank	log(Normalized Score)	log(Elapsed Time)	Confidence
Ease-of-Use Rank	— (—)	0.872475 (0.0000)	0.050902 (0.3845)	0.046793 (0.4241)	-0.19504 (0.0008)
Preference Rank	0.872475 (0.0000)	— (—)	0.009285 (0.8740)	0.07005 (0.2311)	-0.22578 (0.0001)
log(Normalized Score)	0.050902 (0.3845)	0.009285 (0.8740)	— (—)	-0.08943 (0.1260)	-0.2236 (0.7041)
log(Elapsed Time)	0.046793 (0.4241)	0.07005 (0.2311)	-0.08943 (0.1260)	— (—)	-0.25239 (0.0000)
Confidence	-0.19504 (0.0008)	-0.22578 (0.0001)	-0.2236 (0.7041)	-0.25239 (0.0000)	— (—)

Table 1. Correlation coefficients between dependent variables, with significance probability.

beam directions, and was also typically used as a "best-beam-direction-so-far" marker to which the subject would return for the final solution after further exploration elsewhere. Many subjects expressed a desire to have more than one marker. Most subjects did not make use of the context provided by dodges uniquely colored in HLS space for reference. Only one subject, whose own research is concerned with the use of color, found the colors useful—so useful, in fact, that the markers were never used.

Steering Mode Summaries

Immersion (IMM). Immersion mode produced significantly worse scores than Orbital, Spaceball, and Joystick modes, and it appeared to have instilled less confidence in the subjects than the other modes. This may be a result of the subjects' being able to see only a small portion of the model at any time, which, combined with the lack of any head-motion parallax, could have hindered the subject's development of a complete mental picture of the model. In addition, subjects were required to evaluate prospective beam orientations by looking in one direction and then in the other direction, with no clear indication of where the boundary of the beam was. Immersion mode did, however, have the advantage of providing the ability for the subject to use muscle memory in navigation. Even without a complete global understanding of the model, subjects knew how they had to orient their heads to get back to a particular beam direction.

Orbital (ORB). Despite the fact that there is no real-world metaphor for this steering mode, Orbital mode produced significantly better scores than Immersion, 6-D Mouse, and Walk/Rotate modes. This may have been due to the unique combination of several factors. Orbital mode provides a beam's-eye view of the model, which at once gives the subject an external global view of the model and allows the subject to easily determine which dodges intersected the beam. Another contributing factor is the aid to navigation through muscle memory provided by Orbital mode.

Walkaround (WLK). Walkaround mode produced the longest mean task completion time, but was undistinguished in score and subject confidence. The long task completion time is not surprising, given the difficulty of walking about in the virtual world in a HMD that seals off any view of the real world. Most subjects found this mode very awkward and time-consuming, and ranked Walkaround low in ease of use and preference. Interestingly, this mode more than any other was used for systematic searches. One subject repeatedly circled around the model, inspecting the model at different heights with each loop. Another subject opted to walk less and inspect the model vertically at regular intervals around the model. Perhaps the awkwardness of the mode instilled in these subjects a need for a disciplined, efficient approach.

Walkaround/Rotation (WKR). Walk/Rotate mode did not perform any better than Walkaround mode, but fared better in ease and preference rankings. The model rotation capability was used to different degrees by the different subjects. Most subjects walked very little and spent most of their time standing still and rotating the model as in 6-D Mouse mode. Some trials showed no rotation at all, perhaps indicating a reluctance in the subject to lose the navigational advantage provided by a fixed model reference frame.

Joystick (JOY). Joystick mode ranked very high in ease-of-use and preference, probably because most of the subjects worked with computers and were somewhat familiar with video games. Even so, performance with Joystick mode was not notable. Trial replay revealed that most subjects used only principal axis rotations, i.e. they rotated models mostly vertically and horizontally and very little diagonally. This was probably due to the mechanical action of the joystick, which required slightly more effort to move diagonally. The effect of this restriction is unclear, for while it forced subjects to decompose their movements into a series of principal axes rotations, it provided a precision of movement not available with the other non-

head-tracked modes.

6-D Mouse (SDM). Compared to subjects' preference for Joystick mode and dislike for Walkaround mode, response to 6-D Mouse mode was relatively flat. Its performance was undistinguished from the other modes. Trial replays showed that this mode suffered greatly from tracker latency, which greatly hindered both precise alignment and movements large enough to require more than one grab-release cycle. Consequently, beam source traces for 6-D Mouse mode were characterized by a very jagged appearance with large direction changes separating relatively small rotations.

Spaceball (SPC). The performance of Spaceball mode is relatively undistinguished, but its preference rankings are weighted toward the low end. Many subjects found the Spaceball fatiguing and difficult to use for precise movements.

General Comments

Perhaps most compelling is the large inter-subject variance seen this experiment, which may have masked significant differences between steering modes and between the collective head-tracked modes and the non-head-tracked modes. Standardized tests of spatial orientation and spatial visualization [4] may provide a normalizing factor to reduce this variance.

Another interesting observation is the large variation seen in the preference and ease-of-use histograms of the head-tracked modes. There was no general consensus about which of the four modes was the best, although Walkaround was generally considered the worst. This suggests that to be widely accepted, an HMD-based targeting tool should have an adaptable user interface that lets users choose the steering mode they want to use. One must also consider, however, that a task so critical as targeting of treatment beams demands optimal performance. Orbital mode provides better performance than the other three, and will be carried over into the next experiment, involving true, anatomical beam-targeting. Since score is not correlated with mode preference, it is expected that performance of users who do not like Orbital mode will not suffer from having to use it.

CONCLUSIONS

Collected data show no significant difference between head-tracked steering modes and non-head-tracked steering modes in the performance of an abstract beam-targeting task. Orbital mode provided the best overall performance, Immersion mode the worst. The three non-head-tracked modes were not distinguished by performance.

ACKNOWLEDGEMENTS
Support for this research was received from:
Defense Advanced Research Projects Agency, Contract No. DAEA 18-90-C-0044.
Digital Equipment Corporation, Research Agreement No. 582.
National Science Foundation, Grant No. CDA-8722752.
Office of Naval Research, Grant No. N00014-86-K-0680.

REFERENCES

1. Ware, C. and Osborne, S., Exploration and virtual camera control in virtual three dimensional environments. In Proc. 1990 Symposium on Interactive 3D Graphics (Snowbird, UT, Mar. '91). Computer Graphics, 24, 2 (Mar. 1991), 175-183.

2. Ware, C. and Slipp, L., Exploring virtual environments using velocity control: A comparison of three devices. In Proc. Hum. Factors Soc., 35th Ann. Mtg. (San Francisco, Sep. '91). HFS, 1991, pp. 300-304.

3. Mackinlay, J.D., Card, S.K., and Robertson, G.G., Rapid controlled movement through a virtual 3D workspace. Computer Graphics, 24, 4 (Aug. 1990), 171-176.

4. McGee, M.G., Human Spatial Abilities. Praeger, New York, 1979.

Interactive Manipulation and Display of

Two-Dimensional Surfaces in Four-Dimensional Space

David Banks
Department of Computer Science
University of North Carolina at Chapel Hill

Abstract

Surfaces in 4-space generally produce self-intersections when projected to 3-space. The geometry of the projected surface changes as the surface rotates rigidly in 4-space. This paper presents techniques for interacting with such a surface, for recovering the geometry and depth information that the projection destroys, for computing the intersections and the surface when projected to 3-space, and for computing the silhouettes and the surface when projected to the screen. These techniques are part of an interactive system called Fourphront, which uses Pixel-Planes 5 as the graphics engine.

1 Introduction

Versatile high-performance graphics machines let us interactively manipulate surfaces in four dimensions. The projective geometry and linear algebra required for the job are well known [Semple], but surfaces in 4-space present challenges in designing a user interface and a set of visualization cues. This paper presents techniques to address these problems, using Pixel-Planes 5 as the graphics platform. In particular, we present techniques for gathering 3D input to manipulate a surface in 4-space, for providing visualization cues, and for applying 4D depth cues. These techniques are at the heart of an interactive system called "Fourphront."

Why study surfaces in 4-space? One reason is that topologists have yet to classify all the 3-dimensional compact surfaces, but have succeeded with the 2-dimensional surfaces (k-holed donuts and their non-orientable counterparts). Many of the 2-dimensional surfaces require four dimensions in which to imbed, and none of the compact 3-dimensional surfaces can imbed in three dimensions of Euclidean space. It might be enlightening to examine and compare surfaces that are topologically equivalent and that inhabit four dimensions of space. Do they look alike or not?

It is difficult even to illustrate the 3D classification problem with genuine examples; these are volumes without boundaries, residing in up to seven dimensions of space. Even the 2-dimensional surfaces may require four dimensions for their imbedding. Interactive computer graphics can be of service by providing a window on these surfaces in 4-space.

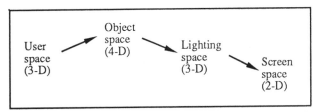

Figure 1. A user in 3-space manipulates a surface in 4-space, which projects to 3-spac and then onto the screen.

The three steps of our task (figure 1) are (§2) mapping input from user space to object space, (§3 and §4) projecting from object space to illumination space, and (§5) projecting from illumination space to the screen.

2 Mapping User Input to World Transformations

The illusion of reality is strongest when the user controls what scene it is that he views. Dynamic control of the transformation matrices requires an input device that offers a natural means for producing the object's motion. There are ten degrees of freedom that we wish to control for manipulating objects in 4-space: four extents of translation in the axial directions (x, y, z, w), and six Euler angles of rotation within the axial planes (xw, yw, zw, xz, yz, xy). The 4D rotations look very much like their 3D counterparts, although it becomes more appropriate to think of rotations occurring within a plane rather than occurring about an axis (figure 2). In 3-space, rotations leave a 1-dimensional subspace fixed; that subspace is the rotation axis. In 4D, rotations leave a 2-dimensional subspace fixed, while permuting the points within the 2-dimensional rotation plane and within the bundle of planes parallel to it. In general, the rotation matrix A for the $x_i x_j$ plane $(i < j)$, contains the elements $a_{ii} = a_{jj} = \cos t$, $a_{ij} = -a_{ji} = (-1)^{(i+j)} \sin t$, and the remaining elements $a_{kl} = \delta_{kl}$. For a more thorough treatment on Euler angles in 4-space, and how to specify orientation, see [Hoffman]. The challenge in assigning the ten degrees of freedom in 4-space to input devices that exist physically in 3-space is to promote kinesthetic sympathy: the similarity of input-motion to object-motion [Gauch].

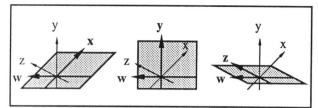

Figure 2. *These are three of the six axial planes in xyzw-space, defined by the axis pairs xw, yw, and zw. The other three axial planes (xz, yz, and xy) lie in the 3-dimensional xyz-subspace.*

2.1 Mapping 2D Input to 3D Transformations

The fact that an input device is constrained within a physical 3-dimensional world will impair kinesthetic sympathy. The question is, how much? This problem is very familiar in a different guise, namely, how to affect direct 3D manipulations with a 2D locator such as a mouse. In this case there are six degrees of freedom (three Euler angles and three orthogonal translations) to associate with a 2-dimensional input space. The popular techniques are to overload the input space, to partition the input space, to discard a dimension of control, or to create a cross-product of the input space by using multiple locators. The following is a highly compressed review of these techniques.

2.1.1 Overloading the Input Mapping

We can overload the input space (x', y', z') by extracting x' and y' components of the locator's velocity, and assigning the magnitude of circular acceleration to the z' component [Evans]. Converting these components into translations in x, y, and z preserves sympathy for x and y, and naturally suggests a screw-translation for z. An important drawback to mapping the input space this way is that the locator's velocity and acceleration are not decoupled. If the user wants to change the direction of the locator's motion, that change necessarily produces a circular acceleration and hence a z-translation in world space (figure 3).

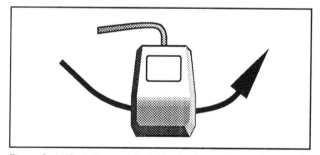

Figure 3. *At the bottom point of this circular trajectory, the mouse's velocity is purely horizontal, while its acceleration is purely vertical.*

2.1.2 Partitioning the Input Space

We can partition the input space into components, each of which maps the locator motion to the object motion in a different manner. The partition can be explicit, by determining in which of several control areas a cursor lies [Chen]. The partition can be implicit, by comparing the motion of the 2D locator to the orientation of a 3D cursor that is projected to input space [Nielson]. Whichever mapping is employed, the user must be prepared to change his motion when the input space switches context, and must be aware of which mapping is being invoked.

2.1.3 Discarding Input Mappings

There are several ways to discard a degree of control in order to eliminate a dimension from the range of the input mapping. For example, two angles determine a position on the unit 2-sphere. Rather than specify three Euler angles, we can use the locator's velocity vector to determine a rotation of the unit 2-sphere and hence of the 3-space it inhabits. Alternatively, we can map the input space to the tangent space at a point on a surface [Nielson, Bier, Hanrahan, Smith], in order to control the motion of the object by controlling its motion within that tangent plane. Of course the locator's motion becomes less sympathetic as the tangent plane deviates from the image plane. A more abstract problem is that path-planning can become very difficult when it requires a route through successive tangent planes to reach a target orientation. A surface in 3-space that isn't closed or that isn't everywhere differentiable may possess a Gauss map that does not cover the unit sphere. Such a surface is difficult or impossible to orient by controlling it through its tangent or normal space.

2.1.4 Taking a Cross Product of the Input Space

By using k locators, each with n degrees of freedom, we permit n^k degrees of freedom in the input space. These can be realized either as k physical locators, as one logical locator with a k-way selector to map physical-to-logical, or as a hybrid of the two. Thus, a single mouse button can select between two mappings of the mouse position into the world [Chen].

2.2 Mapping Spaceballs and Joysticks to 4D Transformations

What does the experience of mapping 2D input to 3D manipulation suggest for mapping 3D input into 4D manipulation? Consider each of the four approaches outlined above. (1) Overloading the input space can produce transformations in 4-space as side effects of an attempted 3D manipulation – side effects which novice users cannot easily undo. (2) Nielson's method for partitioning a locator's 2-dimensional space extends to 3D for translation, but it does not lend itself to rotations. (3) There are problems with discarding one or more dimensions of manipulation. First, mapping a velocity vector in 3-space into rotations of the unit 3-sphere in 4-space is a promising idea, but it is difficult to restrict the input so as to rotate the projection of the object within its projected 3D subspace. Second, the bigger the dimension of the space, the less of it can be visited by excursions in a 2D tangent plane to a point on a surface, so exploiting local surface properties pays a much smaller dividend than it did in 3-space. (4) Using multiple input devices can be inconvenient, requiring ten sliders or dials, five mice, four 3D joysticks, or two six-degree-of-freedom spaceballs.

What choice is best? There may be no single optimal technique, but multiple input devices at least promise a great deal of kinesthetic sympathy if their input space is 3-dimensional. The relative novelty of interactive manipulation in 4-space is a powerful motivation for designing a sympathetic interface. Not many people have developed a sense of how surfaces look as they rotate in 4-space. Consequently, we do well to approximate that motion as closely as possible by the motion of the input device. Of the devices listed above, spaceballs and joysticks provide the most degrees of freedom. How then can we use them to create sympathetic motion in 4-space?

Translations and rotations within an input plane $x'y'$ can sympathetically and uniquely map to motion within an image plane defined by the xy plane in world space. But the projection from 4-space to the screen will annihilate two orthogonal directions z and w, together with the 2-dimensional plane they define. This plane will apparently go "into" the screen at each point. Translation in the z or w directions and rotation in the xw, yw, xz, or yz planes thus present a problem. If the input device moves toward the screen, we can legitimately map that motion either to z or w. Either choice preserves kinesthetic sympathy, but the map is not unique. Rotation in the zw plane is also problematic. There is no physical rotation of a 3D input device sympathetic to this 4D rotation, since (in our physical 3-space) such a rotation would be confined to the 1-dimensional input space z'. The sympathetic maps are tabulated below (figure 4).

x'y'z' Input Space Translation Direction	xyzw World Space Translation Direction
x'	x
y'	y
z'	z or w

x'y'z' Input Space Rotation Plane	xyzw World Space Rotation Plane
x'y'	xy
x'z'	xz or xw
y'z'	yz or yw
??	zw

Figure 4. The mappings of 3D input space to 4D world space that promote kinesthetic sympathy.

Despite the ambiguities, there are still reasonable ways to convert input from a spaceball or a joystick into 4D transformations. A spaceball offers six degrees of freedom: three translations (x',y',z') and three rotations $(x'y',x'z',y'z')$. To extract ten degrees of freedom requires two spaceballs, either physically or logically.

The mapping from input space to object space can be defined as follows. $Spaceball_1$ assigns (x',y',z') to (x,y,z) for calculating translations and rotations. $Spaceball_2$ re-interprets the z' coordinate, assigning it to w instead of to z. $Spaceball_2$ also makes the exception that rotations in its $x'y'$-plane map to rotations in the world's zw-plane. This rotation is not sympathetic, but, as pointed out above, no rotation in input-space can be sympathetic to a zw rotation. Note that two physical spaceballs compete to produce x and y translations under this scheme; it is necessary then to squelch one spaceball's input to these translations. This makes the two-spaceball solution somewhat unattractive.

3D joysticks that use twist (about the joystick axis) as the third degree of freedom can map in a similar way to the spaceballs, using two joysticks to mimic the mappings of a single spaceball. The joystick rotates in each of three planes based at a common origin. Two of the rotations feel like translations for a short interval: when the joystick is centered, a rotation in its $x'z'$ or $y'z'$ planes is momentarily a linear translation in the x' or y' direction (figure 5). We exploit this duality to sympathetically map these two motions into either rotation or translation in 4-space. Twist is not kinesthetically sympathetic

to translation, but is at least suggestive of forward motion that results from rotating a screw.

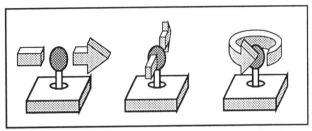

Figure 5. The 3D joystick rotates in the x'z', y'z', and x'y' planes, which can produce a momentary translation in the x and the y directions. In the input space coordinates, x' is rightward, y' is forward, and z' is vertical.

We need four (physical or logical) joysticks in order to supply the ten degrees of freedom necessary in 4-space. We can map pairs of (logical) joysticks the same way we map the spaceballs. Each pair allocates translations to one joystick and rotations to the other. Since joysticks have a small range of motion, it is wise to treat their input as velocity rather than position when gross manipulations are desired.

The two mapping schemes are summarized in the following table (figure 6). The subscripts indicate which logical locator supplies the input.

Spaceball Translation Direction	Joystick Rotation Plane	World Translation Direction
x_1'	$x_1'z_1'$	x
y_1'	$y_1'z_1'$	y
z_1'	$x_1'y_1'$	z
x_2'	$x_2'z_2'$	x
y_2'	$y_2'z_2'$	y
z_2'	$x_2'y_2'$	w

Spaceball Rotation Plane	Joystick Rotation Plane	World Translation Direction
$x_1'y_1'$	$x_3'y_3'$	xy
$x_1'z_1'$	$x_3'z_3'$	xz
$y_1'z_1'$	$y_3'z_3'$	yz
$x_2'y_2'$	$x_4'y_4'$	zw
$x_2'z_2'$	$x_4'z_4'$	xw
$y_2'z_2'$	$y_4'z_4'$	yw

Figure 6. The mappings of spaceball and joystick input that promote kinesthetic sympathy in 4D world space.

It is inconvenient to re-home the hands from one set of joysticks to another in the midst of manipulating an object. Fourphront therefore uses only two physical joysticks, one for each hand, multiplexed as four logical ones. One physical joystick functions as a logical pair that always maps (x',y',z') to (x,y,z). This physical joystick embodies logical joysticks 1 and 3 in the table above. The other physical joystick (corresponding to logical joysticks 2 and 4 in the table) maps (x', y', z') to (x, y, w), with the same caveat that it nonsympathetically maps rotations from the x'y' input plane to the zw world plane. A binary state variable (governed by a joystick button) determines whether to produce translations or rotations.

It is not uncommon to decouple the positioning and orientation operations in the input domain. Experience shows that that users also decouple 4D manipulations (the ones that involve the w-axis in world space) from 3D manipulations [Hoffman] in order to inspect the change that was made to the 3D projection moving the model in 4-space. So there is some justification in this splitting of the joystick control into four parts. The other natural decomposition would assign logical joysticks 1 and 2 to one device, and joysticks 3 and 4 to the other.

3 Projecting to 3D: Intersections, Transparency, and Silhouettes

The same technique for projecting surfaces from 3-space to 2-space applies to projection from 4-space to 3-space. A perspective projection requires an eye point eye_4 in 4-space. In (non-homogeneous) normalized eye-space coordinates, the point (x, y, z, w) projects to $(x/w, y/w, z/w)$ in the 3-dimensional image volume. A second eye point eye_3 within that volume determines a further projection to the final image plane (figure 7).

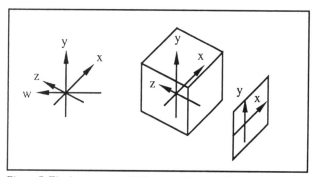

Figure 7. The (x y z w)-axes (left) project in the w-direction to the (x y z)-axes (middle), which project in the z-direction to the (x y)-axes of the image plane.

The typical side-effect of projection is that the resulting surface intersects itself in 3-space, even if it has no intersection in 4-space. Why is that? The self-intersections arise when a ray from eye_4 strikes the surface twice, since both of the intersection points must map to a single point in 3-space. This is the usual situation for a closed surface in 4-space, just as it is for a closed curve in 3-space: the shadow of a "curvy" space curve exhibits self-intersections through most of its orientations .

A surface is *imbedded* if it has no self-intersections or singularities. An imbedded surfaces locally looks like a neighborhood in the plane – no creases, no crossings. If a surface imbeds in three dimensions, there's little need (from the standpoint of topology) to study it in four; thus the interesting surfaces are generally the ones that contain self-intersections when projected to 3-space, because they fail to imbed there. None of the one-sided surfaces imbed in 3-space. Happily, all tof he topological surfaces have incarnations that imbed in 4-space.

Typically a surface that we transform and rotate on our graphics machines is the boundary of a solid object, whether the object

be a house or a mountain range. Such a surface may be geometrically complex, but it dutifully performs a crucial topological service: it separates 3-space into an inside and an outside. We can tour the surface from the inside (as with a building walkthrough) or from the outside (as with a flight simulation over rugged earth) until we have developed a sufficiently complete mental model of it. We need not cross the surface to the other side.

By contrast, a self-intersecting surface separates 3-space into any number of subsets. If the surface is opaque, some or most of its pieces remain hidden during a tour of a particular volume that it bounds. Rotating the surface in 4-space may reveal a patch of surface that was previously hidden, but only at the expense of another portion of the surface that is now obscured. The fundamental problem of displaying such surfaces is that they continually hide their geometry from us. Three popular ways to tackle this problem are to use ribboning, clipping, and transparency. Overall, transparency is the most helpful, but it has certain drawbacks which we repair in §5.

3.1 Ribboning

To reveal the geometry of a self-intersecting surface, we can slice it into ribbons [Koçak]. The gaps between ribbons reveal parts of the object that would otherwise be obscured. One advantage of ribboning is that it can be performed once, at model definition time, and then left alone. Some of the drawbacks are that (1) any already-existing non-ribboned datasets must be remeshed and ribboned, (2) the high-frequency edges of thin close ribbons attract the attention of the eye, at the expense of the geometric content of the surface, and (3) ribbons can produce distracting moiré patterns when they overlap.

These drawbacks do not mean that ribboning is a clumsy technique. On the contrary, for surfaces that can be foliated by 1-dimensional curves, ribboning is a very elegant means of visualization. The compact surfaces that admit such a foliation are the torus and the Klein bottle. Banchoff has made productive use of this technique to illustrate the foliation of the 3-sphere in 4-space by animating a ribboned torus that follows a trajectory through the 3-sphere.

Surfaces with other topologies do not admit such a simple ribboning. We can slice a surface along level cuts as it sits in 4-space, but the cuts will sometimes produce x-shaped neighborhoods in the ribbons. Morse theory determines whether a surface can be successfully ribboned: the singularities of a Morse function on a surface must all be degenerate with the topology of a circle [Milnor, Morse].

3.2 Clipping

Rather than pre-compute sections of the surface to be sliced away, we can clip them out dynamically. The chief advantages are that (1) many graphics machines implement fast hither-clipping as part of their rendering pipeline; (2) no special treatment is required for the representation of the model; and (3) by clipping the surface as it moves, the user can inspect views of it that a single static segmentation cannot anticipate.

There are drawbacks to clipping. We usually think of clipping a surface against a plane. In fact, clipping is properly a geometric intersection of a surface against a 3-dimensional volume whose boundary is the clipping plane. In 4-space a plane does not bound a volume, just as a line does not bound an area in 3-

space. Instead, a 4-dimensional halfspace clips the surface, and the boundary of the halfspace is a 3-dimensional flat, or hyperplane. It is true that a user could interactively specify the position and orientation of the 4D halfspace that does the clipping, just as he can control the position and orientation of the surface under scrutiny. But consider the problem of providing visual feedback to show where that clipping volume is. The shape of the clipped surface implicitly defines where the boundary of the clipping volume is. In 3-space we can mentally reconstruct the orientation of that volume from the clipped edges it leaves behind. It is much harder to reconstruct the orientation of a clipping volume in 4-space based on the shape of the region it clips away. We might indicate the orientation of the 4D clipping halfspace by volume-rendering its boundary. Unfortunately, that boundary will tend to hide the surface that remains after clipping.

Recall that the immediate problem is to view the component pieces of a self-intersecting surface. In particular, to see beyond a patch of surface that hides another patch behind it, "behind" being in the z-direction of the 3-dimensional space to which the surface has been projected. If this is truly the driving problem, we can sufficiently address it by clipping in that 3-dimensional space, and clipping strictly in the z-direction. This amounts to nothing more than hither clipping. To summarize: clipping in 4-space is mathematically easy but interactively hard. For the purpose of revealing hidden interiors, however, hither clipping suffices.

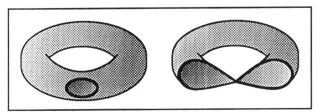

Figure 8. Clipping into a torus produces a figure-eight contour. Clipping reveals internal geometry, but complex contours can confuse the shape.

Hither clipping has other problems. The shape of the surface region that gets clipped away can be very complex. A simple shape is one that is topologically equivalent (homeomorphic) to a disk. In general it is easier to make sense of surfaces whose clipped regions have simple shapes rather than complex shapes [Francis], but intersections and saddle points on a surface cause the clipped regions to look complex (figure 8). Secondly, a clipping plane cuts into a concave region of a surface only by cutting into the neighboring regions as well. This is not necessarily the effect a user wants to achieve. Both of these shortcomings can be remedied by using more exotic, custom-shaped clipping volumes. Thirdly, clipping the frontmost patches of a surface exposes some of the hindmost patches, which may be behind the center of rotation for the objects. The visible part of the surface then seems to rotate in the direction antisympathetic to the input motion. This shortcoming is independent of the shape of the clipping volume.

3.3 Transparency

Ribboning and clipping simulate transparency via a binary classification. Both classify parts of the surface as completely opaque and the other parts as completely transparent. Why not use transparency outright? Ideally a semi-transparent surface presents all of its self-intersecting components on the screen so that the shape of each layer is discernible. In practice the effect

is dramatic and helpful for many surfaces. But there are several things that can hinder the usefulness of transparency.

Disappearing intersections. The intersection of two opaque surface patches A and B is readily apparent whenever their colors differ. On one side of the intersection we have A atop B (yielding A's color); on the other side B atop A (yielding B's color). As the patches become simultaneously more transparent, their colors blend and the intersection becomes less distinguishable. Intersection curves figure prominently in the study of nonimbedded surfaces, so it seems a shame to apply transparency at their expense.

Disappearing silhouettes. A surface with many self-intersections may require a great deal of transparency to make the deep layers visible, but then the outermost layer becomes nearly invisible. In particular, it becomes difficult to see the outline, or silhouette, of a very transparent surface, because the silhouette includes the rim of the nearly-invisible outermost layer.

Reduced performance. Rotations in 4-space change the geometry of a surface's 3D projection. Polygons that were disjoint one frame ago now interpenetrate. Polygons that were on the outermost side trade places with polygons on the innermost. Opaque polygons can be rendered in any order, so long as only the nearest polygons (in screen depth) survive the rendering process. On the other hand, transparent polygons can be rendered from back to front or from front to back, but in any case they must be rendered in sorted order. The dynamic 3D geometry caused by 4-space rotations prevents us from ordering the model by a static data structure in 3-space, such as a binary space partition (BSP) tree [Fuchs83]. Does the BSP tree extend to surfaces in 4-space? Alas it does not; a polygon partitions 3-space by the plane in which it lies. But a plane does not separate 4-space.

In short, to render transparent polygons we must be prepared to sort them dynamically, perhaps even splitting them to eliminate interpenetrations. But that is computationally expensive, and hence slow.

Loss of 3D depth cue. It is true that an opaque self-intersecting surface hides parts of itself that we want to see, but that opacity serves a positive purpose: to disambiguate 3D depth on a 2D display. Obscuration is a powerful depth cue. A hidden polygon is obviously farther away than the visible polygon atop it. Transparency reduces or eliminates this depth cue, leaving us to rely on other cues to recover 3D depth. One especially helpful cue is specular reflection.

Specular highlights reveal surface geometry in two ways. The shape of a surface is easy to see along its silhouette, but is not so apparent in the neighborhoods that are viewed head-on. Phong highlights help exaggerate the curvature, thereby distinguishing the shape of a neighborhood. Where two translucent surface patches interpenetrate, the Phong highlights can disambiguate which surface is in front, especially when we rock the surface back and forth. Moreover, the highlights can disambiguate the different layers that transparency reveals. The benefit diminishes, of course, as the number of transparent layers increases, but the effect is appreciable through three or four layers.

Transparency is an essential tool for studying surfaces in 4-space, since it reveals the behavior of the patches that intersect each other, and since any given surface is likely to exhibit self-intersections when it is projected to 3-space. But transparency comes with a price. It subdues intersections and silhouettes. It makes rendering slower. It makes depth more ambiguous.

In order to redeem transparency as a tool for rendering surfaces in 4-space, we can address these demerits in the following ways. (1) Highlight the intersection curves; (2) Highlight the silhouette curves. (3) Order the polygons in sub-linear time. (4) Apply Phong shading to recover some sense of 3D depth.

Finding the intersections and silhouettes could be slow, and these curves will often change with every frame. In §5 we discuss techniques for computing them after the second projection, from 3-space to the screen. The algorithms exploit the logic-enhanced memory on board Pixel-Planes 5. Fourphront uses these techniques in the presence of transparency and Phong shading by taking advantage of the underlying algorithms on Pixel-Planes: multipass transparency and deferred shading. In (back-to-front) multipass transparency, the model is sent to the SIMD renderers multiple times. On each pass, a pixel processor retains the geometry of the backmost polygon that it has not previously retained, then blends the shaded result into a temporary frame buffer. This technique requires two z-buffer areas per pixel processor. Deferred shading extracts the shading operation common to all primitives, and posponed applying the operation until after all the primitives have been z-buffered. Thus, only the necessary state information (*e.g.*, color, reflectivity, normal, transparency) is stored per pixel at the time the geometry of the primitive is rendered.

4   Projecting to 3D: Depth Cues

There are several cues that lend a 3D effect to images on a computer screen. Among them are obscuration, shadows, illumination, perspective, parallax, stereopsis, focus, and texture. These are natural cues that we use every day to derive a 3D model of our world from the 2D image of it on our retinas.

But now we confront a serious problem. By projecting the image of a surface in 4-space down to a 2-dimensional screen, not only do we lose depth information in the z-direction, but we lose it in the w-direction as well. What 4-dimensional depth cue does our retina employ that we can now supply when we render the surface? Evidently there is none. Since both the z and the w directions are perpendicular to the screen, we might try applying some of the usual z-depth cues as w-depth cues. This strategy risks ambiguating the two depths, of course. The alternative is to invent w-depth cues that have no basis in our physical experience. How do the usual z-depth cues extend to four dimensions?

4.1   Obscuration and Shadows

We can drop down a dimension and liken the situation to viewing 1-dimensional curves in 3-space. Space curves rarely obscure or cast shadows on each other: only at isolated points, in general. Similarly, surfaces in 4-space only obscure each other or cast shadows on each other along mere isolated curves (in general). The result is that these cues are not especially helpful for recovering w-depth.

4.2   Illumination

Again we consider the lower-dimensional analog to our problem. Illumination is ill-defined along a curve in 3-space, since a space curve has an entire plane for its normal directions.

The usual illumination equation does not apply. Several researchers have observed that any surface with co-dimension 1 submits to ordinary lighting techniques, and have jumped ahead to illuminating 3-dimensional surfaces in 4-space [Burton, Carey]. Burton lets a polygon inherit the normal vector of the 3-dimensional volume whose boundary includes it. This is like illuminating a polygonal surface in 3-space, but only displaying the result on the polygonal mesh. The problem with non-orientable surfaces imbedded in 4-space is that they do not bound any volume at all. Hansen inflates a surface to a small 3-dimensional volume, like wrapping a tube around a space curve, and then illuminates that bounding volume in 4-space and volume-renders it [Hansen]. The images are satisfying, but the technique is fairly slow, since rendering volumes is considerably slower than rendering polygons.

Illuminating surfaces in 4-space is thus an unresolved problem. Fourphront postpones illumination until the surface is projected into 3-space, so that shading looks familiar and realistic on the projected surface, and so that this strong z-depth cue is preserved. This strategy is at least as old as 1880, when it was used to shade polygonal faces as though they were illuminated in 3-space [Stringham]. The obvious drawback with this approach is that the shading in 3-space reveals more about the shape of the projected surface than about the shape of the surface as it lies in 4-space.

4.3   Perspective

A perspective projection from 3-space to 2-space behaves like an orthogonal projection where 3-space is pre-warped: planes parallel to the image plane are first shrunk or magnified according to their distance. A perspective projection from 4-space to 3-space has the same general effect. Volumes shrink that are distant from, and parallel to, the volume of projection, but volumes grow that are close to the center of projection eye_4. In particular, translating a neighborhood in the w-direction causes its projection to shrink and approach the origin. This behavior can disambiguate relative w-depth. The nearer neighborhood changes size faster than the farther one.

4.4   Stereopsis and Parallax

Parallax and stereopsis are side-effects of perspective projection, and they offer additional w-depth cueing [Armstrong]. Consider the effect of translating the eye. Objects at various depths in the world change their relative positions when the eye shifts in the x or y directions. But which eye position (eye_4 or eye_3), and which depth (z or w)?

Let us again drop down a dimension and examine the situation. Consider a viewpoint eye_3 in 3-space, and the image plane to which the world projects (figure 10). Within that plane there is a second viewpoint eye_2 and an image line to which the scene projects further. Two spheres A and B in the 3D world project to two disks A' and B' in the image plane, and then to two segments A" and B" in the image line. Suppose A" and B" are only slightly separated. If eye_2 shifts to the right and A" shifts to the right relative to B", we conclude that A' is farther away than B'. But that does not imply that the source object A is farther from eye_3 than B. It can be the case that shifting eye_3 to the right causes A" to shift left instead (relative to B"). Translating eye_3 and eye_2 together couple these behaviors. The situation in 4-space is the same. We have a choice of where to apply a translation. Applying it before the projection from 4-space to 3-space produces nonintuitive motion, due to the parallax from the w direction: the projected object is no longer rigid under the expected isometries, although the source object, of course, still is.

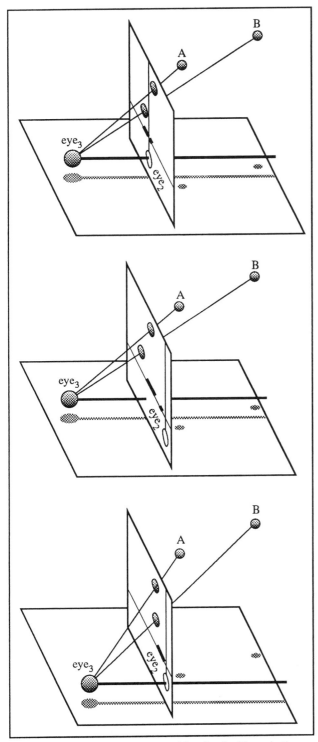

Figure 10. *When there are two eye positions involved in projecting an image, either of them can produce parallax. In this figure, spheres A and B project from 3-space onto a 2-dimensional plane as disks. The disks project to a 1-dimensional line as segments. By tilting the page obliquely, you can see what the second eye sees. Moving an eye to the right will make the farther object seem to move to the right o the nearer object. Which sphere looks closer? It depends on which eye does the measuring. A is closer to eye_3 than B is. But the projection of B is closer to eye_2 than the projection of A is.*

4.5 Texture

The texture applied to a surface can be defined dynamically in world space, so that as the surface moves in the **w** direction, the texture changes. One of the simplest textures is color modulated according to depth. This texture is well-known as intensity depth cueing. In 3-space there is a convenient metaphor for an intensity depth cue – the object looks as though it were obscured by fog, and the fog's color prevails as the object recedes. In practice, the 4D fog-metaphor is considerably less convincing, perhaps because the usual 3D interpretation is so much more natural.

Encoding **w**-depth by color is nonetheless a useful tool, especially for locating level sets according to the color they share. The idea is evidently pretty obvious, since there are very old examples of its use [Hinton]. A more modern treatment of the strategy might be to apply a dynamic texture to a surface, where the texture continually flows in the **w**-direction [Freeman, van Wijk].

4.6 Focus and Transparency

The human eye can focus at various depths. Neighborhoods of a surface that lie within the focal plane in 3-space appear crisp. Neighborhoods that are nearer or farther look increasingly blurry. There are various techniques for producing this effect during rendering [Haeberli, Mitchell, Potmesil].

In 4-space we could define a focal volume at some particular distance in **w**. Neighborhoods within this volume would appear crisp, while neighborhoods outside would be progressively blurry. In general this is not a fast process, since blurry polygons are effectively semitransparent, and hence incur some of the cost of computing transparency. But we can approximate the effect cheaply by simply modulating transparency by **w**-depth. If the focal volume is at the yon distance, transparency will unambiguously determine **w**-depth. Recall that neighborhoods near to eye_4 are generally large due to perspective, and often enclose the far-away neighborhoods that have shrunk toward the origin. If the outermost patches of a surface are opaque, they hide the interior geometry. This is the motivation for choosing a focal volume at the yon, rather than the hither, distance: it is more likely to reveal the interior of a self-intersecting surface. Unfortunately, the eye does not resolve transparency with a great deal of resolution, so this technique is best applied for gross classification of relative distances in the **w** direction.

5 Finding Silhouettes and Intersections During Projection to 2D

This section describes a screen-oriented technique for locating silhouette curves and intersection curves. In §3 we described the powerful advantage transparency gives for visualizing self-intersecting surfaces, but noted that although transparency lets us see more layers of the surface, it strips those layers of some of their geometric content. In particular, the intersections and silhouettes are less apparent on transparent surfaces.

We can estimate the amount of computation required for calculating the geometry of these curves and for rendering semi-transparent surfaces. The conclusion is that even for a modest-sized polygonal model, the burden on the traditional front end of a graphics system becomes too great. Programmable SIMD renderers let us shift some of the computation away from the math processors on Pixel-Planes 5,

203

which makes it possible to display silhouettes and intersection curves of a dynamic 3D (projected) surface at interactive rates.

5.1 Calculating in 3-space

Consider the task of manipulating a surface composed of $n = 2000$ triangles (this is a skimpy polygon budget to spend on self-intersecting surfaces). The cost of transforming and ordering these semi-transparent triangles, along with calculating their silhouettes and intersections, is substantial. Depending on the particulars of the algorithms we employ, we can easily spend $O(n \log n)$ floating-point operations sorting the polygons (as required for transparency) and computing their intersections. Since the geometry is dynamic in 3-space as the surface rotates in 4-space, this cost is charged per frame. The transformations and projections from 4-space to the screen can take another $250n$ floating-point operations. So we easily face over 1.5 million floating-point operations for this meager data set. These estimates disregard all other necessary operations; the front-end system must sustain well over 30 MFLOPS in order to calculate the intersecting geometry at interactive speeds of 20hz. By using multiple CPUs to achieve this speed, we incur substantial communication cost or memory contention. In either case, the time complexity is super-linear in the number of polygons. The conclusion: avoid sorting and avoid analytically computing the intersections in 3-space.

Pixel-Planes 5 offers programmable SIMD logic-enhanced frame-buffers (the renderers) that can offload much of the burden from the geometry processors [Ellsworth, Fuchs89]. In particular, we can use the SIMD renderers to order the polygons, to find the silhouettes, and to find the intersections. For the case of 2000 triangles, the renderers can relieve the geometry processors of over half their floating-point burden and reduce their communication cost.

5.2 Silhouette Curves

Analytic Solution. There are several ways to define a silhouette. In common usage, a silhouette is the boundary of the projection of a surface onto the image plane. But a more generous definition counts any point on a differentiable surface as a silhouette (or contour) point if the eye vector lies within the tangent plane to the surface at that point. The second choice is preferable for self-intersecting surfaces, since we wish to highlight the silhouettes of the component patches that nest inside a transparent image. A simple way to find a silhouette (whose transverse is non-inflecting) is to locate every edge that is shared by two polygons, one facing forward and the other facing backward from the eye. But if the polygon data is distributed among many processors, the processor that owns a given polygon will not necessarily hold the neighboring ones, even for a mesh that is static in 3-space. Note too that this technique only identifies silhouettes along mesh boundaries of a polygonal representation of the model, and not in the polygons' interiors.

We can analytically compute the silhouette for surface patches that are defined parametrically [Schweitzer, Lane], but this does not take advantage of the SIMD renderers of Pixel-Planes.

Screen-based Solution. Consider a screen-oriented approach to finding silhouettes. As a routine step in Phong-shading, the Pixel-Planes renderers hold the information necessary to locate silhouettes, namely, the interpolated surface normals and the eye vector. Each renderer covers a region on the screen and holds hundreds of bits of information per pixel in the region.

These pixels are operated on in SIMD fashion. If the normal to a point on a polygon is orthogonal to the eye vector, the point lies on a silhouette curve.

We can use the renderers to perform a dot product between the normal vector and the eye vector at every pixel, which identifies the silhouette if the dot product is zero. (If the eye is sufficiently far away, the projection is nearly orthogonal, and it suffices to test just the z-component of the normal.) This yields, at best, a 1-pixel-thick line on a curved surface; at worst, it misses most pixels on the silhouette because of the imperfect sampling of the normal vector. We might treat a pixel as a silhouette point if the dot product is within some threshold ε of zero, thereby enlarging the silhouette's thickness on the screen (figure 11).

But thresholding has problems. As ε gets large, false silhouettes appear wherever the surface is sufficiently edge-on to the eye, and the silhouette becomes much fatter in some places than in others. The false silhouettes are inherent to thresholding since, for example, a planar section of the surface, and containing the eye, may have an inflection whose tangent lies arbitrarily close to the eye vector. The inflection point will appear as a silhouette point, even though there may be no silhouette in its vicinity.

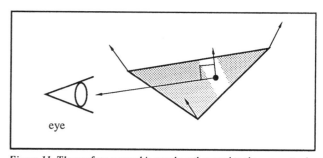

Figure 11. The surface normal is nearly orthogonal to the eye vector in the vicinity of a silhouette curve.

The reason that the thresholded silhouette has varying thickness is that the curvature of the surface may vary from place to place. A silhouette point with a large magnitude of normal curvature in the silhouette's transverse direction will witness its normal vector changing direction quickly along a path toward the eye. A large value of ε may still produce a thin silhouette region. Meanwhile, a silhouette point with a small magnitude of normal curvature in the transverse direction will witness its normal vector changing direction slowly along a path toward the eye. The same value of ε produces a thick silhouette, since there are points over a large area (even as seen from the eye) whose normals are nearly perpendicular to the eye vector.

Note that silhouettes need not be computed when a polygon first enters the pixel's memory. We need only look for silhouettes on visible polygon fragments that ultimately survive z-buffering. We defer shading until after the polygons have been transformed and their z-buffered geometry (including normal) has been stored in the pixel memory. Thus we incur the expense of silhouette computation only once per frame (or, for multipass transparency, only once per pass), rather than once per polygon.

Having found a silhouette, what do we do with it? The question concerns visualization in its abstract sense. How can we effectively map the internal state at a pixel onto the available dimension of output (*e.g.*, red, green, and blue)? A simple solution is to map silhouettes to a particular color that is known to be absent elsewhere in the rendered surface. Such a color may not, of course, exist. But assigning a constant color on the silhouette of a smoothly shaded surface is often, in practice, a sufficient visualization. In the case of a transparent image, it can also be effective to assign complete opacity to a silhouette in order to make it stand out. In fact, we can relax the binary classification of silhouttes in favor of a real-valued measure of "silhouetteness." If the intrinsic opacity of the surface at a point is α, let the effective opacity be $1-(1-\alpha)^{1/d}$, where d is the dot product of the eye vector and the normal vector. Surfaces then become increasingly opaque near their silhouettes, which mimics the natural behavior of transparent laminas. Viewed away from the normal by an angle whose cosine is d, a lamina of width w intercepts a ray through a distance w/d.

5.3 Intersection Curves

If the projected surface in 3-space were static, we could analytically compute the intersection curves [Baraff, Moore] once and for all. Since transformations in 4-space make its 3-space projection change shape dynamically, we recompute it each frame. This can be accomplished easily within the SIMD renderers. The straightforward approach to finding intersections is to modify the usual z-buffer algorithm. We test the z-value of each incoming polygon at each pixel against the contents of the z-buffer, retaining the polygon's state information if the polygon is closer. If the new value matches the z-buffer, we count it as an intersection. If we have flagged an intersection and then a closer polygon comes along, we unset the intersection flag. The result is that all the frontmost intersections will be flagged.

The proof of correctness is easy. Let $\{P_i\}$ be the set of polygons that cover a pixel, indexed by the order in which they arrive, and let P_j and P_k ($j<k$) be two of them that participate in the front-most intersection at that pixel. The z-buffer must contain z_j after P_j is processed. Since P_j is frontmost at the pixel, the z-buffer still contains z_j when P_k is processed, thereby setting the intersection flag. Since P_k is frontmost at the pixel, the flag will not be unset. At the end of the pass, we have found an intersection. By piggy-backing on the multipass algorithm for transparency, we can find all the interior intersections, since they will be frontmost intersections at some particular pass.

Two polygons that share an edge formally intersect each other along it. Polygons whose edges pass through pixel centers will "intersect" at those pixels. These are spurious intersections, and not the kind of intersection we are trying to show. We could be careful not to scan-convert pixels more than once on the common boundary of adjacent polygons. This technique presents a problem for a machine like Pixel-Planes, which is suited to rendering entire polygons as primitives, without maintaining connectivity information. But in fact the pixel already holds sufficient information to eliminate spurious intersections: surface normals. The intersections we wish to highlight are those of polygons diving through each other, whose normals are different where they interpenetrate. Since the SIMD renderers interpolate vertex normals, that information is available per pixel. We can thus modify the z-comparison, requiring that the dot product of the new normal with the old normal be less than unity in magnitude.

Exact matching against the z-buffer can identify at best a 1-pixel-wide intersection curve. At worst it misses much of the curve due to imperfect sampling (just as is the case with silhouette curves). We remedy this problem by thresholding. If the incoming pixel is within ε of the z-buffer value, we consider it an intersection point. This introduces the same artifact of variable-width curves on the screen. If two polygons intersect each other at a shallow angle, their separation remains small over a large area of the screen, and the curve that satisfies $|z_{new} - z_{old}| < \varepsilon$ is many pixels wide. If they intersect each other at a steep angle, a short excursion to neighboring pixels will find them separated far apart. We can use the interpolated normals of the polygons at pixels near the intersection in order to approximate a fixed-width intersection curve. But note that the added computation is charged per polygon, and cannot be deferred to end-of-pass unless we retain the geometric state of both polygons. Also note that most implementations of the z-buffer algorithm interpolate reciprocal-z across the polygon. Over small extents or for large original values of z, thresholding produces nearly the same behavior even when using the reciprocal. But for locating intersections across large ranges, it is wise to recover the true depth.

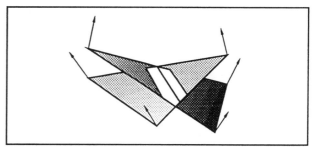

Figure 12. At their common intersection, two polygons share z-values. The z-values are within some threshold of each other along a thickened intersection curve.

Another artifact of thresholding is that the thickened intersection curve gets trimmed near silhouettes, since the depth-comparison is strictly within the z-direction rather than the normal directions of the participating polygons. This artifact is hard to overcome without using pixel-to-pixel communication.

6   Future Work

There are several research areas that this project has identified. A hemi-3-sphere can be mapped to the input space of a spaceball. How effective are the induced rotations in 4-space, and can the user produce the rigid motion within the 3-space to which a surface projects? Surfaces can be clipped in 4-space against volumes with 3-dimensional boundaries. Are there effective ways to shape, to position, and to display the volume or its boundary interactively? Is there an effective algorithm (like the BSP tree) for precomputing the rendering order for polygons projected from 4-space to the screen? Is there a speedy and natural way to illuminate surfaces in 4-space? What is the best interface for producing uncoupled parallax in either 4-space or the 3-space to which it projects? In what ways can texture be used as a w-depth cue? A quadric approximation to a surface contains curvature information, which can improve both the silhouette and intersection calculation for fixed-width curves. What are fast ways to produce this second-degree approximation and fast ways to use it on a per-pixel basis? Our consideration of silhouettes was motivated by the loss of geometric content that transparency produces. Hence we discussed silhouettes as seen by *eye₃*. What useful information do *eye₄* silhouettes add to a surface?

7   Conclusions

The shape of surfaces in 4-space can be difficult to comprehend. Interactive computer graphics provides an excellent tool for making the surfaces seem more real, since we can manipulate them ourselves. The effort is full of trade-offs. In order to control all the degrees of freedom in 4-space, we need multiple input devices in 3-space. We can apply transparency in order to reveal the interior of a self-intersecting projection, but then we lose the intersections and the silhouettes. We can then highlight those special curves, but at the expense of the system's performance or memory. We can steal some of the usual z-depth cues and use them as w-depth cues, but that tends to make z-depth more ambiguous again.

This paper has focused on shortcomings of the various techniques in order to encourage other people to enter the fray and invent solutions. Until the advent of the powerful graphics computers we have today, mathematicians could only imagine interacting in four dimensions. Experience with Fourphront demonstrates that the effort can pay off, that we can open a window on the truly "virtual world" of four dimensions. The collateral spinoffs are algorithms that can be of service to the more pedestrian problems in three dimensions.

8   Acknowledgements

Fourphront is a descendant of interactive applications that were written for Pixel-Planes by Trey Greer (Front), Howard Good (Pphront), and Vicki Interrante (Xphront), all based on a PHIGS-like library developed for Pixel-Planes. Many people had a hand in improving its function and performance. Among them are Greg Turk (debugging), Howard Good (callback functions, one-sided picking), Brice Tebbs (algorithm designs), David Ellsworth (animated cursor, parallel pick), Andrew Bell (multipass transparency), Marc Olano (conditional executes, parallel pick), and Carl Mueller (frame dumps). Greg Turk was instrumental in creating the prototype on Pixel-Planes 4. Jeff Weeks (University of Minnesota) was the first to suggest using the flat imbedding of the torus in 4-space. Nelson Max (Lawrence Livermore National Labs) suggested displaying intersection curves. Robert Bryant (Duke University) and James Stasheff pointed out connections to Morse Theory. Oliver Steele (Apple Computer) helped devise certain parametric models in 4-space. Fred Brooks provided the initial support for this project, and Stephen Pizer currently directs it. Thanks also go to the reviewers, who proposed visualizing silhouetteness by mapping it to opacity.

9   References

William Armstrong and Robert Burton, "Perception Cues for n Dimensions," *Computer Graphics World* (Mar 1985), pp. 11-28.

David Baraff, "Curved Surfaces and Coherence for Non-penetrating Rigid Body Simulation," *SIGGRAPH '90 Proc.* (1990), pp. 19-28.

Eric Bier, "Skitters and Jacks: Interactive 3D Positioning Tools," *Proc. 1986 Workshop on Interactive Graphics,* (1986) pp. 183-196.

Robert Burton, "Raster Algorithms for Cartesian Hyperspace Graphics," *Journal of Imaging Technology* (**15**:2 Apr 1989), pp. 89-95.

Scott Carey, Robert Burton, and Douglas Campbell, "Shades of a Higher Dimension," *Computer Graphics World* (Oct 1987), pp. 93-94.

Michael Chen, Joy Mountford, and Abigail Sellen, "A Study in Interactive 3-D Rotation Using 2-D Control Devices," *SIGGRAPH '88 Proc.* (1988), pp. 121-130.

David Ellsworth, Howard Good, and Brice Tebbs, "Distributing Display Lists on a Multicomputer," *Proc. 1990 Symp Interactive 3D Graphics.* (1990).

Kenneth Evans, Peter Tanner, and Marceli Wein, "Tablet-based Valuators that Provide One, Two, or Three Degrees of Freedom," *SIGGRAPH '81 Proc.* (1981), pp. 91-97.

George Francis, *A Topological Picturebook*, Springer-Verlag (1987).

William Freeman, Edward Adelson, and David Heegar, "Motion Without Movement," *Proc. 1991 Symp Interactive 3D Graphics.* (1991) pp. 27-30.

Henry Fuchs, Greg Abram, and Eric Grant, "Near Real-Time Shaded Display of Rigid Objects," *SIGGRAPH '83 Proc.* (1983) pp. 65-69.

Henry Fuchs *et al.*, "Pixel-Planes 5: A Heterogeneous Multiprocessor Graphics System Using Processor-Enhanced Memories," *SIGGRAPH '89 Proc.* (1989), pp. 79-88.

Susan Gauch, Rich Hammer, Dals Krams, Teresa McBennett, and Dabby Saltzman, "An Evaluation of Factors Affecting Rotation Tasks in a Three-Dimensional Graphics System" TR87-002 Dept Comp. Sci, UNC-Chapel Hill (1987).

Paul Haeberli and Kurt Akely, "The Accumulation Buffer: Hardware Support for High-Quality Rendering," *SIGGRAPH '90 Proc.* (1990), pp. 309-318.

Pat Hanrahan and Paul Haeberli, "Direct WYSIWYG Painting and Texturing on 3D Shapes," *SIGGRAPH '90 Proc.* (1990), pp. 215-224.

Andrew Hansen and P. Heng, "Visualizing the Fourth Dimension using Feometry and Light" *Visualization '91.* (1991).

Charles Hinton, *The Fourth Dimension* [Frontispiecs], London and New York, 1904.

Christoff Hoffman and Jianhua Zhou, "Visualizing Surfaces in Four-Dimensional Space," Technical Report CSD-TR-960, Computer Sciences Department, Purdue University (Mar 1990).

Hüseyín Koçak, Frederic Bisshopp, Thomas Banchoff, and David Laidlaw, "Topology and Mechanics with Computer Graphics: Linear Hamiltonian Systems in Four Dimensions," Advances in Applied Mathematics **7** (1986), pp. 282-308.

J. Lane, Loren Carpenter, Turner Whitted, and Jim Blinn, "Scan Line Methods for Displaying Parametrically Defined Surfaces," *Communications of the ACM* **23**:1 (Jan 1980), pp. 23-34.

J. Levine, "Imbedding and Immersion of Real Projective Spaces" *Proc. Amer. Math. Soc.* **14** (1963).

Don Mitchell, "Spectrally Optimal Sampling for Distribution Ray Tracing," *SIGGRAPH '91 Proc.* (1991), pp. 157-164.

John Milnor, *Morse Theory*, (*Annals of Mathematical Studies* **51**), Princeton University Press (1969).

Matthew Moore and Jane Wilhelms, "Collision Detection and Response for Computer Animation," *SIGGRAPH '88 Proc.* (1988), pp. 289-298.

Marsden Morse, *The Calculus of Variations in the Large*, American Mathematical Society (1934).

Gregory Nielson and Dan Olsen, "Direct Manipulation Techniques for 3D Objects Using 2D locator Devices," *Proc. 1986 Workshop on Interactive Graphics,* (1986) 175-182.

A. Noll, "A Computer Technique for Displaying n-dimensional Hyperobjects" *Comm. ACM* **10** (1967).

Michael Potmesil and Indranil Chakravarty, "Synthetic Image Generation with a Lens and Aperture Camera Model," *ACM Transactions on Graphics* (Apr 1982).

Dino Schweitzer and Elizabeth Cobb, "Scanline Rendering of Parametric Surfaces," *SIGGRAPH '82 PROC.* (1982) pp. 265-271.

J. Semple and G. Kneebone, *Algebraic Projective Geometry*, Clarendon Press, Oxford (1952).

David Smith, "Virtus Walkthrough" [Macintosh application and user manual].

Stringham, "Regular Figures in n-Dimensional Space," *American Journal of Mathematics* (1880).

Jarke van Wijk, "Spot Noise-Texture Synthesis for Data Visualization," *SIGGRAPH '91 PROC.* (1991) pp. 309-318.

Hassler Whitney, "The Singularities of a Smooth n-manifold in (2n-1)-space" *Ann. of Math.* **45** (1944).

10   Illustrations

The surfaces in the color plate section were rendered on Pixel-Planes 5. Each surface was transformed, illuminated, and rendered on 5 in 0.2 seconds or less, and each has between 4k and 10k polygons. There are two light sources: one slightly left of the eye, and one above and to the right of the eye.

Visualizing Hyperbolic Space:
Unusual Uses of 4×4 Matrices

Mark Phillips   Charlie Gunn

The National Science and Technology Research Center for
Computation and Visualization of Geometric Structures
(The Geometry Center)

December 15, 1991

Abstract

We briefly discuss hyperbolic geometry, one of the most useful and important kinds of non-Euclidean geometry. Rigid motions of hyperbolic space may be represented by 4×4 homogeneous transformations in exactly the same way as rigid motions of Euclidean space. This is a happy situation for those of us interested in visualizing what life in hyperbolic space might be like, because it means we can use existing graphics hardware and software libraries to animate scenes in hyperbolic space. We present formulas for computing reflections, translations, and rotations in hyperbolic space. These are a bit more complicated than the corresponding formulas for Euclidean geometry, which emphasizes our need for graphics libraries which allow completely arbitrary 4×4 transformations.

The use of 4×4 transformations to represent isometries of hyperbolic space is not new; it has been used since the discovery of non-Euclidean geometry in the 19-century. The new part of our work is the application of this theory to real-time 3D computer graphics technology, which for the first time ever is allowing mathematicians to interactively explore hyperbolic geometry.

The Geometry Center is funded by the National Science Foundation, the Department of Energy, Minnesota Technology, Inc., and the University of Minnesota. The authors may be reached at: The Geometry Center, 1300 South Second Street, Minneapolis, MN 55407. (612) 626-0888. Email: mbp@geom.umn.edu, gunn@geom.umn.edu.

Introduction

The use of 4×4 matrices to represent affine transformations of Euclidean 3-space is well-known in computer graphics. Most graphics languages include provisions for specifying 4×4 transformations, and most interactive graphics workstations have the ability to multiply 4×4 matrices in hardware. These capabilities were designed with Euclidean geometry in mind, because we think of the space in which we live as Euclidean 3-space.

There are, however, alternate systems of geometry which are of interest in mathematics and physics research and education. One of the most important of these is hyperbolic geometry. Hyperbolic space arises naturally, even more so than Euclidean geometry, in the study and classification of 3-manifolds. It is also frequently taught in introductory geometry courses because it is in some sense the simplest and most elegant type of non-Euclidean geometry. Learning hyperbolic geometry forces one to challenge many assumptions which are usually taken for granted, in the process strengthening one's geometric reasoning skills.

The "space" of hyperbolic geometry consists of the interior of the unit ball in $\mathbf{R}^3$; the boundary of the ball, the unit sphere, is "at infinity". Distance is redefined to approach infinity as we move closer to this sphere. From a hyperbolic point of view, therefore, we can never actually reach the boundary sphere. We can think of hyperbolic space as consisting of points, lines, planes, surfaces, etc, just as in Euclidean space. In hyperbolic space, however, some of the rules of geometry are different. Specifically, Euclid's fifth postulate is not valid: in the hyperbolic plane there are many lines through a given point which do not intersect a given line. Another non-Euclidean property is that the sum of the angles in a planar polygon is always less than 180 degrees. It is possible, for example, to have a "regular right pentagon" (all five sides are equal and all five angles are 90 degrees). Figure 1 shows a tesselation (tiling) of hyper-

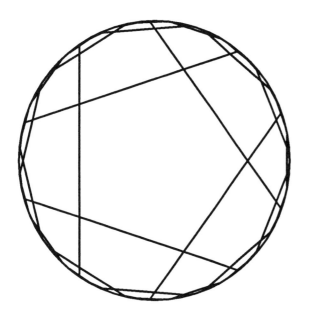

Figure 1: Tiling of the hyperbolic plane by regular right pentagons. All angles in this picture are right angles in the hyperbolic metric, and all pentagons are congruent.

bolic 2-space by such pentagons.

These differences between Euclidean and hyperbolic space mean that the intuition which we have from living in what we perceive as essentially Euclidean 3-space is of little value, and may actually hinder us, in an effort to understand hyperbolic geometry. It would be extremely useful, therefore, for researchers and geometry students alike, to be able to experience some of what life in hyperbolic space might be like.

Fortunately, since the transformations of hyperbolic 3-space can be represented as 4×4 matrices in much the same way as with Euclidean transformations, we can use the matrix capabilities of many graphics languages and hardware systems to create images and to animate motions in hyperbolic space. We must, however, be able to use completely arbitrary 4×4 transformations, because the matrices which arise in hyperbolic geometry are different from those of Euclidean geometry.

Hyperbolic Space

In the following discussion we think of vectors as column vectors; so $\mathbf{a} \in \mathbf{R}^4$ represents the 4×1 matrix $\begin{pmatrix} a_1 \\ a_2 \\ a_3 \\ a_4 \end{pmatrix}$ and its transpose $\mathbf{a}^T$ the 1×4 matrix $(a_1 \ a_2 \ a_3 \ a_4)$. Thus $\mathbf{a}^T\mathbf{b}$ is the usual dot product of $\mathbf{a}$ and $\mathbf{b}$, and $\mathbf{a}\mathbf{b}^T$ is a 4×4 matrix, sometimes called the *outer product* of $\mathbf{a}$ with $\mathbf{b}$.

In computer graphics points in Euclidean 3-space are commonly represented by homogeneous coordinates — i.e. vectors in $\mathbf{R}^4$, where any two vectors which are scalar multiples of each other are considered to represent the same point. The 3-dimensional coordinates (a_1, a_2, a_3) of a point in $\mathbf{R}^3$ are called its *affine coordinates*. We can convert affine coordinates to homogeneous coordinates by appending a 1 as the 4-th coordinate to obtain $(a_1, a_2, a_3, 1)$, and we can convert arbitrary homogeneous coordinates (a_1, a_2, a_3, a_4) to affine coordinates by normalizing to obtain $(a_1/a_4, a_2/a_4, a_3/a_4)$ (assuming $a_4 \neq 0$). The advantage of homogeneous coordinates is that rigid Euclidean motion (isometries), as well as perspective projections, can be represented by multiplication by 4×4 matrices. The isometries of $\mathbf{R}^3$ correspond to the semidirect product of the 3-dimensional orthogonal group $O(3)$ with the 3-dimensional translation group. Recall that an orthogonal matrix $\mathbf{M}$ is one which preserves the inner product of vectors: $\mathbf{Ma} \cdot \mathbf{Mb} = \mathbf{a} \cdot \mathbf{b}$. The inner product in this case is

$$\mathbf{a} \cdot \mathbf{b} = a_1b_1 + a_2b_2 + a_3b_3,$$

where we assume that $\mathbf{a}$ and $\mathbf{b}$ are normalized.

Using other inner products yields non-Euclidean geometries. The inner product

$$\langle \mathbf{a}, \mathbf{b} \rangle_s = a_1b_1 + a_2b_2 + a_3b_3 + a_4b_4.$$

yields spherical geometry, and

$$\langle \mathbf{a}, \mathbf{b} \rangle_h = a_1b_1 + a_2b_2 + a_3b_3 - a_4b_4.$$

yields hyperbolic geometry. Our treatment of hyperbolic geometry is in terms of $\langle \cdot, \cdot \rangle_h$; analogous derivations using $\langle \cdot, \cdot \rangle_s$ instead would yield the corresponding formulas for spherical geometry. Note that the Euclidean inner product, by ignoring the 4-th coordinate, can be seen as a bridge between these two inner products.

$\langle \cdot, \cdot \rangle_h$ is called the *Minkowski inner product*. The Minkowski inner product can also be described as follows. Let

$$\mathbf{I}^{3,1} = \begin{pmatrix} 1 & 0 & 0 & 0 \\ 0 & 1 & 0 & 0 \\ 0 & 0 & 1 & 0 \\ 0 & 0 & 0 & -1 \end{pmatrix}.$$

Then $\langle \mathbf{a}, \mathbf{b} \rangle_h = \mathbf{a}^T \mathbf{I}^{3,1} \mathbf{b}$. The group of 4×4 matrices which preserve the Minkowski inner product is denoted $O(3, 1)$.

Now consider the vectors $V_- = \{\mathbf{a} \in \mathbf{R}^4 \ || \ \langle \mathbf{a}, \mathbf{a} \rangle_h < 0\}$. The set V_- forms a solid cone along the 4-th axis with vertex at the origin. Hyperbolic 3-space, denoted $\mathbf{H}^3$, is the projectivization of V_-, with the metric induced by the Minkowski inner product; vectors in V_-

210

correspond to the homogeneous coordinates of points in $\mathbf{H}^3$. Each point in $\mathbf{H}^3$ is represented by a unique vector with 4-th coordinate 1, which can be obtained from any vector in V_- by normalization, just as in the Euclidean case. (The fact that the vector lies in V_- guarantees that the 4-th coordinate is nonzero.) This gives a model of $\mathbf{H}^3$ consisting of those points of V_- with 4-th coordinate 1; this is the same as the interior of the unit ball in 3-space. Hyperbolic space thus consists only of the points inside this ball.

Two-dimensional hyperbolic space, also called the *hyperbolic plane*, consists consists of the interior of the unit disk. Although the discussion below is in terms of hyperbolic 3-space, it extends straightforwardly to any dimension. In particular, the illustrations and examples we give are all in two-dimensions (the 3-rd coordinate is 0) to simplify the computations and the figures.

The geodesics (straight lines) in this model of hyperbolic space are the same as the Euclidean straight lines passing through the unit ball, except that we only consider the part of the line inside the ball. Similarly, the hyperbolic planes in $\mathbf{H}^3$ are the same as the Euclidean planes.

The hyperbolic distance between two points a and b with homogeneous coordinates $\mathbf{a}$ and $\mathbf{b}$ is given by

$$d^{\text{hyp}}(a,b) = 2\cosh^{-1}\sqrt{\frac{\langle \mathbf{a}, \mathbf{b}\rangle_h^2}{\langle \mathbf{a}, \mathbf{a}\rangle_h \langle \mathbf{b}, \mathbf{b}\rangle_h}}. \qquad (1)$$

A simple calculation shows that this formula is invariant under multiplication of $\mathbf{a}$ and $\mathbf{b}$ by scalars, and hence depends only on a and b. It is also easy to verify that if a remains fixed and we let b approach the boundary of the unit ball, then $d^{\text{hyp}}(a,b)$ approaches infinity.

The model of hyperbolic space that we are using here is called the *projective* model, or the *Klein* model, after the 19-th century mathematician who popularized it. A more familiar model is the *conformal* model, also known as the *Poincare* model. In the conformal model, geodesics are arcs of circles perpendicular to the boundary sphere (or circle, in two dimensions). Each model of hyperbolic space has its advantages and disadvantages. The projective model seems better suited for visualization and computer graphics, because geodesics appear "straight" and the isometries can be represented by projective linear transformations.

Matrix Formulas

The isometries of $\mathbf{H}^3$ correspond to the matrices in $O(3,1)$, just as the isometries of Euclidean 3-space correspond to the matrices in $O(4)$. We now present formulas for computing the matrices of rigid motions in hyperbolic space.

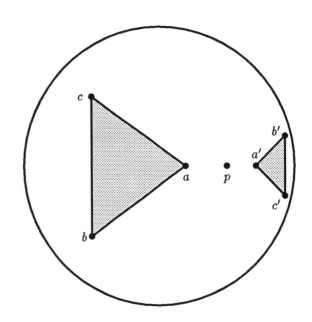

Figure 2: Hyperbolic Reflections. Triangle abc is the reflection of triangle $a'b'c'$ in point p. The two triangles are congruent in hyperbolic space, and hence would appear to be of equal size to an observer inside the space.

Reflections

One of the simplest types of isometries is a reflection. If $\mathbf{p}$ represents the homogeneous coordinates of a point p in $\mathbf{H}^3$, then the 4×4 matrix for the hyperbolic reflection in p is

$$\mathbf{r}_p^{\text{hyp}} = \mathbf{I} - 2\mathbf{p}\mathbf{p}^T\mathbf{I}^{3,1}/\langle \mathbf{p}, \mathbf{p}\rangle_h. \qquad (2)$$

This same formula may be used to obtain the matrix for the reflection in a plane as well. In this case, $\mathbf{p}$ represents the homogeneous coordinates of the plane.

Note: (2) can also be used to give the matrix for a Euclidean reflection, by replacing $\mathbf{I}^{3,1}$ with $\mathbf{I}$ and the Minkowski inner product with the dot product.

To use (2) in an example, let $p = (0.5, 0.0, 0)$, and consider the triangle with vertices $a = (0.2, 0.0, 0.0)$, $b = (-0.5, -0.5, 0.0)$, and $c = (-0.5, 0.5, 0.0)$ — see Figure 2. Then we can use the homogeneous coordinates

$$\mathbf{p} = \begin{pmatrix} 0.5 \\ 0 \\ 0 \\ 1 \end{pmatrix} \text{ to obtain}$$

$$\mathbf{r}_p^{\text{hyp}} = \begin{pmatrix} 1.666 & 0 & 0 & -1.333 \\ 0 & 1 & 0 & 0 \\ 0 & 0 & 1 & 0 \\ 1.333 & 0 & 0 & -1.666 \end{pmatrix}$$

To transform a point, say a, by this reflection, we multiply its homogeneous coordinates $\begin{pmatrix} 0.2 \\ 0 \\ 0 \\ 1 \end{pmatrix}$ by this matrix

to obtain $\begin{pmatrix} -1 \\ 0 \\ 0 \\ -1.4 \end{pmatrix}$ and then normalize to obtain the

point $a' = (0.714, 0, 0)$. Transforming b and c similarly gives $b' = (0.929, 0.214, 0)$, and $c' = (0.929, -0.214, 0)$.

Although the two triangles in 2 look very different from a Euclidean point of view, they are congruent in hyperbolic space. One may verify this by using (1) to compute the hyperbolic lengths of the triangles' edges. For example $\mathbf{d}^{\text{hyp}}(a, b) = \mathbf{d}^{\text{hyp}}(a', b') = 2.074$. (Be sure to use homogeneous coordinates in (1)!)

Translations

We can now define hyperbolic translations in terms of reflections. Just as in Euclidean space, the translation which takes a point a to a point b is the composition of the reflection in a with the reflection in the midpoint m of a and b:

$$\mathbf{T}_{a,b}^{\text{hyp}} = \mathbf{r}_m^{\text{hyp}} \cdot \mathbf{r}_a^{\text{hyp}}. \qquad (3)$$

The homogeneous coordinates $\mathbf{m}$ of the hyperbolic midpoint are given by the formula

$$\mathbf{m} = \mathbf{a}\sqrt{\langle \mathbf{b}, \mathbf{b} \rangle_h \langle \mathbf{a}, \mathbf{b} \rangle_h} + \mathbf{b}\sqrt{\langle \mathbf{a}, \mathbf{a} \rangle_h \langle \mathbf{a}, \mathbf{b} \rangle_h}, \qquad (4)$$

where $\mathbf{a}$ and $\mathbf{b}$ are homogeneous coordinates for a and b, respectively.

As an example, consider the triangle from Figure 2 again. And let $b' = (0.3, -0.7, 0)$. We compute the matrix of translation $\mathbf{T}_{b,b'}^{\text{hyp}}$. Using the homogeneous coordinates for b and b' in (4) gives $\mathbf{m} = \begin{pmatrix} -0.1 \\ -0.733 \\ 0 \\ 1.212 \end{pmatrix}$

for the midpoint. Using (2) and (3) then gives

$$\begin{pmatrix} 1.676 & 0.814 & 0 & 1.572 \\ -1.369 & 0.636 & 0 & -1.130 \\ 0 & 0 & 1 & 0 \\ 1.919 & 0.257 & 0 & 2.179 \end{pmatrix} \qquad (5)$$

The images of a, b, and c under this transformation are $a' = (0.744, -0.548, 0)$, $b' = (0.3, -0.7, 0)$, and $c' = (0.846, -0.095, 0)$; see Figure 3.

To continue this example, we can translate b' again by (5) and obtain $b'' = (0.585, -0.771, 0)$, which lies on the line containing b and b'. The points b, b', and b'' lie at equally spaced intervals along this line in the hyperbolic metric.

An important fact about hyperbolic translations is that each has a unique axis. This is different from Euclidean translations, where it is only the direction of the axis that matters, not the particular choice of axis.

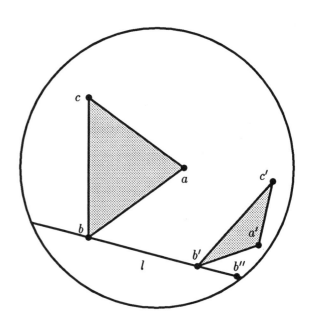

Figure 3: Hyperbolic Translation. Triangle $a'b'c'$ is obtained by translating triangle abc along line l from b to b'; the two triangles are congruent in hyperbolic space.

Rotations

A rotation of $\mathbf{H}^3$ about an axis l through the origin is the same as the Euclidean rotation about the same axis, since this rotation preserves the unit ball. To compute the matrix of rotation about an axis not passing through the origin, we first translate l the origin, do the rotation there, and then translate l back to its original position. The concatenation of these three transformations gives a rotation about the original axis. In order for the angles to work out right, we must translate along the unique line through the origin perpendicular to l. If l_0 is the point of l closest to the origin, this is the translation $\mathbf{T}_{l_0,0}^{\text{hyp}}$.

Specifically, suppose a and b are points in $\mathbf{H}^3$ and we wish to rotate through an angle of θ about the line l through a and b. The point l_0 of l closest to the origin is given by

$$l_0 = \frac{a \cdot (a-b)}{(a-b) \cdot (a-b)} b + \frac{b \cdot (b-a)}{(b-a) \cdot (b-a)} a. \qquad (6)$$

Note that in (6) a and b are the *affine* (not homogeneous) coordinates of points in $\mathbf{H}^3$, and $\cdot$ is the usual dot product. The desired hyperbolic rotation is then

$$\mathbf{R}_{l,\theta}^{\text{hyp}} = (\mathbf{T}_{l_0,0}^{\text{hyp}})^{-1} \cdot \mathbf{R}_{u,\theta}^{\text{euc}} \cdot \mathbf{T}_{l_0,0}^{\text{hyp}} \qquad (7)$$

where $\mathbf{R}_{u,\theta}^{\text{euc}}$ is the Euclidean rotation of $\mathbf{R}^3$ through an angle of θ about an axis in the direction of u, where

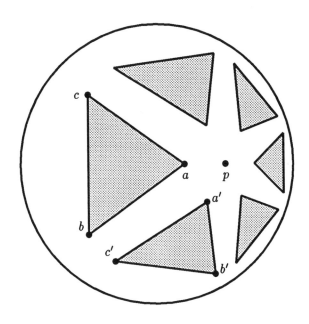

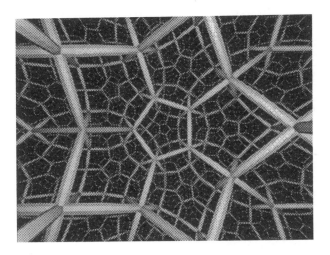

Figure 5: Scene from the video *Not Knot*. This scene shows a tesselation of hyperbolic space by regular right dodecahedra — analogous to a tesselation of Euclidean space by cubes.

Figure 4: Hyperbolic Rotations. Triangle $a'b'c'$ is obtained by rotating triangle abc about the point p through and angle of $\pi/3$ radians. The other four triangles are obtained by additions rotations through the same angle. All six triangles are congruent in hyperbolic space.

$u = (a - b)/\|a - b\|$ is a unit vector in the direction of l. $\mathbf{R}_{u,\theta}^{\text{euc}}$ is given by ([3], p. 73)

$$\begin{pmatrix} u_1^2 + c(1 - u_1^2) & u_1u_2c_1 - u_3s & u_1u_3c_1 + u_2s & 0 \\ u_1u_2c_1 + u_3s & u_2^2 + c(1 - u_2^2) & u_2u_3c_1 - u_1s & 0 \\ u_1u_3c_1 - u_2s & u_2u_3c_1 + u_1s & u_3^2 + c(1 - u_3^2) & 0 \\ 0 & 0 & 0 & 1 \end{pmatrix}$$

where $c = \cos(\theta)$, $s = \sin(\theta)$, and $c_1 = 1 - \cos(\theta)$.

To give another example using the above triangle, we compute the rotation about the line l through the points $p = (0.5, 0, 0)$ and $q = (0.5, 0, 1)$. This line is perpendicular to the x-y plane (in both the Euclidean and hyperbolic metrics) and hence this rotation preserves the x-y plane.

The point l_0 from (6) is, of course, just p. Using $u = (0, 0, 1)$ in (7) we obtain

$$\begin{pmatrix} 0.333 & -1 & 0 & 0.333 \\ 1. & 0.5 & 0 & -0.5 \\ 0. & 0 & 1 & 0. \\ -0.333 & -0.5 & 0 & 1.167 \end{pmatrix}. \qquad (8)$$

The images of a, b, and c by this transformation are then $a' = (0.364, -0.273, 0)$, $b' = (0.421, -0.789, 0)$, and $c' = (-0.308, -0.692, 0)$. Figure 4 shows the resulting triangle, as well as the next five images under the transformation (8).

Applications

Three recent projects at the Geometry Center have applied these ideas. One is the video *Not Knot* [4]. This video, whose purpose is to illustrate some of the basic concepts of knot theory and the theory of 3-manifolds, includes a fly-through scene of hyperbolic 3-space; see Figure 5. During this fly-through one easily notices that apparent size changes more rapidly in hyperbolic space than in Euclidean space. Angles appear to change as we move closer to them. In fact, however, they are not changing — what changes is our perception of them.

Another project which has used 4×4 matrix technology in this way is a flight simulator for hyperbolic space written by Linus Upson, a Princeton University undergraduate working as a research assistant during the summer of 1991. Patterned after the popular SGI flight simulator, Upson's program allows one to navigate through a scene in hyperbolic space; see Figure /ref-fig:hfly. The program is excellent for conveying a sense of how angles and distances seem to change with motion. The intuition which one gains from this experience is hard to pinpoint but extremely valuable in understanding hyperbolic geometry.

The third Geometry Center project using hyperbolic transformations is a general graphics library which we call the "Object Oriented Graphics Language" (OOGL), begun by Pat Hanrahan in the summer of 1989. This library provides a general framework in which geometric objects and the actions which operate on them may be specified arbitrarily. This makes it easy to define and manipulate objects in hyperbolic space. The interactive viewing program which accompanies OOGL (*MinneView*) has a "hyperbolic mode" in which the translations and rotations controlled by

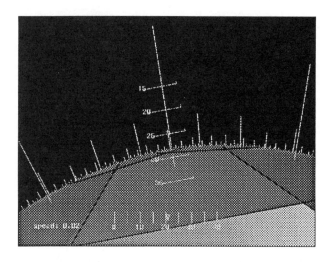

Figure 6: Hyperbolic space flight simulator. This scene shows the view from the cockpit of an airplane flying over a hyperbolic plane in hyperbolic 3-space. The plane is tesselated with regular right pentagons — it is essentially a copy of Figure 1.

mouse motions are hyperbolic rather than Euclidean. A version of this program for SGI IRIS workstations may be obtained on the Internet via anonymous ftp from host `geom.umn.edu` (IP address 128.101.25.31).

Acknowledgements

Figures 1, 2, 3, and 4 were generated by the program *Hypercad*, written Mark Phillips and Robert Miner. This program may be obtained on the Internet via anonymous ftp from host `geom.umn.edu` (IP address 128.101.25.31).

Figure 5 is a frame by Charlie Gunn from [4].

Figure 6 was generated by the hyperbolic flight simulator program written by Linus Upson.

References

[1] Beardon, Alan F. *The Geometry of Discrete Groups*, Springer-Verlag, New York, 1983. Chapter 7 contains many useful formulas for hyperbolic geometry and trigonometry.

[2] Coxeter, H.S.M. *Non-Euclidean Geometry*, University of Toronto Press, 1965. This book provides a comprehensive introduction to hyperbolic geometry, with an emphasis on its definition in terms of projective geometry.

[3] Faux, I.D. and M.J. Pratt. *Computational Geometry for Design and Manufacture*, Wiley and Sons, New York, 1979.

[4] Gunn, Charlie, et. al. "Not Knot" [videotape] Jones and Bartlett. Copies of this video may be ordered by contacting Jones and Bartlett Publishers, Inc, 20 Park Plaza, Suite 1435, Boston, MA 02116-9792.

[5] Thurston, William. *The Geometry and Topology of Three-Manifolds*, volume 1. Princeton University Press, to appear. Chapters 1 and 2 provide a good introduction to hyperbolic geometry.

Human Engineering the User Interface to Spaceland

Stuart Card, Xerox Palo Alto Research Center

As we spread our wings in an attempt to escape user interface Flatland, it is useful to set current work on interactive 3D systems in the context of work on human-computer interaction generally.

Taking the long view, we can see the history of human-computer interface design as a set of inventions having different relative impact. In fact, it is interesting to plot these on a sort of seismic scale of innovation according to how much they shake the status quo. 3D animated interactive graphical user interfaces look like they will belong on the high end of this scale. We can look in more detail at where we are by plotting the work of this conference against a characterization of work in human-computer interaction broadly defined. Such an analysis reveals work mainly on the computational side, with some attention to applications. In the end, computer systems to be successful involve arranging a fit among the system, the context of use, and human characteristics. It is work on the fit to human characteristics that is most lacking. Technology often develops through a cycle of point designs, abstraction, characterization, and articulation of design principles (not necessarily in that order). While much of the progress in interactive 3D interfaces will continue to be the result of intuitive and analogical point design, it is my contention that we can already begin to pursue the abstraction and characterization of parts of the design space.

I will give examples of abstractions that attempt to relate the missing human characteristic point of the system-use-human triangle. These will include perceptual, motor, and cognitive interactions and also the characteristics of the task environment. Such abstractions can be used in design as "tools for thought" to speed the identification of interesting parts of the vast new user interface Spaceland now open for exploration.

Author Index

Color
Plate
Section

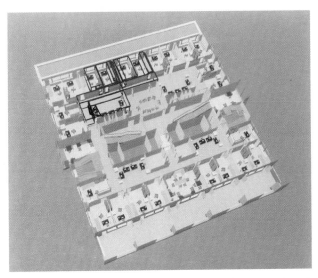

I. The sixth floor of the building model (242,668 faces). The eye-to-cell visibility set (30,265 faces) for a typical observer viewpoint is outlined in blue.

IV. Another typical observer viewpoint. Visible objects are rendered using the highest level of detail for every object (23,468 faces are drawn).

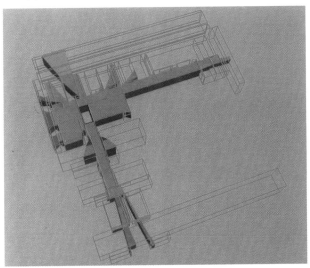

II. Cell-to-cell visibility and polyhedral bounds on the visible portions of reached cells for the cell containing the observer of Plate I.

V. Same viewpoint as in Plate IV. Detail has been reduced for objects that appear small to the observer (7,555 faces are drawn).

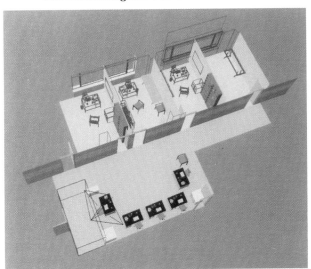

III. Eye-to-object visibility for the observer of Plate I. Wireframe objects are incident upon visible cells but not in the potentially visible set.

VI. Same viewpoint as in Plate IV. Shading represents the level of detail chosen for each object in Plate V. Darker shades represent higher levels of detail.

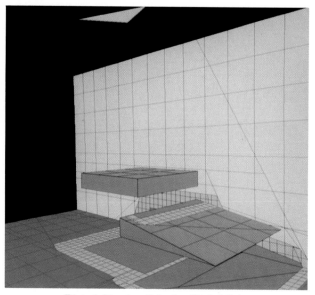

Plate 1 Simple solids classified, 1 light.

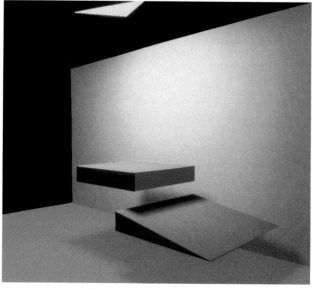

Plate 2 Simple solids illuminated, 1 light.

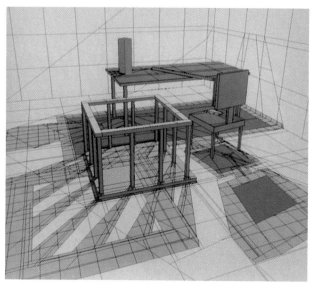

Plate 3 Room scene classified, 1 light.

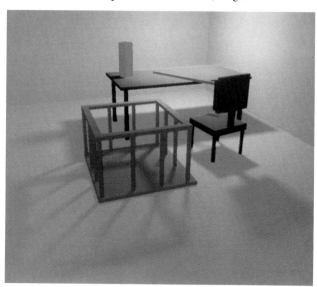

Plate 4 Room scene illuminated, 1 light.

Plate 5 Room scene without playpen illuminated, 2 lights.

Plate 6 Room scene illuminated, 2 lights.

Chin and Feiner, "Fast Object-Precision Shadow Generation for Area Light Sources Using BSP Trees"

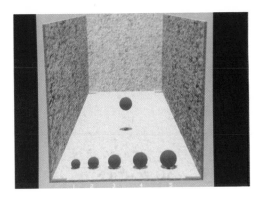

Figure 1: A sample trial from Experiment 1: Effect of shadow sharpness on the perception of object size and position.

Figure 2: Shadow sharpness levels used in Experiments 1 and 3. The sharpness levels are (from left to right): no shadows, hard shadows, and soft shadow.

Figure 3: .A sample trial from Experiment 2: Effect of shadow shape on the perception of object size and position.

Figure 4: Shadow shape levels used in Experiment 2. The shape levels are (from left to right): no shadows, true shadows, and bounding volume shadows.

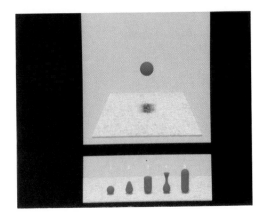

Figure 5: A sample trial from Experiment 3: Effect of shadow sharpness on the perception of object shape.

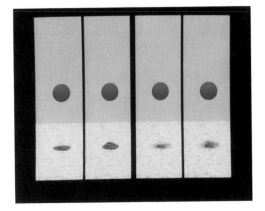

Figure 6: An example of the detrimental effect of soft shadows in experiment 3. The ball and pear shapes (left and right objects in each image pair respectively) are distinguished by the tapered end of the pear shape when hard shadows are present. The feature is obscured under soft shadows (the pair of images to the right) causing confusion between the two shapes.

Wanger, "The Effect of Shadow Quality on the Perception of Spatial Relationships in Computer Generated Imagery"

Color Plate 1: Color detail of MusicWorld. "Device Synchronization Using an Optimal Linear Filter" Martin Friedmann, Thad Starner & Alex Pentland.

Gish and Tanner, "Hardware Antialiasing of Lines and Polygons".

PLATE 1: Front-to-back antialiased rendering without sub-pixel bit masks.

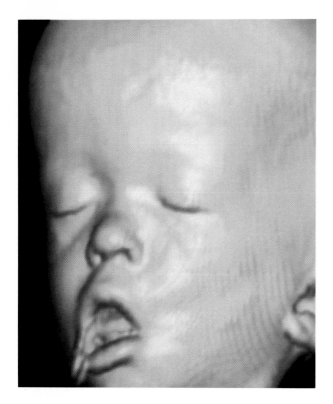
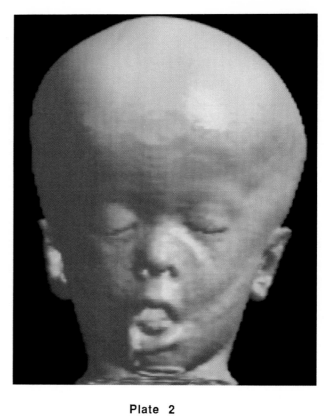

Plate 1   **Plate 2**

128×128×124 CT-study of a child.
Data is courtesy of Dr. Frans Zonneveld,
Philips Medical Systems, The Netherlands.

Neumann, "Interactive Volume Rendering on a Multicomputer"

Photo 1 - Living Room in Walkthrough[2]

Photo 2 - Kitchen in Walkthrough[1]

Photo 3 - Fireplace with Animated Fire[2]

Photo 4 - Landscape in Head-Mount Bike[1]

Photo 5 - Environment Mapped Teapot[3]

Photo 6 - Animated Water Waves[1]

[1] 640x512 resolution one sample/pixel
[2] 1280x1024 resolution one sample/pixel
[3] 1280x1024 resolution 56 samples/pixel
Permission granted to reproduce these pictures.

Rhoades, Turk, Bell, State, Neumann, and Varshney, "Real-Time Procedural Textures"

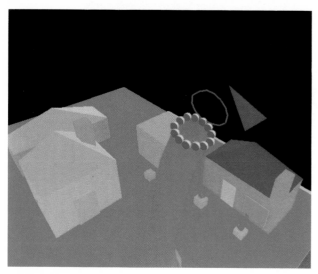

Color Plate 1
A tree trunk being extruded.
The user is roughly five times
taller than the houses.

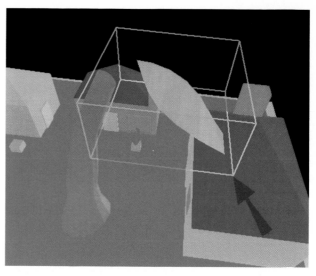

Color Plate 2
A palm branch is being marked for
copying using a rubber banding box.

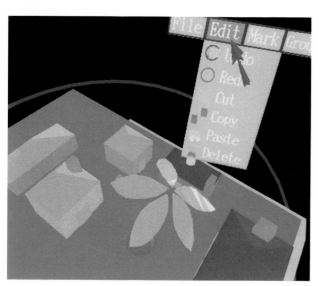

Color Plate 3
The branch has been copied four times.
Part of a toolbox menu is visible.
The red ring is the "magic carpet",
showing the tracker range.

Color Plate 4
The user is now normal size.
The airplane is the cursor, which indicates
that the "flying" tool is being used.

Butterworth, Davidson, Hench, and Olano, "3DM: A Three Dimensional Modeler Using a Head-Mounted Display"

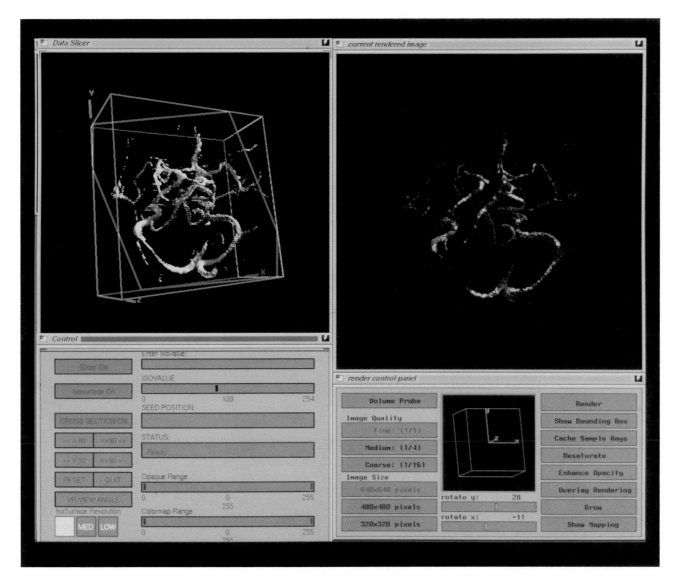

Plate 1: This shows the screen presented to the user in the Volume Seedlings system. The slicer/isosurface interface is in the upper left. The purple outline indicates the slicing plane. The red areas of the isosurface indicates areas on or near the slicing plane. Areas behind the slicing plane are rendering using "screen door" transparency. Seeds can be deposited on the slicing plane which will then effect the subsequent rendering of the volume in the upper right.

Cohen, Painter, Mehta, and Ma, "Volume Seedlings"

Plate 1: (upper left) Helo-cow stalking a M-106 Self-propelled mortar.

Plate 2: (upper right) Results of collision between a M-35 2 1/2 ton truck traveling at medium speed and a tree.

Plate 3: (middle left) The Helo-cow's round nearly impacts with an M-2FAADS tank.

Plate 4: (bottom left) Multiple formations of tanks and aircraft on tracks generated by NPSNET-MES. V-22 Ospreys and AH-1T Cobras provide close air support.

Zyda, Pratt, Monahan, and Wilson, "NPSNET: Constructing a 3D Virtual World"

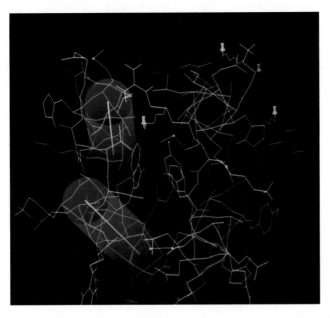

Plate 1: Protein with 760 atoms.

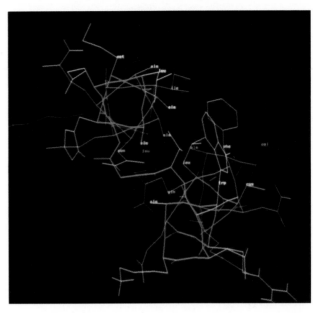

Plate 2: Two helices before rotations.

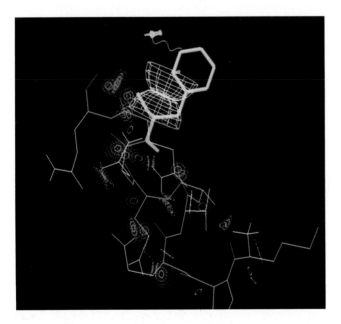

Plate 4: Non-bonded interactions represented
with partial wireframe spheres.

Plate 3: Two helices after rotations.

Surles, "Interactive Modeling Enhanced with Constraints and Physics—With Applications in Molecular Modeling".

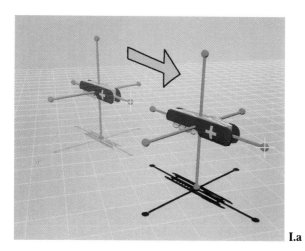

I.a

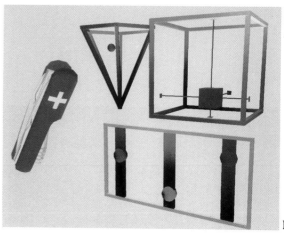

II.

Color Plate II. Three interdependent color picker widgets demonstrate the relationships between color spaces. Sliders are on the bottom, an HSV cone and RGB color cube are on top. Changing any widget determines the color of the pocket knife's case as well as the values of the other widgets.

I.b

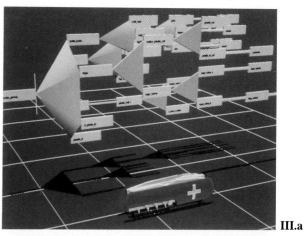

III.a

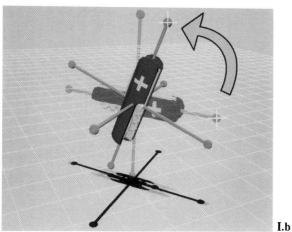

I.c

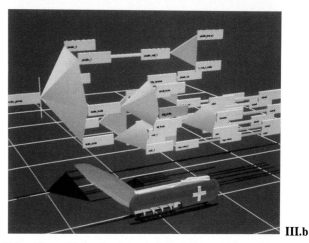

III.b

Color Plate I. Object handles are used to constrain geometric transformations to a single plane or axis. Handles can be applied to any geometric object in the scene, in this case, a model of a pocket knife. Dragging one of the spheres at the end of a handle can translate, rotate or scale the knife depending on which mouse button was pressed. First, the knife is translated along its x axis (**a**). Next, the knife is rotated around a single axis (**b**). The direction of the user's initial gesture determines which of the two axes perpendicular to the handle is used as the axis of rotation. Finally, the knife is scaled along one axis (**c**).

Color Plate III. An implementation of Xerox PARC's cone tree is used to visualize the geometric hierarchy of a pocket knife (**a**). Nodes represent hierarchical components of the knife's geometry. Clicking on a node initiates two behaviors (**b**), one that rotates the node to the front, another that highlights and animates the corresponding element of the knife's geometry, in this case, the large blade.

Conner, Snibbe, Herndon, Robbins, Zeleznik, and van Dam, "Three-Dimensional Widgets"

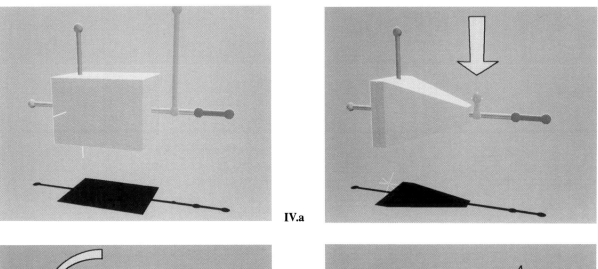
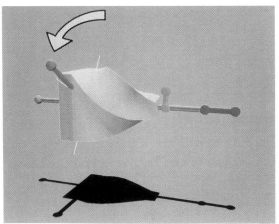
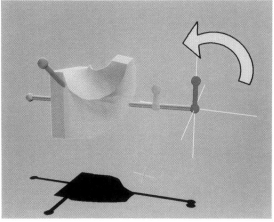

Color Plate IV. The rack widget is used to perform deformations on any geometric object, here a cube (**a**). Dragging the blue handle downward tapers the cube (**b**). Deformations are applied to the region of the cube between the blue and pink bars. Rotating the pink handle twists the cube about the gold bar (**c**); pulling the red handle upward bends the cube (**d**). Finally, below, we deform a geometric model of a pocket knife using the rack (**e**).

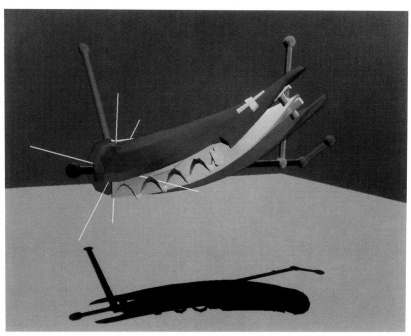

Conner, Snibbe, Herndon, Robbins, Zeleznik, and van Dam, "Three-Dimensional Widgets"

Color Plate 1. One of the models used in the abstract beam targeting task. The white lines, which were not displayed to the subject, represent the double cone of HLS color space, in which the dodge balls are randomly distributed and colored according to their position in HLS space. The multi-colored target ball is at the center of the double cone.

Chung, "A Comparison of Head-tracked and Non-head-tracked Steering Modes in the Targeting of Radiotherapy Treatment Beams"

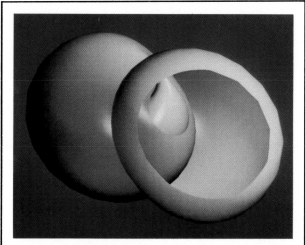

A topological sphere knotted in 4-space. The hither clipping plane in 3-space reveals some of the internal geometric complexity of the surface.

Torus imbedded in 4-space as (cos *s*, *sin s, cos t, sin t*). The inner core of the torus is farther in **w** than the outer core, hence its color is more amber, and its size is diminished by perspective.

The knotted sphere sliced into ribbons. The inter-ribbon gaps are semi-transparent to suggest the continuity of the geometry. Note the moiré patterns emerging in the middle.

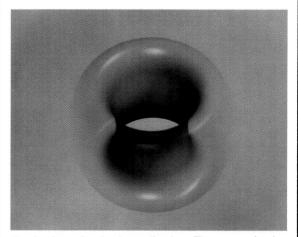

Opacity increasing in the **w**-direction. The opaque interior reinforces the interpretation that the inner part of the torus is farther away in **w** than the outer part.

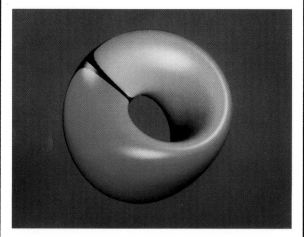

Klein bottle imbedded in 4-space, with color growing more amber in the **w**-direction. The surface self-intersects in 3-space (black line) but not in 4-space, as revealed by the differing colors on either side of the intersection curve.

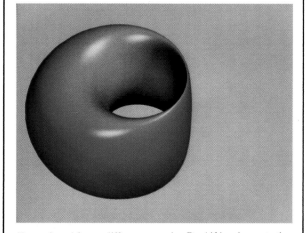

Torus viewed from a different eye point. By shifting the eye to the right in 4-space, we see farther neighborhoods shift right relative to nearer neighborhoods. Thus the farther, inner core of the torus slides right compared to the outer core.

Banks, "Interactive Manipulation and Display of Two-Dimensional Surfaces in Four-Dimensional Space"

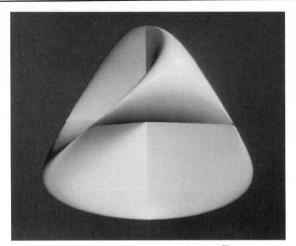

A projective plane that self-intersects in 4-space. The upper part of the vertical self-intersection persists under all rotations in 4-space.

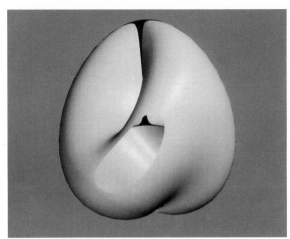

Hither clipping the opaque projective plane reveals the bottom of the black intersection curve. The curve is thinner where the intersecting patches dive steeply through each other.

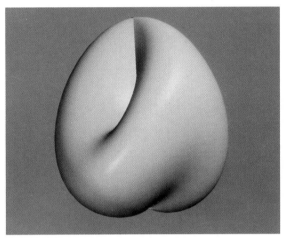

Rotated view of the projective plane. The intersection curve has a terminus at the top of the figure and another terminus midway down the surface, which the frontmost neighborhood hides.

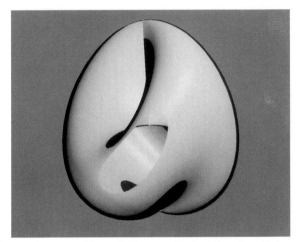

Clipping to reveal internal silhouettes. Their width varies with the surface's curvature. There is a false silhouette where the bottom of the surface inflects in the eye plane across the curve.

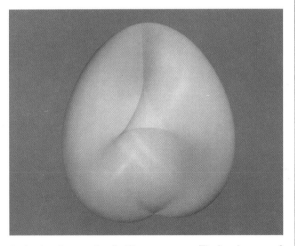

Projective plane rendered with transparency. The interior parts of the surface are visible, showing the lower terminus of the intersection curve. But the intersection curve is less prominent.

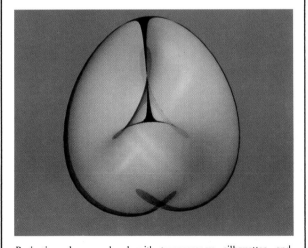

Projective plane rendered with transparency, silhouettes, and intersections.

Banks, "Interactive Manipulation and Display of Two-Dimensional Surfaces in Four-Dimensional Space"